Envisioning the Worst

Envisioning the Worst

Representations of "Hottentots" in Early-Modern England

Linda E. Merians

Newark: University of Delaware Press
London: Associated University Presses

© 2001 by Rosemont Publishing & Printing Corp.

All rights reserved. Authorization to photocopy items for internal or personal use, or the internal or personal use of specific clients, is granted by the copyright owner, provided that a base fee of $10.00, plus eight cents per page, per copy is paid directly to the Copyright Clearance Center, 222 Rosewood Drive, Danvers, Massachusetts 01923. [0-87413-738-1/01 $10.00 + 8¢ pp, pc.] Other than as indicated in the foregoing, this book may not be reproduced, in whole or in part, in any form (except as permitted by Sections 107 and 108 of the U.S. Copyright Law, and except for brief quotes appearing in reviews in the public press).

Associated University Presses
440 Forsgate Drive
Cranbury, NJ 08512

Associated University Presses
16 Barter Street
London WC1A 2AH, England

Associated University Presses
P.O. Box 338, Port Credit
Mississauga, Ontario
Canada L5G 4L8

The paper used in this publication meets the requirements of the American National Standard for Permanence of Paper for Printed Library Materials Z39.48-1984.

Library of Congress Cataloging-in-Publication Data

Merians, Linda Evi.
    Envisioning the worst : representations of "Hottentots" in early-modern England / Linda E. Merians.
    p. cm.
    Includes bibliographical references and index.
    ISBN 0-87413-738-1 (alk. paper)
    1. Khoikhoi (African people)—Public opinion. 2. Khoikhoi (African people)—Social life and customs—16th century. 3. Khoikhoi (African people)—Social life and customs—17th century. 4. Cape of Good Hope (South Africa)—Description and travel. 5. Cape of Good Hope (South Africa)—Discovery and exploration—English. 6. Travelers' writings, English. 7. Public opinion—England—History—16th century. 8. Public opinion—England—History—17th century. 9. Racism—England—History—16th century. 10. Racism—England—History—17th century. I. Title.
DT1058.K56 M47   2001
942.05—dc21
00-048916

PRINTED IN THE UNITED STATES OF AMERICA

To Helene L. Blum
grandmother and matriarch extraordinaire

Contents

Acknowledgments	9
Introduction	13
1. First Contact	32
2. Spreading the Word	60
3. The Story of Cory	87
4. "Hottentots" at Home and Abroad	118
5. Challenging the Constructions	151
6. An Information Age	176
7. "The Most Wretched of the Human Race"	207
Conclusion: Remembering "Hottentots"	238
Notes	245
Bibliography	271
Index	284

Acknowledgments

THE LIBRARIANS AND STAFFS OF RECORD OFFICES AND LIBRARIES ON three continents have provided me with much help and assistance, and I hope I adequately expressed my gratitude to them throughout the time I worked in their collections. There are some, however, who deserve special mention. Many, many thanks to Phil Lapsansky (Library Company of Philadelphia), John Pollack and Virginia Tinkler-Moor (University of Pennsylvania), Frances Harris (British Library), Joan Sussler (Lewis Walpole Library), and Eithne Bearden and Stephen Breedlove (Connelly Library, La Salle University).

I have profited from conversations about my subject with Brijraj Singh, Marie McAllister, Beth Lambert, Kevin Berland, Jim May, Patricia Tatspaugh, Nandini Bhattacharya, Kate Marsters, Joan Stemmler, Nancy Grayson, Leeds Barroll, Marjorie Bayersdorfer, James Walvin, and Ted Braun. Thank you one and all. I would also like to express my grateful thanks to Betty Rizzo, Jim Butler, Susan Iwanisziw, Mary Margaret Stewart, Jane Otten, Sarah McKibben, and Susan Zimmerman for their careful and thoughtful reading of sections of my manuscript. Marilyn Lambert listened to drafts of every conference paper I delivered on my subject. Don Mell proved to be my knight, rescuing my manuscript. April London and Ann Kelly showed me on many occasions their impressive range of knowledge about literature, history, and human nature. I am deeply grateful to them for their wisdom and friendship.

I owe Francine Lottier, Kevin J. Harty, Jim Butler, Gabriel Fagan, F.S.C., Stephen P. Smith, and John Kleis much for the support they lent me during my years in the English Department at La Salle University. My greatest debt is to my family. The love and support they direct my way every day enriches my life more than words can say.

Envisioning the Worst

Introduction

> For the soil about the Bay; it seems to be very good, but the Sun shines not upon a people in the whole world more barbarous than those which possess it; Beasts in the skins of men, rather than men in the skins of beasts.
> —Edward Terry, *A Voyage to East-India*, 1655

> MY Design, in writing this *Paper,* being chiefly to expose such *Barbarians,* who think themselves exempt from those Laws of *Hospitality* . . . I hope I shall, *even in my own Country* find Persons enough to join with me in a hearty Detestation of a certain *Country-Squire,* at the Relation of the following *Fact* . . . Good God, said the *Doctor* to himself, (when he had got out of Gunshot) what a *Hottentot* have I been talking to! who so little values the Life of a Gentleman, and as it happen'd that very Gentleman, to whom the Nation hath in a particular manner been obliged.
> —Thomas Sheridan and Jonathan Swift, *The Intelligencer,* 18 May 1728

> I'll Skiver you like a Rabbit you French Hottentot son of a whore.
> —Moses Mendez, *The Double Disappointment*, 1745

I

THIS STUDY EXAMINES HOW AND WHY THE EARLY-MODERN ENGLISH constructed "Hottentots" as the world's most beastly people. A society named "Hottentot" did not exist when England's contact with Khoikhoi clans in southern Africa began in 1591, but the descriptions of the people at the Cape of Good Hope recorded by English sailors and merchants in the late sixteenth and early seventeenth centuries provided part of the fuel necessary for its creation. By the start of the seventeenth century, when English voyage narratives began to be written and circulated on a regular basis, authors and editors were quick to realize how the negative depictions of the Cape Khoikhoi could work in provocative and politically useful ways. English constructions of "Hottentots" became a crucial component of early-modern England's definition of itself as the world's most superior society. In short, those who imagined themselves as humanity's best found it equally necessary to envision humanity's worst.

The sheer number of English "Hottentot" representations alone is suggestive. Still more remarkable is the range of different discourses they served from the seventeenth through the nineteenth centuries: literary, political, scientific, religious, imperialist, and abolitionist. In this study, I present the entire course of precolonial English representations of "Hottentots." Tracing the constructions of "Hottentots" and "Hottentotism" operative in early-modern England allows us to see the birth and development of a prejudice that contributed in significant ways to larger constructions of nation, race, and gender. More seriously, the case the English developed against the "Hottentots" licensed the erasure of the Cape Khoikhoi people from British colonial history.

My focus is on early-modern English constructions of "Hottentots," and I must here address my use of the name. I place "Hottentot(s)" within quotation marks throughout my study because I mean this term to stand for the constructions invented and developed by the English and to distinguish the imagined people from the real society. I do not mean "Hottentot" to stand for the Cape Khoikhoi. We do well to heed Dan Jacobson's reminder that "Names like 'Bushmen,' 'Hottentots, and 'Coloureds,' have long been naturalized in English speech. It must not be imagined, therefore, that they carry within them no cultural and racial presuppositions, no historical charge or burden."[1] My study examines the stories the English came to write and tell about "Hottentots" for over two hundred years. The name "Hottentot" appeared in print for the first time in an English imprint in 1670. Most likely, it was an invention of seventeenth-century Dutch sailors, who might have heard the Cape Khoikhoi chant a similar sounding word.[2] English descriptions of the Cape Khoikhoi and, later, the envisionings of "Hottentots" tell us little, if anything, about the actual people who resided at the Cape of Good Hope. A brief introduction to them and the history of their contact with Europeans helps to keep them separate and distinct from the subject of my analysis.

The numerous clans of Cape Khoikhoi all hailed from the Khoisan peoples of southern Africa. The name Khoikhoi means "real man" or "men of men." Anthropologist Isaac Schapera places Khoikhoi societies into four ethnic divisions: the Cape, the Eastern Cape, the Korana, and the Nama. Alan Barnard and others suggest three subdivisions by location: Western, Central, and Eastern

Cape Khoikhoi.³ There were considerable physical, linguistic, and lifestyle differences among the divisions and the clans themselves, but as Europeans moved into the larger Cape region, they preferred to call them all "Hottentots." Ogilby's *Africa* (1670) records the names of the clans in the Cape region as: Goringhaiconas; Gorachouquas; Gorinhaiquas; Cochoquas or Saldanhars; Great and Little Cariguriquas or Hosaas; Chainouquas; Cabonas; Sonquas; Namaquas.

The Khoikhoi peoples had come to the Cape as early as A.D. 400 from regions in present day Zimbabwe and eastern Botswana. Alan Barnard's *Hunters and Herders of Southern Africa: A Comparative Ethnography of the Khoisan Peoples* (1992) describes their social and political structure as patrilineal, with precedence established by primogeniture. They lived in groups that anthropologists describe as "mobile and unstable."⁴ Their kraals or camps ranged in size and number but, according to the European representations, the Cape Khoikhoi could break down a camp easily and quickly. Kinship ties were of tremendous value to them. Although there were groups of captains who could limit the chief's authority, chiefship was hereditary. The earliest depictions detail that the Cape Khoikhhoi were capable healers of the sick, had systems in place to punish offenders of their laws, and that livestock could be owned individually. In many regards, Khoikhoi and European societies clearly had similar traditions, especially in regard to hereditary leadership and the ownership of livestock. It is significant, therefore, that English authors usually failed to see any links between their society and "Hottentot" culture unless a satiric figurative connection suited their purpose or intention.

Khoikhoi-European contact initially occurred between the clan known as the Gouriqua and the Portuguese sailors led by Bartholomeu Dias. In February 1488, after the ships in Dias's command rounded the Cape, they landed eastward of it at what is now Mossel Bay. In November 1497, Vasco da Gama's expedition made landfall before they rounded the Cape, at what they named St. Helena's Bay, where they encountered and skirmished with San peoples. After passing through the Cape, they put in at Mossel Bay, where they traded with Khoikhoi clans, and then sailed up the southeastern African coastline on their way to India. For the next one hundred years, Europeans did not generally seek to land at the Cape, although shipwrecks sometimes set them there. These early European sailors often found trading with the Cape people to be dangerous and difficult. In 1510 the Portuguese sent Francisco d'Almeida to India, but he and others were killed in a skirmish with the Khoikhoi. In 1552, according to some of their slaves who escaped, the European survivors of the shipwrecked *Sao Joao* disappeared without a trace after some contact with local inhabitants. Sailors on other Portuguese and Spanish ships that stopped at the Cape during the early decades of the sixteenth century did not enjoy much better luck at the Cape.

It was not until the 1590s that Europeans began to put in at the Cape on a regular basis for refreshment supplies. Depending on what the weather and wind conditions allowed, their ships usually dropped anchor in Table Bay or slightly north at Saldanha Bay. Between 1597 and 1601, at least sixty Dutch East India Company ships stopped there, as opposed to only three English ships during the same period.[5] England showed little interest in claiming the Cape as a colonial possession. At the close of the sixteenth century, domestic concerns predominated in the minds and actions of those governing England. In 1591, the year English sailors first stepped on Cape soil, England was heading into a chaotic decade. Serious outbreaks of plague erupted in London during 1592 and 1593, growing unease about Elizabeth's failure to produce an heir sparked conflicts and animosities among the aristocracy, famine and bad harvests diminished food supplies, rebellion in Ireland escalated into war, the attempts to establish a colony in Virginia failed, and a continuing inability to generate new wealth all combined to drain England's energy, strength, and potential to achieve dominance as Europe's greatest economic and military power. Moreover, the monarch and her policy makers did little to encourage the exploration and development of trading opportunities in distant lands. The Queen's motto, *semper eadem* (always the same), captures well the governing style and ethos of her court.[6] Lawrence Stone believes that the core of the aristocracy followed suit to such an extent that the supreme virtues in England at this time were "obedience and the avoidance of change."[7]

Two Englishmen, Andrew Shilling and Humphrey Fitzherbert, claimed the Cape for England on 1 July 1620, but King James I's Privy Council ignored their action. The English court, again distracted by personal and sectarian rivalries, was anything but forward-looking during this period, and neither was the general public. John Parker believes that the general English population was also hesitant to embrace the possibilities of overseas travel and exploration: "England's new position in the reign of James as an emerging imperial power did not excite any large segment of the English population, and even among those interested in travel abroad there was a conservatism that attempted to hold Englishmen to patterns of interest and conduct that were traditional and secure."[8] While the Cape's resources and people thrilled and horrified English sailors, the public at home had no particular interest in the place or its people.

The Dutch came to see the colonial potential of the Cape earlier than the English. In 1649, a memorandum written by Leendert Janssen assured the governors of the Dutch East India Company that the Cape people were not cannibals, and that they "responded to kindness and learnt Dutch easily."[9] Three years later, the Dutch East India Company sent men there to build a fort and hospital, and to cultivate a vegetable garden that would help their sailors recover from the physical ravages of long sea voyages. Jan Van Riebeeck, who did not share Janssen's positive view of the Cape people, led a group of about one hundred East India Company employees in the initial colonial party, which landed in Table Bay on 6 April 1652. In his diaries, Van Riebeeck describes the Cape people as "black stinking dogs," "dull, stupid and odorous," and "people living without a conscience."[10]

To ensure consistent resupply of its ships, the Dutch East India Company wanted all its stations to establish as good relations as possible with the local inhabitants. Regulations stipulated that local indigenous populations were not to be enslaved, and, indeed, this policy was adhered to at the Cape. The first slaves from the Guinea coast and Angola were brought to the area in 1657/8, and after Dutch and French Huguenot settlers began development of the Cape region, additional slaves were brought from Mozambique, Madagascar, the East Indies, India, and China. Throughout the Dutch colonial period, the Cape Khoikhoi were never transported as slaves the way other Africans were, but they certainly were pressed into service and treated cruelly by the white colonial farmers. Over the century and a half of Dutch colonial rule, there were numerous outbreaks of hostilities between the Cape Khoikhoi and the European settlers. In 1659, in the Table Bay area, there was a short war over land between the Dutch and Cape Khoikhoi clans that ended with an understanding rather than a capitulation of either side. In 1673 the Dutch and the Cochoqua inhabitants of Saldanha Bay, under their chief Gonnema, began a protracted struggle over land rights that lasted until 1677. Peace was reached in 1677, and soon thereafter Dutch expansion into the north and east began to pick up in pace.[11] French Huguenots started to settle in the area in the late 1680s, founding, in particular, the Cape's wine industry. European population in Cape Town and in other regional towns and interior settlements increased from 125 in

1670 to approximately 20,000 in 1798.[12] Cape Town grew rapidly during the eighteenth century. *The Oxford History of South Africa* estimates that in 1714, there were 254 houses in the town, and by 1786 this number had increased to 1,200.[13] By the end of the eighteenth century, Cape Town had become—for Europeans—a prototypical colonial city, with all the social and cultural establishments and hierarchies one might expect.

The Cape Khoikhoi suffered because of the European presence at the Cape, and many began to disperse into the interior of the country. For those who remained in the vicinity, demands placed on them for their livestock reduced their stocks, epidemics of smallpox (especially in 1713, 1735, and 1767) decimated their populations, and the seizure of their land by Europeans placed them in great peril. Jan Van Riebeeck estimated the population figures of two of the clans in the Table Bay area at the start of the Dutch colonial period to be "300 Gorinhaiquas capable of bearing arms" and 6,000 to 8,000 men among the Saldanhars or Gochoquas.[14] A census taken at the Cape in 1815 records the local "Hottentot" population as: Cape Town, 384 men, 436 women; Cape District, 381 men, 357 women.[15] With the Dutch and, later, the British, colonial expansion into the Cape regions and beyond, the demise of autonomous Cape Khoikhoi societies was certain. Nineteenth-century colonial British administrators and their supporters, who never had actual Cape Khoikhoi societies in their ken, generally showed little unease as they spoke more and more frequently about the "Hottentots" as a dying and extinct people. Surviving Khoikhoi individuals incorporated themselves into other southern African societies or colonial European communities, and their twentieth-century descendents were often counted as part of the "Cape Colored" community.

II

Early-modern English descriptions of indigenous societies, such as those included in Hakluyt's *Principal Navigations* (1588, 1598) or Purchas's *Purchas His Pilgrimage* (1613, 1614, 1617, 1626) and *Purchas His Pilgrimes* (1625), suggest that English sailors and merchants were quick to judge these inhabitants as different from and inferior to them almost immediately upon first contact. In fact, their representations of Irish, American, and African societies demonstrate how much they came to depend on difference, not only in their descriptions of "otherness" but also as a psychological strategy to reassure themselves of the primacy of their own culture and nation. Describing the physical characteristics, the religious systems, and the political and lifestyle preferences of these "other" societies helped the English to create narratives that allowed and encouraged them to believe they were superior to all those they observed.

Of all the indigenous societies that England came into regular contact with during the seventeenth century, why did the English select the Cape Khoikhoi as their model for humanity's worst people? Most crucially, they were of Africa. Chinua Achebe believes that the general European selection of Africa as its negative foil derives from a psychical gap. He refers to a "need" of "Western psychology to set Africa up as a foil to Europe, a place of negations at once remote and vaguely familiar in comparison with which Europe's own state of spiritual grace will be manifest."[16] Anti-African literary and visual representations were not a new phenomenon of England's or Europe's early-modern period. As many scholars have noted, classical authors such as Herodotus, Solinus, and Pliny began a tradition in western literature of imagining Africans as physically ugly and monstrous, sexually promiscuous and brutal, and technologically backward in comparison with Europeans.[17] Margaret T. Hodgen describes the formulaic quality of the representations in their works: "each people—European, Asian, African, or the tribal components of each—was submitted to description, but the description was formalized and repetitious, the shorter the better; and included value judgments contrasting national virtues and iniquities. Each people thus described became a familiar entity in the iconography of the Middle Ages: arrested types of human beings, represented over the passing centuries as performing unvarying ceremonies, in unvarying costumes, and with unvarying characteristics."[18] The extremely popular late-sixteenth- and early-seventeenth-century English translations of classical texts generally make no attempt to correct or contextualize the descriptions presented within them. Consequently, these works helped to reinforce English fear of and anxiety about both geographical and cultural unknowns. They participated, like coconspirators, in a demonization of Africa that was reenergized by political unrest in England and by the advent of New World slavery.

The Cape Khoikhoi also came under particular negative scrutiny because Europeans knew less about them than they did about other societies in east and west Africa. Moreover, the authority English readers gave to classical geography texts meant they had a particularly high comfort level with a literary tradition that envisioned southern Africans as the most demonic of all Africans. Pliny's description of Africa's southernmost people is, of course, included in his *Natural History*. There he presents what was to him a fantasy of people he had never seen, but it is telling that Edward Aston, an early-seventeenth-century English translator, presents Pliny's wild imaginings as if they were as likely and trustworthy in 1611, the year his *The Manner and Customs of All Nations* appeared, as they were when Pliny dreamed of a place no Roman had seen.

> The last people, and the utmost towards the South bee the Ichthiophagi, which inhabite in the gulph of Arabia, upon the frontiers of the Trogloditae, these carry the shape of men, but live like beasts: they be very barbarous and go naked all their lives long, using both wives and daughters common like beasts: they be neither touched with any feeling of pleasure or grief, other then what is naturall. Neido [*sic*] they discerne any difference betwixt good and bad, honesty and dishonesty.[19]

English (mis)perceptions about indigenous peoples grew and developed because early-modern English geographers and authors of travel narratives, often hoping to make their own works more literary and/or authoritative, let themselves be influenced by texts like Pliny's. Thomas Herbert, for example, who was at the Cape in the late 1620s, borrows and quotes liberally from Pliny and others in his narrative. Indeed, Herbert reaches into Pliny's work for the word "Troglodite," which he employs in his description of the Cape people.

Another factor contributing to the demonization of the Cape Khoikhoi is the fear Europeans felt on the often tumultuous seas around the Cape of Good Hope. This area, where the South Atlantic and Indian oceans come together, has consistently frightened mariners and claimed their ships. Indeed, history records that Bartholomew Dias originally named it the Cape of Torments ("Tormentoso") in the late fifteenth century, but either he or Portugal's King John II changed the name to the Cape of Good Hope. Twelve years before any English man would step ashore at the Cape, Thomas Stephens, an English Jesuit missionary sent to the East Indies and India in 1579, recorded the sheer and consuming terror he felt as the ship he was on struggled to survive its battle with the seas at the Cape.

> . . . but alwayes making our supplications to God for good weather and salvation of the ship, we came at length to the point, so famous & feared of all men: but we found there no tempest, only great waves,

where our Pilot was a little overseene . . . he thinking himselfe to have winde at will, shot so nigh the land that the winde turning into the South, and the waves being exceeding great, rolled us so nere the land, that the ship stood in less than 14 fadoms of water, no more than five miles from the Cape, which is called Das Aguilias, and there we stood as utterly cast away: for under us were rockes of maine stone so sharpe, and cutting, that no ancre could hold the ship.[20]

Stephens's letter presents the earliest English eyewitness account of a Cape of Good Hope passage, and it makes clear that the author's fear of the sea extended to the Cape people. Stephens's high level of anxiety is evident in his description of them, made despite the fact that he was miles away from the possibility of any physical encounter with them: "the shore so evill, that nothing could land, and the land itselfe so full of Tigers, and people that are savage, and killers of all strangers, that we had no hope of life nor comfort, but only in God and a good conscience." It is relatively easy to see that there is far more fiction than fact in Stephens's description, but his highly emotional account, which appeared in both editions of Hakluyt's *Principal Navigations* (1588, 1598), had the chance to make a significant impact on generations of English readers.

With fear, sickness, and desperate need influencing their responses to the Cape people, it is not surprising that the English who stopped at the Cape, especially those who were on the English East India Company's earliest expeditions, often had trouble complying with the prescription to write detailed and systematic accounts of their encounters with this unfamiliar people and land. Their representations demonstrate an awareness of the emerging generic rules and regulations of travel writing, yet their descriptions digress or shy away from the subject at hand with such a high degree of self-consciousness that their shifts or abrupt endings suggest the high level of anxiety and/or conflict they must have been feeling at the Cape. In many of these cases, the authors excuse or rationalize their evasion by claiming that since so many others have described the Cape people they do not feel the need to do so. This astonishing and utterly false claim was made as early as 1608, by John Jourdain, when he was on only the fourth English East India Company expedition to the East. After ending his description of the Cape people's eating habits with a damning conclusion, "I think the world doth not yeild a more heathenish people and more beastlie," Jourdain begins his next paragraph with the following dismissal: "Off these kinde of people and there behaviour I neede not to write, because it is sufficientlie knowne to many of our countrymen."[21] It is not engaging in overstatement to say that these first descriptions reveal the English sailors and merchants partially, at least, losing their facility to use language to impose order and sense on their experiences and observations.

For the English, the Cape of Good Hope's very name carried, as we shall see, suggestive and symbolic layers of meaning, which lent the people there a special, albeit dubious, distinction. This seems to be the case for at least two reasons. Firstly, the Cape and its people contested deeply held Christian values. Christians believed that a garden or "Paradise," for that is what Reverend Patrick Copland called the Cape in 1611, should not have such seemingly beastly people in it. As Christians, the English believed that disobedient and degenerate "man" was driven from Eden, yet to them the paradise at hand, the Cape, was inhabited by a people who represented the living embodiments of fallen Man. As J. M. Coetzee explains, "In its isolation from the great world, walled in by oceans and an unexplored northern wilderness, the colony of the Cape of Good Hope was indeed a kind of garden. But the future promised by the Cape seemed to be less of the perfection of man in a recovered original innocence than of the degeneration of man into a brute."[22] That the first generation of English sailors, preachers, and merchants did not appreciate the cosmic joke or irony their perceptions of the place and its people lent them is suggested by the vehemence of their condemnations and judgments of the Cape Khoikhoi people. Secondly, since the paradise-fallen Man theme could so easily be adopted for domestic political and religious allegory, English authors of representations and editors of travel collections and geography books seem, in many cases, to have invested more literary energy in their discussions of the Cape and its people. They clearly understood the symbolic potential their Cape descriptions and sections carried, and they often used them to discuss English concerns and problems.

Both Benedict Anderson and Gerald Newman have addressed how the "imagined political community" searches for motifs, myths and stories that ensure consensus about a nation's distinct identity.[23] As early-modern England's consensus narrative about itself was being written, it was simultaneously being challenged. The English belief that their society had progressed to a more highly evolved or advanced level than other societies (both European and non-European) was shaken by what they saw as the "degenerate" lifestyles of the Cape people and others. What the English took as proof of the extreme beastliness of the Cape people, such as their clothing or diet, intensified their fears about "going native." Moreover, the Cape people's subsistence manner of living also seriously challenged emerging English notions about the value of land cultivation and capital exchange. It is not surprising, therefore, that in their descriptions and reports of the Cape people (and others), we find English authors wondering if members of their society would ever "fall" to such a low level if they lived in, ironically, an equally hospitable landscape?

The uncertainty of the English colonial project in America also played a distinct role in the negative reception of the Cape people. The failure of the English settlers in America to become fully self-sufficient certainly framed depictions of native Americans, and, to some extent, it might well have added extra negative energy to the descriptions of the Cape people also. As the success of their early-seventeenth-century colonial settlements often depended on the help and instruction the settlers received from the native inhabitants, it thus behooved the English to acknowledge the native Americans as having some skills and practices that were superior to their own. In their depictions of life in America they could then present themselves as learning the new and necessary skills that would allow them to successfully extend England's dominion and, at the same time, pacify or civilize the native population. Indeed, early-seventeenth-century English representations of Native Americans demonstrate that—when they had to—the English could create a rhetoric and find the necessary language to represent an indigenous society in a sometimes complimentary and generous way.

The English regarded Native Americans as savage but, ultimately, capable of Christianity and, thus, having the potential to be "civilized." The "savagism" ascribed to Native Americans, writes Bernard Sheehan, still "placed no permanent impediment in the way of progress. Even when the Indian was portrayed in bestial terms, there was still hope for his salvation. He participated to some degree in the common human inheritance which, in Christian terms, meant that he would benefit from the preaching of the Gospel."[24] Native Americans also won their more favorable judgment because they were in the New World and on land England had "claimed." In short, the English colonization of America allowed (and forced) authors to place native Americans within a narrative of progress. Because England had no colonial interest in the Cape, this story line did not apply to the Cape people. The denial of such a narrative for the Cape people and, later, the "Hottentots," is evident in the contrast between the contemporaneous "stories" written about Pocahontas and "Cory," a man from the Cape, who was taken to London three years before the American Indian princess.

The ongoing rebellion in Ireland also played a significant role in why and how the English became so invested in their negative constructions of the people they came to call "Hottentots." Indeed, the English tendency to develop its own identity against its definition of an indigenous nation is most evident in early-modern representations of the native Irish. Andrew Hadfield and Willy Maley, editors of *Representing Ireland,* argue that "the development of 'Englishness' depended on the negation of 'Irishness'."[25] Relatedly, they suggest that it is possible to read English representations of Ireland "as a series of negative images of Englishness."[26] The development of such a rhetoric and representational style for depictions of native Irish is not surprising when put in the context of England's longstanding plans for the subjugation of the native Irish and Ireland.

Seventeenth-century descriptions of the Cape people demonstrate conclusively that English eyes and minds certainly saw (and felt) correspondences between the native Irish and the Cape people. In his travel narrative, Thomas Herbert links their languages and their styles of dress. Other travelers note that the Cape people's huts resemble native Irish ones. Descriptions of the bodies of Cape women and men are, as we will see, nearly identical to depictions of the native Irish. Additionally, when and if the English remembered the Anglo-Irish, who in their eyes "degenerated" to the low level of the native Irish, they received discomforting reminders that they might not, in fact, be so superior to and different from the Cape people. Thus, while it is remarkable, it is certainly not coincidental that early-modern English representations of the native Irish and the Cape people share a style of diction and syntax; it suggests the presence of a mode of thinking as well as a developing rhetoric for the delimitation of indigenous groups that have been deemed disobedient or dangerous in some way.

Despite all the negative associations they did make between the native Irish and the Cape people, the English could do something with their ideas and images of the Cape people that they could not do with those they held of either the native Americans or the native Irish. That is, they could, literally and figuratively, use the Cape people to perform what Hayden White calls "ostensive self-definition by negation": "in times of sociocultural stress, when the need for positive self-definition asserts itself but no compelling criterion of self-identification appears, it is always possible to say something like: 'I may not know the precise content of my own felt humanity, but I am most certainly not like that'.[27] In this completely unique way, the example of the Cape people offered the English a chance to assemble positive ideas and images of themselves against an unequivocal negative background. Descriptions of the Cape people gave English authors a significant degree of power and control to make definitive assertions of their own superiority without offering proof and without the burden of history. Since the English were neither colonizing the Cape nor engaged in a war with its people, they could dismiss, adapt, or depart from the reality of the Cape people whenever they wanted. They could envision the Cape people and, later, the "Hottentots," in ways that unabashedly contributed to self-serving individual and/or national narratives. As we will see, in the eighteenth century, this is exactly what happened.

III

Employing Hans Blumenberg's concept of a "zero point," Rose Zimbardo believes the Restoration period to be a moment, "in cultural history when an epistemology is collapsing and simultaneously a new epistemology is arising."[28] What emerged from it, among other things, was a new construction of race that was determined to a significant extent by skin color. Numerous historians have identified the second half of the seventeenth century as the time of the shift, when, as Philip D. Curtin writes, "culture prejudice" slipped into "color prejudice."[29] Soon after Charles II regained the throne, his ministers and bureaucrats began to piece together the structures necessary for the nation's profitable entrance into the burgeoning mid-Atlantic slave trade. The monopoly right given in 1663 the Company of Royal Adventurers to Africa, and nine years later the issuing of a new monopoly to the Royal African Company, demonstrates how eager England was to ensure that it would be able to both supply its colonies with slaves and profit from the business of slavery. The nation's deepening involvement in slavery played the major role in the emerging construction of race at this historical moment. Winthrop D. Jordan argues that "the development of the slave trade was beginning to transform the Negro's color from a marvel into an issue."[30] England's investment in the mid-Atlantic slave trade grew so quickly that it simultaneously prompted and required a rhetoric that both justified colonial slavery and argued that the black race was naturally inferior to the white race, which served to license their enslavement. James Walvin finds an increasing articulation of the connections between the new construction of race, blackness, and slavery in English publications early on in the Restoration period: "English publications from the 1670's onwards, came to assume that there was an immutable link between blackness and slavery."[31] The emerging constructions of "Hottentots" played a unique role in arguments for and against slavery and in discussions of race, nature, and skin color.

Restoration and early-eighteenth-century descriptions of the color of those who were beginning to be referred to as "Hottentots" threatened to upset the emerging color-based construction of race. More specifically, the confusion expressed about the skin color of "Hottentots" in Restoration and early-eighteenth-century English and European representations of them posed a complicated challenge to the emerging construction of race that created a binary opposition between black and white and, in relation to slavery, linked blackness with slavery and whiteness with unslaveable. The debate that ensued in England over "Hottentot" skin color suggests the escalating English investment in color-based racial categories as well as their growing fascination with "Hottentots." Since the end of the sixteenth century, if not before, the English had thought of the Cape people as black or as darkskinned people, and, in this regard, identical to other sub-Saharan Africans. Indeed, all the initial English descriptions of the Cape people that reported on the subject depicted them as having black skin. Uncertainty about "Hottentot" skin color, however, began to emerge in the Restoration era because the majority of English and European representations asserted that "Hottentot" infants are born white-skinned. They routinely depict "Hottentots" as being fairer-skinned than Negro African societies, all of which served to call into question the presumption that they are black like African Negroes. Some accounts compare the skin color of "Hottentots" with that of English skin color rather than holding it up to the standard of African Negro societies.

With the fairness of their skin color subverting a major determinant of the new construction of race, "Hottentots" had to be classified as a distinct race of people. And so they were, at least for a while. In a 1707 report sent from the Cape to the members of the Royal Society, John Maxwell describes "Hottentot" skin color as "naturally as White as ours," and, therefore, he considers them "a race unto themselves."[32] As we will see, "Hottentots" were judged to be worse and lower than African Negro societies on the human ladder. At the same time, however, the English and other Europeans judged "Hottentots" to be "unfit" for slavery. It is interesting to speculate how and if the relative "fairness" of their skin color prompted the English to conceive of them as unslaveable. Moreover, the fair "Hottentot" skin color seems to have prompted a willingness on the part of the English to ponder other issues of "sameness" between themselves and "Hottentots," and not only for satiric purposes. By the end of the eighteenth century, however, "Hottentots" were again generally considered in the same category as "Negroes." Interestingly, once Britain took possession of the Cape at the start of the nineteenth century, the legal status of "Hottentots" as colonial subjects served to diminish the issue of their skin color.

The highly charged and peculiarly negative nature of English constructions of "Hottentots" in relation to race and skin color becomes even clearer when we briefly consider how these issues figure in the constructions developed by other European nations. The Dutch construction of "Hottentots" was far less conflicted than the English one. The matter-of-factness of the description in Willem Ten Rhyne's 1673 account suggests he felt little to no confusion in relation to questions of skin color and character. He and other Dutch colonial settlers saw the Cape people as black and inferior.

> The human race as a whole, apart from local and national peculiarities, is provided at birth with a character proper to itself; . . . distinct from those of other men, expressive alike of the inner and the outer man, and constituting an indefinable difference between one individual and another. Thus the Hottentots as a race have everywhere a dark and swarthy skin, as if scorched by the sun, and are generally endowed with a dry, warm blood. Yet the faces of some show much fairer, departing from their native dusky hue. Nevertheless the darkest are the loveliest in their eyes, and they think themselves never so finely adorned as when they sprinkle divers coloured earths upon their hair, or rub them, mixed with fat, upon their faces.[33]

Michael Streak links views like Ten Rhyne's to the "Primitive Calvanism" of the Dutch colonists: "In the eyes of the early colonists, by the unalterable decrees of God, the Blackman had been provided for their use, and it was therefore necessary that, when dealing with the Hottentots, Bushmen and Bantu, these people of colour should at all times be impressed with the superior authority of the Whiteman.[34] Significantly, the Dutch did not debate the "Hottentots' " place in the human world as did the English.

Comparing British representations with the ones that formed the foundation of the more positive French construction also suggests the conflicted character of the English response. Buffon, for example, saw skin color on a continuum, and he had an answer to the controversy surrounding the proper racial classification of "Hottentots": "it is evident that the Hottentots are not real negroes, but a people of the black race, approaching to the whites, as the Moors of the white race do to the black."[35] Skin color plays no role in Rousseau's vision of "Hottentots" as living examples of his Natural Man or Noble Savage. In *Discourse on the Origin and the Foundation of Inequality Among Men* (1755), Rousseau presents images of "Hottentots" as humane and virtuous people, and he sets them in telling opposition to the figures of "Civilized" or "Social Man," which he wished to criticize. Even more forcefully and emotionally than Rousseau, Abbé Raynal and Denis Diderot employ a "Hottentot" figure to critique European society, and "Hottentot" skin color is not an issue at all. In Raynal's *A Philosophical and Political History of the Settlements and Trade of the Europeans in the East and West Indians* (Geneva, 1780 and London, 1783), there appears a romantic comparison of the "Hottentot" way of life to the European lifestyle:

> But it may be asked, whether these Hottentots are happy? And in return, I shall ask, where is the man so prejudiced in favor of the advantages of our social institutions, and so great a stranger to our sufferings, as not sometimes to return in idea into the midst of the forests, or at least to envy the happiness, innocence, and tranquillity of a patriarchal life? This is exactly the life of the Hottentot. Are you fond of liberty? He is free. Are you desirous of health? He knows no illness but old age. Are you delighted with virtues? He has inclinations which he satisfies without remorse, but is a stranger to vice. I know very well that you will separate yourselves with disgust from a man, wrapped up, as it were, in the entrails of animals. Do ye think, then, that the corruption in which ye are plunged, your hatred, your perfidy, and your duplicity, are not more disgusting to my reason, than the uncleanliness of the Hottentots is disgusting to your senses?[36]

Only late-eighteenth-century British radicals expressed agreement with the sentiments espoused by Raynal and Diderot. Most representations, however, still find ways to mark "Hottentot" skin color and paint the society as an example of degeneration and lack of civilization.

In the nineteenth century, advocates for Britain's imperial project in Africa, India, the Middle East, the Orient and other parts, believed that the people falling under their colonial umbrella would benefit from their nation's protection and benevolence.

This attitude suppressed to some degree the questions related to the skin color of "Hottenots." With the British takeover of the Cape of Good Hope, select "Hottentots" (i.e., Christian "Hottentots") were thought to have a chance to improve and lift themselves up from the lowest rung of humanity's ladder because they had new colonial masters who were more understanding and tolerant of their natural limitations.

IV

Throughout this book, I focus for the most part on literary and visual representations that were recorded before Britain assumed control of the Cape Colony. I have organized the book chronologically in order to give readers a sense of how different constructions emerged over the course of roughly two hundred years and how at any given historical moment there could be constructions of "Hottentot" that served a variety of discourses. What becomes evident is early-modern England's creation and appropriation of constructions of "Hottentots" into its own consciousness, and its subsequent reliance on them as it wrestled with its own images and definitions of self and nation.

Chapter 1 examines the English representations of the Cape Khoikhoi written mainly between 1591 and 1634, although some accounts were later revised. The majority were written by English East India Company sailors and merchants, who were required to record their voyage experiences. English East India Company officers and others read and studied all available documents like these at the company's archives before they set sail themselves. Some accounts appeared in print as individually published narratives or as excerpts in Samuel Purchas's collections. This chapter also examines the earliest representations of the Cape people in the context of English depictions of the native Irish. The comparison demonstrates how a full complement of historical and literary styles of representation were imposed on the emerging constructions of the people soon to be named "Hottentots."

Inscription of the Cape people as the most beastly of human societies occurred relatively quickly. Chapter 2 discusses the etymology and the early descriptions of "Hottentots" that appear in Purchas's collections and in seventeenth- and early-eighteenth-century geography texts. Chapter 3 analyzes the two narratives (one English, one continental European) of Cape men who were exposed to English and European lifestyles and values, but refused to embrace them or renounced them when the opportunity arose. For the English, the story of Cory emerged first in the seventeenth century, although it was rewritten and retold throughout the eighteenth century. The Cory story also seems to have served as an urtext for narratives that chronicle African-European contact. Examining some of them in relation to the Cory story helps us to see how and why the English maintained their extremely negative construction of "Hottentots." A discussion of a competing continental European tale that captured English attention in the 1730s, but never managed to displace the Cory story in their consciousness, helps us to evaluate the Englishness of the Cory story. Unlike Cory, the protagonist in the continental narrative embraced a European lifestyle, but ultimately he also rejected it to return to his "Hottentot" traditions.

Subsequent chapters focus on eighteenth-century English "Hottentot" representations in a wide variety of genres. Chapter 4 shows how images and ideas of "Hottentots" first appearing in travel narratives were appropriated into the domestic literary landscape to represent individuals or movements thought to be degenerate and dangerous to the English nation. The fifth chapter is concerned with the reception of the few depictions that challenged the dominant representations of "Hottentots." The English translation of Peter Kolb's *The Present State of the Cape of Good Hope* (1731) was the first to create such a stir. The response by the popular press shows how strongly the English were invested in their negative rendering of the Cape people. The sixth chapter examines later eighteenth-century scientific travel narratives, geography books, and encyclopedias that make visible a shift in some constructions or challenged stereotypical notions about "Hottentots."

The final chapter explores the two parallel tracks of representation that took shape as the nineteenth century ensued. The British colonial presence at the Cape demanded a reconfiguration of the traditional constructions that had disallowed "Hottentots" true religious faith and the potential of progressing to the status of being a "civilized" people. Also, with the British replacing the Dutch as the colonial power, it became useful to represent "Hottentots" as the victims of Dutch colonial cruelty. Many nineteenth-century representations envision British rule as rescuing at least some "Hottentots" from the doomed fate of their entire society. Other facets of the traditional constructions, however, especially ones related to unnatural gender roles and perverted sexualities persisted. My examination purposely stops at the advent of British colonization of the Cape. What emerged as Cape Colony discourse during what we might call the first period of English-language South African literature is a subject unto itself, and one that has been ably handled by others. The conclusion briefly explores how the "Hottentots" are remembered in twentieth-century literature and popular culture. I broaden my focus to include a brief look at American "Hottentot" representations because I want to make the point that the "Hottentot" phenomenon is present in any nation that likes to think one skin color or one religion or one language or one sex is superior to any other.

The theoretical foundation of my study rests on the premise first developed by Edward Said in *Orientalism* (1979), which argues that a dominating culture, such as early-modern England's, invented "others" to suit its own purposes. Orientalism, Said writes, "was ultimately a political vision of reality whose structure promoted the difference between the familiar (Europe, the West, 'us') and the strange (the Orient, the East, 'them')."[37] More recent postcolonial readings, such as those offered by Mary Louise Pratt, David Spurr, Sara Suleri, Jyotsna G. Singh, Simon Gikandi, and Ann McClintock, which examine European-authored novels, travel narratives, works of personal testimony (journals, letters, autobiographies), and other cultural artifacts, employ and test Said's foundational theories to explore how a dominating culture as well as its authors rely on strategies of selection, arrangement, and characterization to serve ideological ends and reinforce the metropolitan culture.[38] These persuasive and valuable works, however, mainly address nineteenth-century texts and imperial structures or look backward to earlier ones from a secure colonialist promontory.

Focusing as it does on representations produced over the course of two centuries when England and, later, Great Britain, had little desire for and no plans to place the Cape of Good Hope and the people there under its dominion, my study refines existing theoretical constructs that tend to rely on binary oppositions from which the "Hottentots" are, in some measure, exempt: the opposites of self and other, sameness and difference, metropolitan and colonial cultures. As we will see, precolonial English constructions of "Hottentots" reveal the semi-articulated voice of what later became the ambivalent and assertive language and rhetoric of colonialism. Envisioning the worst gave early-modern England a crucial boundary marker as it began to examine and judge what it found when it looked both inside and outside of itself.

1
First Contact

WHAT DID THE ENGLISH ENVISION ABOUT THE INHABITANTS OF THE southernmost region of Africa before their ships began to stop there on a regular basis? From the most popular classical and medieval geography texts, such as Pliny's *Natural History* and Boemus's *Omnium Gentium Mores,* and sixteenth-century works, such as William Prat's *Description of the Country of Africa* (1554) and William Cunningham's *The Cosmographical Glasse* (1559), English readers received fantastical and negative images of Africans. In 1599, George Abbot argued that these privileged works communicated unreliable information about Africa: "From beyond the hils of *Atlas maior,* unto the South of *Africa,* is nothing almost in antiquitie worthie the reading, and those things which are written for the most part are fables."[1] But Abbot's complaint did not stop some of his countrymen from envisioning the worst. Richard Zouch's *The Dove: Or Passages of Cosmography* (1613) includes two stanzas about southern "Afrique" that sound very much like a poetic rendering of Pliny's descriptions.

> In ZANZIBAR, neare to that Southern Cape,
> Which lately from GOOD HOPE deriv'd his name,
> If no: by Nature, many an ugly shape
> Have beene brought forth by Monster-making Fame,
>   Such Creatures hardly could produced be,
>   But by th'assistance of her Midwifery.
> There headlesse some are framed, as *Momus* would,
> With eyes and mouth, like windowes, in their breast;
> Others as cast in *Polyphemus* mould,
> Of one Light in their fore-head stand possest:
>   Some Pygmyes, Men Diminutives, maintain
>   Like Pawnes tall squadrons in a chesse-boord plaine[2]

An educated reader in the early seventeenth century might not have believed in the accuracy of this poetic depiction, but studying contemporary descriptions in geographies and travel narratives would not necessarily have lent him (or her) any more reliable and accurate ideas about the peoples in southern Africa.

Late-sixteenth-century English accounts of the Cape contributed little elucidation on the subject. The second edition of Richard Hakluyt's *Principal Navigations* (1598) includes three English-authored accounts of the Cape of Good Hope, two of which had appeared in the first edition also. Thomas Stephens's semihysterical description of the Cape, quoted in the introduction, contrasts with Sir Francis Drake's brief description of the delight he felt at the Cape: "This Cape is a most stately thing, and the fairest Cape we saw in the whole circumference of the earth."[3] A new entry in the 1598 edition chronicles the first contact between English sailors and the people of the Cape. On 1 August 1591, a three-ship expedition commanded by Captain George Raymond sailed into Table Bay after close to four months at sea.[4] Hakluyt's source, Edmund Barker, who served as a lieutenant to James Lancaster, the captain of the *Edward Bonaventure*, relates that when the sailors went ashore, they encountered, "certaine blacke salvages, very brutish, which would not stay, but retired from them."[5] After a brief period of time, during which the English foraged for themselves, "we got a negro, whom we compelled to march into the country with us, making signs to bring us some cattell; but at this time we could come to the sight of none; so we let the negro goe, with some trifles."[6] Eight days later, however, more trading ensued. As Barker explains, the "negro" they had earlier compelled, "with 30 or 40 other negros, brought us downe some 40 bullocks and oxen, with as many sheepe; at which time we bought but few of them."[7] Resupplied and refreshed, two of the three ships set sail for the East, but they met with disaster soon after. The sole ship that managed a safe return to England was the one that left the Cape to limp back to London with the sailors who were too ill to continue the voyage. According to Foster Rhea Dulles, of the one hundred and ninety-eight men who doubled the Cape with Lancaster and Barker, only twenty-five eventually made it home.[8] This expedition's failure hardly presented the English court with an argument to fund or sanction a return visit to the Cape of Good Hope. In fact, ten years passed before an English sailor again placed his feet on Cape soil.

Dutch ships stopped at the Cape with far greater frequency than English ones. English translations of late-sixteenth-century Dutch travel narratives that included descriptions of the Cape people appeared in 1597 and 1598. *The Description of a Voyage Made by Certaine Ships of Holland into the East Indies* (1598) chronicles a voyage undertaken in 1595 by three Dutch ships, on one of which sailed Cornelius Houtman. Houtman's representation of the Cape people is far more detailed than Barker's. He records a friendly exchange of goods between the Dutch sailors and the Cape people.

> We went into the country and spake with the inhabitants, who brought divers fresh victuals aboard our ships, for a knife, or small piece of iron, & c. giving us an ox, or a sheep, &c. three oxen and five sheep for a bill, an axe, a shovel, a great iron nail, a knife, and other little pieces of iron not worth four livres.[9]

His description of their physical appearance is relatively matter of fact. In contrast to English-authored accounts, his prose makes relatively few judgmental comments about the Cape people.

> The inhabitants are of small stature, well jointed and boned. They go naked, covering their members with foxes and others beasts tails. They seem cruel, yet with us they used all kind of friendship; but are very beastly and stinking, in such sort, that you may smell them in the wind at least a fathom from you. They are apparelled with beasts skins made fast about their necks. Some of them, being of the better sort, had their mantles cut and raised chequerwise, which is a great ornament with them.[10]

Even when he employs an emotionally charged simile, such as when he details the eating habits of the Cape people, Houtman still does not delimit them from the human race. "They eat raw fish as it is new killed, and the entrails of beasts without washing or making clean, gnawing at it like dogs; and meneaters, where they take the advantage."[11] Significantly, allegations of cannibalism had currency for decades to come. Indeed, as we shall see, a number of seventeenth-century English representations also claim the people of the Cape were "meneaters," but none ever offered proof of the charge.

Immediately following the one-sentence indictment, Houtman's description returns to simple description and comparison. Crucially, he sees sameness as well as difference in his reference to Europeans who share characteristics with the Cape people.

> Under their feet they tie pieces of beast skins instead of shoes, that they may travel in the hard ways. We could not see their habitations, for we saw no houses they had, neither could we understand them; for they speak very strangely, much like the children in our country with their pipes, and clocking like turkey-cocks; or like the Germans that live

upon the mountains of Switzerland toward the Julian Alps, who by drinking spring and snow water very cold, have always swellings in their throats.[12]

A curious illustration accompanies this representation, and it also suggests sameness.[13] It depicts a European-looking male figure dressed in a cape or mantle that covers his back, shoulders, one arm, and a loincloth of sorts that covers his genitalia. He wears sandals on his feet and holds a spear in one hand. He is gazing at a slightly bigger "Cupid-like youth," holding arrows, who is reported to be a "native of Madagascar."

Similitude is also suggested in another Dutch representation. The 1598 translation of John Huighen van Linschoten's *His Discourse of Voyages into ye Easte and West Indies* employs a biblical reference that captures the paradox of European perceptions of the Cape and its people: "they cover themselves with the like apparell that Adam and Eve did weare in Paradise."[14] Through the simile, Linschoten declares that what we have here is a garden, yet its inhabitants "live like beastes or wild men."

> Most part of the Caffares live like beasts or wild men, yet they have their houses in troups or heaps, like coûtry villages, whe they assemble and divel together and in every Village they have a Lord or King, to whome they are subject and obedient, they are commonly in warres one with an other, and one place or Village against an other, and have law and Justice among them with some small Policie, concerning their worldly affaires and gouernment: but as concerning Religion and faith, they know not what it meaneth, but liue like beastes without any knowledge of God.[15]

It is interesting that Linschoten here gives the Cape people credit for having a system of government, because English representations of them generally did not. Linschoten's representations are not specific to the people of the Cape; he intended them to describe all southern Africans. In fact, he did not actually stop at the Cape. A visual image of four Africans accompanies Linschoten's text. As Van Wyk Smith points out, the figures in this illustration "attest to a markedly Eurocentric vision."[16] They are represented as Adam and Eve figures. Their bodies are well proportioned and handsome, and they both appear to be relaxed. Significantly, they do not carry any weapons. The woman is given a physical appearance that would become an iconographic cliche in early-modern European visual representations of African women. She has large breasts and she appears to be nursing a baby who is perched across her shoulder. A loose fitting apron of material covers the mother's waist and groin. We can also see specific markers in relation to the depiction of the African male figure. He is naked, and there is a decoration on his penis that seems to be a ribbon or tassel of some sort. In other words, the viewer's attention is directed to his genitalia.

The first English-edited work about Africa that received authoritative status, John Pory's version of Leo Africanus's *The History and Description of Africa* (1600), presents a more negative picture of Africans than his source text. Pory himself wrote and added "A General Description of Africa," in which he emphasizes the Cape's danger: "this cape the mariners were woont to cal the lion of the Ocean, and the tempestuous cape, by reason of the russling and roring of the windes, which they found there for the most part very boisterious: for the sea thereabout is exceeding rough, by reason of the continual fury of the windes; neither will any navigators touch upon the cape, except they be enforced by meere necessitie."[17] In another section added by Pory, entitled "A Description of Places Undescribed by John Leo," he creates a sort of allegory of his own, implying that if a man survives the peril of the seas, he will find a garden on the land: "In the midst of this cape lieth a plot of ground of that beautie and delight, as that without any humane industrie it may compare with the most artificiall gardens of Europe. On the top of this place, nature minding as it were to excelle her-selfe, hath framed a great plaine, which for beautifull situation, fruifulness of herbes, varietie of flowers, and flourishing verdure of things, seemeth to resemble a terrestriall paradise."[18]

The next paragraph presents Pory's description of the Cape people, which sets them in stark contrast to the land they inhabit. The details of Pory's representation are drawn from the recently translated Dutch narratives: "The Hollanders in the yeere 1595 . . . had conversation and truck with some of these Cafres, whom they found to be a stoute and valiant people, but very base and contemptible in their behavior and apparell, being clad in oxe and sheeps skins wrapped about their shoulders with the hairie sides inward in forme of a mantle."[19] Signficantly, Pory also includes a digression on their skin color that establishes a connection between lawlessness and blackness.

> The people of this place called in the Arabian toong Cafri, Cafres, or Cafates, that is to say, lawlesse or outlawes, are for the most part exceeding blacke of colour, which very thing may be a sufficient argument, that the sunne is not the sole or chiefe cause of their blacknes;

for in divers other countries where the heate thereof is farre more scorching and intolerable, there are tawnie, browne, yellowish, ash-coloured, and white people; so that the cause thereof seemeth rather to be of an hereditarie qualitie transfused from the parents, then the intemperature of an hot climate, though it also may be some furtherance thereunto.[20]

Critics have recently argued that Leo's vision of dark-skinned Africans is in itself suspect. Kim Hall finds in Leo "a disdain" that he shares with European readers "for the darkest African peoples."[21] Add to this Pory's own cultural bias, which is, according to Anthony Barthelemy, evident in his selection of diction, and what we have is a text that reveals the high level of his, and by implication, the English, anxiety over "difference."[22]

The earliest English visual representation of the Cape people also emphasizes their supposed beastliness. Executed for a map by John Speed, it depicts one figure eating what appears to be the intestine of an animal. Speed pays scant attention to detailing the body of the Cape figure, dressing him simply in a loincloth and cape; he clearly wishes to direct the viewer's gaze to the intestine.[23] Interestingly, the 1606 map by Hondius the elder, which Speed used as a model for his own figure, shows both a male and female inhabitant of the Cape. The two figures are wearing capes, loin coverings, and some decorative objects, and both are eating animal intestines.

These and other texts lent English readers the opportunity to learn about violent previous encounters between Europeans and the Cape people. The story about the Cape people's 1510 killing of the Portuguese viceroy Francisco de Almeida and over fifty of his men was fairly well known. Also in circulation was a description of a November 1598 skirmish between Cape people and Dutch sailors that was written by John Davies, an English navigator who worked as a pilot on Houtman's ship.

> The Flemings offering them some rude wrong, they absented themselves three dayes, in which time they made great Fires upon the Mountaines in the Countrey. The nineteenth hereof there came great troups of them to us, bring much cattel with them, and in the time of bartering, suddenly taking their advantage, they set upon us, and slue thirteen of our people with hand Darts, which a foure Pikes length could not offend.
> Notwithstanding, the Flemmings fled before them like Mice before Cats, throwing away their weapons most basely. And our Baase, to save himselfe stayed aboord, and sent us Corselets, Two-hand-swords,

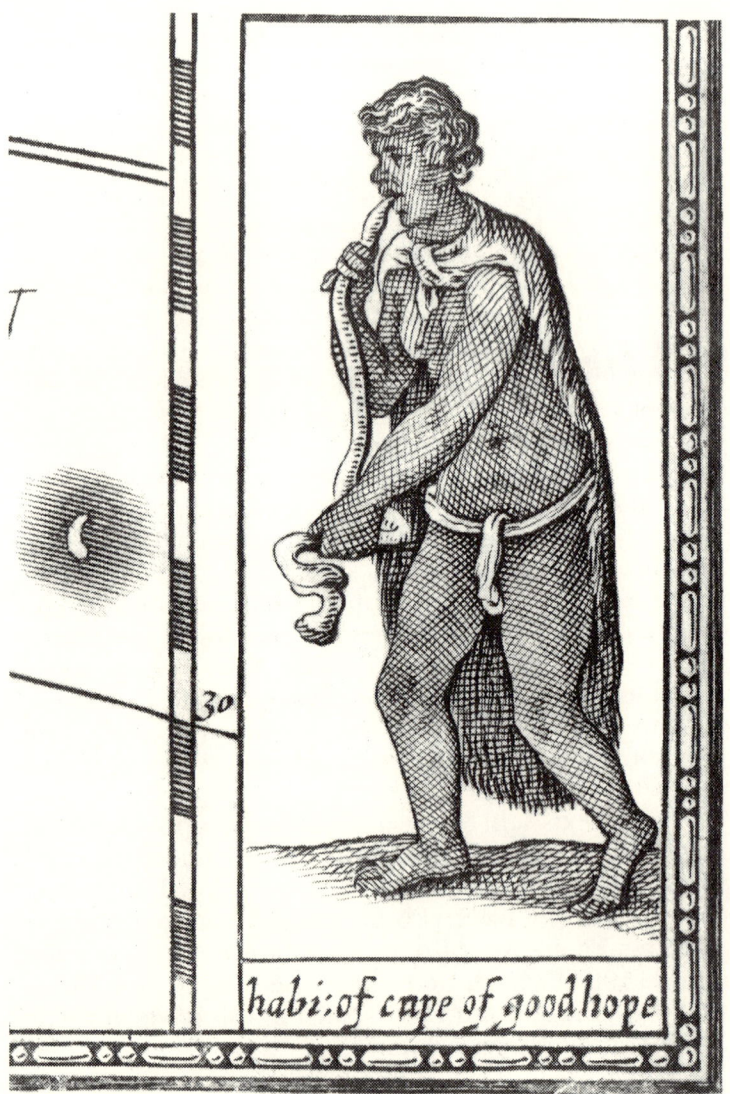

John Speed, from *A Prospect of the Most Famous Parts of the World*. Beinecke Library, permission of Yale University.

Pikes, Muskets, and Targets, so that we were armed and laden with weapons, but there was neither courage nor discretion. For we stayed by our Tents, being belegred with Canibals and Cowes; we were in Muster Giants, with great armed bodies, but in action Babes, with Wrens hearts. Hereupon Master Tomkins and my self undertook to order these Fellowes. . . . Some consented to us, but the most part unwilling, and divers ranne to the Pottate Pot, for they swore it was dinner time. This night we went all aboord, only leaving our great Mastive Dogge behind us, who by no means would come to us. For I thinke he was ashamed of our Companie.[24]

Davies's castigation of the Dutch sailors is both amusing and suggestive. He basically dismisses the Cape people from any serious consideration. He clearly expected his comrades to fight more bravely against the "Canibals and Cowes" facing them, and thus his disappointment in them assumes precedence in his representation.

The information about the Cape people that appeared in accounts written before 1601 are uniformly negative. Subsequent representations did little to erase this assortment of negative ideas and images. In 1601, the English East India Company launched its first expedition, led by Cape veteran James Lancaster. It left England on 20 April, but the four boats did not reach the Cape of Good Hope until September. The long sea voyage took its toll; one hundred five men died before landfall was accomplished. Only the crew on James Lancaster's boat escaped a widespread outbreak of scurvy; their experienced captain ordered them to swallow a spoonful of lime juice every morning. The other crews, however, had been so depleted that they could not drop anchor without help from Lancaster and his men. An anonymous hand on the expedition recorded that the Cape's vast supply of fresh food provided "so royall refreshing that all our men recovered their health and strength, onely foure or five excepted."[25] It is certainly a shame that this author does not provide any details about the "royal refreshing," although the phrase suggests the relief the Cape provided the men.

A 1603 publication, *A Letter Written to the Right Worshipfull the Governours and Assistants of the East Indian Marchants in London,* presents a more detailed picture of near disaster. Less complimentary about the Cape, and far more begruding about the native trading partners, it summarizes the fleet's arrival and stay at the Cape in two sentences: "The 19. day of September we came to Anchor at *Saldaina,* being in very great distresse by reason of the scurvy disease then raging among us. The *Ascention* and *Susans* company were scarce able to let fall their Anchors without the helpe of other ships, there we staied and refreshed our men with fresh victuals, as Beefe and Mutton in great aboundance which cost us little or nothing, there we staied about seaven weekes, and had staied there longer if the inhabitantes had continued to bring us fresh victuals, so we departed thence the 9. of October."[26] This implied criticism of the Cape people, that they are too parsimonious in their exchanges of food supplies for trinkets, appears frequently in English representations. It, and the dangerous wind and sea conditions around the Cape, prompted the English East India Company to prefer other ports for the refreshment of its ships.

Orders to ignore the Cape were issued to Henry Middleton, the commander of the English East India Company's second expedition, but he and his fleet stopped there nonetheless. The record suggests he had little choice. His convoy of four ships left England on 25 March 1604, and they did not come into sight of the Cape until Friday, 13 July.

> The wind at south-west, a gentell gale, the Generall commaunded the tackes aboord, intending to go about the Cape. But our sick men cryed out most lamentably; for at that present there were sicke of the scurvy at the least 80 men in our ship, not one able to helpe the other; who made a petition to the Generall, most humbly entreating him, for Gods sake, to save there lives and put in for Saldania; otherwayes they were but dead men.[27]

The prose describing the expedition's stop at the Cape is driven by its need to make certain and specific sense out of an incident. According to Hayden White, this is what any historian does.[28] But English disorder handed the author of this narrative a particularly challenging assignment. He had to inscribe the English sailors as the winners of what was, in reality, a losing exchange caused by their own lack of discipline.

As the account makes clear, some initial trading took place after the ships landed, but the English were not able to secure all the goods they needed. They considered the withdrawal of the Cape people as uncivil behavior. The narrative's explanation for the disappearance of the Cape people (that they "disliked" the fact that the English were establishing a camp of sorts) is nothing more than mere projection, but it was believed and adapted in subsequent accounts.

> Our Generall and the captains went to barter with them for small peeces of iron, and bought some 12 sheepe; and more [they] would have sould us, till that they saw us begin to set up our tents; which as it seemed was to their disliking, for that incontinent they pulled downe their houses and made them fast upon their beasts backes, and did drive away; yet all meanes possible was sought to drawe them to sell us

more: but in no case they would abide any longer with us, but drove away with all the speed they might. (9–10)

The suggestion that the breakdown in trade negotiations is the Cape people's fault is intended to indict them as blameworthy for subsequent events.

The next section presents a decidedly pro-English version of the violent encounter. The English leaders at the Cape evidently discussed how they should respond to the Cape people's disappearance. Some argued for the use of force: "It lay in the Generals power to have taken them all from them, as some counselled him to doe; but he in no case would give eare thereunto, but let them depart; not doubting but that they would returne again, seeing we offered them no wrong, when it was in our powers to dispossesse them of all their cattell" (84). The sub-textual implication here is that a civil Englishman like Middleton uses reason while any response on the part of the Africans is dictated by their emotions. Middleton tried to solve the trading impasse by presenting a less threatening presence. He ordered four men to go forward to the Cape people and negotiate a resumption of trade between the groups. In fact, between 26 July and 2 August, the Cape people sold to Middleton's party far more livestock than they had to the 1601 expedition led by Lancaster.

> But the generall caused all the company to make a stand; and then sent 4 to them, with a bottell of wine and victuals, with a taber and a pipe. They, seeing no more in company, came to them, and did eate, drinke, and daunce with them. So they, seeing with what kindnes they were used, tooke hart unto them and came along with our Generall to our tents; where they had many toyes bestowed upon them, as pins, points, beads, and branches [brooches]. And so they returned, all very well pleased, making signes to returne the next day with cattell; but foule wether prevented them 3 dayes. The forth day after, being the 26, they brought us 44 sheepe, and the next day 23 sheep and two kine, and the next day 15 sheepe and one bullocke; and the 30 day we bought 120 sheepe and 6 beeves, the next day 9 sheepe and three beeves, and the 2 of August 3 sheepe. (10–11)

The anonymous author makes two interesting assumptions here about the people of the Cape: that they understand the "kindness" of the English and that they are "very well pleased" with the trades.

Six days later, however, relations between the two groups broke down again. Evidently, Middleton had ordered a party of twelve men to trade with the people for more food, but they returned with only two sheep. On being asked why they returned with so few provisions, the leader of the group replied that the people of the Cape "would abuse them, in snatching their yron from them, and not to suffer them to drive the cattell away they payd for" (12–13). The description of what happened next forms the largest section of the narrative, and in it we can see how the Cape people are blamed for the fiasco that ensued.

With one hundred twenty of his men in tow, Middleton planned to ambush the Cape people during the next negotiating session. In the interim, three sailors—who had been drinking—became separated from their troop and ended up hiding in the bushes from the country people. The author's use of repetition here is striking: he repeats three times and in three different ways that the English sailors were unarmed.

> At that time, the sunne being up halfe and houre after these fellowes had hid themselves, came our weaponlesse merchants from the tents and beganne to barter with them for two or three sheepe, which of purpose they had sent downe to our people to keep them busie while they were getting their herds of cattell to runne away; which our merchants perceiving, they presently, unarmed as they were, went amongst them, and sent worde by one of them to the Generall to come away, with all his people, for that he and all his companie were discovered. (13)

Before Middleton could "rescew" his men, one of them was wounded. Not surprisingly, the author is very conscientious about providing the exact details: "they had wounded one of our men with foure dartes sticking in his body" (13). The strategies employed here show the author wanted his readers to see the three drunk sailors as innocent victims.

With his readers still in mind, the author uses the penultimate section of the narrative to establish a rhetorical victory for the English troop. The Cape people are described as fleeing to the countryside, which allows the author to depict the English as being in control of the battle. The use of metaphor masks English disorder. "Our men, as then having the raines in their owne handes, pursued after them in such scattering maner that, if the people of the countrey had been men of any resolution, they might have cut off most of them" (13–14).

The account goes on to relate that Middleton ordered a trumpet to signal a retreat, but his forces were in evident disarray. Yet here again the author finds a way to create another negative picture of the "countrey people," implying that if they had any sense, they might have defeated the English:

> Yet the Generall tooke it greevous to see his men scatterred over all the Playne, & scarce three of them together in a company: which if the people of the countrey had joyned together and set upon them, beeing so scattered, they had cut most of them off, which thing the Generall greatly doubted, yet God be thanked it sorted better. (14)

The final sentence of the paragraph awards a moral victory to the English; they managed, after all, to secure the additional livestock they wanted ("and so retorned homewardes with a hundred Kyne and Calves, which was welcome to our sicke men" [14]).

The concluding paragraph shows how keen this anonymous author was to present the English in a positive light. Forced to account for the accidental drowning of some English sailors who rushed to help their comrades on land, the last sentence depicts the English as driving the Cape people from the area: "This night, and the next after, our sentenels had spied the cuntry people lurking about our tents; so that alarome was given, and they fled" (14–15). This fiasco at the Cape is thus remembered as a victory for the English. The diction used to represent the Cape people is wholly negative in connotation: they are the ones lurking, and they are the ones who flee after the (alert) English sentries sound the alarm. Victory complete, the English sail off to continue the expedition. Written in order to bolster the public's support for the efforts and aims of the English East India Company, *The Last East-Indian Voyage* was entered in the stationer's register in May 1606, just two weeks after the expedition returned to London. It was crucial for the fledgling English East India Company that the public consider this expedition a success; clearly, this pamphlet was intended as propaganda for the company.

What passed for information and knowledge about the Cape people increased as more English East India Company sailors and merchants recorded their impressions of what they saw at the Cape during their refreshment layovers at Table Bay and Saldanha Bay (slightly north of Table Bay). This first English generation of representations, written between 1601 and 1633, have identifiable patterns that testify to how English sailors and merchants were awed by the Cape but shocked by the people they found there. The accounts also reveal the strategies that helped to develop an anticipatory Cape discourse. The most prominent of them are (1) a marked tendency to separate the people from the landscape; (2) the development of a rationale that finds the Cape people undeserving of the land because they do nothing to develop it; (3) the use of unflattering references, allusions, and figurative language to castigate the Cape people for everything from their dietary habits to their clothing to their trading practices to their seeming lack of religion.

Many narratives make clear that the long voyage to the Cape (and beyond) presented extraordinary physical and emotional challenges to the sailors. All expeditions suffered from outbreaks of scurvy and other illnesses. In the narrative he wrote in 1616, Edward Terry uses a revealing and remarkable phrase to describe the physical hardships of the long sea journey: "I say our people when they have come hither with very crazie bodies, have often found here much good refreshing."[29] After enduring passages of four or more months at sea, the relief and excitement felt by English sailors and merchants when they finally landed at the Cape should not be underestimated. It is not surprising, therefore, that the language found in the early representations suggests the intensity of their emotions. Superlatives are consistently employed to describe the rich and vital resources of the Cape. Seeing how well the place "agrees with English bodies," Patrick Copland calls it a paradise: "The Bay of Soldania and all about the Cape is so healtfull and fruitfull as might grow a Paradise of the World."[30] Twenty-two year old Thomas Herbert was so captivated by what he saw during his eight-day stay at the Cape in July 1627, that, in the first edition of his narrative, he declares: "in all my life I never saw Ground more pleasant for view or healthfull for use."[31]

The abundant refreshment offered at the Cape delighted English sailors and merchants, and it prompted them to resent the people who lived there. The relief felt by an anonymous author on the 1605 expedition led by Sir Edward Michelbourne is evident. In two sentences, he emphasizes the "goodly countrey" and the "excellent good refreshing," yet he twice repeats the word "savage" in reference to the Cape people: "The ninth [of April], wee went on shore, finding a goodly Countrey, inhabited by a most savage and beastly people as ever I thinke God created. In this place wee had excellent good refreshing, in so much that I thinke the like place is not to be found among savage people."[32] Then his stocktaking begins. As Mary Louise Pratt and others have noticed, inventories are often featured in colonial discourse, although these earliest English descriptions of the Cape demonstrate that they were a part of precolonial discourse as well.[33]

1: FIRST CONTACT
45

> For we neither wanted Beefe, Mutton, nor Wilde-Fowle all the time we lay there. This Countrey is very full of Oxen and Sheepe, which they keepe in great Heards and Flocks, as we do our Cattle in England. Moreover it doth abound with store of wild Beasts and Fowles, as wild Deere in great abundance, Antelopes, Babious, Foxes, and Hares, Ostriches, Cranes, Pelicans, Herons, Geese, Duckes, Pheasants, Patridges, and divers other sorts of most excellent Fowles. Of which Fowles wee killed great store with our Pieces. It is also most pleasantly watered with wholesome springs, which have their beginning from the tops of exceeding high Mountaines, which, falling into the Vallies, make them fruitful.[34]

What is so interesting about this description is what the author fails to mention: the English traded with the Cape people for the meat and livestock. This tendency to separate and to erase the Cape people from the landscape is common in English representations.

For Christian sailors such as the English and, as we saw, the Dutch, the symbolic potential of such a rich and restorative place is hard to ignore. The complicating and serious flaw that prevents the Cape from being positively Edenic, however, is the people who inhabit it. In the opinion of the English, the Cape people do not deserve to live in a land so rich and so beautiful. Captain Thomas Elkington judges them to be "unworthy so good a Land, which in likelihood with culture would be very fertile."[35] Ralph Standish, a surgeon on the *Hosiander,* which stopped at the Cape in June 1612, states quite directly that he thinks the Cape people are unworthy of the land.

> the Counttrey being firtille ground and pleasantt and a counttrey verie temperatt but the people bruitt and savadg, without Religion, without language, without Lawes or government, without manners or humanittee, and last of all withoutt apparell, for they go naked save onelie a pees of a Sheepes Skyn to cover their Members that in my opinion yt is a greatt pittie that such creattures as they bee should injoy so sweett a counttrey.[36]

The English judged the Cape people to be doubly guilty because they did little to improve the land. The emerging English colonial sensibility wanted to see such a rich place planted and worked, and to the sailors and merchants who stopped at the Cape, the Cape people lived without performing any industry. The English had difficulty accepting the subsistence lifestyle of the Cape's inhabitants, which clearly clashed with the increasing value they placed on industry and capital exchange. Abdul R. JanMohamed sees this response as central to the mentality of European colonialism. He writes, "the Europeans disrupted a material and discursive universe based on use-value and replaced it with one dominated by exchange-value."[37]

Although England had no explicit plan to claim and develop the Cape at this point, it is possible to find a procolonialist mentality even in these early representations. At this time, English visitors clearly perceived the land as belonging to no one (*res nullius*). In their eyes, the Cape people, who did not perform labor on the land, did not have any claim to it. The Cape's potential inspired some colonial dreams and plans. As early as 1608, John Jourdain advised the East India Company about the location's potential:

> Beinge planted and sowne in due time, and kept as it ought to bee, if this countrye were inhabited by a civill nation, haveinge a castle or forte for defence against the outrage of those heathenish people and to withstand any forraine force, in shorte time it might bee brought to some civillitie, and within fewe years able of it selfe to furnish all shipps refreshinge, for the countrye at present doth abound with fishe and fleshe in greate plentie.[38]

The language Jourdain employs in relation to the Cape people ("the outrage of those heathenish people") is contrasted with his own cultural assumptions. His use of the word "civill" is of particular interest. At this point in time, civility was one of England's most cherished values. To the English, therefore, only civil and Christian men could perfect the garden at the Cape.

The very existence and presence of the Cape people—so uncivil and so imperfect—at such a paradisiacal location deeply upset and troubled some of the English. The vehemence in Edward Terry's condemnation of the Cape people is striking.

> For the soyl about the Bay, it seems to be very good, but the Sun shines not upon a people in the whole world, more barbarous than those which possess it; Beasts in the skins of men, rather than men in the skins of beasts, as may appear by their ignorance, habit, languages, diet, with other things, which make them most brutish.[39]

Terry's use of synecdoche ("the soyl about the Bay") to call the land "good," and thus separate it from the people who are "bad," gives the English who stopped there a kind of reprieve, a way to remain unpolluted by the people who were ensuring their continued sustenance. The English separated themselves from the Cape people by creating distance, by insisting that this "other" people were animal-like and did not have systems, such as language, religion, and law, which the English considered signifiers of humanity and civility. This is why Ralph Standish, among others, could hear the implosive sounds of the Cape language, yet declare them a people "without language,"[40] and still use the word "language" when describing the sounds.

Since all the exchanges the English had with the people of the Cape were driven by a need to resupply their ships with food and fresh water, the earliest representations often include information about the negotiations between the two groups. These passages have a twofold purpose. They help to establish difference by presenting the English as "winning" these encounters, and they implicate the Cape people as untrustworthy trading partners. The triumph of the English traders is secured, rhetorically speaking, by the use of telling facts and European standards of value. A journal kept during the Michelbourne expedition (1604) says that "For a piece of an old yron Hoope, not worth twopence, you might buy a great Bullocke, and for a piece of yron, not worth two or three good Horse Nayles, you might buy a Sheepe."[41] Robert Coverte believes the Cape people are ignorant of real worth because they "chiefly desire Iron, esteeming it more than either gold or silver. For with our old iron, we bought all our Cattell and any thing else that we had of them."[42]

The earliest trade negotiations between the English and the people of the Cape were accomplished through sounds. The Purchas version of the 1601 expedition explains that Lancaster "spake to them in the cattels language (which was never changed at the confusion of Babell), which was moath for oxen and kine, and baa for sheepe; which language the people understood very well without any interpreter."[43] A number of accounts report that the English could not imitate or learn the Cape people's language. A representation from the Lancaster-led 1601 expedition records, "the sharpest wit among us could not learne one word of their language; and yet the people would soone understand any signe wee made to them."[44] *A True and Large Discourse of the Voyage of 20, April 1601* (1603) similarly explains that "their language is very hard to be pronounced, by reason of a kinde of clacking with the tongue; so that we could not learne one worde of their language."[45] Significantly, in these accounts the Cape people are not given credit for being intelligent enough to understand English, and the sailors are not faulted for their failure to understand the Cape tongue. Jourdain writes, "To these people we made signes for cattle and sheepe; which by our signes they understoode us."[46] The suggestion here is that the English "signes" were what facilitated the comprehension. In this way, the English often gave themselves credit for facilitating discussions.

The language spoken by the Cape people became a subject of discussion for the next two centuries. In fact, the English often insisted that it was not a language at all, a strategy which allowed them to cast doubt on the humanity of the Cape people. John Milward called it "a chattering rather than a language."[47] Those who recognized it as a language still found ways to demonize the people who spoke it. In his *A Relation of Some Yeares Travaile* (1634), Thomas Herbert explicitly connects the native Irish and the Cape people: "their pronunciation is like the Irish: their customes not much unlike the rude ones of antique times."[48] For the 1638 second edition, Herbert revised this passage to include an assertion that the Cape people copulate with apes: "Their language is apishly sounded (with whom tis thought they mix unnaturally) . . . being voyced like the Irish."[49] This assertion of beastly correspondence between the Cape people and apes, and the simultaneous reference to Irish suggests how eager the English were to demonize through negative association.

English accusations against the people of the Cape for stealing are also strikingly similar to contemporaneous complaints made about the native Irish. In his *Itinerary* (1617), Fynes Moryson castigates the Irish for honoring theft ("Theft is not infamous but rather commendable among them"), which he links with their native idleness.[50] The accusation that the people of the Cape were given to stealing can be found in many of the early accounts. The 1603 narrative of the Lancaster expedition relates that "They will picke and steale, although you looke on them."[51] Similarly, a journal keeper on a voyage led by William Keeling complains that "they doe apply all their witts unto filchinge and stealinge."[52] John Jourdain's 1608 representation makes the same charge, and it also suggests how frustrated the English were by their dependence on the Cape people.

> And many tymes, having sould them to us, yf we looked not the better to them, they would steale them agayne from us and bringe them agayne to see; which we were fayne with patience to buy agayne of them, without givinge any foule language, for feare that they would bringe us noe more. As lykewyse yf they stole any thinge, yf yt weare of smale valewe, wee would not meddle with them butt suffer them to carry yt awaye; which they tooke very kindly, in soe much that they brought such plentye downe, more then wee were able to tell what to doe withall. Yett we refused noone, for feare lesse in soe doeinge they would bring noe more.[53]

The use here of the word "feare" suggests the high level of vulnerability on the part of the English. Their inability to provide themselves with an adequate amount of fresh food, and thereby ensure their own survival, was heightened by their horror for the Cape people's diet. Could they still consider themselves as vastly superior to the Cape people if they were "reduced" to such staples?

The diet of the Cape people became a major signifier of their savageness and strangeness. Indeed, oftentimes a description of it appears as the first piece of evidence the writer uses to argue that the Cape people are the most beastly on earth. A representation from the Sir Edward Michelbourne expedition of 1604 says that the people of the Cape feed "in most beastly fashion."

> In all the time of our being there they lived upon the guts and filth of the meate which we did cast away, feeding in the most beastly fashion, for they would neither wash nor make cleane the guts, but take them and cover them with hote ashes, and before they were through hote, they pulled them out, shaking them a little in their hands, and so eate the guts, the excrements and the ashes. They live upon raw flesh, and a certaine kind of roote which they have, which groweth there in great abundance.[54]

The attention to detail given in this description suggests the author felt a certain level of fascination as well as repulsion. Descriptions of the diet often produce negative pronouncements. The record kept by Thomas Roe during his 1615–18 ambassadorial mission to the court of Jehangir in India describes the "5 or 600 people" at "Soldanya" as "the most barberous in the world, eating Carrione, wearing the gutts of sheepe about their Necks for health, and rubbing their heads (curled like Negroos) with dung of beasts and durte."[55]

The disgust the English felt at the dietary habits of the Cape people often also results in the imposition of distance and difference based on religious or ethnic boundaries. Captain Robert Coverte, for example, marginalizes the people at the Cape as "Ethiopians" in his *A True and Almost Incredible Report of an Englishman, That (Being Cast Away in the Good Ship Called the* Assention*) (1612)*, where he writes that they "are by nature very brutish or beastly people, especially in their feeding." After providing a graphic description of how the people "eate the guts & garbedge, yea even the very panch where the dung & filth lieth," Coverte says that "it could almost have stifled one of us to come by them."[56] Others used the Cape people's dietary habits to enforce distance based on religion.

John Jourdain maintained that "noe Christian" could endure coming within a "myle" of the dead seals "the Saldanians fed very hartilie on."[57]

The use of overstatement in representations of dietary practices is prevalent and striking. Edward Terry uses it and simile when he writes that the Cape people eat like dogs, although not English dogs: "yea, they will eat that which a ravenous dog in *England* will refuse."[58] Nicholas Withington employs the same simile: "They will eate any garbage both rawe and fowle. When we had killed an oxe or a sheepe at annye time, they would scramble for the offall, like doggs, and eate yt."[59] Jourdain offers their diet as proof that the people at the Cape are cannibals: "in soe much that my opinion is, that if without danger they could come to eate mans flesh, they would not make any scruple of it, for I think the world doth not yeild a more heathenish people and more beastlie."[60] Herbert echoes Jourdain's belief about their cannibalism and goes one step more: "One word of their food, tis dead Whales, Seales, Grease, raw Puddings, or mans flesh, which rather then want they will digge Christians out of their Graves."[61] Herbert's outrageous claim that the Cape people will cannibalize Christians identifies religion as a major component of how the English tendency to boast about their own religion, and, at the same time, insist that the Cape people and, later, the "Hottentots" lived without religion, served as a useful, suggestive, and emotional part of their argument.

The English sailors also reacted strongly and emotionally to what they saw as the dirtiness of the bodies of the Cape people. Nicholas Downton's log suggests how deeply shocked he was by it.

> These people are the filthiest for the usage of there bodyes that ever I have heard of, for besides the naturall uncleanes (as by Sweat or otherwise) whereto all people are subject, which the most by washing cleare them selfes of, contraryewise these people doe augment by annointing there bodyes with a filthy substance which I suppose to be the Juice of hearbes, which one there bodyes sheweth like Cowe doung, and the wooll of there heades is so baked like a scurfe of greene hearbes.[62]

It is not surprising that the English, coming from a homeland that is relatively unused to powerful rays of sun, had an especially difficult time comprehending the people's use of ointment to protect their skin. As we will see, subsequent representations also demonized this practice.

The self-referential element in the English horror at the bodily appearance and eating habits of the Cape people is related to the general European taboo against dirt. Mary Douglas contends in *Purity and Danger* that "there is no such thing as absolute dirt: it exists in the eye of the beholder."[63] The English associated dirt with a degenerate lifestyle, and somehow this association seriously discomforted them and challenged their own sense of identity. Perhaps the English antipathy to dirt is related to the undeniable connection or root they recognized between themselves and the native Irish. They regarded the native Irish as a dirty and degenerate people, and, more crucially, they viewed some of the English settlers there as having degenerated to that low level. Thus, their own narrative in Ireland challenged them with a historical precedent that shook them. English contact with the Cape people and, more frighteningly, with the levels of dirtiness that they themselves endured on the voyages to the Cape, showed them that any people, be they from the Cape or from England, could be dirty. Condemning the dirty skin and food of the Cape people allowed the English to reimpose order on themselves.[64] Their insistence that the Cape people were beastly was a way for the English to reassert their own sense of superiority and reassure themselves that they had not and would not degenerate.

Perhaps more than anything else, the clothing and the anatomy of the Cape people marked their very humanity, and so the English had to find rhetorical strategies to neutralize them. Not surprisingly, the Cape people's clothing (or lack thereof) receives consistent negative attention in these early representations. Thomas Herbert's first edition declares "They contemne apparell, not comparable to the antiquitie of their weare," and what they did wear he describes as "Their clothing at best is a stinking beast skinne, the haire inverted, reaching from head to wast."[65] Mario Perniola explains how clothing helps to define identity and, to some extent, authority: "Clothing prevails as an absolute whenever or wherever the human figure is assumed to be essentially dressed, when there is the belief that human beings are human, that is, distinct from animals, by virtue of the fact that they wear clothes. Clothing gives human beings their anthropological, social and religious identity, in a word—their being."[66] The English tendency to see the Cape people as naked rather than clothed also helped to establish difference. The representations suggest that an English man considered a Cape person to be naked if that person's genitalia was visible or only slightly covered up. A description written during the Sir Edward Michelbourne expedition of 1605 records the people of the Cape as "naked, save onely that they weare upon their shoulders a Sheepe skin, and before their privities a little flap of skin, which covereth as much as if they had none at all before them."[67] Patrick Copland's depiction of the Cape people dancing demonstrates that he also sees them as naked despite the fact that he credits them with wearing something: "They dance in true measure all naked, only weare a short Cloke of sheepe or Seale skinnes to their middle, the hairie side inward, a Cap of the same, and a kind of Rats skinne about their privities; some had a Sole on their feet, tyed about."[68]

Close attention was paid to the bodies of the Cape inhabitants, although specific body parts were of particular interest to the English at different times. Descriptions of the genitalia of Cape men can often be found, especially in this first generation of representations. The journal kept by John Milward, who sailed east with David Middleton in 1614, reports that the men are "naked, save a short cloake of skinnes on their shoulders, and a Fox-skinne before their privities: have but one stone, naturally or ceremoniously I know not."[69] Herbert is more literary, saying that "Most have but one stone, the other is forced away in their infancie, that Venus allure them not from Pallas," and in the second edition he calls the men "Semi-Eunuchs."[70] Like so many others, Patrick Copland speaks generally, and, we might assume, uses his own and other Englishmen's bodies as a silent standard of comparison. He writes that the Cape people are "of middle size, well limmed, very nimble and active."[71] Ralph Standish, a member of the same 1612 expedition as Copland, uses more direct comparison to describe their faces: "Ther persons are preporcionable butt ther Faces like an Appe or Babownne, with flat nosses and ther heads and faces both beastlie and fillthye."[72] The comparison with an ape or baboon had resonance for a long time to come.

Fewer of these first generation of representations present detailed observations about the breasts and genitalia of Cape females. Descriptions of the women as immodest are common, although some representations say the reverse. Copland reports that their breasts "hang to the middle," and he says the women "were shamefac't at first; but at our returne homewards they would lift up their Rat-skinnes and shew their privities."[73] A patriotic comment of sorts drives Herbert's description of the women's immodesty: "They are very ceremonious in thanksgivings, for, wanting requitals, if you give a woman a piece of bread, she will immediately pull by her flap, and discover her pudenda. A curtesie commanded them, I suppose, by some Dutch-ill-bred Sayler, for taught it they are, they say, by Christians. And English men, I know, have greater modestie."[74] *Purchas His Pilgrimage* relates that the women took measures to cover themselves up: "The men and women were clothed, or rather a little couered, with hairy skinnes, the women beautifying this their beastly habite with the tailes of the beasts, hanging downe before and behinde to couer their shame."⁷⁵ In his description of the breasts and the nursing methods of Cape females, Edward Terry compares them and the native Irish, who were also often pictured nursing their children over their shoulders. Terry reports the women "carry their suking Infants under their skins upon their backs, and their breasts hanging down like Bag-pipes, they put up with their hands to their children, that they may suck them over their shoulders."⁷⁶ Herbert maintains that "the women give their Infants sucke as they hang at their backes, the uberous dugge stretched over her shoulder."⁷⁷ He also claims some knowledge about the Cape female's genitalia, reporting that "the female sexe are for the greater sort excised in their hidden parts."⁷⁸ His second and subsequent editions claims this practice stems "not from a Notion of religion but as an ornament."⁷⁹

The first English visual representation to accompany a travel narrative can be found in Herbert's work. Even allowing for an enormous lack of artistic talent on his part, his depiction of "A man and woman att the Cape of good Hope" is strikingly different from the earlier Dutch images. Herbert's picture makes the two Cape figures seem strange, horrible, and not quite human. There appears to be a purposeful attempt to demonize the female figure more than the male figure; she is presented as nothing less than a maternal devil. She holds a dripping intestine up to the pointed end of the man's spear as she simultaneously nurses a child. Her breast, slung over her shoulder, defies gravity and anatomy. The child on her back appears to be perched there without the benefit of gripping her, as its hand merely touches her shoulder. The tattoos on her leg and arm, her vacant and menacing facial expression, her bony hand, and her bent over and strange one-footed stance give her a demonic quality. The picture also separates the two figures from the Cape landscape. Almost like monsters, they tower over it.

Herbert renders the Cape man in an equally strange fashion. Looking straight ahead, he appears to have little relation to the Cape female. But he is armed, and whether he means to steal the intestine from the female figure or give it to her is unclear. His body tattoos, earring, and what appears to be an elongated ear make him seem even stranger. His physique is meant to be impressive and intimidating. He is clearly extremely strong, and his mus-

Thomas Herbert, "A Man and Woman at the Cape of Good Hope." Library Company of Philadelphia.

cles appear to be well developed. He carries a mantle on his shoulder, and he wears a loincoth over his genitalia. Van Wyk Smith calls Herbert's image "a vicious caricature," and he correctly points out that it had enormous influence on later English visual representations.[80]

English sailors judged the people of the Cape to be savage and beastly due to several factors, but their skin color was rarely mentioned in this regard. Indeed, these early English representations suggest that the Cape people's skin color was not as crucial an issue as their dietary habits or the sounds of their language. Certainly it is true that the earliest English visitors to the Cape brought with them their own preconceived negative notions relative to non-white skin and to Africans. P. J. Marshall and Glyndwr Williams believe that "when white Englishmen first encountered black Africans, preconceptions of distate, even repulsion, already existed."[81] If Kim Hall is correct, after Elizabeth's death, the idea of blackness carried with it a new capacity for negative and self-reflexive expression. Hall believes that as early as 1605, "blackness had become part of the linguistic currency of James's rule. Not only did James keep Africans at court as part of his passion for oddities: the actual excesses of the court seem to have been perceived as 'Oriental'. Racial difference, particularly in descriptions of the perceived decadence of the court, was a priviliged idiom for self-description and critique."[82] Significantly, the first English travelers to the Cape sometimes noted the skin color of the Cape people, but it rarely appears as an issue for discussion or debate.

As we have seen, the first Englishmen at the Cape found the people there to be "blacke salvages [sic], very brutish."[83] The 1603 pamphlet chronicling the Lancaster-led expedition reported that "the people are blacke," although the account of the voyage that appeared in the 1614 and 1617 editions of *Purchas His Pilgrimage* say "the people are of a tawnie color."[84] *The Last East-Indian Voyage* (1606) does not present any sort of description of them beyond calling them "negroes."[85] As we have shown, that volume was far more concerned with relating the skirmish between Middleton's men and the Cape people. An unpublished log chronicling the Keeling voyage calls the people "heathenish and brutish" but makes no mention of their skin color, nor does John Jourdain in the journal he kept during his 1608 outward passage from England.[86] Similarly, Nicholas Downton's 1610 stop at the Cape prompted him to comment on how filthy the people of the Cape are, but he saw their dirty appearance as stemming from their practice of skin greasing. He does not mention their skin color in his description.[87]

English visitors to the Cape during the second decade of the seventeenth century did not display any greater interest in skin color. Patrick Copland says nothing about it, and Ralph Standish, who, as we saw, thought "yt is a greatt pittie that such creattures as they bee should injoy so sweett a counttrey," specified other reasons for reaching the judgment he did about them. Nicholas Withington, also on the 1612 Best expedition along with Copland and Standish, simply calls the people of the Cape, "Negrose," without supplying any additional commentary.[88] Edward Terry makes no mention of the Cape people's skin color when he begins to delineate why he thinks the Cape people are "beasts in the skins of men." At another point in his narrative, Terry describes their skin color as "very tawny."[89]

Although the Cape people's skin color was not at this time an absolute marker for their demonization, their "blackness" was not doubted. There were then competing theories about the significance and the variety of human skin color. The classical theories of Hippocrates, who wondered if blackness is caused by leaking nutrients and heat, and Herodotus, who believed the color of the parent's sperm is the determinant of skin color, had been displaced by the beginning of the seventeenth century.[90] Others argued that climate and geography determined skin color, but the dark skin color of the Cape people was often used as proof to refute this theory.[91] Although the English did not yet have any scientific proof as to what caused blackness, they were quite ready to see black skin as the direct opposite of white skin. Richard Eden had expressed this notion in his *The Decades of the Newe World or West India* (1555): "One of the marveylous thynges that God useth in the composition of man, is coloure: whiche doubtlesse can not bee consydered withoute great admiration in beholding one to be white and an other blacke, beinge coloures utterlye contrary."[92] Seeing black and white skin color in such a way lent both tremendous symbolic potential, especially because the Elizabethans idealized the fair skin of their monarch. Winthrop Jordan believes that such a love of "fairness" carried special signficance for them: "It was important, if incalculably so, that English discovery of black Africans came at a time when the accepted standard of ideal beauty was a fair complexion of rose and white. Negroes not only failed to fit this ideal but seemed the very picture of perverse negation."[93]

In late-sixteenth- and early-seventeenth-century England, many cited the biblical story of Noah and his sons, perhaps because it assigns blackness as a punishment. George Best's *True Discourse of the Three Voyages of Discoverie* (1578) was one of the first texts to promote such a connection between blackness and disobedience.

> Which good instructions and exhortations notwithstanding, his wicked sonne Cham disobeyed, and being persuaded that the firstborne after the flood (by right and law of nature) should inherit and possesse all the dominion of the earth, he, contrarie to his fathers commandement, while they were yet in the Arke used company with his wife . . . for the which wicked and detestable fact . . . God would a sonne shuld be borne whose name was Chus, who not only itselfe, but all his posteritie after him, should be so black and lothsome that it might remaine a spectacle of disobedience to all the world. And of this blacke and cursed Chus came all these Blacke Moores which are in Africa.[94]

Significantly, Best goes on to make specific reference to the people at the Cape of Good Hope: "these black men are found in all partes of Africa, as well withoute the tropicks as within, even unto Capo d'buona Speranza southward, where by reason of the sphere should be the same temperature that is in Spayne, Sardigna, and Sicilia, where all be of very good complexions. Wherefore I conclude that the blacknesse proceedeth, not of the hotnesse of the clime, but as I sayd of the infection of bloud, and therfore this their argumente gathered of the Africans blacknesse is not able to destroy the temperature of the middle zone."[95] Benjamin Braude argues that early-modern English and European versions of the Bible as well as a general English tendency to misread Mandeville's *Travels* helped to create this "willful Africanization of Ham," which, in turn, led to a link between blackness and slavery.[96] According to Braude, "between 1589 and 1625, a change took place in English attitudes toward the Curse of Ham. Slavery had started to make it credible."[97]

The emerging English preference to view skin color as a marker of superiority (in the case of whites) and inferiority (in the case of non-whites) became more crucial to them as their nation's involvement in mid-Atlantic slavery increased. The revisions Thomas Herbert made to his narrative demonstrate the growing seventeenth-century English embrace of a racialist, if not racist, way to interpret skin color. In the first edition, Herbert describes the complexion and physique of the Cape people in a matter-of-fact tone: "The people are of a swarthy darke colour (I cannot say complexion) well limmed and proper, nor want they courage (though discretion) to their limmes."[98] As he revised the work, however, he added subjective commentary to his description. The comparable sentence in the 1638 second edition has the Cape people represented as "ugly black" instead of "swarthy darke." Additionally, the rest of this sentence depicts them as physically threatening, as he goes on to call them "strongly limbd, desperate, crafty, and injurious."[99] More tellingly, by making an allusion to Ham, the second edition demonstrates how use of the biblical story could help to seal a negative judgment: "The Country is rich and fruitfull in her womb, but owned by an accursed Progeny of Cham, who differ in nothing from bruit beasts save forme."[100]

With English participation in the slave trade increasing significantly after the Restoration, it is not surprising that in the third (1665) and fourth editions (1677) Herbert's description of the Cape people's skin color were revised again to include still more condemnatory moral judgments: "The Natives being propagated from *Cham,* both in their Visages and Natures seem to inherit his malediction."[101] Significantly, these two editions also express a far more negative view of Africans generally. In the second edition, the concluding sentences in the Cape section present Herbert's conclusion about them, "And as simple as they seeme they are witty enough in craft, revenge, and villany," as well as a historical reminder and warning to Englishmen who might stop at the Cape:

> Yet le me advise our Men to avoid needlesse bravadoes, and not contemne them from their indefensive nakednesse, or by a supercilious conceit of their owne weapons and field practises. *Exempla docent. Almeyda* the bravest Captaine the Portugals ever had, after many glorious achievements in *Asia* and *Africk,* thought invicible, and returning home *anno* 1510 out of *India:* Hee, eleven Captaines and many other gallant men, upon a small affront putting some of the Savages to death (who grew desperate in revenge) were set upon by these naked Barbarians, and slaine every one of them.[102]

The 1665 and 1677 editions extend these final remarks even more forcefully: "and for a farewell, take that which *Leo* gives the *Lybians,* They have no letters, faith, nor law, living (if it be a life) like wild beasts for ignorance, like devils for mischief, and like dogs for poverty."[103] Rather than relying only on references to classical works, Herbert's return to his native language at this point in the text is significant. His strong declaration against the Cape people moves beyond the literal or human world. He sees them as other than human, more like "wild beasts," "devils," and "dogs."

This chapter opened with the question, what did the English envision about the Cape people before contact between the two groups began on a regular basis? It closes with a brief comment about what the English actually saw. When English sailors went ashore at the Cape, both the unfamiliar and the familiar appeared before their eyes. All that was unfamiliar served to emphasize how they were different from the Cape people. In relation to skin color, the Cape people did not look like they looked. The two groups voiced language differently, valued different kinds of objects, wore different kinds of clothes, and organized their days around different principles. But the familiar also stood toe to toe with the English, and this fact might well have been harder for them to contemplate and accept. Any comparison of their bodies, especially their genitalia, proved they were men greeting men. Although they prepared food differently, they had the same need for it. The English were, quite literally, dying for fresh food and water, and the Cape people sold it to them. Both groups had leaders and followers, and, presumably, Khoikhoi and Englishmen alike suffered similar kinds of wounds in their violent encounters with each other. Perhaps this first group of English travelers to the Cape had such a need to express, often quite explicitly, their judgment of the Cape people as the most beastly of all human societies because they were not all that sure of themselves and their vaunted civility, especially after enduring the long and dangerous passage to Table Bay.

2
Spreading the Word

THE ENGLISH VERY QUICKLY JUDGED THE CAPE PEOPLE TO BE HUMANity's most base society. This dubious distinction took hold partially because of Samuel Purchas, whose collections of travel narratives presented descriptions of the Cape and its people that, in many instances, would not appear in any other publications. Even more crucially, Purchas introduced a dynamic that prompted the English to invoke the Cape and its people when their own domestic agendas would be served by such a comparison. He was the first of many to use representations of the Cape people to discuss national concerns, in this case the divisiveness of religious sectaries. Purchas's volumes did not dominate the market for long, however. The seventeenth-century emergence of geography as a popular as well as an academic subject also helped to disseminate a considerable amount of (mis)information about the Cape people. These sources together ensured that negative images and ideas about the Cape people found their way into the collective English imagination.

Samuel Purchas is often described as Richard Hakluyt's disciple or heir, but such an easy classification often fails to consider both his editorial style and his personal ambition. Knowledge of both is essential to understanding his works and their influence on subsequent representations of the Cape and its people. Appointed as a vicar in Eastwood (Essex) in August 1604, Purchas lived for at least ten years near to the port at Leigh-on-Sea. Philip L. Barbour suggests that it was here Purchas's fascination for the stories of sailors began.[1] It is impossible now to know how he got the idea for *Purchas His Pilgrimage* (1613), but we need not speculate about his goal for the work. He expresses that clearly in the preface, where he confides his hope that the volume's publication will result in his "Leaping out of the dungeon of Obscuritie."[2] As we will see, the work's political subtext ensured that it would attract the sort of attention its author sought. Soon after the first edition appeared in print, Purchas won the notice and the patronage of George Abbot, then archbishop of Canterbury (and previously the author of *A Briefe Description of the Whole World* [1599]). In 1614, Purchas was selected to be a chaplain to Abbot, and he was also named as rector of St. Martin's, Ludgate (London). *Purchas His Pilgrimage* appeared in three subsequent editions during the next thirteen years (1614, 1617, 1626), and two other publications, *Microcosmos* (1619) and *Hakluytus Posthumus, or Purchas His Pilgrimes* (1625) brought Purchas additional literary renown.

Scholars have presumed that Purchas was acquainted with Richard Hakluyt, and *Purchas His Pilgrimage* at least suggests that he was familiar with his fellow clergyman's great collection.[3] *Purchas His Pilgrimage*, however, did not champion English exploration and enterprise the way *Principal Navigations* did. In fact, it can be argued that Purchas looked abroad in order to describe and comment on the domestic political landscape.

Representations of the Cape of Good Hope proved to be crucial to Purchas. *Purchas His Pilgrimage* (1613) introduces the use of the Cape and its people as a specific foil for the English. Purchas returns to a pun several times, which suggests his awareness that descriptions of the Cape and its people could provide sufficient cover for his subversive commentary on his own nation.

> But now we see it made a daily matter to the Portugall, English and Dutch, so capable of *Hope of Good*, that the *Cape* of *Good hope* is nothing feared: (579)

The clause immediately following this colon suggests that once Purchas conceived the pun, he knew what to do with it. Indeed, he repeats it in order to level criticism at some countrymen.

> although at home many have no good hope of publicke good, and wish that they would carry out of Europe lesse money, and bring home more men. For my own part, I wish so wel to Navigation and Discoveries, that I could wish such complaints to be but calumnies and to be the Navigations of false discoverers. I cannot omit, that upon the top of this Promontory, Nature hath as it were, framed herself a delightfull bower, heere to sit and contemplate the great Seas. (579)

Purchas's playful interjection in the penultimate sentence of his own hopes for the adventurers includes another verbal slight at those "many" who "have no good hope." Here he accuses them of being "false discoverers." The next sentence lends him the vantage point and the authority (he is a true discoverer on "this Promontory") to contemplate a sea of his fellow citizens, especially those "false discoverers."

Previous commentators on Purchas's work have stressed the religious lesson he attempts to teach in it. To that end, they often cite his statement of purpose as it appears in the preface: *"Religion* is my more proper aime" (4). They fail to consider, however, that in 1613 such a "religious" purpose was tantamount to having a political purpose as well. Indeed, other references make clear that Purchas intended a level of political meaning from the start. Why else would he assign an anniversary of the Gunpowder Plot (5 November) for the date of the dedicatory epistle, as well as express his hope that his history of religion will teach his readers about "the Unnaturalnesse of FACTION and ATHEISME" (3)? At this point in time, James's court was in disarray. Indeed, the factions of courtiers fighting personal, political, and religious battles included George Abbot, Purchas's patron, as one of the major players. Tensions between the cliques organized around the earls of Northampton and Suffolk, on one side, and those of Abbot and the earls of Pembroke, Ellesmere, and Coke, on the other, were at a high pitch. Derek Hirst calls the years 1612–14 "unfortunate years," and writes that during them "extravagance and corruption grew."[4]

The prefatory material identifies Purchas's targets. *Purchas His Pilgrimage* has an especially anti-Spanish (thus anti-Catholic) thrust to it because Pembroke, Abbot, and others in their circle were advocating that James renew an alliance with Holland and risk war with Spain. Others argued that England should play the role of Europe's peacemaker and, according to Hirst, James himself was partial to this view.[5] Of course, religious differences in England factored into this debate as well. Those who were sympathetic to Catholicism adopted the antiwar position, while many mainstream Protestants (and others) argued for an alliance with the Dutch. Purchas, not surprisingly, uses the excerpts of travel narratives to establish a connection in the minds of his readers between the "heathens" and "pagans" described therein and those men who opposed the position embraced by Abbot, Pembroke, and their circle. For example, at the conclusion of an extended discussion about the excessive cruelty Spanish sailors and soldiers inflicted on natives in the Americas, Purchas strongly expresses his own anti-Catholic feelings. His use of visual imagery here is striking, especially in regard to how he connects blackness, the devil, and disobedience.

> For me, I want fit words to paint them in their blacke colours, my hand with reluctance trembleth at the writing, my tongue faltereth in the speaking, and wholly I seeme to my self surprised with distraction, and not to be my selfe, whiles the view of this Spanish *Medusa* transformeth me into a stone: the rather when I thinke such should our English Conversion have beene, if in that dismall year 1588. England had as well succeeded to them as the Indies: or if since, our Catholike Preachers had prevailed in their Powder-projects, in the year of 1605 who for a Temple, chose a Vault, that their workes of darkenesse might be done in the darke, and their work-house might bee neerer to Hell, thence to borrow at hand supplies of devillish devises, and in neerer familiaritie to consult with the Divell. (751–52)

The frequency with which this passage and the next one allude to the Gunpowder Plot suggests exactly why 5 November is the date assigned to the dedicatory epistle.

Using his pilgrim persona, Purchas keys the reader's attention to the signficance of the anniversary: "Friend, I draw neere my port, and leaving America behind me, still red with this bloud; now also having England in sight, which (as from a great height) was neere to a more dangerous fall: . . . And now me thinkes I see the shores of England, from which my lingring Pilgrimage hath long detained me: I heare the Bells, and see the Bon-fires, with publike acclamations of thankfulnesse for that Deliverance, all singing their *Hallelu-iahs*, and saying, *This is the Day which the* LORD *hath made, we will rejoyce and be glad in it*" (752). In the subsequent sentences, Purchas presents a call for unity in England: "And now I see a better sight then all my Pilgrimage could yeeld, Christian Churches, without Heathenish, Jewish, or Antichristian pollutions: a Royall King, truely entituled Defender of the Faith: a learned Clergie, wise and Honorable Counsellers; peaceable and loyall Commons" (752). His plea here is certainly an appropriate one, coming as it does from a "pilgrim," but Purchas's obvious political agenda undermines his sincerity.

When Purchas leaves the domestic landscape and turns his attention to the world abroad, he also makes an argument for unity. In the section devoted to the "Land of the Negros," Purchas reviews the various theories concerning the variety of human skin colors. Signicantly, he refers to the blackness of the Cape people, which he knows undermines one of the current theories.

> Now if any would looke that wee should here in our discourse of the Negro's assigne some cause of that their black colour: I answere, that I cannot well answere this question, as being in it self difficult, and made

more, by the variety of answeres that others give hereunto. Some alledge the heat of this Torrid Region, proceeding from the direct beames of the Sunne; . . . And if this were the cause; why should Africa yeeld white people in the Melinde, and neare the Line, blacke at the Cape of *Good Hope* in five and thirtie? Some leaving the hot impressions in the Aire, attribute it to the drynesse of the earth; as though the Libyan Deserts are not more drie, (and yet the people no Negro's) and as though Niger were here dryed up. Some, to the hidden qualitie of the soile; . . . Some ascribe it (as *Herodotus*) to the blackness of the Parents sperme or seede; . . . Some ascend above the Moone, to call some heavenly constellation and influence into this consistorie of Nature: And there will I leave them. (545–46)

Purchas does not have an explanation to provide about the variety of human skin colors, which is appropriate for his persona as a pilgrim: "yea, I will send them further to him that hath reserved many secrets of nature to himselfe, and hath willed us to content our selves with thinges reveiled" (546). Indeed, his lack of a definitive answer to the question suits his pretended call for unity in England: "that wee also might serve that *one-most God;* the tawny Moore, black Negro, duskie Libyan, Ash-coloured Indian, olive-coloured American, should with the white European become *one sheepe-fold,* under *one great shepheard*" (546). Significantly, Purchas's last work, *Purchas His Pilgrimes* (1625), indicates a change in his position about skin colors. As Benjamin Braude points out, *Pilgrimes* includes a description of black slaves from a George Sandy travel narrative that supports the "Ham" theory. Sandy's narrative asserts that they and "all of that complexion" are "descended of Chus, the Sonne of cursed Cham . . . from the Curse of Noe upon Cham in the Posterities of Chus."[6] Purchas's use of this work suggests that by 1625, he was willing to link blackness and slavery.

Contrary to its statement that it would present a history of religions, *Purchas His Pilgrimage* communicates no information whatsoever about the religious practices of the Cape people. Nor does it include much information recently available from several English East India Company expeditions. In fact, the representation of the Cape in the first edition is significantly out of date. Purchas includes in his section on the "Land of the Caphars" the basic definition of "Caphar" from Pory's work (1600), and he cites information deriving from Houtman's and Linschoten's narratives (1598), and from Lancaster's first voyage under Raymond as it appears in Hakluyt's *Principal Navigations*. The only new material Purchas incorporates comes from Robert Coverte's *A True and Almost Incredible Report of An Englishman,* which first appeared in print in 1612. As we saw in the previous chapter, Captain Coverte recorded negative impressions about the eating habits of the Cape people. For his summary, Purchas condenses Coverte's six-paragraph representation into four sentences:

> The *Ascension* [Cap. Rob. Covert.] built their Pinnesse *Anno*. 1608. at Soldania, about fifteene or sixteene leagues from the Cape of Good Hope, and there tooke in for their provision about foure hundred head of cattell, as Oxen, Steeres, Sheepe, and Lambes, together with fowles and fresh water. They filled their boat with Seales at the Ile Pengwin, a little from thence. Such was the brutish nature of the inhabitants, that when the English had cast out of their shippe one of those Seales, and the same had lien fourteene dayes, and now swarmed with crawling Maggots, they would take them up and eate them; as they would also doe the guts, garbage, and panch of the beasts. They more esteemed iron, than gold or silver. (580)

Significantly, Purchas's summary fails to mention that Coverte and his men found the Cape people to be willing traders. Coverte's original did: "For with our old iron, we bought all our Cattell and any thing else that we had of them."[7] In this way, Purchas's omission of material portrays the Cape people in a more negative light than the original.

Purchas concludes this Cape section of *Pilgrimage* with a summary and quotation from Linschoten's *His Discourse of Voyages into ye Easte and West Indies* (1598). Purchas must have known that the Dutchman did not stop at the Cape of Good Hope. Still, this did not stop him from (mis)placing in his discussion of the Cape people, Linschoten's gruesome description of body mutilation and an allegation of cannibalism concerning those who live near "Mosambique."[8] Many subsequent geographers and travelers used it to charge that the Cape people were cannibals, believers in a devil, and cruel surgeons of their prisoners of war. For example, Peter Heylyn's extremely successful *Microcosmus* (1621) also presents this account. Purchas corrected his mistake in the second and subsequent editions of *Purchas His Pilgrimage,* where the description was moved to a different location, but the assertion of cannibalism would not be forgotten.[9]

The 1614 second edition of *Purchas His Pilgrimage* has a revised chapter title for the section, which is "Of Caphraria, The Cape of Good Hope, and Soldania," and the contents include more current information. One new paragraph early in the chapter summarizes the dire condition of the crews on Lancaster's 1601 expedition and also incorporates information about the Cape people from narratives deriving from Houtman's (1595), Michelborne's (1605), and Middleton's (1604) expeditions, only some of which had been published previously. The excerpts from these English and Dutch expeditions relate descriptions of the blackness of the Cape people's skin color, their diet, the trade between the two groups, and the violent encounter between the Dutch and Cape people. Significantly, no reference is made to the 1604 skirmish Middleton's men had with the Cape people, which had been described in such great detail in *The Last East-India Voyage* (1606). Also new to this section is a curious and suggestive use of a 1503 Italian travel narrative. Among other things, the reference claims the Cape people have no religion.

> *Giovanni da Empoli* telleth, That neere the Cape the Countrey-people would give them a Cow for a little bell. The men and women were clothed, or rather a little covered with hairie skins, the women beautifying this their beastly habite with the tailes of the beats, hanging down before and behind to cover their shame. These women had large and deformed pappes. Religion they could observe none amongst them, and thought that they eate their flesh raw. (866)

Coming as it does immediately after the more recent accounts, and since it confirms the descriptions presented in them, Purchas lends the information a sort of historical authority.

Two completely new paragraphs conclude the chapter in the 1614 edition. Purchas includes previously unpublished information from the journal of Patrick Copland (1612) and from accounts written by several men on Downton's expedition (1614). Most crucially, Purchas here refers to Cory, a man abducted from the Cape and brought to England in 1613.

> The *Hector* brought thence one of these Salvages, called *Cory*, which was carried againe, and there landed by the *Newyeeres-gift, June 21.* 1614. in his Copper Armour, but returned not to them whiles the Shippes continued in the Roade, but at their returnes in *March* was twelve-month after, hee came, and was ready to any service, in helping them with Beeves and Sheepe.[10]

Purchas's *Pilgrimage* is the first text to print any reference to Cory.

There are no substantive revisions in the third edition's representation of the Cape and its people, nor are there any additions, which is curious because a number of English expeditions stopped there in the intervening years between the two editions. Significantly, the chapters in *Pilgrimage* that Purchas did take the time to revise after 1616 concern the areas of America where the English had colonial settlements. The fourth and final edition of *Purchas His Pilgrimage* (1626), produced after Purchas recovered, albeit only for a short time, from a bout with a "dreadfull infection," also does not present any fresh descriptions of southern Africa. This edition, however, does include two new dedicatory epistles. The first is addressed to the recently installed King Charles, and the second is directed to the honoree of the earlier editions, George Abbot, archbishop of Canterbury. In both, Purchas expresses his gratitude for the support he received from Abbot and the late King James.

Purchas's evident loss of interest in *Purchas His Pilgrimage* must be due to the fact that he had already begun work on his next major project. In 1616, Purchas bought the papers of the recently deceased Richard Hakluyt, which he used to compile his third and final work, *Hakluytus Posthumus, or Purchas His Pilgrimes* (1625). This must have been an overwhelming task. *Purchas His Pilgrimes* has failed to win praise from twentieth-century historians, but as it was the only collection of voyage narratives that appeared between 1626 and 1699, its impact on seventeenth-century readers should not be underestimated. An unnamed source calls Purchas's editorial method "irregular and curtailed or contracted" and refers to his intrusions into the text as "often silly, and always little to the purpose."[11] Philip L. Barbour charges that Purchas suffered from a lack of good "editorial sense" in this work:

> Lacking a sound editorial sense, or a bent for thematic anthologizing, Purchas reprints books already on the market only to surpress 'intriguing' manuscripts with a bare hint of what they contained; he lops off the beginning or the end of many an invaluable account because somebody else has written on the same subject, and he inserts editorial comments where they are truly superfluous; in some instances he discards dates and other logbook details from vital accounts, and in others perpetuates original blunders without questioning their accuracy, and so on; and through all this he gives no clue to what prompts his course of action.[12]

While the dubiousness of Purchas's editorial decisions are a consideration in any modern analysis of the work, readers who perused the volumes in the seventeenth century were not so discerning. Much of what they read about the Cape of Good Hope and its people was familiar to them if they had read *Purchas His Pilgrimage*, although there is a fresh twist to the Cape section as well as to the work as a whole. What is different about *Purchas His Pilgrimes* from the earlier work is that now the author is far more enthusiastic about overseas trade and colonialism.

John Parker believes that Purchas's decision to include in *Pilgrimes* excerpts or references to works that advocate the increase of trade, such as Thomas Mun's *Discourse of Trade* (1621), Dudley Digges's *The Defense of Trade* (1615), and Edward Misselden's *Free Trade* (1622), shows that the preacher-editor now "espoused merchandizing over missionizing."[13] During the late 1610s and 1620s, the competition between Dutch and English factors and sailors in the East Indies became fierce and, sometimes, violent. In relation to the Cape of Good Hope, no European power had yet made a move to colonize it, but Purchas seems to hint in *Pilgrimes* that England should act on the claim for the nation that Humphrey Fitzherbert made at the Cape in 1620. His position is suggested by the excerpts he selected to use in the section. Two of the five sentences he includes from the journal of Captain Thomas Elkington speak to how the land is not being cultivated by the Cape people.

> The thirtieth of June we set saile from the Bay of *Soldania*. Heere at this time which is their dead of Winter, it was temperate, rather inclining to cold then heate. We had little refreshing but water and fish. The people are wretched, neither sow nor plant, dwell in small Cottages made of Hides, and so joyne many of them in a round Circle, having their Cattle in the middest. They are browne, but by greasing themselves become almost blacke, and in the wind unsavourie a doozen yards off, filching, trecherous, unworthy so good a Land, which in likelihood with culture would be very fertile.[14]

As discussed in the previous chapter, *Pilgrimes* also includes representations deriving from the expeditions led by James Lancaster (1601), Henry Middleton (1604), Edward Michelbourne (1606), David Middleton (1607), William Keeling (1607), Thomas Best (1612), Walter Peyton (1613), and Nicholas Downton (1614).

When we compare the representations of the Cape people and Native Americans in *Pilgrimages* and *Pilgrimes*, we can see the emergence of two separate rhetorics for the representation of a native people. Generally, depictions of America and its inhabitants stress the positive, while descriptions of Africans accentuate the negative. Purchas's representations of Native Americans, in particular, ensures them a welcome embrace from English readers. Also, his advocacy for American plantation is expressed emphatically.[15] In the first edition of *Pilgrimage,* Purchas refers to the native inhabitants of Virginia as savages, but he is quick to add that they "were now in good termes with the English, their plantation at *James Towne* where they had built a Church and many Houses, in some reasonable manner flourished."[16] Having become friends with John Smith in 1611, Purchas also includes his friend's descriptions of Virginia.[17] In fact, Purchas puts Smith forward as a trusted authority: "This the Captaine saith, that hee hath beene in many places of Asia and Europe, in some of Africa and America, but of all, holds Virginia by the naturall endowments, the fittest place for an earthly Paradise."[18] Purchas's use here of a garden metaphor is especially suggestive of his favorable attitude toward the English colonization of America; the land certainly did not present anything like the kind conditions and the rich resources the Cape of Good Hope offered its residents and visitors, yet he employs the identical metaphor.

Although the English regarded Native Americans as savage, they did not consider them as undeserving inhabitants of the land, which is how they perceived the Cape people. Any shock felt by the English settlers in Virginia at the physical appearance or the customs of the Native Americans goes unreported. According to Bernard Sheehan, the English saw Native Americans as handsome and not unattractive: "Creatures of the devil and ignoble savages the Indians may have been, but the English found them remarkably attractive physically. The native skin color was free of the negative connotations that the English attached to blackness."[19] The English regarded Native Americans as part of their cultivation project in Virginia. They were more hopeful for the development of Native Americans as civilized beings than they were for the Cape people at least partly because some of the natives, or so they liked to think, converted to Christianity. Seventeenth-century English texts often mention conversions. For example, Pocahontos's embrace of Christianity is related in the third edition of Purchas's *Pilgrimages:* "They tooke *Pokohuntis* (*Powhatans* dearest daughter) prisoner, a matter of good consequence to them, of best to her, by this meanes being become a Christian, & married to Master *Ralph*, an English Gentleman."[20] It was not until the eighteenth century that geographies would dare to challenge conversion stories like Pocahontos's.[21]

Purchas and other English writers and editors saw a shared human history between themselves and the Native Americans. They admitted that "the Inhabitants of the great Britannie have bin in times past as savage as those of Virginia" in order to establish that Native Americans could improve themselves.[22] Conversely, the eighteenth-century representations of "Hottentot" that imagined a likeness between them and ancient Britons did so in order to caution against British degeneration rather than to argue for "Hottentot" progression. Also, we see in the depictions of Native Americans that Purchas and others were willing to acknowledge shared signifiers of culture, although they steadfastly refused to extend this generosity to the Cape society.

After Purchas's death in 1626, English readers were denied any new collection of travel narratives until William Hacke produced one in the very last year of the century. There were, however, several important academic and popular geography books that continued to serve up a steady stream of information about the Cape and its people. By no means was geography a new subject for the English. Enterprising printers had kept the classical geographies in print throughout the sixteenth century, but the new age of expedition created a renewed enthusiasm for geography.

At the start of the seventeenth century, several Oxford colleges could boast about the contributions made by their geographers in residence. According to J. N. L. Baker, John Prideaux of Exeter College played a major role in the rising fortune of geography as a science. He greatly influenced Robert Stafforde's *A Geographical and Anthologicall Description of All the Empires and Kingdomes Both of the Continent and Ilands in This Terrestrial Globe* (1607, 1618, 1634).[23] Stafforde's work describes the inhabitants of Africa very negatively: they "are generally very blacke, of countenance rude, barbarous, and of uncivil behaviour, addicted to all sorts of religion, of *Gentiles, Jewes, Turkes, Christians,* and such like."[24] More specifically, Stafforde describes the inhabitants in the southern region of Africa, then often referred to as "Ethopia inferior," as "very Savage, cruell, and for the most part great Idolaters, so much contemning Christianitie, that in the Province of *Douos,* no man can marry untill he hath killed . . . Christians."[25]

Prideaux also influenced Nathanael Carpenter, another Fellow of Exeter College, whose own *Geography Delineated Forth in Two Bookes* (1625) is an interesting theoretical work that was used as a textbook in the universities.[26] Baker notes Carpenter's debt to the mathematical theories of the day for his description of the earth, and credits him for having "a larger conception of geography than most of his contemporaries."[27] Carpenter's book includes a chapter on "Natural Disposition," which maintains that in all nations of man there are "certaine naturall or nationall vertues or vices, which neither time nor Lawes could ever change or correct . . . And howsoever many means have bin put in practise, either by the severity of lawes to curb such enormities, or the subtilty of discourse to shroud these vices under the name of vertues: yet these markes are found to stick as close as the spots unto the Leopard, as neither altering their pristine hue, or yeelding to time or statutes."[28] In the eighteenth century, David Hume, among others, would revisit this subject.

Peter Heylyn, elected as a fellow of Magdalen College in 1618, was the most influential English geographer of the seventeenth century. He did not remain at Oxford, however. Heylyn became a pastor and controversial pamphleteer, as well as the author of the century's most reprinted geography books. Borrowing the tittle word from Purchas's own 1619 geography, Heylyn's *Microcosmus: A Little Description of the Great World* (1621) is geared to the educated general reader as well as to the Oxford student. It proved to be extremely popular, with editions appearing in 1621, 1625, 1627, 1629, 1631, 1633, 1636, and 1639. Keeping the more general audience in mind, Heylyn makes an attempt to entertain as well as to instruct his reader. He presents quotations from classical texts in both Latin and English, and he keeps geographical theory to a minimum. His general description of man, which puts an emphasis on difference, shows how he mixes original prose and borrowed sources.

> The Earth thus being described, it is necessary wee should speake somewhat of the Lord of the Soyle, *viz.* Man: who was created last of all, as the creature in whose constitution on the Perfections of all the rest were united. This Epitome of the great Volume of Nature, borroweth from the angels, soule; from the bruite Animals, sense; from the plants, life; from other creatures, bignesse: and above all inferiours, is endowed with this prerogative, which *Ovid* thus affordeth us: *Met I.*
>
> > *Pronaque cum spectent animalia caetera terram,*
> > *Os homini sublime dedit, coelumque videre*
> > *Iussit, & erectos ad sydera tollere voltus.*
> > And where all beasts looke downe with groveling eye:
> > He gave to man lookes mix't with majesty,
> > And will'd him with bold face to view the skie.
>
> Men thus one by originall, are of divers complexions of body and conditions of minde: according to the divers climates of the Earth: of whom *Du Bartas* in his Colonies.
>
> > O see how full of wonders strange is Nature,
> > Sith in each Climate, not alone in stature,
> > Strength, colour, haire, but that men differ doe
> > Both in their humors, and their manners too.

> The Northern man is faire, the Southerne foule,
> That's white, this blacke: that smiles, and this doth scoule,
> Th'ones blith & frolicke, th'others dull and froward,
> Th'ones full of courage, th'other a fearefull coward, & c.[29]

Heylyn's decision to quote from Du Bartas's work, with its race and color based binary oppositions, suggests the emerging early-modern European construction of race.

Microcosmus presents more specific descriptions of the world and its people than any of the other geographies of the time, but its representation of the Cape and its people does not suggest that Heylyn had any particular interest in the place. Only two of seven sentences present any information about the Cape people, and the description itself is vague and familiar: "The people live like beasts, are black as pitch, and therefore when they would represent any ugly thing, to make it white: they have flat noses and thick lippes. They have some villages in which they live together; and in every village a king or lord to whom they are subject."[30]

The numerous editions of *Microcosmus* and Heylyn's next work, *Cosmographie In Four Books* (1652), gain in significance when we consider that they very largely kept depictions of the Cape people before the eyes of the reading public. Except for Edward Terry's narrative, written in 1616 but not published until 1655, no new English-authored descriptions of the Cape people appeared in print between 1635 and 1687. Heylyn expanded and reworked *Microcosmus* into a new work, calling it *Cosmographie In Four Books* (1652). It quickly became the standard geography of the later seventeenth century, reappearing in new editions throughout the Restoration period (1652, 1657, 1666, 1669, 1670, 1670, 1674, 1677, 1682) and into the early eighteenth century (1703), when it was finally supplanted by more up-to-date works. Stylistically, *Cosmographie* anticipates the privileging of travel narratives, which became such a hallmark of "new" geography.

The first edition of *Cosmographie* (1652) presents a six paragraph section on "Cafraria" that steals freely from previously printed accounts. Indeed, many of the phrases and sentences are hardly rewritten at all.

> Exceedingly well watered, and as liberally stored with Woods and Forrests: the Hils thereof so intermixt with grassie Vallies, that pity 'tis so beautiful and rich a Country should be inhabited by so barbarous and rude a people; who being utterly unprovided of towns and houses, live in woods like beasts. Of colour black, thick lips, flat noses, long-shaped heads, and most monstrous ears; extended far beneath their shoulders,

by hanging in them iron chains, glasse, bullets, Bels, and such ponderous bables. These Ornaments common to both sexes, who also use (for their greater beauty) most hideously to slash themselves in all parts of their bodies, even their very bellies; as if no lace could better sort with their naked skins; with which only, except some flap of leather to hide their privities, they are here apparelled.[31]

In subsequent paragraphs, Heylyn essentially reprints other representations from previously published accounts, and he provides a survey of European visitations to the region.

The concluding paragraph of the Cape section in *Cosmographie* is especially interesting and suggestive. It demonstrates that Heylyn, like Purchas, takes the opportunity to use his representation of the Cape people to offer some domestic political commentary of his own. Heylyn was an avowed royalist; he had published many controversial tracts in support of the monarch during the civil war era. After the establishment of the Commonwealth government, both Heylyn's house and livelihood were taken from him as punishment for his pro-royalist views. His wife and family were forced to live with friends, and he, according to the *Dictionary of National Biography*, "wandered in disguise from house to house where he could find entertainment."[32] In the last paragraph of *Cosmographie's* Cape of Good Hope section, Heylyn remembers the 1620 claim that King James and his council had ignored, and he argues that the English monarch is the rightful owner of the Cape. In 1652, however, there was no king residing in England, a point Heylyn underscores with a jab at the Commonwealth ministers, calling into question their moral fitness as "lawyers and statesmen." For a royalist like Heylyn, no man in Cromwell's ministry could be a rightful "chief" or king.

> The Country is not subjected unto any one Prince, the *Natives* being governed by the *Chiefs* of their several *Clans;* nor finde I hitherto that either the *Portugals* or *Spaniards* have took possession of any one part of it, in the name of the whole. So that for ought I know, the best title to it doth belong to the King of *England;* for whom possession was taken of it in the reign of King *James*, by one *Captain Fitz-Herbert,* who called the *Ascent* unto the *Table* King *James his Mount*. But whether this Act of his beget any good title, or whether the title of a Country lying so far off be held worth the owning, I leave to be determined of by *Lawyers* and *Statesmen*.[33]

Heylyn's book evidently went to press before he knew that the Dutch East India Company had just established a permanent settlement at the Cape. Thus, although it makes a strong political point, its argument was no longer relevant to the actual situation at the Cape.

Heylyn lived long enough to revise his work only once. The second edition of *Cosmographie* (1657) presents more (mis)information about the Cape people than the first one, adding one completely new paragraph and tacking five sentences on to another. The new paragraph is indebted to the first edition of Edward Terry's narrative, which was published for the first time in 1655. It does not present any fresh information, but its emphasis on the beastliness of the Cape people helped to paint a more negative picture of the Cape people than that presented in Heylyn's first edition.

> Their best habits for the most part are the Hides of Beasts, undressed, unfashioned, just as they tear them from the flesh; but when they cloath themselves with Sheep-skins, they have so much wit as to wear the fleece next to their bodies in cold weather, which at other times they expose (with no small pride and glory) to the open view. Their voice so inarticulate, that it is hard to be distinguished into words and syllables; which, being composed with that bruitishnesse, which commonly appeareth in all their actions, makes it hard to say, whether the people generally may be thought to be men in the skins of beasts, or beasts created in the likenesse, and shape of men. But they make a greater use of their Cattle, than for Garments onely, their raw flesh serving them for food, and the Guts for Ornament, which hang about their Necks uncleaned, and with all the filth in them, in as great a bravery as Ropes of Pearle, or Chains of Gold in more civil Countreys. Gold here so vilified, that they exchange it gladly for Brasse, or Iron, and that quantity for quantity, and weight for weight, but in such senselesse disproportion, as rendreth Brasse and Iron the more excellent metals.[34]

The sentences Heylyn adds to the next paragraph include his summary of Terry's account of Cory. The importance of Heylyn's retelling of the Cory story should not be underestimated. As we will examine in the next chapter, the creation of the Cory myth provided the cornerstone for the negative constructions of "Hottentots." After Heylyn's death in May 1662, his work was revised by other hands. The "Cafraria" section, however, did not change in any substantive way until the last revision in 1703, when the name "Hottentots" was finally inserted into the text ("none are more barbarous than those whom they call the *Imbians*, they call themselves *Hottentots*").[35]

In addition to Heylyn's *Cosmographie*, there were other geographies that succeeded in the lively literary marketplace. Samuel Clarke, a contemporary of Heylyn's and, curiously, a pastor as well, produced *A Geographical Description of All the Countries in the Known World* (1657). Its Cape section is clearly indebted to the second edition of Herbert's narrative (1638) and Heylyn's *Cosmographie*, and its representation of the Cape people is damning. Clarke clearly wrote his work for a more general audience. He does not reprint Herbert's sentence detailing the immodesty of the women, preferring instead to speak more generally: "but the women, when they receive any thing, return their gratitude by taking up that flap, and discovering their shame."[36] Nor does he include Herbert's joke about "Mistress Venus alluring them not from Pallas." Clarke also has little use for all the classical texts Herbert cites, and he does not call the Cape people "Trogloditcs." Clarke's work evidently sold quite well. In 1671, he attached the fourth edition ("very much Enlarged") of his geography to a work more in keeping with a man of his profession, *A Mirrour or Looking-Glass Both for Saints, and Sinners, Held Forth in Some Thousands of Examples*.

A Geographical Description of All the Countries in the Known World was so popular that in 1689, an author who identifies himself as S. Clark brought out *A New Description of the World*, which pretends to have much in common with Clarke's work.

> let you know that my care has been to present you with Geographical and Historical Description of the World, as it formerly stood, and at present stands: and though upon first thought it may seem strange, that in so small a Volume so large a one can be contained, yet upon perusal you will find that nothing material is omitted, that can be required to render satsifaction upon this occasion.[37]

The description of "Cafraria" is different from the one presented in Clarke's *A Geographical Description*, although it is also extremely negative. At every opportunity, Clark stresses the brutishness of the Cape people. The extraordinarily long first sentence presents a catalog of visual images and details:

> A third Division of this *Aethiopia*, is a Country greatly abounding with Herds of Cattle, Deer, Antelopes, Baboons, Foxes, Hares, Pelicans, Ostriches, Herons, Ducks, Geese, Pheasants, Partridges; exceeding well watered, but deficient in Corn, by the neglect of the Natives, who choose rather to live idly upon the bounty of Nature, than to improve it by Art; making their Aboads in Woods and Forrests, and building, for the most part, their Houses of Branches of Trees, interwoven Hurdle-waies, and are black of Colour, thick Lipped, flat Nosed, long

Headed, but longer Eared, which reach beneath their Shoulders, occasioned by their hanging extraordinary Weights in them for Ornaments, as Rings, Chains, & c.[38]

The process of demonization continues in another long sentence, which focuses on the "Imbians" who live "not far from the Cape." The emphasis he places on the "Imbians' " cannibalism is so overdramatic that it is almost comical.

And in this Tract live the *Imbians,* not far from the *Cape of Good-hope,* Tall, and of considerable Strength, living by War and Rapine, feeding on the Flesh of their conquered Enemies and dying Friends, whose Deaths they hasten, that they may the Sooner Eat them, and make Drinking Cups of their Sculls; and in their Wars they fight with Poisoned Arrows, and a long Pole, hardened at the end with Fire, carrying likewise Fire before them, signifying thereby that they intend to Roast and Boil all they shall overcome; and these were they that Eat up the King of *Mambaza* and his People; their King if such a Monster deserve that sacred Epithete, accounting himself Lord of all the Earth; and when at any time the Heat or Rain offends him, he darts his Poisoned Arrows at Heaven, by way of defiance.[39]

Clark's description does not provide the reader with any way to identify the separate peoples he is describing; indeed, they all merge into one collective people of the Cape region. English readers could find copies of Clark's work for decades to come; other editions or pressings of it appeared in 1708, 1712, and 1719.

Neither Samuel Clarke or S. Clark puffed his geography as a "new" one, but both men clearly perceived the special power of telling stories from contemporary travel narratives. The emergence of "new" geography as a popular science was a true innovation of the Restoration era, and the many geographies published during this time provide ample evidence that the public's fascination with places and peoples beyond England was growing. Catalogs of books, auctions, and estate sales demonstrate that Restoration and eighteenth-century readers often had several geographies in their personal libraries.[40] Indeed, geography books and travel narratives complemented rather than competed with each other. Restoration era geographies style themselves as "new" for at least two reasons. Firstly, they aim to present the most recent information available. Their title pages often boast that the information therein is "Collected according to the latest Discoveries, and agreeing with the Choicest and Newest *Maps.*"[41]

The two styles of geography texts that came to be especially popular during the Restoration period testify to the subject's popular appeal. Dictionaries, gazettes, or simple geographies provided a relatively inexpensive way to learn about the world beyond England. They generally give basic information about a location and its landscape and inhabitants in one short entry. Edmund Bohun's *A Geographical Dictionary* (1688) provides a representative example of the form's simple presentational style.

> *Caffreria*, a country of *Africa*, of large extent. It lies from the Kingdom of *Angola*, on the North to the *Cape of Good Hope;* and is bounded East, West, and South with the Ocean; the South-eastern part is very fruitful, and well peopled, the rest is barren, Mountainous, and little peopled. The Inhabitants are so barbarous, that they are called by this Name from their rude way of living, which signifies the Lawless-People, and they were all heretofore Man-eaters, and many of them continue such to this day. They call themselves *Hottentots*. Mr. *Herbert*, an *English* man, will scarce allow them to be perfect men, and saith they sell Mans flesh in the Shambles.[42]

There was enough of a market for Bohun's work that Charles Brome, his printer, produced, without the author's permission, subsequent editions in 1691, 1693, 1695, 1702, and 1710. In fact, when a startled Bohun saw an advertisement in May 1691 for the second edition of his work, he wrote that it "pierced my heart like a clap of thunder."[43] The pirated second edition presents the same description of the Cape people as the first edition. The third and subsequent editions, however, add a long sentence after the reference to Herbert, and assert that the Cape people worship a God, which is something that other geographies would deny: "They acknowledg a Soverain Being under the Name of *Humma*, which they adore when he sends good Weather: But in cold and rainy, or very hot Seasons, they change their Praises of him, into Complaints against him."[44]

Restoration readers also had the option to purchase more formal, comprehensive, and expensive geography texts. These works were often folio-sized and multivolumed, and they often included colored maps and engravings. They frequently present discussions of classical as well as modern theories of geography and navigation, give instructions concerning the use of a globe, review recent literature, and provide a general introduction to the earth's continents and seas along with lengthy articles on specific regions and the nations.

Restoration England's first folio-sized new geography text cites a celebrated French geographer in its title, *A Geographical Descrip-*

tion of the Four Parts of the World Taken from the Notes and Workes of the Famous Monsieur Sanson, Geographer to the French King, and Other Eminent Travellers and Authors (1670), but it gives a description of the Cape that is all English. Editor Richard Blome, one of the era's most "bold" and "impudent" compilers, does not acknowledge the works of Terry or Heylyn, although he steals freely from them.[45]

> The *Inhabitants* are Black, have thick Lips, flat Noses, long Ears, and in a word, very ill-shapen. They are more barbarous and brutish than the rest of *Africa*, they *are Man-eaters;* their chief ornaments in their Apparel, are Chains of *Iron, Brass, Beads, Bells,* of the like; and cutting and slashing their skins in several shapes. Cloathing they have none, onely in the cold season they wrap themselves about with skins of *Beasts. Towns* they have none, or very few; for the most part living in the *Woods and Forests*, like brute *Beasts*.[46]

Blome reprints this same description in his *Cosmography and Geography in Two Parts* (1682), which is his translation of Varenius's *Geographia Generalis*, first published in Amsterdam in 1650. Varenius's text was regarded throughout Europe as the authoritative academic geography of the late seventeenth century. Isaac Newton edited Latin editions of it in 1672 and 1681, and it remained the standard text at English universities until the start of the eighteenth century, when Edward Wells's *A Treatise of Antient and Present Geography* (1701) replaced it as the standard text.

Like Blome, John Ogilby was a veteran author and literary hustler of sorts. Having curried the favor of Charles II through the publication of works celebrating the restoration of the throne, Ogilby won fame and fortune by specializing in the production of fine folio English translations of Virgil, Homer, and Aesop. *Africa* (1670) was the first in a series of volumes he planned on countries outside Britain. It presents the most detailed information about the people of the Cape then available, and, significantly, it introduces English readers to the word "Hottentot." Despite the fact that Ogilby's title page boasts that it is "Collected and Translated from most *Authentick Authors*, And Augmented with later Observations," the volume is largely a translation of Olfert Dapper's *Naukeurige Beschrijyinge der Afrikaensche Gewesten van Egypten, Barbaryen, Libyen, Biledulgerid, Negroslant* (1668). Dapper's book was itself a collection of sources; the information about the Cape of Good Hope area derives from letters written by Georg Frederick Wreede, a German who was there circa 1659–63.[47]

Ogilby was not a geographer, and nothing he had done previously suggests he had any expertise in geography. Until this late point in his life, he had served as a dancing master, tutor, and scribe in the earl of Strafford's household, as a deputy master and master of revels in Ireland, and as translator of Virgil and Homer. Still, before he died in 1676, he was named the king's cosmographer and geographic printer. In *Africa* (1670), Ogilby's lack of expertise in his subject shows. More often than not, his introduction reveals his extremely Eurocentric opinions, especially in regard to Africans: "For Valour and Courage, they are much inferior to the *Europeans;* neither understanding to handle Arms, nor willing or forward to learn."[48] He goes on to blur sexual categories, when he calls into question the male virility of African warriors: "A great number of them not long since, by their effeminancy were conquer'd by a few *Portugues:* One strong Fort of *English* or *Hollanders,* are able to rout whole Armies" (24). In this regard, *Africa* anticipates many eighteenth-century representations of "Hottentots" and others that would link Africans to sexual perversions. Like Purchas and Heylyn before him, Ogilby tries to demonize fellow English citizens, usually the members of dissident religious sects, by bringing "Hottentots" into the domestic landscape. He draws connections between them and "Hottentots": "The *Caffers,* or *Libertines,* who hold many Atheistical Tenets . . . like our *Familists* or *Adamites,* following their sensuality and unbridled lust, inhabiting from *Mosambique* to the *Cape of Good Hope*" (34).

The sections of Ogilby's text that do not derive from Dapper's source reveal a significant level of editorial recklessness and/or carelessness. Ogilby's introduction, which is not based on Dapper's text, relates that the Cape people "are the blackest" of all Africans (24), yet it also reports they are "yellowish" in color (43). Dapper's text presents a different report, stating that they are of a "tawny colour, like *Mulleto's*" (589). Ogilby's assertion that the Cape people are "the blackest" Africans might well be based on English sources. Whatever the reason, it is wise to question the general accuracy and reliability of his translation. Schapera suggests that Ogilby often omits or paraphrases important information.[49] Significantly, the inaccuracies and deletions in Ogilby's translation consistently serve to depict "Hottentots" in a more negative fashion than they are portrayed in Dapper's text. In fact, his textual alterations seem deliberate, and his tendency to be as negative as possible about those he refers to as "Hottentots" is evident from the first paragraph about them, where he claims that the "Kaffers" exist without law or religion.

> *Kaffrarie*, or according to *Marmol*, *Quefrerie*, took Denomination from the *Kaffers*, the Natives thereof, which others name *Hottentots*, by reason of their lameness and corruption of Speech, without either Law or Religion. (576)

Schapera's early-twentieth-century edition of Dapper's original work, which is recognized as a reliable translation, presents a far more neutral rendering of these lines

> The country or land of Kaffraria (or, according to Marmol, Quefrerie) is so named after the Kafirs, its native inhabitants. They are commonly known to our countrymen as Hottentoos or Hottentots, because their language is so clumsy and difficult; and they live without any laws of religion.[50]

Close comparison shows us that Ogilby's translation does not recognize their speech as language, but Dapper's text does, albeit that it is for Europeans "clumsy and difficult." Moreover, Dapper's text says "they live without any laws of religion," not that they are without laws and religion.

The last eight pages of Ogilby's chapter on "Hottentots" relate general information about their bodies, customs, and practices. While Dapper certainly did not seek to depict "Hottentots" in a particularly positive light, he, at least, recognizes their essential humanity. Ogilby's translation often does not. For example, his translation of a paragraph about how "unlearned" the Cape people are differs significantly from Dapper's text. Ogilby's choice of the words "dull" and "clownish," as well as his failure to mention that some of the Cape people are successful at learning, demonstrates how his translation delivers a more negative representation than the original work.

Ogilby's translation:

> All the *Kaffers* are void of Literature, stupidly dull and clownish, and in understanding are more like Beasts than Men: but some by continual converse with *European* Merchants, shew a few sparks or glimmerings of an inclination to more humanity. (590)

Dapper (Schapera translation):

> All the Kafirs or Hottentots are people bereft of all science and literature, very uncouth, and in intellect more like beasts than men. Some, however, through steady intercourse with our countrymen, gradually let the sparks of their human nature come to light, just as several at the Fort are also beginning to grasp the Dutch language.[51]

At best, Ogilby grants the "Hottentots" "an inclination to more humanity," but only if they come into contact with Europeans. Conversely, Dapper's text implies that their human nature can be developed through increased exposure to Europeans.

The question of Ogilby's reliability and accuracy notwithstanding, his work had clear influence and significance. Most crucially, it introduced English readers to the name "Hottentot." Subsequent works, like the fourth edition of Herbert's travel narrative (1677) and the 1678 English translation of Jean Baptiste Tavernier's *Les Six Voyages de Jean Baptiste Tavernier* (1676) also called the Cape people "Hottentots. By the late 1680s, the majority of contemporaneous geographies refer to the Cape people as "Hottentots."

Only two highly regarded geography texts do not place the name "Hottentot" in a revision or reprint. Blome does not use it in his editions of Varenius's work, nor does Robert Morden in his *Geography Rectified: Or, A Description of the World* (1680, 1688, 1693, 1700), even though he revised his entry for the second edition.

Once English writers and readers had this name in their vocabulary, negative depictions of the people called "Hottentots" seemed to receive a special kick of energy. Edmund Bohun uses the name in his *A Geographical Dictionary* (1688). "Hottentot" appears in the "H" section of the English translation of Moréri's *Dictionary* (1694), although it simply refers the reader to the "Caffraria" entry, which does not use it. The name also appears in the second edition of Laurence Echard's *A Most Compleat Compendium of Geography* (1691). The first edition, which appeared earlier in 1691, presents old information in a rather matter-of-fact way.

> The *Caffers* have not the least sign of Religion or Worship, living without both Law and Government. Their Language such as no man could ever understand but themselves, being so inarticulate, it resembles the Clucking of Hens and Gabling of Turkies. They have no Town, so nothing is here remarkable but the *Cape of Good Hope*, being the most Southern Point in all *Africa*.[52]

In the second edition, however, Echard incorporates the name "Hottentot" in the paragraph preceding his representation of them. The account in Echard's second edition, when compared to that in the first, reveals one crucial addition about their "Manners" that serves to pass a far more condemnatory judgment on "Hottentots."

> The *Caffers* themselves have not the least sign of Religion, or Worship, living for the most part without Law, Reason, or Government. Their

> *Language* is such as no Man could ever understand but themselves, being so inarticulate; it resembles the clucking of Hens, and gabling of Turkeys; and as to their Manners, no Persons can be supposed to be more irrational and brutish.[53]

Echard's work was in circulation for over twenty years. The third and fourth editions, printed in 1693 and 1697, present no substantive changes to the second edition, nor do any of the early-eighteenth-century editions (1700 [5th ed], 1704 [6th], 1705 [7th], 1713 [8th]).

Like Echard, Patrick Gordon added the name "Hottentot" and made other significant revisions to the second edition of his geography book. The first edition of *Geography Anatomiz'd: Or, The Compleat Geographical Grammar* (1693) does not use the name "Hottentot," and neither does it discuss the Cape people specifically. The entry speaks generally about the inhabitants in the region known as "Ethiopia Exterior."

> The Inhabitants of these various Countries are generally a savage kind of people, and many of them are said to be very treacherous, especially those of *Biafara*, who are also much given to thieving; those inhabiting the *Cafres* do live mostly in Woods and Caves in manner of wild beasts.[54]

The second edition, which appeared in 1699, mirrors what we found in Echard's geography. The use of the name "Hottentot" increases the representation's negativity.

> But of all the Inhabitants of these various Countries, there's none more observable for their manners of living than a certain People near unto, and upon the Cape, and commonly call'd by the Name of *Hottantots*. They're so term'd from a frequent Repetition of that, or such like word, and may be reckon'd the most Nasty and Brutish of all reasonable Creatures, having nothing save the Shape of Man, that can lay claim to that noble Character.[55]

The concluding sentences in Gordon's later section on "Manners" move from a discussion of skin greasing to what might be considered a joke about cannibalism. Interestingly, this marks the first time in any text that the "Hottentots" are dismissed in such a lighthearted way. Perhaps Gordon is delivering a sly commentary on all those accounts that alleged the "Hottentots" are cannibals, or perhaps it simply marks the emergence of the eighteenth-century tendency to belittle and delimit them (and those like them) through the use of humor.

> Their Bodies are usually besmear'd with common Grease, or some worse stinking Stuff, which occasions a very loathsome smell. Their ordinary Habit is a Sheep-Skin just as 'tis pull'd off from the Carcase; and they use (as Ornaments) the Guts, *cum puris Naturalibus*, wrapt about their Legs and Arms two or three Inches deep, on which they frequently feed when scarce of fresh Provisions. Notwithstanding of the unparallel'd nastiness of this People; yet some Travellers talk of a certain Inland Canibal Nation, (term'd *Cobonas*) who make frequent Incursions into their Neighbouring Countries, and spare none they catch, no not the Swinish *Hottantots* themselves, who ('twould seem) should make but a very unsavory Repast.[56]

In the remainder of the entry, Gordon relates the same kind of misinformation that so many geographies communicate: that the "Hottentots" do not have a language ("only a confus'd and inarticulate Noise and Bellowing"), and that they are irreligious "the numerous Inhabitants of these many Countries . . . [particularly the *Hottantots* abovemention'd] do live without any sign of Religion, being destitute both of Priest and Temple; and never shew any token of Devotion among 'em, except we reckon their Dancing at the Full and New Moon for such."[57] Nineteen editions of *Geography Anatomiz'd: Or, The Compleat Geographical Grammar* appeared between 1693 and 1754, and so we can assume that close to three generations of English readers were (mis)informed by the work.

Although several other Restoration-era geographies appeared in new editions or were reprinted in the early eighteenth century, the growing English appetite for travel narratives challenged them to incorporate the most recent information about familiar as well as unfamiliar regions of the world. This was especially true after the 1699 appearance of the first English travel collection since Purchas's *Pilgrimes*. Captain William Hacke's *A Collection of Original Voyages*, was soon eclipsed, however, by John and Awnsham Churchill's *A Collection of Voyages and Travels* (1704) and John Harris's two-volume *Navigantium atque Itinerantium Bibliotheca: Or, a Compleat Collection of Voyages and Travels* (1705).

Dutch born Herman Moll, a cartographer and geographer, understood the changing nature of the geography book trade. His perceptiveness is impressive, especially when we consider that he had only lived in London for three years before his first work appeared.[58] Moll's *A System of Geography: Or, a New and Accurate De-*

scription of the Earth (1701) pitches itself as a fair replacement for Heylyn's *Cosmography*.

> Dr. Heylin's *at the time it was written, was undoubtedly the best in our Language. But Geography has receiv'd so many and Great Improvements since his Time, that we hope it will not be call'd Presumption, to Offer at a new Work on the same Subject; wherein, from the many Corrections and Discoveries made of late years by the Skill and Industry of Modern Astonomers and Travellers, the Deffects of that may be supply'd.*[59]

Moll himself became an important force in English geography and cartography. Indeed, Swift salutes Moll in *Gulliver's Travels*, when Gulliver refers to him as "my worthy friend Mr. Herman Moll."[60] Moll's *System of Geography* remained in print a long time, and his maps appeared in many of the most highly regarded eighteenth-century geographies. Indeed, the presence of his maps in any volume lent it special credibility.

The Africa section in the first edition of Moll's *System* relies on the work of J. Luyts, a professor at the University in Utrecht. Moll assures his English readers, however, that Luyts had consulted the works of travelers, albeit mostly continental European ones. The representation of the "Hottentots" includes one piece of information that might well have shocked English readers whose knowledge of them derived solely from English-authored geography texts. It reports that the "Hottentots" are of "an artificial black Colour."

> The *Hottentots* of these Parts, whose Speech is scarce articulate, are most sordid Brutes, altogether ignorant of the use of Money, of a low Stature, Lean, of an aritificial black Colour, and very swift in running; to which purpose they usually out [*sic*] off one of the Testicles of their male Children, that are newly born: They are also most expert Archers, and extremely skilful in the application of Medicinal Herbs.[61]

Continental European representations of "Hottentots" had been debating a definitive classification of their natural color since the middle of the seventeenth century, and soon Restoration era and early-eighteenth-century English travel narratives also began to pay much attention to this subject.

The 1709 edition of *The Compleat Geographer*, produced by the Churchill brothers, is essentially an expanded and reworked version of Moll's *A System of Geography* (1701). Its representation of the people of the Cape is unabashedly negative, and it makes no pretense to specificity or objectivity. The assertion in its very first sentence, that Europeans degenerate through interaction with the "Hottentots," suggests the high levels of anxiety they triggered in the eighteenth century: "The great Barbarity of these People has been the Occasion that no *Europeans* have ventur'd among them; and the little there is to be got by running such Hazards, has made Men backward in exposing themselves."[62] Moll and the Churchill brothers relied on Willem Ten Rhyne's narrative *A Short Account of the Cape of Good Hope* (1673), which did not appear in English until they translated it for their massive 1704 collection. According to B. Farrington, a twentieth-century translator of Ten Rhyne's work, the Churchill translation is "a poor version, full of mistakes and omissions, quite unfit to be reprinted."[63]

The lengthiest account of the "Hottentots" to appear in a geography text in the early eighteenth century demonstrates the enormous impact of recent travel narratives. The editor of the *Atlas Geographus: Or, A Compleat System of Geography (Ancient and Modern) for Africa* (1714) devotes twenty-four pages to a chapter on *"The Cape of* Good Hope, *or the Country of the* Hottentots *or* Hodmadod." The discussion seems to include a reference to or quotation from almost every source, travel narrative or geography that includes a description of "Hottentots." There is little organization to the chapter devoted to the region and the people of southern Africa. Quoting one representative paragraph in its entirety shows the amount of material thrown at the reader in a sort of explosion of citations and "facts."

> *Dapper* tells us, they are extremely ignorant; but by their conversation with the *Dutch*, they begin to be refin'd. In the mean time they have some bright Beams of natural Reason, and understand the Laws of Nations and Nature. He commends them for their mutual Love, Fidelity, Sincerity, and Generosity, and says, that they never commit any Insult but when they are intoxicated by eating the Root *Dacha*, or drinking the Water in which 'tis infus'd. And if any, reduc'd by extream Poverty, take the Opportunity to pilfer any thing, they severely punish them. They are also very jealous of their Honour. When they go to the Fort at the Cape, they set themselves off with the fattest and most shining Skins, and adorn themselves with Ear-Pendants, Necklaces, Bracelets, and Rings of Tin. They think one Habitation no better than another, and 'tis common for those of one Village to take Arms rather than submit to their Neighbours; and if the Fortune of War be favourable to the one, the other must obey, and be for a long time expos'd to the Insolence of the Conqueror. *Tavernier* says, both Sexes are not asham'd to shew their Nakedness, and calls them a Sort of Humane Beasts. *Heylin* says, they live by War and Rapine, and feed on the Flesh

of their Enemies and Friends, using their Skulls for Drinking Cups. He adds, that when they go to the Wars, they always carry Fire before them, with which they threaten to roast or boil all that they overcome. They reckon the *Portuguese* Masters of all the Seas; and their King, whom they count the Lord of the whole Earth, shooteth his poison'd Arrows against Heaven as often as the Rain or Heat offends him. In 1589, about 80000 laid all *Zanzibar* waste as far as *Mombaza*, and devour'd the People. In short, *Gordon* says, they are the most nasty and brutish of all reasonable Creatures. *Dampier* tells us, they are abominably lazy, and chuse rather to be miserable, than to be at Pains for Plenty, in a Country which would so easily produce it; for *Lockyer* says, that as they knew not the least Part of Husbandry before the *Europeans* came among them, so now they practise nothing of it; whereupon the *Dutch* were forced to encourage Foreigners to transport themselves hither, which the *French* Refugees embrac'd in such Numbers, that 'tis said there are above 500 Families of 'em that live here in good Fashion. He adds, that the greatest Mark of Respect they shew to *Europeans* is to retire to a small Distance; but that he thinks that Compliment rather forc'd than natural.[64]

The tendency present in this text for the citation of so many sources is indicative of an English stylistic preference. Judging from the travel narratives, collections, and geographies that became popular in England throughout the century, the English had neither the desire nor the expertise to discriminate between accurate and inaccurate representations of the people they now called "Hottentots." The name came to communicate all they felt they needed to know about a society they thought beastly and uncivilized.

3

The Story of Cory

As SEVENTEENTH-CENTURY ENGLISH READERS WERE BECOMING MORE familiar with the land and people of the Cape of Good Hope, they began to find accounts of a man who in 1613 was abducted by English East India Company sailors from the Cape and taken to London to be kept as a virtual prisoner for about seven months before being returned home. How the public received and transformed that which became the Cory story is linked inextricably to the negative constructions of the society called "Hottentot."[1] Indeed, the story of Cory became far more than a tale for merely the literate audience. A consensus narrative developed that depicts Cory's rejection of English values and his sheer happiness at returning to his "guts and garbage" existence. So completely did the Cory story find its way into the early-modern British consciousness that the specter of this unregenerate Cape man figures in the larger eighteenth-century narrative of human progress as well as in the establishment of generic conventions for antislavery literature and other works that deconstruct an absolute frame of cultural reference in relation to African-European contact.

Two men were seized by English East India Company men in June 1613, and put aboard *The Hector* as the ship began its return voyage home. Only one of the Cape men survived the journey. After arriving in London in September, he was kept, at least through February 1614, at the house of Thomas Smith (also spelled Smythe), the first governor of the East India Company. The governors of the English East India Company planned for the man to learn English; they wanted him to serve as a sort of agent when English sailors negotiated with the Cape people for supplies. Cory, as he came to be called, was returned to the Cape of Good Hope in June 1614, sailing from England in early March on the *New Year's Gift*, the flagship of an expedition led by Nicholas Downton.

References to Cory in a variety of documents suggest that the

English East India Company made an investment in him that was emotional as well as material. The English clearly hoped that Cory would do more than just ease and improve trade for them; they wanted him to adopt the values of their culture as well. Nicholas Downton's use of the word "love" demonstrates this high level of feeling for him: after returning Cory to the Cape, Downton reports that he let him go "in hope of his better performance and nothing doubting of his love."[2] Cory, however, did not fulfill English expectations, and the resentment voiced against him in East India Company documents is remarkably strong. Believing that the Cory experiment actually made trading with the Cape people more expensive than before, Edward Blitheman writes that "itt had been good in my opinion if he had been hangd in England or drowned homeward."[3] Edward Dodsworth, the purser on the *New Year's Gift*, also blames Cory (whose name he spells as Quore) for changing the dynamics of their trade: "the *Salldanians* broughte us downe some fewe cattell, which as formerlie we bought for copper, but nowe that comoditie plentifull amongste them theie alltogether desired brasse, of which metle we supposed that Quore, which retorned with us, had geven them knowledg off."[4] Significantly, Dodsworth's journal sarcastically discusses the "kindnes he requited us," and describes Cory's leavetaking: "for beinge got ashoare with his tinckerlie treasure, he never afterwardes aforeded us the sighte of his persone."[5]

For years to come, English sailors continued to blame Cory when their negotiations with the Cape people ran into difficulties. When John Jourdain was at the Cape of Good Hope in February 1617, he fingered Cory as the chief reason why the Cape people were driving harder bargains: "That dogge Corye is the cause of all this rogerye, for that hee understanding our manner hath made them soe bould, thatt they doe not greatlie care for a peece."[6] Interestingly, Jourdain's representation describes a change in the Cape people's eating practices in favor of one that might have won English approval: "whereas before they were accustomed to eate rawe stinking meat, they are now content to eate the best and boyle itt themselves in potts which they carry with them for that purpose."[7] Clearly, however, he was far more concerned that trading at the Cape would become too expensive: "Soe that heare after within fewe yeares there will be no victualls to be had butt att deare rates."[8]

The English extended their negative response to (what they saw as) Cory's failure to the Cape people as a group. Thomas Elkington, also on the expedition that brought Cory home, denounces all the Cape people ("being ingratefull dogges all of them") in a letter to the East India Company's governors, in which he argues that they should not undertake another such experiment with a Cape person. His description of Cory's disappearance supports Dodsworth's account.

> Wee landed ther the Saldanian . . . but after he once gott ashore with such things as your Worships bestowed on hym wee could never see hym more; so doe greatly fear he mought be cause of our worser intertaynment, for which he had no ocation given, being all the voyadge more kindly used then he any waies could deserve, but being ingratefull dogges all of them not better to be expected; and would have bynn much better for us and such as shall come hereafter yf he never had seene Ingland, which your Worships hearafter may please to give order to prevente.[9]

The use of the word "ingratefull" in a number of accounts suggests that the English believed they were offering Cory (and his people) a way of life worth far more than "tinckerlie treasure." What was first seen as Cory's rejection of language and material wealth became, in the story of Cory, proof positive that the Cape society could never become civilized.

The English wanted and, perhaps, needed this negative reading of the Cape people. The authors of the myth generally ignored documents which suggest that Cory had proved to be helpful to the English. In a letter written just one year after Cory's return, Richard Baker reported that "Cory the Saldanian is returned to his old bitts of gutts around his necke: he hath done some good and some harme there."[10] It is not a coincidence that when the English were able to secure all the supplies they needed, Cory was not referred to so harshly in their letters. In June 1615, Walter Peyton, on the outward bound leg of a voyage, recorded a happy reunion and a successful trade negotiation between English sailors and Cory. His description records Cory (and his people) simply as "heathenish" rather than as "dogges."

> Heare *Corey* came downe, & welcomed us according to his heathenish manner, by whose meanes the Contrye people wheare nothing soe fearfull of us nor soe thievish as in former tymes, for they brought us downe sheepe and cattel in great aboundance which we bought in trucke of copper shreds as before.[11]

Peyton goes on to relate an expedition to what must have been Cory's village or kraal. Peyton's account suggests that Cory had a prominent place in his society, and that he had not, contrary to the myth that developed, thrown away "his tinckerlie treasure." Significantly, Peyton's description of the Cape people's friendly reception to the English was not incorporated into the myth.

> *Coreye* caryed of our people who desyred to see the Contrey & shewed them his house, wyfe & children at a towne distant from Saldania 8 English myles, conteyning about 100 housen or smale Cottages; all or most part of theise people saye to us (as it semeth they have learned of Coree) *Sir Tho: Smithe English Shipps* which they often repeat & that with great glorye, their wyves & childeren came often downe to us, to whom wee gave bugle [bead] bracilitts & the lyke, which gave them great content; there weare 2 or 3 of the Contrey people desyred to goe for England with us, because they ystemed *Corey* to have spedd soe well, returning rich with his shuite of copper, which yett hee keepeth verry charylie in his house, seene theare by some of our people; alsoe *Corey* determineth to retorne for England with us & to carrye one of his sonnes, when our Shipps toutche at the Cape homeward bound.[12]

This inland excursion was probably the first time English sailors had ventured so far into the Cape countryside. It is a shame that Peyton makes no attempt to describe the settlement or the people who lived in it; what he recorded relates almost solely to English interest and value.

Positive encounters between English sailors at the Cape and Cory actually continued for several years. According to a letter written by Nathaniel Salmon in July 1617, Cory guided English sailors inland to look for supplies. They "put him in apparel, and he brought us cattle enough."[13] During the 1620s, far fewer English expeditions touched at the Cape, and so references to Cory are scant. In July 1624, a man referred to as "young Corey" went aboard an English ship "with a couple of his consorts" and received some gifts.[14] Evidence suggests that Cory was executed by the Dutch in or by 1627. An anonymous sailor from Wales recorded in his logbook that the people of the Cape "hate the duchmen since they hanged one of the blackes called Cary who was in England & upon refusall of fresh vituals they put him to death."[15]

Before the first printed version of Edward Terry's *A Voyage to East-India* appeared in 1655, English readers could find details about Cory in only two printed texts. As we have seen, the earliest references appear in Samuel Purchas's *Purchas His Pilgrimage* (1617 and 1626 [third and fourth editions only]) and *Purchas His Pilgrimes* (1625), although neither of these sources present anything more than a slight mention. Significantly, *Purchas His Pilgrimage* depicts Cory as being helpful to the English:

> The *Hector* brought thence one of these Salvages, called *Cory*, which was carried againe, and there landed by the *Newyeeres-gift, June 21.* 1614. in his Copper Armour, but returned not to them whiles the Shippes continued in the Roade, but at their returnes in *March* was twelvemonth after, hee came, and was ready to any service, in helping them with Beeves and Sheepe.[16]

Purchas's later work, *Purchas His Pilgrimes* (1625) presented extracts from Captain Nicholas Downton's journals: on 17 June 1614, "Choree the Saldanian presented me with a young Steere," and on the next day, "Choree the Saldanian departed from us, carrying with him his Copper Armour and Javelin, with all things belonging to him, promising to come againe to us the third day after, but he never came againe."[17] When taken together, Purchas's accounts of Cory are neutral. By the early 1620s, Purchas had read a copy of Terry's manuscript, from which he extracted excerpts for *Purchas His Pilgrimes* (1625). Purchas's failure to select any references to Cory for his last work is noteworthy. English sailors and those who read their accounts surely had a variety of opinions and, perhaps, even personal memories of Cory, but the fact that no story about Cory began to take shape in the late 1610s and 1620s suggests that the English did not yet find it useful.

The Cory narrative that came to assume mythic proportions differs significantly from the representations written by English East India Company men. The first full draft of the Cory story appeared in print in Edward Terry's *A Voyage to East-India* (1655). Not really a travel narrative per se, Terry partly recounts the experiences he had as a chaplain to the 1616 ambassadorial delegation Sir Thomas Roe led to the court of Jehangir, the emperor of Hindustan. This volume also includes long sections of Terry's philosophical, religious, and political reflections. Why Terry waited close to forty years to publish a work stemming from a 1616 expedition must, necessarily, remain a mystery. He might well, of course, have published a more conventional travel narrative immediately or soon after his return. In 1622 he did, in fact, present some sort of account of his voyage in manuscript form to Charles, prince of Wales, and possibly other people. This narrative is what Purchas read for *Pilgrimes*. But Terry never saw his manuscript through to print in the 1620s. In 1629, he was appointed rector to the church in Great Greenford (Middlesex), and he served in that role until he died in 1660.

Terry was not, however, a quiet country vicar: he was an outspoken royalist. During the English Civil War, he published at least two highly charged sermons that testify to his deep concerns about the spiritual and political direction the nation seemed to be adopting. On 16 August 1646, Terry preached a sermon before the lord mayor of London at St. Paul's Cathedral.[18] The dedicatory epistle to the published version of the sermon presents its theme, which is that England is turning away from its blessed existence and ruining itself:

> For surely there were never any people under heaven that enjoyed and wanted more instruction than we doe: when we seriously consider how that Almighty God hath laid wide open before us the Books of his *revealed will,* of his *mercies,* of his *judgements,* yet though we have been taught abundantly by precepts, we have not *learned:* been prest upon by mercies, we have not *regarded.*[19]

Three years later, on 6 September 1649, Terry delivered another like-minded sermon to caution those who were leading the nation down what he thought to be a shameful path: "For us, that considering the variety of mercies wee formerly enjoyed, till wee sinned them away; to provoke us to love God, these two particulars seriously considered, wee may conclude against our selves, that the Sunne shines not upon a more vile, wretched, ungodly people, than wee of this Nation are, considered collectively, and together."[20] Significantly, the phrase—"that the Sunne shines not upon"—is repeated in a description of the Cape people in the work Terry finally published in 1655 ("but the Sun shines not upon a people in the whole world more barbarous than those").[21] His reuse of the phrase suggests that in Terry's mind, at least, the Cape people and the English people are interchangeable.

Like Purchas before him, Terry clearly understood how a travel narrative could accommodate a political purpose. The last section of *A Voyage to East-India*, which he styles the "Corollarie and Conclusion," emphatically expresses his hope that his work will inspire reflection: "I shall take liberty in this my last section, to enquire into some causes and reasons, why those Heathens, compared with us, but a wilderness, should be so fruitful in many moral good performances, and we, compared with them a Garden enclosed, should be so barren and fruitless."[22] It is in the Cape section and, even more specifically, in the Cory sections that we find Terry making full use of his voyage experiences (whether real or imagined) to speak allegorically about England's domestic situation.

3: THE STORY OF CORY

Telling Cory's story enables Terry to give full expression to some of his most political and philosophical conclusions. The following reflection precedes his first description of Cory:

> Me thinks when I have seriously considered, the Dresses, the Habitations, and the Diet of this people, with other things, and how these beasts of Mankind live all like Brutes, nay worse, I have thought that if they had the accomadations we enjoy (to make our lives more comfortable) by good dwelling, warm clothing, sweet lodging, and wholesome food, they would be abundantly pleased with such a change of their condition; For as Love proceeds from Knowledge, and liking, and we can neither love nor like any thing we cannot know: so when we come to a sensible understanding of things wee knew not before; when the Belly teaches, and the Back instructs, a man would believe that these should work some strong convictions. But I shall here insert a short story.[23]

It is telling that Terry himself refers to his narrative about Cory as "a short story."

Immediately following his brief introduction to it, Terry explains how Cory came to be in England in the first place:

> About three years before I went to *India*, it happened, that one of the Company-ships returning thence, and arriving at this Harbour, after a little stay, when she was ready to set sail for *England,* and having then two of these Salvages aboard, her Commander resolv'd to bring them both home with him, thinking that when they had got some *English* here, they might discover something of their Country which we could not know before. These poor wretches being thus brought away, very much against both their mind, one of them (meerly out of extream sullenness, though he was very well used) died shortly after they put to Sea, the other, who call'd himself *Cooree* (whom I mentioned before) lived, and was brought to *London,* and there kept, for the space of six months, in Sir *Thomas Smith's* house.[24]

What we find here is Terry's tendency to blame the victims, be it the man who died enroute ("meerly out of extream sullenness") or Cory himself for his homesickness. For Terry, these men, not the English, are the ones responsible for the failure of the English East India Company's plan.

The moral lesson of the story begins to unfold in Terry's dubious description of Cory at Thomas Smith's house. Terry never claims that he saw Cory in London. He was matriculated at Oxford's Christ Church College during the Cape man's stay in England. If Terry had a source outside of his own imagination for his description of Cory's mental and physical states, it remains unknown to this day. He depicts Cory as disdainfully rejecting material and spiritual improvement:

> he had good diet, good clothes, good lodging, with all other fitting accomodations; now one would think that this wretch might have conceived his present, compared with his former condition, as Heaven upon earth, but he did not so, though he had to his good entertainment made for him a Chain of bright Brass, an Armour, Breast, Back, and Headpiece, with a Buckler all of Brass, his beloved Metal; yet all this contented him not; for never any seemed to be more weary of ill usage, than he was of Courtesies; none ever more desirous to return home to his Countrey than he: For when he had learned a little of our Language, he would daily lie upon the ground, and cry very often thus in broken English, *Cooree home go, Souldania go, home go.* [25]

Despite the fact that Terry's description of Cory is clearly embellished or plainly false, it was believed and taken to heart by English readers.

The accuracy of Terry's depiction of Cory's behavior after his homecoming in June 1614 is equally questionable. Terry was not at the Cape to witness it, and so it is not surprising that his description contradicts the accounts written by those who actually were present for the occasion. As we have seen, Dodworth and Elkington represent Cory as disappearing with his English wares. Yet, Terry's account is the one that provided the seeds for the story. His representation has Cory discarding his English clothes along with any hope for becoming civilized, or even fully human.

> And not long after, when he had his desire, and was returned home, he had no sonner set footing on his own shore, but presently he threw away his *Clothes*, his *Linnen*, with all over *Covering*, and got his sheeps skins upon his back, guts about his neck, and such a perfum'd Cap (as before we named) upon his head; by whom that Proverb mentioned, 2 Pet 2.22. was literally fulfill'd, *Canis ad vomitum; The dog is return'd to his vomit, and the swine to his wallowing in the mire.*[26]

Terry's use of the biblical citation, which likens Cory to a dog and pig, emphatically denies the Cape man any humanity. The subsequent paragraphs suggest that Terry also has others in mind, however. They are the antiroyalists who, in Terry's mind, turned their collective back on English civility and culture with their deposition and execution of the king.

Terry goes on to deliver a rather lengthy sermon in prose and poetry for the conclusion to this part of the Cory story. As he did in his 1640s sermons, Terry wants to emphasize that even civil men and women in England, if led by degenerate forces, will descend to a level of brutishness like that displayed by Cory and the Cape people. The lesson is delivered in prose: "From all which wee may draw this Conclusion, that a continued Custome may make many things that seem strange and loathsome to some, even naturall to others, and that the most brutish life may seem civill, and best to a most brutish man; and he thus pleading for it."[27] Curiously, the moral is restated in twelve unskillful heroic couplets, interrupted by a reiteration in prose.

> 'Tis most strange that a Creature who hath any thing of Reason in him, should thus degenerate, thus plead, or thus doe, but it is most true in these, as of millions more of brutish Heathen in the world, who live as if they had nothing at all of man left in them.
>
> > For man the worst of brutes, when chang'd to Beast,
> > Counts to be civiliz'd, to be opprest;
> > And as he tames Hawks, & makes Lions mild
> > By Education: so himself growes wild.[28]

The last couplet's use of the figures of a hawk and lion, which have symbolic connections to royalty, presents a pointed reminder that men can change the nature of fierce animals, but not, apparently, their own nature. Terry also implies that the English, especially at this point in time, seem to be unable to squash their own tendency to wildness.

His conclusion made, Terry returns to his much-neglected narrative, explaining that after the Cape man was returned to his homeland, trade became more difficult for the English: "that we had never after such a free Exchange of our Brass and Iron for their Cattel."[29] Terry then relates a discussion he says he had with Cory when he stopped at the Cape on the Roe mission. It is impossible to know if this conversation ever actually took place; certainly it exists in Terry's narrative text in order to create the occasion for the long reflection that follows. This purported exchange between Cory and Terry makes little sense unless one brings Terry's discontent with his own people into the dialogue, as he himself does:

> It was here that I asked *Cooree* who was their God? he lifting up his hands answered thus, in his bad English, *England God, great God; Souldania no God.* Now if any one desire to know under whose Command these Brutes live or whether they have any Superiority & Subordina-

tion amongst themselves, or whether they live with their females in common, with many other questions that might be put, I am not able to satisfie them.[30]

Terry goes on to set himself in contradistinction to Cory and all the other "brutes" in the world, some of whom, quite pointedly, have degenerated "from the loyns of *Civill & Christian Parents*":

> But this I look upon as a great happiness not to be born one of them and as great nay a far greater misery to fall from the loyns of *Civill & Christian Parents*, and after to degenerate into all brutishness as very many doe, *qui Gentes agrunt sub nomine Christianorum;* the thing which *Tertullian* did most sadly bewail in many of his time, who did act *Atheisme* under the Name of *Christianity*, and did even shame Religion by their light and loose possessing of it. When *Anacharsis* the Philosopher was sometime upbraided with this, that he was a *Scythian* by birth he presently returned this quick and smart answer unto him that cast that in his teeth; *Mihi quidem Patria dedecus, tu autem Patriae*, my Country indeed is some disparagement to me, but thou art a disgrace to thy Country, as there be many thousands more beside, who are very burdens to the good Places that give them *Breath* and *Bread*. Alas, *Turkie*, and *Barbary*, and these *Africans*, with many millions more in that part of the world & in *America*, and in *Asia*, I and in *Europe* too, would wring their hands into peeces, if they were truly sensible of their condition, because they know so little.[31]

Terry concludes this reflection with a prophetic warning that would make sense only to a Christian audience, and might well have had terrifying resonance for those who fought against the royalist forces during the English Civil War.

> And so shall infinite numbers more one day born in the visible Church of God, *in the valley of visions*, Es. 22.1. have in their very hearts broken into shivers, because they knew so much, or might have known so much, and have known and done so little; for without all doubt, the day will one day come, when they who have sinned against the strongest means of Grace and Salvation shall feel the heaviest miserie, when their means to know God, in his will revealed in his Word, shall be put in one Balance, and their improvement of this means by their Practice in the other, and if there have not bin some good proportion betwixt these two, manifested in their lives, what hath been wanting in their *Practice* shall be made up in their *Punishment*.[32]

Having employed the Cory story to make this moral and political point, Terry has no need to return to it. Indeed, the next four pages of his volume are devoted to narrating an equally purposeful story—that of ten English convicts who were taken to the Cape in 1614 as part of some undefined penal experiment. The few who survived a stay at the Cape pleaded with returning sailors to take them home and, perhaps predictably, were hanged for new crimes soon after they returned to England.

The English remembered Terry's account of Cory far longer than they could recall any details about the vicar's voyage to the East Indies. Indeed, the Cory story quickly found its way into the nation's collective consciousness. As was mentioned in the previous chapter, Peter Heylyn, who in 1655 was at work on the second edition of his *Cosmography*, incorporated a summary of it in the 1657 second edition. Heylyn remains true to Terry's description of Cory in London, hardly changing a word.

> I have heard that some of our *English* ships in their return from the *East-Indies*, seized on two Savages, living near this Bay, whom they brought on ship boord, with an intent to carry them into *England*, to the end that having learned the *English* tongue, we might be more particularly informed by them of the Estate and Affairs of this Countrey. One of these who was called *Coore*, being brought to *London* (for the other died upon the way) was dieted and cloathed according to the *English* fashion, gratified also with brasse Rings, Beads and such other things, by which they thought they might most gain upon him to affect the change of his condition. But *home, is home, though it be but homely*, as the saying is. For this poor wretch having learned so much *English*, as to bemoan his own misfortunes, would throw himself upon the ground, and cry out with great anguish, and vexation of spirit, *Coore home go, Soldania go, Coree home go*, out of which unquietnesse of humour, when they could not get him, they sent him back in the next ships which were bound for the *Indies*.[33]

Heylyn's representation of Cory after his return home, however, differs from Terry's. Heylyn puts him back into his native dress, but there is no mention of him discarding his English clothes upon landfall. Additionally, Heylyn does not borrow Terry's citation from the Bible.

> After which time, as oft as he saw any ship with *English* colours, he would very joyfully make towards the Bay with Guts and Garbage hanging about his neck (as their custome is) and readily perform all good Offices towards them; yet so that it was found withall; that by discovering to the Natives how low esteem the *English* had of Brasse and Iron, they thenceforth raised the value of those richer Metals, which formerly they had parted with for such sorry trifles, as have been spoken of before. (994)

This version of Heylyn's account appeared in all subsequent reissues and or new editions of *Cosmography* (1665, 1666–67, 1669, 1670, 1674, 1677, 1682, 1703).

Ten years after its first publication, and five years after Terry's own death, another edition of his narrative appeared in print, but it is far different than the original 1655 edition. Only the travel narrative, stripped of all its reflections and commentary, appears as a supplement to G. Havers's edition of *The Travels of Sig. Pietro della Valle, a Noble Roman, into East-India and Arabia Deserta* (1665). Terry's account is puffed up as "one of the Exactest Relations of the Eastern parts of the World."[34] Terry's Cory story is reduced to two paragraphs that describe the Cape man's stay in London, his return to the Cape, and the negative effect Cory's return to the Cape had on the trade. The language and the biblical reference remain true to the original text, however.

> And not long after, when he had his desire, and was returned home, he had no sooner set footing on his own shore, but presently he threw away his *Clothes*, his *Linnen*, with all other *Covering*, and got his sheeps skins upon his back, guts about his neck, and such a perfum'd Cap (as before we named) upon his head; by whom that Proverb mentioned, 2 Pet. 2.22 was literally fulfill'd, *Canis ad vomitum; The dog is return'd to his vomit, and the swine to his wallowing in the mire.* (1665, 333)

Terry's full 1655 text resurfaced only in an edition printed in London more than a century later in 1777. The Cory story, however, was not forgotten during this one hundred and twenty-two year interval. Indeed, new versions of it appeared throughout this period of time.

Ten years after the first publication of Terry's narrative, a far different account of Cory appeared in the Restoration editions of Thomas Herbert's *Some Yeares Travels into Divers Parts of Asia and Afrique* (1665 and 1677). The first two editions of Herbert's work (1634, 1638) included no mention of him at all. Herbert probably did not know about Cory until he read Terry's narrative after its 1655 publication or saw excerpts from it in Heylyn's *Cosmography*. For his third edition, Herbert inserts his Cory story into a paragraph about trade. Herbert does not depict Cory as shedding his English clothing. Indeed, unlike both Heylyn and Terry, Herbert states that Cory was successfully civilized, but that he was "butchered" by his own people when he returned home. Needless to say, there is no source that supports Herbert's version of Cory's return and demise.

An example we have in Cory, a Savage brought thence into *England* in the year 1614. where being civilized, he returned in a few years after to his Country, where to express how nobly he had been treated, entring the Woods in a copper gilt armour; whether in revenge of his departure, or to be possest of so great a treasure, is not known; but instead of a kind reception which he thought he should have had, they butchered him.[35]

That only one of the many subsequent English retellings of the Cory story paid any recognition to Herbert's version suggests it did not have much appeal to the nation's collective imagination.

S. Clark's *A New Description of the World* (1689) borrows Terry's story generally. While it does not depict Cory throwing off his English clothes in any act of defiance, the description of the Cape man's mental state, especially at his return home, communicates the same lesson as Terry's narrative. Curiously, Clark's version is the only one that depicts Cory as an enthusiastic helpmate of the English.

It happened that some English Ships, in their way home from the *Indies*, fortuned to take two of the Natives, near the Bay of *Soldania*, in order to learn from them, when they could be brought to speak English, a farther account of the Country, and one of them, named *Coore,* they brought to *London,* the other dying by the way, when the better to please him, they not only arrayed him in fine Cloaths, but gave him Beads, Bells, and other things, wherein the Natives of his Countrey most delighted. yet not these, nor the sumptuous Fare he met with, could alter his inclination, for he altogether appeared Dogged and Melancholy; and when he had a smattering of English, he would often throw himself upon the Ground, in a melancholy posture, and passionately cry'd out, *Home go* Saldania, *go* Coore *home, go.* So that all hopes being lost of bringing him to any better manners than what he had naturally imbibed, they sent him back again by the next Ships, and set him, to his no small joy, on shore where they found him: So that at any time when he saw Ships with English Colours, he would come running to the Bay with Gut and Garbidg about his Neck, to them, doing them all the good Offices he could, being more pleased with that Beastly manner of Living than any other.[36]

If taken within the context of England's increasing trade and colonization at the start of the eighteenth century, it is easy to see how Clark's version of the Cory story better serves the nation's new economic sensibility and agenda. It imagines the English as intending to improve him ("So that all hopes being lost of bringing him to any better manners than what he had naturally imbibed"), but their hopes are dashed because of his "inclination" or nature. Clark's Cory story was not revised in any way for the three subsequent editions of his work (1708, 1712, and 1719).

Additional representations of Cory appeared throughout the first half of the eighteenth century, and they also demonstrate how his story was still evolving. John Harris's travel collection, *Navigantium atque Itinerantium* (1705), includes early seventeenth-century material "chiefly out of the journals" kept by both Nicholas Downton and Thomas Elkington, but the representation of Cory derives from Terry's and/or Heylyn's texts. Harris himself adds a somewhat ironic tone when he makes room for Herbert's imagined death of Cory.

> We lost here the Company of *Coree* the *Soldanian;* who having been transported into *England,* had lived there a pining disconted Life, and could never be easie till he was brought back to the beastly Company of the *Soldanians.* All the good Usage of the *English,* all the Toys and Trifles given to please him; Sports, Company, good Victuals and Apparel, signified nothing to this Brute out of his own dirty Element. Nothing could make him a sufficient amends for the loss of those agreeable Pleasures and Diversions which his Native Soil afforded him. To run about the Woods with the rest of that wild and brutish Herd, to dance and roul in the Mud, and eat raw Guts and Garbage: To be dress'd in Sheep-Skins, according to his Country mode, and rubb'd all over with Grass and Cow-dung: These Enjoyments the poor Creatures droop'd and quite languish'd after, and could not possibly hold out any longer in that State of cruel separation from them.
>
> To ease him therefore of his Burthens he was brought back hither again, where we had his Company for a little while, but then he pack'd up all his things, and went up into the Country, promising to be with us again, tho' we never saw him after that time. So 'tis possible that either he was so powerfully engaged by the Pleasures of his happy state then renew'd upon him, that he was not able to break loose from them so long as he visited us; or else that the *Soldanians* knock'd him o'th Head, as one that they suspected to have lost the purity of the manners and breeding of his own Country, by a debauching Acquaintance with another.[37]

Harris's tentative embrace of Herbert's version is very interesting. In suggesting, albeit ironically, that the Cape people might have regarded Cory as one who "lost the purity of the manners and breeding of his own Country, by a debauching Acquaintance with another," we can see a projection of the "going native" fear. For the English, Cory was a discomforting figure precisely because he did not "go native" and mimic them when he was kept in England.

Another indication of how the Cory story found its way into English minds is how often Cory-like stories appear in early-eighteenth-century travel narratives. Despite the fact that the authors of them could not, of course, have seen Cory, they still wanted to incorporate his story in their own works. William Funnell's *A Voyage round the World* (1707) includes an account that matches Terry's account of Cory, although it depicts two "Hodmandods" held by the Dutch. Their rejection of European clothes, however, mirrors Cory's.

> I was told a story by the Person with whom I lodged here, that some years since, the *Dutch* sent two of these *Hodmandod* Men to *Holland;* where they were very well cloathed, had a good maintenance allowed them, and for the space of four years were sent up and down to see the several parts of *Holland* and other countries adjacent: The *Dutch* thinking this would be a means of bringing them to a more civilized way of living. But it proved ineffectual: For the two *Hodmandods* at their return, as soon as they got ashore, tore off all their Cloaths, and returned to their old beastly way of living.[38]

Twenty years later, in his *A New Account of the East Indies* (Edinburgh, 1727; London, 1737), Alexander Hamilton depicts a better schooled and less homesick Cory. Still, this youth also rejects English clothes. According to Hamilton, an English Captain

> had the Curiosity to detain a Youth that came on board his Ship, and, being ready to sail, carried him to *England,* where he staid some Years, clothed well after the *English* fashion, and kept at School to learn to speak and read *English;* and, when the East-India Company thought him well enough qualified to serve for an Interpreter, they sent him back to his own Country, very well clothed. As soon as he appeared ashore among his Friends and Relations, he pulled off his *English* Apparel, and put on his Country Habit, which is a Sheep's Skin about his Shoulders.[39]

John Green, the editor of Astley's *A New General Collection of Voyages and Travels* (1745–47), actually invokes Cory to try to make the Cape more appealing to the growing British colonial appetite. It is interesting to note that this Cory is cleaner and less brutish than the imagined original: he is not wearing the "guts and garbage" that is featured in almost every other version of his story.

> In 1614, Captain *Downton* set ashore here a *Hottentot,* called *Koree,* who had been brought over to *England* (in Company with another, who died) the preceding Year; and was cloathed and entertained by Sir *Thomas Smith,* . . . This *African,* far from rejoicing at his good Usage,

though he had a Suit of Brass Armour given him, continually sighed for his own Country, so that the Company sent him home by that Commander; and he no sooner got ashore, but he threw away his Cloaths, and returned to his old Way of Living. But whenever any *English* Ships, touched here, *Koree* was sure to be very serviceable in getting them Cattle, and what Refreshments they wanted.[40]

Interestingly, Green places his version of the story in a chapter that chronicles the history of the Dutch colony. Locating the story here helps Green suggest that Cory's service to a colonizing force is being carried on by his descendents.

The Cory story told in the fifth volume of Thomas Salmon's *Modern History* (1755), a full century after Terry's travel narrative first appeared, has some curious departures from all the above-mentioned versions. Some of what Salmon relates derives from Funnell's 1707 narrative, but he names England as the destination rather than Holland. Salmon also introduces his own phrase to relate how eager the two men were to renounce ("rejoiced beyond measure") their English experience.

> but the two Hottentots only learnt English enough to bewail their misfortune in being brought from their country and their friends; and, after two years trial of them, being again set on shore at the Cape, they immediately stripp'd off their European cloaths, and, having taken up the sheep-skin mantle again, rejoiced beyond measure for their happy escape from the English.[41]

Salmon's story was retold as late as George Augustus Baldwyn's *A New, Royal, Authentic, Complete, and Universal System of Geography; Or, a Modern History and Description of the Whole World* (1794).

The specter of Cory can also be found in Restoration and eighteenth-century English belles-lettres. A character named Coree appears as an American Indian in the "Third Vision" of Edward Pettit's heavily political *The Visions of Government etc. Wherein the Antimonarchical Principles and Practices of all Phanatical Commonwealths-Men, and Jesuitical Politicians are Discovered, Confuted, and Exposed* (1684 and 1686). This Coree is depicted as "a poor Indian Savage, that can indeed speak English, but has scarce shak't off his Soot and Grease, and is just polisht enough for the common Civilities of life."[42] He is a more positive than negative character, which is consistent with the more positive English constructions of Native Americans. Through the instructions of his English "master," he has embraced Christianity and other English values and preferences. He is also obedient: when his master tells him to assault a Jesuit, he carries out the order in a most enthusiastic manner:

> *and then turning to his* Indian, *hark you,* Coree, *thou art* Christian *enough to encounter that* Tanto Devil; *therefore beat him soundly, and tell him, I bid you do so.*
> The *Jesuit* seeing the *Indian* coming up to him in good earnest, began to run for it; however, he soon overtook him, and gave him half a dozen *American* Complements with his *Indian Bill* in exchange for his *Bill of Exclusion*. (212)

The appropriation of Cory for such a political message suggests Pettit learned a lesson from Terry's work.

Another Restortion-era representation of Cory shows how easy an examplar he became. In *An Essay Concerning Human Understanding*, John Locke refers specifically to Cory as part of his proof that the idea of God is not innate in human beings: "But to intercede with your Lordship for a little more . . . Coore, an inhabitant of the country, who could speak English, assured Mr Terry that they of Soldania have no notion of God."[43] Cory remained in the British consciousness throughout the eighteenth and into the nineteenth centuries. A vision of him came into Horace Walpole's mind as the disgruntled author tried to find a way to express his exasperation in February 1774: "But how could any Gentleman oppose it?—could they hesitate?—were they tired of being honest? Hottentot-like, would they return to their garbage?"[44] At the start of the nineteenth century, Maria Edgeworth remembers the lesson of the Cory story in her novel *Leonora* (1806), where she has one character saying to another about a third: "It is lost labor to civilize him, for sooner or later he will hottentot again."[45]

The widespread dissemination of the Cory narrative late in the seventeenth and early in the eighteenth century positioned it to act as a kind of urtext for works that depict points of contact between Africans and Europeans, most of which were a product of the slave trade. Despite the fact that the Cape Khoikhoi were never seized as slaves for the Atlantic trade, the Cory myth provided readers with an image of an African person whom they could regard as ignoble, savage, and different enough from them that he was suitable for slavery. Equiano's *The Interesting Narrative of the Life of Olaudah Equiano, Written by Himself* (1791) challenges what he believes to be a general notion of Africans that had emerged by the end of the eighteenth century. He does so by directly addressing the basic (un)truth the Cory story helped to establish in many British minds: "And yet you assert that they are incapable of learning; that their minds are such a barren oil or moor that culture would be lost on them; and that they come from a climate where nature, though prodigal of her bounties in a degree unknown to yourselves, has left man alone scant and unfinished, and incapable of enjoying the treasures she has poured out for him!"[46]

In a complementary fashion, the influence of Cory's story can also be found in the representations of Africans who embraced English systems and values as a result of the slave trade. These men, whether real or imagined, are the very reverse of Cory, and they are often depicted heroically. Educated and literate, they believe in a God and, not coincidentally, in monarchy. Moreover, they are almost European in physique or dress, and they seem to hail from aristocratic families. Behn's *Oroonoko* presents its hero as a "gallant *Moor*," accepting of an European tutor, admiring of the Romans, informed about the English Civil War, and sad about the execution of Charles I. Behn writes, "He had nothing of Barbarity in his Nature, but in all Points address'd himself, as if his Education had been in some *European* Court" (13). Thomas Bluett's early-eighteenth-century account of Ayuba Suleiman Diallo, published as *Some Memoirs of the Life of Job, the Son of Solomon the High Priest of Boonda in Africa* (1734), is manifestly devoted to showing that Job does not reject English values, hospitality, or the opportunity to learn cultivation. Unlike Cory, he does not suffer from homesickness when he resides in England. Indeed, the diction seems to stress his positive frame of mind.

> Job's Mind being now perfectly easy, and being himself more known, he went chearfully among his Friends to several Places, both in Town and Country. One day being at Sir *Hans Sloane's* he expressed his great Desire to see the Royal Family. Sir *Hans* promised to get him introduced, when he had Clothes proper to go in. Job knew how kind a Friend he had to apply to upon occasion; and he was soon cloathed in a rich silk Dress, made up after his own Country Fashion, and introduced to their Majesties, and the rest of the Royal Family. Her Majesty was pleased to present him with a rich Gold Watch; and the same Day he had the Honour to dine with his Grace the Duke of *Mountague*, and some others of the Nobility, who were pleased to make him a handsome Present after Dinner. His Grace, after that, was pleased to take Job often into the Country with him, and shew him the Tools that are necessary for Tilling the Ground, both in Gardens and Fields, and made his Servants shew him how to use them. . . . About the latter End of *July* last he embar'k on Board one of the *African* Company's Ships, bound for *Gambia;* where we hope he is safely arrived, to the great Joy of his Friends, and the Honour of the *English* Nation.[47]

The major point behind Job's narrative is, of course, to support the argument that there are moral and economic reasons why Africans and the English could benefit from contact with one another. Equally importantly, it, like Behn's *Oroonoko*, depicts an African male who would not make the English uneasy. Job will do what Cory refused to do. He returns home, the book's conclusion hopes, to "be of considerable Service to us also; and we have reason to hope this, from the repeated Assurances we had from Job, that he would, upon all Occasions, use his best Endeavours to promote the *English* trade before any other" (59–60).

The influence of the Cory myth can also be felt in the generic conventions adopted for the "talking books" made popular by the abolitionist movement in Britain during the closing decades of the eighteenth century. Henry Louis Gates reminds us that these works were written by Africans "to establish and redefine their status within the human community."[48] The authors exhibit their obvious facility with European letters as well as demonstrate their embrace of Christianity in order to present what Gates calls a "testimony of defilement: the slave's representation of the master's attempt to transform a human being into a commodity, and the slave's simultaneous verbal witness of the possession of a 'humanity' shared in common with Europeans" (52). These works also include what the eighteenth-century British readership certainly wanted to see, that is, Africans whose stories do not at all match Cory's story in relation to a rejection of English culture and the civilizing process that it implies.

In *Thoughts and Sentiments on the Evil and Wicked Traffic of the Slavery and Commerce of the Human Species* (1787), Quobna Ottobah Cugoano makes a point of stressing the good use he has made of his escape from slavery. Notice, however, the passive pose he assumes; he was "delivered" from Grenada and taken as a servant to England.

> Thanks be to God, I was delivered from Grenada, and that horrid brutal slavery.—A gentleman coming to England, took me for his servant, and brought me away, where I soon found my situation become more agreeable. After coming to England, and seeing others write and read, I had a strong desire to learn, getting what assistance I could, I applied myself to learn reading and writing which soon became my recreation, pleasure, and delight; and when my master perceived that I could write some, he sent me to a proper school for that purpose to learn.[49]

His change in status, from being a slave to a servant, is, in the English view and, seemingly now his own, an upward move for him and a nonthreatening advance toward them. Judging by a note Cugoano added to his table of contents, he shows an awareness that he as an author and as a former slave needs to strike a sometimes precarious balance between asserting himself as an African and assuming a compliant stance before his readers.[50]

There also emerged a competing narrative to the Cory story. It depicts a "Hottentot" boy who was raised and educated by Van der Stel, an early Dutch governor at the Cape. For a time this "Hottentot" embraced European manners and dress, and, significantly, Dutch commerce. He went to work for the Dutch East India Company in the East Indies, but when a ship he was on stops at the Cape, a reunion with his "Hottentot" family prompts him to renounce his European lifestyle. Different versions of this story appeared in English as early as the end of the seventeenth century, and, variations aside, what they all stress is that this young man, like Cory, rejects "improvement."

The first English reference to this figure occurs in the translation of Simon de la Loubère's *A New Historical Relation of the Kingdom of Siam* (1693).

> The *Hollanders* had educated an *Hotantot* Infant after the *European* manner, and had sent him into *Holland*. Sometime after they caused him to return to the Cape, where he might be useful to them amongst those of his own Nation. But so soon as he found himself again amongst them, he continued there, and renounced the *Dutch* Habit, and Manner of living.[51]

The brevity of this account is striking. It does not claim that the "Hottentot" adopts Christianity, nor does it give him a voice. Indeed, short of the fact that the boy is "educated," the experience described here is similar to the Cory story.

The names and facts change considerably with John Nieuhoff's relation of a narrative that might or might not be related to the story related by Loubère. In any case, English readers could find it included in Nieuhoff's *Voyages and Travels to the East-Indies* (1704). Nieuhoff frames the story with the lesson he hoped to teach: Europeans should not trust "Hottentots." In this account there is no outright rejection of European ways, although the desire to rejoin one's native society is expressed quite emphatically.

> Notwithstanding the *Hottentots* are so stupid, and in my Judgment, the most wretched Nation upon Earth, there are some among them that want not cunning, especially if they are brought up to it; an instance of which we saw in our time, in two young fellows, who being carried

from hence to *Batavia*, where they were instructed in speaking, reading and writing of Dutch. One of them was employed as a Servant by the General Director, *John Maet Zuicker*, and after some time was sent back to the Cape to serve as an Interpreter there. I met with him at my first return from the *East-Indies*, among the *Hottentots*, and ask'd him whether he would not rather be with us where he lived much better? He told me he would rather be with his own Country men.[52]

Nieuhoff gives the story a conclusion that would have appealed to those who believed that in making the decision to rejoin his people, the "Hottentot" committed a crime against his former European friends.

> I understood afterwards that this fellow had proved the occasion of great mischief and differences among the *Hottentots*, and that several had been kill'd in the Quarrel on both sides. At last he fell again into the hands of the Commander of the Cape, who banish'd him to the *Robben Island*, where he dyed.[53]

The mention of Robben Island demands a brief comment. Robben Island functioned as a place of exile and imprisonment from the earliest days of the Dutch East India Company settlement at the Cape until the 1990s.[54]

Although not intended as a travel narrative, John Maxwell's early-eighteenth-century description of the Cape and its people, which was written to be read to the Royal Society twice in June 1707, includes a reference to an adult "Hottentot" male, who was educated by the Dutch and served them and their interests in some capacity. At the insistence of his family, this "Hottentot" figure is forced to return to "their way of Living."

> There was a *Hottentot*, who had liv'd for some considerable time in *Holland* and the *East Indies*, and had learned to speak *Dutch* and *Portugueze* very well, whom, upon his return home, his Wife, Children, or Friends, could not endure, nor would they converse with him, till upon returning his Ancient Habit, Diet, and Customs, he had returned to their way of Living.[55]

Although these three above-cited stories are not identical, they conclude in a markedly similar fashion: a "Hottentot," it seems, will elect to return to the beastly existence of his society, even if he has had an exposure to literacy and an European lifestyle. Interestingly, these stories did not capture the imagination of the British reading public when they first appeared in 1693, 1704, and

1707. At this point in time, the Cory story was clearly the preferred one, perhaps because it more fully represented the English idea of degeneration.

What became the consensus narrative about this "Hottentot" youth raised by the Dutch initially appeared in the editions of Peter Kolb's *The Present State of the Cape of Good Hope* (German edition, 1719; translated into English in 1731). The final lesson of this story is that the youth opts to return to his "Hottentot" way of life. Unlike Cory, however, this youth is portrayed as having been successfully "civilized," at least for a time.

> M. *van der Stel*, Governour of the *Cape*, took a *Hottentot* in his Infancy, and bred him up in the Christian Religion, and in all the proper and genteel Manners, Fashions and Customs of the *Europeans* about him; allowing him little or no Conversation or Intercourse with *Hottentots*. He became well skill'd in the Mysteries of the Faith, and in several Languages; was always sumptuously clad; and, his Manners were very justly form'd after the best *European* Models at the *Cape*. The Governour seeing him so qualified, entertain'd great Hopes for him; and design'd very noble Things in his Favour. He sent him, with a Commissary General, to the *Indies;* where he remain'd employ'd in the Commissary's Affairs, till the Death of that Gentleman; when he return'd to the *Cape*. A few Days after, at a Visit among his Relations, he stript himself of his *European* Apparel, and equipp'd himself *à la Mode de son Païs*, in a Sheep-Skin.

As we have seen, previous representations of this figure end here. Guido Medley's translation of Kolb's text, however, continues and, crucially, gives him a voice.

In his final moments with his Dutch patron, the youth speaks in a reasoned and deliberate manner. His words are both plaintive and patriotic, and they suggest a certain level of friendship on his part for Europeans. His physical action, packing and presenting his clothes to Van der Stel, testifies to his civility.

> This done, he pack'd up his Cast off-Cloaths; and ran with 'em to the Governour's; and presenting himself before His Patron, he lay the Bundle at his Feet, and addres'd His Excellency to the following Effect. "Be pleas'd, Sir, to take Notice, that I for ever renounce this Apparel. I do likewise for ever renounce the Christian Religion. It is my Design to live and die in the Religion, Manners and Customs of my ancestors. I shall only beg you will grant me (and I am persuaded you will grant me) the Collar and the Hanger I wear. I will keep 'em for your Sake." He added not; but turning his Back at once, fled swiftly away, and was never seen in that Quarter again.[56]

His expressed desire to adhere to the "Hottentot" religion directly contradicts all the English accounts that maintain that his society has no religion.

Kolb's version of this story became the standard one. After 1731, authors and editors of most continental European and British geography books and travel collections include it in their own works. For English readers, Kolb's story about Van der Stel's youth appears in a slightly revised version in Astley's *A New General Collection of Voyages and Travels* (1745–47). John Green, the actual editor of the Astley collection, attempts to control how readers will interpret the Cory story by prefacing it with a negative remark:

> THIS appears to be the whole that can be collected as to the *Hottentot* Religion, to which they are invincibly attached. If you attempt to reason with them, they hear you sullenly, or quit you abruptly. They avoid, if possible, entering on any religious Topic. Some of them have dissembled a Belief in Christianity; but when the Motive was removed, they always returned to their native Idolatry: In spite of all the Endeavours of the *Dutch* Missioners at the *Cape*, they have not been able to make a single Convert.[57]

Green summarizes Cory's experiences in just a few sentences, stressing his rejection of European religion and manners more than anything else. He concludes the paragraph with a final negative comment: "In short, the *Hottentots* seem born with a natural Antipathy to all Customs and every Religion but their own" (3:366).

The translation of Astley's collection into both French and German afforded continental European readers the opportunity to find this excerpt from Kolb's work. The French translation, entitled *Histoire Gènèral Des Voyages* (1747) and edited by Antoine Prévost, repeats the story of Van der Stel's youth without Green's editorial and judgmental remarks. Perhaps this is one reason why French readers came to regard Van der Stel's youth as a far more sympathetic character than English readers did. Rousseau was so struck by the story of this boy that he quotes it in its entirety as a note in *Discourse on the Origin and the Foundations of Inequality among Men*.[58] Significantly, an engraving of this youth's departure from Europeans serves as the frontispiece for the first continental European edition of *Discours* (Amsterdam, 1755). The visual representation depicts him already back in his native dress, wearing only a collar, sword, and sheepskin. He does not look like the "wretch" the Astley collection reports him to be. In fact, he appears quite

Frontispiece from *Discours sur l'origine et les fondemens de l'inegalité parmi les Hommes* (Amsterdam, 1755). Annenberg Rare Book and Manuscript Library, University of Pennsylvania.

noble and proud, with his left hand pointing to a native kraal (or village) while his right hand makes a gesture in the direction of his clothes. His European clothes are wrapped in a neat pile in front of him, and behind him five Dutchmen contemplate his action. A fort towering above the scene makes a nice visual reminder of Dutch colonial dominance over the "Hottentots." This engraving did not appear in the 1761 English edition of Rousseau's work.

German readers were familiar with the story of this man from Kolb's original text. Mendelssohn's translation of Rousseau's *Discours* into German in 1756, however, afforded readers the opportunity to react against Rousseau's use of it. Andreas Mielke delineates how Lessing, Wieland, and Riedel objected to the glorification of the man who rejects European ways, but his specter remained in the German consciousness decades later.[59] He is clearly the source of inspiration for a 1773 novella that completely reverses the outcome. Christian Ludwig Willebrand's *Geschichte eines Hottentotten, von ihm selbst erzählt* (1773) depicts a "Hottentot" who, according to Mielke, despises his own culture, adopts the customs of the Dutch, and "completely Europeanized, settles in France."[60] Both the French and German adaptations of the story of Van der Stel's youth, no matter the different paths they take, evidence a flexibility or playfulness that allowed them to reconfigure him so that he becomes more praiseworthy than blameworthy. This is certainly not the case with English adaptations.

English readers had the opportunity to read the story of Van der Stel's youth in many travel collections, geographies, and other encyclopedias of learning. Tobias Smollet was fascinated by "Hottentots."[61] He invokes the story of Van der Stel's youth in a telling way in *A Compendium of Authentic and Entertaining Voyages* (1756).

> We have observed elsewhere, that the natives of Cape, who are called Hottentots from their stammering, are the nastiest people in the world; and the mothers always cut out the right testicle of the male child as soon as 'tis born, in order to make him the swifter of foot. They are for the most part so very stupid, that if you shut them up in a house, with the windows closed, and the door latched, they will have no notion of effecting an escape, being in this respect inferior to beasts, which generally endeavour to free themselves from bondage. Their attachment to their country is surprising; for it has been known that a Hottentot, after his return from Europe, where he has lived for many years, has rejected his manners with his cloaths, and returned to his soot and his garbage.[62]

That Smollet relies so heavily on the figure of Van der Stel's youth to carry his negative conclusion and judgment on "Hottentot" demonstrates that English authors were still content to let Cory or, in this case a figure like him, represent the entire "Hottentot" society.

A representation of Van der Stel's youth also appears in volume five of Thomas Salmon's *Modern History* (1755). It is beholding to Medley's translation of Kolb, but Salmon gives himself some license to augment the original narrative. Salmon depicts this youth asking for "leave to keep the hanger and collar he wore for his sake," but adds the following "which while the governor was deliberating with himself upon, scarce believing the fellow to be in earnest, the young *Hottentot* took the opportunity of running away, and never came near the Cape afterwards, thinking himself extremely happy that he had exchanged his *European* clothes for a sheep-skin and the rest of the *Hottentots* dress and ornaments."[63] The effect of Salmon's additions turn the "Hottentot" into a more negative figure than the youth Kolb depicts.

The version presented in Daniel Fenning and John Collier's *A New System of Geography* (1764) turns the tale into a sort of lament about the failure of missionaries to convert "Hottentots." Fenning and Collier do this by placing the story in a false and misleading frame. Van der Stel was at the Cape decades before the first European missionaries ever arrived at the Cape. Kolb also left the Cape more than twenty years before the arrival of any missionaries.

> We have here given the strange and absurd system of the Hottentot religion, of which they are so fond, that it is not certain any one of them ever died a *Christian*. The Dutch indeed have sent missionaries among them, who have undergone numberless fatigues, and taken the utmost pains to make proselytes; but it was without effect, and they were compelled with sorrow to abandon so good a design, without having made the least impression on the minds of the Hottentots. In confirmation of this, Mr. Kolben gives the following remarkable incident. (375)

Later editions of Fenning's work, beginning with the fourth edition in 1785, include the first appearance of an English engraving of Van der Stel's youth.[64] It provides an interesting counterpart to the engraving in Rousseau's mid-century work. Clearly not intending to idealize or romanticize the "Hottentot" figure in any way, the ambiguities of European colonialistic aims are reflected in quite a theatrical fashion. Van der Stel's youth is far more physically imposing in this rendering than in Rousseau's frontispiece. He wears a chain around his neck, has a sort of feathered boa covering his genitals, and his right arm is reaching out of the picture.

"The Attachment of an Hottentot to the Manners of his Country," Daniel Fenning's *A New System of Geography* (London, 1780). Annenberg Rare Book and Manuscript Library, University of Pennsylvania.

He appears slightly angry as he gazes back at the Europeans, and his left hand holds what appears to be his sheepskin cape. A bundle of European clothes lies on floor between the five Europeans and the "Hottentot." The five Europeans, some of whom are carrying rifles, cower behind a pillar. The subtextual point of the engraving might well be aimed at condemning European soldiers who would be intimidated by a "Hottentot" like this one. The motto is: "The Attachment of an Hottentot to the Manners of his Country, shewn by the Conduct of one of them bred from his Infancy among Europeans."[65]

Other eighteenth-century geographies also relate the story of Van der Stel's youth in ways that serve to emphasize his rejection of European customs. Among them, Charles Theodore Middleton's *A New and Complete System of Geography* (1778) looks to the Astley collection for its source. Middleton frames the story in a similar way, but he uses more pretentious and exaggerated language.

> The Dutch represent the Hottentots as exceeding obdurate of heart, and difficult to be convinced of the propriety of any opinion but their own; for, says an accurate writer, "If you attempt to reason with them, they hear you sullenly, or quit you abruptly. They avoid, if possible, entering on any religious topic. Some of them have disembled a belief of Christianity; but when the motive was removed, they always returned to their native idolatry.[66]

Middleton relates the actual story with no substantive changes in diction until the very last sentence: "Without waiting for a reply, he flew to the woods; here he mixed with his relations, studied their customs, degenerated into their manners, and could never after be drawn from that mode of life by the most persuasive eloquence of the greatest promises, though both were frequently used to recover him to civilized society" (384). The new language signals Middleton's effort to give the story an even more negative slant, insisting as it does that their "idolatry" is "native" to them.

Had all the negative constructions of "Hottentot" not been as stable as they were in eighteenth-century Britain, the British might well have allowed themselves to feel more sympathy for Van der Stel's youth. Any felt connection, however, was renounced and denounced, sometimes with curious vigor. Lord Shelburne evidently showed David Hume the frontispiece engraving of Rousseau's *Discours*. It had such a forceful impact on Hume that he refers to it in a letter to Shelburne, written before he returned to Scotland in December 1761.

> I remember to have seen a picture in your Lordship's house of a Hottentot who fled from cultivated life to his companions in the woods and left behind him all his fine accoutrements and attire. I compare not my case to his; for I return to very sociable, civilized people. I only mean to express the force of habit which renders a man accustomed to retreat and study unfit for the commerce of the great world, and makes it a necessary piece of wisdom for him to shun it after age has rendered that habit entirely inveterate.[67]

That Hume, a Scot, uses this "Hottentot" figure to defend his own people and culture to an English aristocrat is suggestive of the great prejudice against both "Hottentots" and Scots in England.

Throughout the eighteenth century, all English representations of Cory and his youthful counterpart were negative ones. In his *Letters on the Study and Use of History* (1752), Henry St. John, viscount Bolingbroke, cites the story of Van der Stel's youth as the final example in his argument against vanity, "that ridiculous and hurtful vanity, by which the people of each country are apt to prefer themselves to those of every other."[68]

> The Chinese Mandarins were strangely surprised, and almost incredulous, when the Jesuits shewed them how small a figure their empire made in the general map of the world . . . and the Hottentot, who returned from Europe, stripped himself naked as soon as he came home, put on his bracelets of guts and garbage, and grew stinking and lowly as fast as he could.[69]

Three decades later, James Dunbar does not see vanity in the concept of a national identity, but, like Bolingbroke, he uses the story of Van der Stel's youth to make a related point about ignorance. In *Essays on the History of Mankind in Rude and Cultivated Ages* (1780), he presents the "Hottentot's" rejection of European ways as a true sign of ignorance and degeneracy.

> Profound ignorance, and a contrariety, or repugnancy of customs and manners, account for that aversion, or contempt for strangers and foreigners, implied in the partial sentiments of savage and untutored minds. No information, no experience, no conviction can always conquer early prejudice: and the Hottentot, who returned from Europe, relapsed, we may believe, with all imaginable ease, perhaps with additional satisfaction into the established habits of his country.[70]

During the last decade of the eighteenth century, the story of the youth was adapted to service the anti-Dutch and anti-French sentiment that helped pave the way for the British seizure and occupation of the Cape. The following account appears in both *The New Royal Geographical Magazine* (1794) and *Guthrie's Universal Geography Improved* (1795).

> They are so attached to their own country and manners, and such enthusiasts for liberty, that all the attempts of the Europeans, particularly of the Dutch at the Cape of Good Hope, have been hitherto ineffectual for making the least impression on these savage mortals, or giving them the least inclination, or even an idea of the European manner of life. There is even an instance of a Hottentot, who had been taken from Caffraria by the Dutch while an infant, and being instructed in the customs, learning, and religion of the Europeans, became a proficient in literture, but on returning to his native country, he abandoned all the advantages of his education, returned his European dress to his master, put on the sheep-skin mantle, and never more appeared among the Dutch.[71]

As British citizens began to emigrate and settle in the British Cape Colony, Van der Stel's youth was remembered in order to make a point of colonial concern. Published in 1820, the year of the first organized British emigration to the Cape Colony, James Prior's *Narrative of a Voyage in the Indian Seas* uses the story to issue a warning that the emigrants should not become too trusting or dependent on their nonwhite servants. Significantly, this marks the first time the issue of skin color is raised.

> The story of one, who by the means of a Dutch Governor here, had been some years among the whites and on the first opportunity threw off his new dress and manners, to return to his filth and his krawl, is well known. Instances continually occur of confidential servants remaining for years contented in their stations, and then, being suddenly seized with an idle and wandering fit, ramble they know not whither, to exist they know not how.[72]

It is interesting that Prior delimits the "Hottentot" here as "other" than white. Skin color had never before played a significant factor in either the Cory story or the story of Van der Stel's youth, but somehow British colonialism at the Cape demanded a reference to it.

For readers in the seventeenth, eighteenth, and nineteenth centuries, the story of Van der Stel's youth and the Cory myth continued to have tremendous resonance because they supported cultural absolutism at a time when increased contact between Africans and Europeans was beginning to destabilize their trusted frames of reference. Invoking Cory and Van der Stel's youth gave the English a literal and figurative way to demonize figures who dared to reject their value system. At the same time, these two stories allowed the English to explore and test questions about patriotism and other topics that might necessarily need to be redefined due to Britain's growing imperial reach.

4
"Hottentots" at Home and Abroad

I

TRAVEL NARRATIVES ARE WHAT LED WILLIAM PETTY, ONE OF THE original members of the Royal Society, to declare that the "Hottentots" are "the Most beastlike of all men . . . with whom our Travellers are well acquainted."[1] Had Petty not died in 1687, he would have been able to read the late-seventeenth- and early eighteenth-century representations of "Hottentots" that uniformly confirmed his opinion. Philip Edwards does not overstate the case when he maintains that a "new era of voyage literature" began during the Restoration period.[2] The reading public developed a voracious appetite for travel narratives, and printers were able to produce them at ever-increasing rates. Prospective authors were given instructions, most famously, by Robert Boyle, who advised that a "Natural History of a Countrey" must present a "careful account" of inhabitants by including details about "their Stature, Shape, Colour, Features, Strength, Agility, Beauty (or the want of it), Complexions, Hair, Dyet, Inclinations, and Customs that seem not due to Education."[3] Ray William Frantz might well be correct that Boyle and the Royal Society "drafted" travelers "into the service of the New Science," and that a "new traveler," who saw himself as a "collector" rather than an "interpreter" of data, aimed for objectivity, skepticism, and precision.[4] Frantz's definition of new travelers does not, however, hold true for the majority of Englishmen who recorded observerations about the Cape and its people during the Restoration and early eighteenth century. Very few of these men had the literary skills or the powers of observation to put Boyle's strictures into practice. As we will examine in the first half of this chapter, what is most striking about these representations of the people by this time named "Hottentots" is the high level of subjectivity in them, their inordinate use of hyperbolic language, and their general lack of precision.

The wild and fictional quality to many of the representations of "Hottentots" in travel narratives is perhaps what made them so attractive to eighteenth-century readers and authors. If these writers and readers were looking for new and surprising ways to make verbal attacks on personal, political, and national enemies or discuss controversial issues of concern, they found a convenient and easy vehicle for expression in the descriptions of "Hottentots" included in travel narratives. Indeed, eighteenth-century authors consistently imported images and ideas of "Hottentots" to talk about themselves and their nation. Their representations reveal and address the uncertainties of the time, be it in relation to politics, economics, gender, and slavery. As we will see in the second half of this chapter, the numerous literal and figurative references to domestic "Hottentots" demonstrate the extent to which the negative constructions were entrenched in the nation's psyche.

The lively marketplace for travel narratives that emerged during the Restoration era and continued unabated through the early decades of the eighteenth century disseminated descriptions of "Hottentots" that inscribed them as the world's most beastly people. Eighteenth-century readers were, as Percy Adams explains, fully aware of the tradition of "travelers as liars," but they still "wanted to believe that what they read was true."[5] They were certainly ready to believe the worst about "Hottentots." Literal references to "Hottentots" in belles-lettres texts show how the descriptions in travel narratives progressed into poetry and other genres. Richard Blackmore remembers and refers to descriptions of their language in his long poem *The Nature of Man* (1711): "So void of Sense the Hottentot is found, / Whose Speech is scarce articulated Sound. / That 'tis disputed, if his doubtful Soul / Augment the Humane or the Brutal Roll."[6] Similarly, John Dyer's *The Fleece* recalls the depiction of one "Hottentot" custom: "and the rough shore / Of Caffres, land of savage Hottentots, / Whose Hands unnatural hasten to the grave / Their aged parents: what barbarity / And brutal ignorance, where social / Trade is held contemptible!"[7] References like these smoothed the way for figurative constructions of "Hottentots." More crucially, they helped to develop the prejudice against "Hottentots."

That "Hottentots" came to occupy such a central place in the nation's late-seventeenth- and eighteenth-century consciousness at all is remarkable. England had no colonial interest or investment in the Cape until the last five years of the eighteenth century, and very few English men and women wrote travel narratives that actually include descriptions of people called "Hottentots." In fact, for the years between 1660 and 1730, there are only twelve. During this same period, English readers also had access to translations of thirteen continental European travel narratives that included representations of the Cape and its people. Thus, the total number of available descriptions is relatively small, yet they made a most significant impact.

What is particularly striking about these descriptions of "Hottentots" is their highly emotional and emphatic tone. A brief survey of the conclusions reached about "Hottentots" in these works shows that the travelers experienced a heightened reaction to them. Edward Barlow, who spent his life at sea in English ships, was at the Cape circa 1674. He records "Hottentots" as being "the heathenest people that I have ever seen, neither knowing good and worshipping neither God or Devil, going about more like brute beasts than mortal men."[8] John Ovington ranks them somewhere between the human and animal worlds: "of all People, they are the most Bestial and Sordid . . . the very Reverse of Human kind, Cousin Germans to the *Halalchors,* only meaner and more filthy; so that if there's any medium between a Rational Animal and a Beast, the *Hotontot* lays the fairest Claim to that Species.[9] In his *A Voyage round the World* (1707), William Funnell follows suit, and emphasizes his conclusion about them with the word "certainly": "The Natives of this Place . . . are certainly the next to Beasts of any People on the face of the Earth."[10]

John Maxwell is both more specific and measured in the judgment about "Hottentots" that he sent to the Royal Society in 1707. His conclusion, however, is similar to that of his contemporaries:

> By all that I have seen and heard of them and other Nations, they are the most Lazy and Ignorant part of Mankind; by virtue of which two most excellent Qualifications, there are no manner of Arts practised among them, no Plowing or Sowing, no going to Sea in so much as a Boat, no use of Iron or Money, no Notion of God, Providence, or of a future State, no Tradition of Creation or a Flood, no Prayers or Sacrifices, no Magical Rites; nor, in fine, any Notion of any Invisible Being capable of doing them either good or harm, upon the strictest Enquiry that I could make of Men of Sense that had liv'd some time upon the Place; so that I believe their Ignorance hardly can be parallel'd.[11]

In his *A Voyage to the South Sea and round the World* (1712), Captain Edward Cooke allows for the fact that other indigenous societies were still being discovered during this period of exploration: "They are the most filthy beastly People of any yet discover'd, and harden'd in their Brutality; for those who have convers'd with

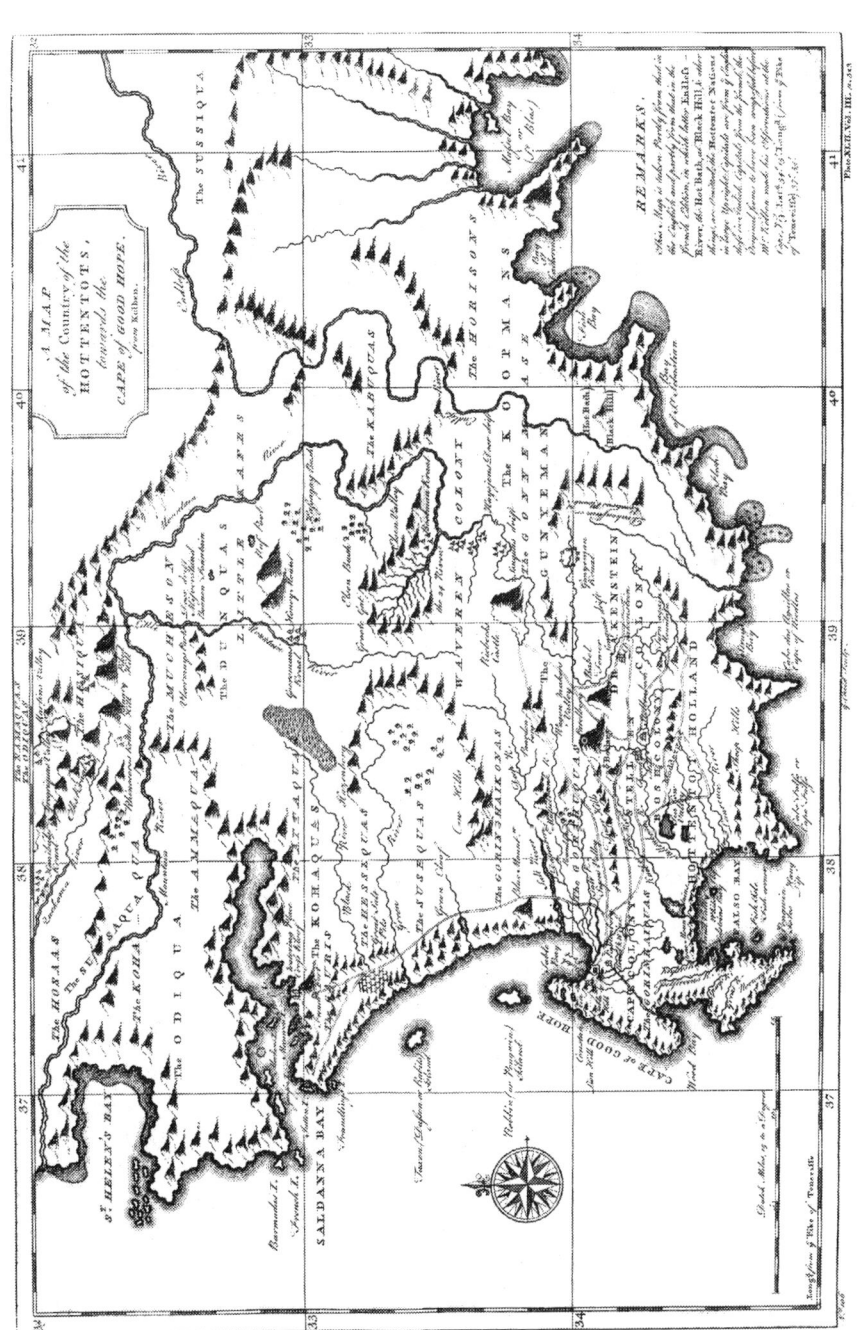

From *A New General Collection of Voyages and Travels* (London, 1745–47). Annenberg Rare Book and Manuscript Library, University of Pennsylvania.

them say it is impossible to reclaim them."¹² By the start of the second decade of the eighteenth century, negative descriptions of "Hottentots" were so widely known that Woodes Rogers expended little effort to describe them in his *A Cruising Voyage round the World* (1712): "This Place having been so frequently describ'd by others, I shall only add, that I found the Character of the *Hottentots* to be very true, and that they scarce deserve to be reckon'd of the Human Kind, they are such ill-look'd stinking nasty People."¹³

Seventeenth- and early-eighteenth-century representations place extra emphasis on what was seen as the negative characteristics of "Hottentots." Diction plays a crucial role in this regard. Ambrose Cowley's gratuitous placement of the word "Nasty" in the initial sentence of his description, the first written by an Englishman during the Restoration era, signals his basic vision and judgment of them. Cowley and others walked "to the Village inhabited by the *Hodmandods,* so called by the *Hollanders,* to view their Nasty Bodies, and the Nature of their Dwellings, which we found to be as followeth: When we came thither, we were scarce able to endure the stench of them, and their Habitations."¹⁴ There seem to be patterns of word choice in descriptions of "Hottentots." "Nasty" appears frequently, as do the words "beastly," "filthy," and "sordid"; they are used individually, as we see in Cowley's representation, or in combinations, as in Rogers' abovementioned conclusion ("most filthy beastly People of any yet discover'd").

The extent to which this second generation of English sailors were confused, offended, and upset by the "Hottentots" is suggested by their word selection, of course, but also by their frequent use of outlandish allusions and comparisons. After presenting his conclusion about the "Hottentots," quoted above, John Ovington goes on to describe, among other things, the sheepskins they wore, and in so doing he employs a Biblical story that would have tremendous resonance for the English (and, presumably, other Christian readers as well).

> The *Hotantots* are as squalid in their Bodies, as they are mean and degenerate in their Understandings. For they are far from being Curious either in their Food or Attire, any further than what they find Nature reaches forth to them. They think it a needless Toil to spend time in dressing of the Hides of Bulls, or in Spinning and Weaving the Wool of Sheep, for Ornaments and Covering their Bodies. They are satisfied with the same wrought Garments that Nature has clad the Sheep with, and therefore without more Labour or Art, they take them from the Backs of the Sheep, and put them presently upon their own, and so

they walk with that Sheep-Skin Mantle about their Shoulders, or sometimes thrown like a Hood over their Heads, which seem to be the Ancienest Garments, according to *Gen.2.21 unto* Adam *and his Wife did the Lord make Coats of Skins.*[15]

Ovington's allusion is clear: the "Hottentots" represent fallen humankind in its most base state, while his audience represents those who have progressed from a degenerate existence.

Another characteristic of these representations is the tendency of the authors to denigrate even those qualities or values they usually praised. For example, the English conceived of themselves as a people who loved liberty so much that they could never be slaves. Indeed, the chorus in "Rule Britannia" (1740), the poem that became an anthem for the nation, captures this sentiment: "Rule, Britannia, rule the waves; / Britons never will be slaves." It is especially interesting, therefore, that the "Hottentots" are recognized as lovers of liberty. Instead of acknowledging this as a shared value, however, English authors regard it as more proof of "Hottentot" beastliness. Daniel Beeckman explains that "there are no *Hottentot* Slaves; for as ignorant and brutish as those People are, they have a great love for Liberty, and an utter Aversion to Slavery: Neither will they hire themselves in your Service longer than from Morning to Night, for then they will be paid, and sleep Freeman, and no Hirelings."[16] Similarly, in 1727, Alexander Hamilton notes their resistance to slavery : "Notwithstanding that they are so brutal and indocile, they know the Value of Liberty, and will by no means be Slaves."[17] Possible references to "Hottentot" resistance appear in unexpected texts. Thomas Southerne might well be addressing the issue in his dramatic treatment of *Oroonoko* (1695), through a character called Hottman, a slave who rails against slavery and promises to "be the head, the hand, and heart" in a fight against it, but then proves himself a coward.[18]

The travelers often equate or link "Hottentot" idleness with their aversion to slavery. Significantly, "Hottentot" idleness begins to be seen as something very close to an ethnic or racial trait. Ovington complains in his *Voyage to Suratt:* "But their Native Inclination to Idleness and a careless Life, will scarce admit of either Force or Rewards for reclaiming them from that innate Lethargick humour."[19] Charles Lockyer comes to the identical conclusion: "The Native *Hotantots* were never fit for Improvements; nay, so Lazy and Ignorant were they, before the *Europeans* came among them, that they knew not the least part of Husbandry, and even now they practice nothing of it."[20]

The assigning of a race to the "Hottentots" became a contentious issue. During the late seventeenth and early eighteenth century, skin color was fast becoming the central determinant used in the classification of race, especially in relation to African Negroes. Although texts such as Ogilby's informed readers that there were variations of skin color among Africans ("Some divide the *Africans* into Black and White, but a curious eye may easily observe a great difference in the colours of those people"), the English tended to regard all dark-skinned African peoples as being of the same color, black.[21] The "Hottentots," however, were not "black" like Negroes. The resulting uncertainty regarding the race of the "Hottentots" was perhaps one of the reasons why Restoration and eighteenth-century representations of them are considerably more negative than contemporaneous descriptions of other Africans. Daniel Defoe's *Atlas Maritimus* (1728) illustrates how "Hottentots" were singled out for special criticism. He characterizes Africans as a "vile accursed race," and he calls the "Hottentots" "the worst and most savage of all savages . . . whose understanding is a thousand times below the meanest class of all the rest of God's rational creatures."[22] Moreover, the shared understanding that "Hottentots" occupied the lowest rung of the human ladder lent authors a strategy by which they could diminish the ranking of other Africans. This is clearly what Stephen Addington has in mind in *The Youth's Geographical Grammar* (London, 1770). He first characterizes "Hottentots" as "Pagans":

> They have some notion of a supreme Being and of a future state; but direct their worship to inferior deities, sometimes to the heavenly bodies, sometimes to departed heroes, and sometimes to a supposed evil spirit to whom they offer sacrifices to prevent or remove calamities of which they imagine him the author.[23]

In the section immediately following, Addington uses this depiction to condemn the religion of "Negroland": "The inhabitants of these parts are Pagans; and their principles and worship are not unlike those of the Hottentots" (182).

As we saw, the late-sixteenth- and early-seventeenth-century English representations of the Cape people described them as black or tawny. Indeed, in these earlier accounts skin color had never really been a point of particular concern or contention. The question of their color became a major point of controversy, however, because some Restoration and early-eighteenth-century travel narratives report "Hottentots" as born white. These accounts caused tremendous confusion. If "Hottentots" were not black, what color were they? Could they be white? Because it marks a significant blurring of the color boundary that was becoming so important to English and European constructions of race, the color of "Hottentots" became one of the most hotly debated questions about them during the Restoration and early eighteenth century.

Many, if not most, Restoration era texts describe the "Hottentots" as white when they are born. The first English-authored account, Ambrose Cowley's *Voyage round the Globe* (1687), reports that "These People, call'd the Hodmandods, are born White."[24] A translation of Loubère's account, *A New Historical Relation of the Kingdom of Siam* (1693) also relates that "They are born as white as the *Spaniards*, but they have their Hair very much frizled, and Features participating somewhat of those of the *Negro's*."[25] William Dampier's popular *A New Voyage round the World* (1697) compares the physical appearance of the "Natural Inhabitants of the Cape . . . the Hodmadods, as they are commonly called" with the Negro and the Indian: Their Faces are of a flat oval Figure, of the *Negro* make, with great Eye-brows, black Eyes, but neither are their Noses so flat, nor their Lips so thick, as the *Negroes* of *Guinea*. Their complexion is darker than the common *Indians;* tho not so black as the *Negroes* or *New Hollanders;* neither is their Hair so much frizled."[26]

Texts often speculated about why and how the "Hottentot" skin color could change from white to black. John Phillips's English translation of *The Six Voyages of John Baptiste Tavernier* (1678) relates, "it cannot be said that either the heat or situation of the Climate makes these *Cafres* so black. Being desirous to know the reason . . . I learnt it from a Girl that was bred up in the Fort, who was tak'n from her Mother, as soon as she was born, and was white like our women in *Europe;* she told me the reason why the *Cafres* are so black is, because they rub themselves with a Grease or Ointment compos'd of several sorts of Drugs.[27] The numerous representations of the Cape people's custom of skin greasing, which was done for protection against the sun, suggest how the English were able, ultimately, to consider the "Hottentots" as far more black than white.[28] As we saw, in his *Voyage round the Globe* (1687), Captain Ambrose Cowley reports the "Hottentots" as being born white, but he continues his description by saying that they "make themselves Black with Sut, and besmear their Bodies all over; so that by frequent Repetition their Skins become almost as black as a Negro's."[29] In *A Voyage round the World* (1707), William Funnell notes how skin greasing deprives the people of their fair skin color:

"They smear or grease themselves very much; which makes them stink abominably; And the thicker they are with Grease, the more they are admired by one another . . . Their Children, when they are young, are something inclining to be White; and were it not for their nasty way of greazing them, they would make likely Men and Women: For they are most of them very well featured."[30]

Some representations insist that "Hottentots" prefer being black. The English translation of Urbain Souchu de Rennefort's account asserts that the inhabitants of the Cape "look upon Blackness as a great Perfection."[31] The translation of William Ten Rhyne's *An Account of the Cape of Good Hope and the Hottentotes* (written circa 1673) told English readers: "The Hottentotes being very much Sunburn't, have generally a tawny Skin, tho' some of them have a tolerable white Skin; but Blackness is the greatest beauty among them."[32] The English interpreted what they saw as the preference of "Hottentots" to be black as further proof of their degenerate state.

John Ovington's confusion about "Hottentot" skin color is clearly evident in his *A Voyage to Suratt* (1696). First he refers to the people of the Cape as "Blacks": "And this fair Country which the Blacks inhabit, is blest with a Soil as pregnant as the Days are pleasant."[33] Subsequently, when he is well into his description of the "Ancient Inhabitants of this Promontory," whom he refers to as "Hotantots," he says "They are more Tawny than the *Indians,* and in Colour and Features comes nearest the *Negroes* of any People, only they are not quite so black." (489–90). After a brief description about their facial characteristics, Ovington returns to the issue of color. He disagrees with those who believe that the color of Negroes derives from the sun, but he does not have a solid counter proposal. In a long digression, he sums up the debate then raging:

> But methinks there is something in Nature which seems to thwart this current Opinion. For under the same Parallels are People of quite different Colours . . . Some are apt to ascribe this to the Air and Climate of the Earth . . . Others resolve much of it into the effect of Food and Diet, which I believe may be of some power . . . And therefore something must be added besides the Sun's Heat, for distinction of Complexion and of Hair under the same Parallels. *Lewenhoock* observes that the Blood of the *Negroes* is of a different Contexture from ours. And *Malpighi* observ'd a small Membrane not transparent between the *Cutis* and *Cuticula,* which caus'd the Blackness. (490–492)

Ovington's confusion finds some stability through his examination of various theories and his use of comparison, but clearly he has no answer to the question of skin color.

John Maxwell's "An Account of the Cape of Good Hope" was the first text to assign the "Hottentots" a racial classification of their own. Read to the members of the Royal Society on 18 and 25 June 1707, it reported that

> The *Hottentots,* Natives of this Place, are a Race of Men distinct both from *Negroes* and *European Whites,* for their Hair is Woolly, Short and Frizled, their Noses flat, and their Lips thick, but their Skin is naturally as White as ours, as appear'd by a *Hottentot* Child brought up by the *Dutch* in their Fort here . . . it is probable, I think, that they were propagated to this Place by the Eastern Coast of *Africa,* the Western being now, and always having been, as far as we know, inhabited by Negroes, from whom it is not very probable, that these of so different a Colour should have sprung.[34]

The extremely tentative nature of Maxwell's conclusion in regard to skin color and race is obvious, although it is significant that he still counts the Hottentots as a "Race of Men."

The conversation about "Hottentot" skin color lasted for decades. At midcentury, Astley's *A New General Collection of Voyages and Travels* (1745–47) summarized the debate as follows: "There are few People who have been, by Authors, so differently represented as the *Hottentots.* Some represent them as Negros in Point of Colour; others say they are at Birth as white as *Europeans;* and *Tachard* speaks of white *Hottentots.*"[35] Of course, the attention the English paid to the questions surrounding the skin color of "Hottentots" reveals how color obsessed they were becoming. But the relative fairness of "Hottentot" skin color created interesting debates and possibilities. Some now saw an equation between them and the English and other Europeans, as is evident in Robert Morden's 1690s geography text, which characterizes the "Hottentots" as being "In Complexion . . . like our Chimney sweepers."[36] With a similarity in skin color established, an even more interesting question arose: can "Hottentots" and the English be similar in character or nature?

This idea was indeed addressed, literally and figuratively, with increasing frequency during the eighteenth century. Alexander Hamilton's reference to the Dutch inhabitants at the Cape as "White Hottentots" serves to register his annoyance at the Dutch East India Company for not admitting English ships into Table Bay.

> The *Dutch* Company has a strong Fort, and a Town on the South Side of a Bay, that serves as a good Road for Shipping in all Winds, except those that blow between the North and West. The *English* call'd gener-

ally there, in their Way to and from India, in former Times, for Refreshments; but of late the white *Hottantots* will not permit the poor *Britons* to carry on board their Ships any Cattle, Sheep or Fowls with Life in them, for the Support or Relief of their dear Friends and Allies, notwithstanding the conscientious Prices we would willingly bestow for their Edibles. The black *Hottentots* would shew the English much more Humanity, if the white did not restrain them.[37]

Hamilton's distinction between white and black "Hottentots" places the Cape Khoikhoi in a favorable light in comparison to the Dutch "Hottentots." Others would follow Hamilton's lead. Miss Emily Brittle composed a jocular verse epistle in which she asserts, "Lord! *Dutch Beaus,* are, at best, but a *Hottentot Race!* / With libations of gin, and tobacco's vile fumes, / They drank, and they smoak'd, us away from the rooms; / And if e'er I repair to their balls anymore, / May I choak, and be poison'd, a thousand times o'er!"[38] As we will see, some English writers use the white "Hottentot" metaphor to chide and insult some of their fellow citizens.

The question of whether or not the "Hottentots" had a religion also proved to be a signficant issue in the eighteenth century. Most English representations maintain that they do not. Granting that "Hottentots" had a religion of any sort would lend them the potential to be civilized by missionaries, but, as we saw, the English were committed already to the idea that they were incapable of any improvement. The investment in seeing "Hottentots" as irreligious created the need for some obfuscation in the representations. English and European representations present descriptions of ceremonies that might easily be considered religious celebrations, but the travelers steadfastly refuse to grant them this classification. John Ovington is quite adamant in his refusal. Notice how his conclusion is placed in front of his extremely slight description.

> They are sunk even below Idolatry, are destitute both of Priest and Temple, and saving a little show of rejoicing, which is made at the Full and the New Moon; have lost all kind of Religious Devotion. Nature has so richly provided for their convenience in this Life, that they have drown'd all sense of the God of it, and are grown quite careless of the next.[39]

Ovington's report proved to be extremely influential.

William Funnell insists that even if the "Hottentots" have a notion of religion, they are still irrecoverable in a Christian sense:

> The Dutch did formerly what they could to bring them to the knowledge of the true God, and to leave their nasty way of living; but never

could prevail with them; they still desiring to live like Beasts. Worship they seem to have none; except at the full Moons; and then they Dance and Sing all or most of the Night; and the brighter the Moon is, the more is their Mirth; For then they think the Moon, which seems to be their God is well-pleased with them: But if the Moon chance to be obscured with Clouds, they then seem much dejected, and fancy their God is angry with them."[40]

Despite what Funnell asserts here about any Dutch attempts to bring Christianity to the Cape Khoikhoi, there was no concerted effort to do so. In fact, except for one short-lived United Brethren station begun in 1736, missionary societies ignored the Cape region until the nineteenth century.

It is curious that the representations that insist the "Hottentots" have no religion often use words with strong religious connotation. A number of accounts acknowledge that "Hottentots" "worship" "Dame Luna," yet there is still a hesitancy to recognize this kind of worship as religious. A representation in Cowley's *A Voyage round the Globe* (1687) stops short of saying the "Hottentots" have a religion, although it acknowledges that they recognize a God.

> They are Worshippers of Dame *Luna,* and when they expect to see the Moon, there will be Thousands of them by the Sea-side, Dancing and Singing: But if it be dark Weather, so that the Moon appears not, they will say, That their God is angry with them; whereas on the contrary when the said Luminary shines, they will say, He is not angry.[41]

Charles Lockyer registered his own doubts, and in so doing is moved to finish his sentence with an emphatically negative phrase: "If the Moon is their God, as some report, they take but small notice of him; at the Full they'll dance till they are weary, and so they will every night while it shines in mild Weather, and at noon-day when their Bellys are full; singing, clapping their Hands, and frisking up and down, as the Maggot bites."[42]

Dampier's *A New Voyage round the World* (1697) does connect the "Hottentot" moon celebrations to what might be considered a religious system. His detailed description, however, tries to deny them the dignity of religious worship, calling it a show of their superstition: "Their Religion, if they have any, is wholly unknown to me; for they have no Temple nor Idol, nor any place of worship that I did see or hear of. Yet their mirth and nocturnal pastimes at the New and Full of the Moon, lookt as if they had some Superstition about it."[43] John Maxwell's account shows that he prefers to see the celebration of a full moon as a custom rather than as a religious observation.

> The only thing that looks like the least knowledge of any thing of this kind among 'em (in as much as I could learn) is a Custom they have in Moonshiny Nights of Dancing in the Fields, of which, if you ask 'em the reason, all their Answer is, that it is a Custom of the *Hottentots*, and was so of their Forefathers.[44]

It is interesting that Maxwell arrests his description at this point in order to refute the opinions of other travelers: "Nevertheless some Voyagers have upon this ground, how truly I will not say, confidently writ, that they worship'd the Moon; and upon Enquiry I could not find that they took so much, nor indeed any such notice of the Sun or Stars; which former at least one would think a People so greatly ignorant would pay some respect to, if they worship'd any God, that being the most Glorious Object of their Senses" (2425–26). Eight years later, in 1715, Maxwell recycles his discussion of "Hottentots" in order to present his own theories about God and religion in *A Discourse Concerning God . . . to Which Is Subjoin'd . . . a Short Account of the Cape of Good Hope* (1715).

Pascoe Thomas's *A True and Impartial Journal of a Voyage to the South-Seas and Round the Globe* (1745) attempts to correct the opinion that "Hottentots" do not worship a God. His failure, however, to present a more persuasive refutation of all the previously published accounts that maintain such a view suggests his own position might not have been based on reliable information, or even any eyewitness experience: "The *Hottentots*, who are Natives of this Part of Africa, are a nasty, beastly People, not in the least differing from the Accounts which has frequently been given of them; only the Notion of their being Atheists, and their believing or worshipping no God, seems not to be well grounded."[45] The final phrase in Thomas's one-sentence-long representation is extremely dismissive: "they have several Customs, which are too barbarous and brutish to admit of any Description here" (340). Whether they had a religion or not, Thomas hardly considers them human.

Later-seventeeth- and early-eighteenth-century representations exhibit a new interest in "Hottentot" genitalia. As we have seen, when early-seventeenth-century accounts mention or describe male genitalia, they do so only in passing. By the end of the century, however, both the travelers and those who read their reports were clearly more interested in the subject. Significantly, it is the first item Pepys mentions in his diary for 30 December 1662:

With the officers I had good discourse, perticularly of the people at the Cape of Good Hope—of whom they of their own knowledge do tell me those one or two things. *viz.*, that when they come to age, the men do cut off one of the stones of each others, which they held doth help them to get children the better and to grow fat. That they never sleep lying, but always sitting upon the ground. That their speech is not so articulate as ours, but yet understand one another well. That they paint themselfs all over with the grease the Duch sell them (who have a fort there) and Sutt. [46]

The rationale that Pepys provides was just one of many that would be given throughout the century, but no one theory came to be regarded as an authoritative one. The fact that the discussion took place at all suggests how, as Mary Louise Pratt puts it, genitalia became the featured part of the "bodyscape scene."[47]

Speculation as to why and how the genitalia of "Hottentot" men were altered is included in many representations. The translation of *The Six Voyages of John Baptista Tavernier* (1678) reports that when a male child is born, "the Mother cut out his right Stone; and presently give him Water to drink, and Tobacco to eat. They cut out the right Testicle, because, say they, it makes them swifter to run. There are some of them that will catch a Roe-Buck running."[48] A number of subsequent accounts largely agreed with this one. Tachard's *A Relation of the Voyage to Siam* (1688) says that "the Men in their youth make themselves half Eunuchs, pretending that that contributes much to the preservation and encrease of bodily agillity."[49] Five years later, another description relates a different theory: that the surgery occurs when the boys are men. *A New Historical Relation of the Kingdom of Siam* (1693), a text purporting to be the narrative of Simon de la Loubère's 1687–88 voyage, reports that at a certain "age of renouncing," the men "make themselves entirely Eunuchs, to deprive themselves wholly of their Commerce, and to enjoy a more vigorous old Age."[50]

The explanation John Ovington provides derives from the stereotypical notion that Negro men have a "Native Heat, which powerfully prompts them to Propagation."

> The Male Children at Eight or Ten Years of Age, are Cut in their Privy Parts, and depriv'd of one of their Testicles . . . For the prevention of a too Luxuriant Increase by Generation because when their Children Increase beyond their Desires, and the just number which they design, to prevent a heavier Charge upon the Parents, they dispatch the Supernumeraries to the other World, without any Remorse for the horrid Crime, or Consciousness of the execrable Sin of Murther, which is the

Reason, I presume, of the *Hotantot's* losing part of their Virility, that they may debilitate that Native Heat, which powerfully prompts them to Propagation.[51]

That Ovington also finds a way to work infanticide into his explanation shows how eager he is to demonize "Hottentots."

All these theories are attacked by John Maxwell in his "Account of the Cape of Good Hope," where he insists that the removal of one testicle is part of the marriage ceremony.

> Being inquisitive to know the truth of this, I had the Curiosity to search several of 'em (who will readily suffer you for a double Stiver to do it) in two of which I could find but one Testicle, they (I suppose) being Marry'd, as the rest who had two were not; which however shews the mistake of *Nieuhoff* and others, who assert, That the *Hottentots* cut out one of the Testicles of all their Male Children as soon as they are born (according to *Nieuhoff*,) or at the Age of nine or ten Years (according to others,) and that, forsooth, to make 'em the more swift and nimble; but how that fancy should come into their Heads, I cannot tell.[52]

As Maxwell's last phrase suggests, he was, at least, more honest than other travelers about what he did and did not know about the Cape people. Similarly, Daniel Beeckman also admits that he has no real explanation for the practice. In his *A Voyage to and from the Island of Borneo in the East Indies* (1718), he, somewhat tentatively, engages in some speculation: "They bruise to pieces the left Testicle of their Male Children when young; for what reason I know not, unless it be in hopes that they may beget more Males than Females, being perhaps of the Opinion of some Naturalists, who hold that the Male Semen comes from the right Testicle, and the Female from the left."[53]

Discussions about the body parts of "Hottentot" females also became more common and strange in Restoration and eighteenth-century accounts. As we saw, any descriptions of Cape females tended to be literal and the tone relatively matter-of-fact in early-seventeenth-century representations. Restoration era descriptions of female genitalia are inconsistent in the information they relate, but they are uniformly emotional. There were many rumors about "Hottentot" female genitalia. A 1682 report on the loss of the ship *Johanna* alludes to them: "ye Wemmon are very disformed in there private parts but as for this I know not ye certainty of it."[54] John Ovington's *A Voyage to Surratt* (1696) is more suggestive about the nature of the public conversation taking place: "There is a vulgar Opinion which has formerly been receiv'd, that the Natives of this

Cape were *Hermophradites*, which was founded only upon Conjecture; for two Gentleman, who were resolv'd not to be liable to this Errour, assur'd me the Report was false, upon the Curiosity they had of knowing the Reason of it, which was because the Female Parts were cut in the Fashion of small Teats hanging down."[55] A translation entitled *A Relation of Two Several Voyages Made to the East Indies* (1700), also indicates the widespread nature of the discussion: "I had often-times been told, that these Women had naturally a little kind of Flap growing over their Privities, like that of a Turkey-Cock's bill, which I had a mind to see if it were true; but upon Examination, I found nothing of Truth in it. My Experience cost me only some Tobacco."[56]

Representations of "Hottentot" female immodesty are included in many narratives. The English translation of William Ten Rhyne's description, published in the 1704 Churchill collection, describes the women's deformity and insists they are proud of it.

> The Women are distinguish'd from the Men by their Deformity, being generally round Shoulder'd, and have this peculiar, among all other Nations, that out of their Privities you see two Labels hanging down, like part of a Man's Yard . . . of these they are so proud, that if a stranger happens to come into one of their Cabbins, or Hutts, (call'd *Krallen*) they will take aside the Leathern Apron, and shew them to the Stranger.[57]

Edward Cooke reports in his *A Voyage to the South Sea and round the World* (1712) that "Hottentot" females are willing to expose themselves for a relatively cheap price: "for a *Dutch* Doubleke they will shew all to the waggish Sailors that ask them."[58] "Hottentot" immodesty, whether real or simply imagined by visitors to the Cape, relates to the larger issue of the general European demonization of "Hottentot" and African females.

Jennifer L. Morgan sees the European representation of the bodies of African women as part of a larger racial construction. "Confronted with an Africa they needed to exploit, European writers turned to black women as evidence of a cultural inferiority that ultimately became encoded as racial difference. Monstrous bodies became enmeshed with savage behavior as the icon of women's breasts became evidence of tangible barbarism."[59] The bodies of "Hottentot" women are often made monstrous. Indeed, it is only as freaks of nature that "Hottentot" females are given any power in travel narratives and other works. Tavernier's account maintains that "The women are of so hot a constitution of Body, that at the times that their monthly customs are upon 'em, they happen to make water, and that an *European* chances to set his feet upon it, it causes an immediate Head-ach and Feaver, which many times turns to the Plague."⁶⁰ Similarly, *The Voyage and Adventures of François Leguat* (1707) employs extremely strong language to portray the dangerous power of "Hottentot" females:

> Notwithstanding all this, the vanity of these ugly Witches is incredible. They fancy themselves the finest Women in the World, and look on us from top to bottom with their Hands to their Sides, disdainfully. 'Tis said, they are of a strange Temper, and that at certain times have a Madness come upon them, during which they emit as strong as Vapour from their Bodies, as those of a Hind in Season.⁶¹

Percy Adams believes that Swift's description of Yahoo women in *Gulliver's Travels* (1726) is based on the depiction of "Hottentot" female breasts in travel narratives written by Herbert, Dampier, Ovington, and Cooke: "Their dugs hung between their fore-feet, and often reached almost to the ground as they walked. Upon the whole, I never beheld in all my travels so disagreeable an animal, or one against which I had naturally conceived so strong antipathy."⁶²

In quite surprising ways, the negative constructions of "Hottentots," and the demonization of the female, in particular, helped to advance the interests of those involved in the slave trade. The English tendency in the eighteenth century to consider African Negroes and "Hottentots" as essentially the same lent proslavery advocates strong material. Edward Long, for example, invokes the "Hottentots" in his *The History of Jamaica* (1774), where he insists that "a general uniformity runs through all these various regions of people; so that if any difference be found, it is only in degrees of the same qualities; and what is more strange, those of the worst kind; it being a common known proverb, that all people on the globe have some good as well as ill qualities except the Africans."⁶³ Long clearly intends his description of "Hottentots," especially of the females, to further prejudice his readers against all Africans.

> Ludicrous as the opinion may seem, I do not think an oran-outang husband would be any dishonour to an Hottentot female; for what are these Hottentot—They are, say the most credible writers, a people very stupid and very brutal. In many respects they are more like beasts than men; their complexion is dark, they are short and thick-set; their noses flat, like those of a Dutch dog; their lips very thick and big; their teeth exceedingly white, but very long, and ill set, some of them sticking out

of their mouths like boars tusks; their hair black, and curled like wool; they are very nimble, and run with a speed that is almost incredible; they are very disagreeable in their persons, and, in short, taking all things together, one of the meanest nations on the face of the earth.[64]

Long's crude insinuation of sexual activity between "Hottentot" females and what he calls the "oran-outang" had precedent. As we saw, Herbert implies this in his early-seventeenth-century travel narrative.

II

The descriptions of "Hottentot" females in travel narratives certainly lent eighteenth-century belles-lettres authors material they could use to construct the "Hottentot" female as the exact opposite of an English woman. The assumption of "difference" is a given. In one of the final issues of *The Spectator* (no. 631, 10 December 1714), Mr. Spectator has the occasion to "throw" together "a few hints upon cleanliness, which, he asserts, is a "mark of politeness." He supports his claim by placing in opposition a "Female *Hottentot*" and an "*English* Beauty." Equally significant is how Mr. Spectator uses "Hottentot" society to represent the most uncivilized society possible, while he credits English society with being the epitome of civilization.

> The different Nations of the World are as much distinguished by their Cleanliness, as by their Arts and Sciences. The more any Country is civilized, the more they consult this part of Politeness. We need but compare our Ideas of a Female *Hottentot* and an *English* Beauty, to be satisfied of the Truth of what hath been advanced.[65]

The negative images of "Hottentot" women served to dimish their maternal potential; as female monsters, they came to embody the sexualized female. The British were eager to set "Hottentot" women in direct opposition to the emerging idealization of the modest British maternal woman. Felicity A. Nussbaum contends that "the invention of the 'other' woman of empire enabled the consolidation of the cult of domesticity in England and, at the same time, the association of the sexualized woman at home with the exotic, or 'savage,' non-European woman."[66] Both Nussbaum and Ruth Perry see this as a specifically eighteenth-century mode of thought: "in the eighteenth century, maternity came to be imagined as a counter to sexual feeling, opposing alike individual expression, desire, and agency in favor of a mother-self at the service of the family and the state."[67]

The sexualized "Hottentot" female became a familiar figure in eighteenth-century belles-lettres. George Alexander Stevens's "A Pastoral" (c. 1780) represents a "Hottentot" female in this stereotypical fashion: "To a Hottentot offals have charms, / With garbage their bosoms they deck; / She sluttishly open'd her arms, / He filthily fell on her neck / On her flabby breasts one hand he plac'd / No towels those breasts ever teaze" (lines 13–18).[68] Matthew Prior and other male poets envision powerful "Hottentot" females, their power stemming from their capacity to seduce English men. Prior's poetic depiction of the "Hottentot" female makes her into a kind of perverse pleasure machine. She has the ability to feed the "ogling Youth's" physical and sexual hunger, although she might elect to flee the scene and he will, thus, be left unsatisfied on both counts.

> In our Fantastic *Climes* the Fair
> With cleanly Powder dry their Hair:
> And round their lovely Breast and Head
> Fresh Flow'rs their mingl'd odors shed.
> Your nicer HOTTENTOTES think meet
> With Guts and Tripe to deck their feet:
> With down-cast looks on TOTTA's legs,
> The ogling Youth most humbly begs,
> She would not from his Hopes remove
> And once his Breakfast, and his Love:
> And if the skittish Nymph should fly;
> He in a double Sense must die.[69]

Such a proclivity to tease English men became yet another reason to demonize the sexualized "Hottentot" female. As we shall see, the English public's interest in the body parts and in the seductive capacity of "Hottentot" females reached its awful culmination in the early nineteenth century when the "Hottentot Venus" was put on display in London.

The representations of "Hottentots" in travel narratives also allowed eighteenth-century authors to ponder similarities as well as insist on differences. Indeed, British authors discovered that having license to draw on "sameness" rather than insist on difference had considerable symbolic potential. Not surprisingly, a wide range of authors found this strategy useful, especially in periods of time when they wanted to examine or question the nation's sense of identity and direction. John Locke was one of the first to wonder about the roles geography and culture play in the capabilities of individuals. *An Essay Concerning Human Understanding* presents the question: "Had you or I been born at the Bay of *Soldania*, possibly our Thoughts, and Notions, had not exceeded those brutish ones of the *Hotentots* that inhabit there."⁷⁰

John Ovington addresses the question of sameness on a national scale. In his *Voyage to Suratt* (1696), he compares "Hottentots" and "Antient Britains," finding many similarities.

> Thus the *Hotantots* have degenerated into the strangest kind of Rationals, and have successively surviv'd the Noble and common Instincts of Humanity; but in their Innocence of Life, the Customs of the Ancient *Britains* did in many things resemble the Inhabitants of this Promontory, in their drinking Water, and the simplicity of their Food, which was upon Acorns or Berries, or such natural Productions; sometimes upon Milk, or what they could gain by Hunting. A great part of their Bodies too was uncover'd, especially their Arms and Legs, and their Cloathing was the same with that of the *Hotantots*, made generally of the Skins of Beasts.⁷¹

Ovington's observation that the "Hottentots" represent human degeneration suggests how they were used in the conversation taking place throughout the century on the question of progress. Constructions of "Hottentots" helped to make the point that individuals and nations can certainly regress to a state as degenerate as that of the people at the Cape. Of course, Ovington also wants to make the point that societies can progress to a state of high cultivation. Thus, his image of "Antient Britains" shows his audience that their own society has progressed from its own "Hottentot-like" state to their present level. Ovington's desire to make his point without summoning up images of the Scots and native Irish, whom the English often saw as degenerate, is thereby accomplished through his "Hottentot" representation.

Throughout the eighteenth century, the English regarded Scottish, Irish, and Welsh populations as "Hottentots" of sorts and degrees. As we saw earlier, Thomas Herbert likened the "Hottentot" language to the Irish tongue. Abraham Cowley points out a connection between the huts of the "Hottentots" and what he calls the "wild" Irish: "They build their Houses round (with their Fireplace in the middle of them) almost like the Hutts, which are built in *Ireland* by the wild Irish."⁷² "Hottentots" serve in a crucial capacity in Samuel Johnson's rumination about progression, regression, and nationhood, written as he toured the Scottish Highlands with Boswell in 1775:

> Yet men thus ingenious and inquisitive were content to live in total ignorance of the trades by which human wants are supplied, and to supply them by the grossest means. Till the Union made them acquainted with English manners, the culture of their lands was unskilful, and their domestic life unformed; their tables were coarse as the feasts of Eskimeaux, and their houses as filthy as the cottages of Hottentots.
>
> Since they have known that their condition was capable of improvement, their progress in useful knowledge has been rapid and uniform. What remains to be done they will quickly do, and then wonder, like me, why that which was so necessary and so easy was so long delayed. But they must be for ever content to owe to the English that elegance and culture, which, if they had been vigilant and active, perhaps the English might have owed to them.[73]

To some extent, of course, Johnson's well-known prejudice against the Scots heightens his English chauvinism.

The associations between what some thought to be inferior native British cultures and "Hottentots" lasted into the nineteenth century. Dorothy Wordsworth's journal of the tour she and William took in Scotland in 1803 reveals a moment when images of "Hottentots" came into her brother's mind.

> *August 26th, Friday.* We did not set off till between ten and eleven o'clock, much too late for a long day's journey. Our boatman lived at the pretty white house which we saw from the windows: we called at his door by the way, and, even when we were near the house, the outside looked comfortable; but within I never saw anything so miserable from dirt, and dirt alone: it reminded one of the house of a decayed weaver in the suburbs on a large town, with a sickly wife and a large family; but Wm. says it was far worse, that it was quite Hottentotish.[74]

The English also linked the Welsh with "Hottentots." Richard Ayton, for example, compares a Welsh woman to a "Hottentot" in his *A Voyage round Great Britain Undertaken in the Summer of the Year 1813:* "One of the women seized hold of my umbrella, and began to examine it with eager attention; but after pulling and twisting it about with truly Hottentot awkwardness, she returned it to me without having made any discoveries as to the nature of the machine."[75]

While the English were clearly willing to entertain the idea that groups in their society had degenerate lifestyles, especially in comparison with their own, they refused to accept the possibility that "Hottentots" could ever become "civilized." Eighteenth-century belles-lettristic representations often express this opinion through sheer exaggeration. Evan Lloyd's "Conversation" suggests the unlikeliness of "Hottentot" progress. Indeed, the very notion of it strikes the persona as so fantastical that he incorporates Swift's Yahoos into the picture.

> The Wilds of *Afric,* temper'd by the plough,
> In time might be what *England's* plains are now
> A *Hottentot* might wear a classic air,
> If you but plant another *Oxford* there,
> *Yahoos* themselves might learn to be polite [76]

Many authors offered similar dismissals of the idea that a "Hottentot" could become "civilized." Any envisioning of a "civilized Hottentot" had to be an ironic one, as it is in Joseph Thurston's "The Fall" (1732): "The powder'd *Hottentot* his miss shall boast, / And *Cannibals* no more devour, but toast."[77] Not surprisingly, the possibility of progress was denied to "Hottentots" until Britain became the ruling colonial power at the Cape.

Writers with subversive intentions could also use the connection seen between "Hottentot" and segments of British society in order to make their points. For example, in his *Letter on the Fishery* (1734), Jonathan Swift uses the commonplace link between the native Irish and the "Hottentot" to place emphasis on the extent to which the Irish are oppressed. By having his speaker equate the misery of the "Hottentots" to the oppression endured by the Irish, Swift emphasizes the suffering of his own people: "I believe the People of *Lapland,* or the *Hottentots,* are not so miserable a People as we; for Oppression supported by Power will infallibly introduce slavish Principles."[78]

While Swift and other Irish writers often use their works to implicitly or explicitly argue that their countrymen and women are used and treated like slaves, those who campaigned against the slave trade were not quick to attack the negative constructions of "Hottentots." Indeed, some of the leaders of the abolitionist movement in eighteenth-century Britain relied on them in order to advance their own cause. The abolitionist movement grew in strength and influence because it was able to publish works that presented sympathetic portraits of slaves or former slaves, sometimes written by the Africans themselves, but the movement's authors did not at first view "Hottentots" in such a kindly fashion. In a 1781 sermon, John Wesley considers them in the same paragraph as he does African slaves, but he does not show them the same pity. Wesley recalls only the most familiar negative images and reports of them, which leads him to wonder how "Hottentots" can be a part of God's creation.

Who cares for those outcasts of men, the well-known Hottentots? It is true, a late writer has taken much pains to represent them as a respectable people. But from what motive it is not easy to say; since he himself allows (a specimen of their elegant manners) that the raw guts of sheep and other cattle are not only some of their choicest food but also the ornaments of their arms and legs; and (a specimen of their religion) that the son is not counted a man till he has beat his mother almost to death. And when his father grows old he fastens him in a little hut and leaves him there to starve! O Father of mercies! Are these the works of thy own hands? The purchase of thy Son's blood?[79]

Equiano's *The Interesting Narrative of the Life of Olaudah Equiano, or Gustavus Vassa, the African* (1792) simultaneously plays with and uses the stereotypical notion of the "Hottentot" in order to attack an act passed by the assembly of Barbadoes: "It is an act at once unmerciful, unjust, and unwise; which for cruelty would disgrace an assembly of those who are called barbarians; and for its injustice and *insanity* could shock the morality and common sense of a Samaide or Hottentot."[80] The abolitionist movement turned its attention to the slaves and the "Hottentots" at the Cape only after the British seized it at the start of the nineteenth century.

As we have seen, authors engaged in advancing political causes had long been finding "Hottentots" useful for their arguments. It is not a coincidence, therefore, that the political uncertainty of the 1710s and 1720s produced more belles-lettristic figurative references to "Hottentots" than any other until the last two decades of the century. The uncertainty of the Hanoverian succession, coupled with the fear that English Catholics and the Pretender would upset the power vested in the monarchy and the Church of England, led Gilbert Burnet to bring out a concluding volume to his earlier *The History of the Reformation of the Church of England* (1679–81). He is blunt about his purpose in *An Introduction to the Third Volume of the History of the Reformation of the Church of England* (1714): "to awaken a Nation, that has perhaps forgot past Dangers, and yet may be nearer them than ever."[81] Burnet uses a "Hottentot" reference to address what will happen if the forces he fears triumph. In his opinion, the country would degenerate to such an extent that the English would become like "Hottentots."

> Can it be possible that any are so depraved as to wish we had no Religion at all, or to be Enemies to the Christian Religion? Would these Men reduce us to be a sort of *Hottentots*? And yet this must grow to be the Effect of our being without all Religion. Mankind is a Creature, by

his Make and Frame disposed to Religion; and if this is not managed by true Principles, all the Jugglings of Heathenism would again take Possession of the World. If the Principles of Truth, Justice, Temperance, and of universal Love do not govern Men, they will soon grow Curses and Plagues to one another: And a Crew of Priests will grow up, who will teach them to compound for all Crimes, and to expiate *the blackest* Practises by some Rituals.[82]

Burnet's linking "blackest Practises" with "Hottentots" suggests how the English envisioned the "Hottentots" as black, especially when it suited their own agenda.

One of Burnet's enemies also employed "Hottentot" references to great effect. Charles Leslie (1650–1722) had been attacking Gilbert Burnet in print since the early 1690s, when he published *Some Reflections upon the Second of Dr. Burnet's Four Discourses* (1694). Leslie, a prolific nonjuror and Jacobite, added his voice to many of the most highly charged political-ecclesiastical pamphlet wars of the 1690s and early 1700s. He also published attacks on Quakers, Jews, and Deists, and edited *The Rehearsal* (1704–09), a periodical that promoted a patriarchal political theory first articulated by Robert Filmer in *Patriarcha, or the Natural Powers of Kings Asserted* (1680). Angered by Burnet's attacks on him during the Sacheverell impeachment, Leslie wrote, but published anonymously, *The Good Old Cause, or Lying in Truth* (1710). Benjamin Hoadly identified him as the author of *The Good Old Cause* in *The Jacobites Hopes Revived* (1710). The publication of *The Good Old Cause* and the backlash it created resulted in a warrant being issued for Leslie's arrest. He wrote his next two works, *Beaucoup de Bruit pour une Aumelette: or, Much Ado about Nothing* (1710) and *The Finishing Stroke* (1711), while he was in hiding and before he made his escape to the court of the Pretender in April 1711.[83]

As the title suggests, in *The Finishing Stroke* Leslie means to have the last words, especially against Whig churchmen Hoadly and William Higden.[84] In one section of the work, Leslie uses the dialogue form to present what he calls "A Battle Royal Between Three Cocks of the Game," identifying the speakers as Mr. Higden, Mr. Hoadly, and Mr. Hottentote. Leslie's Mr. Hottentote "argues against all *Government* whatsoever, for the *Natural* State wherein some suppose them to be."[85] In response to a question from Hoadly early on, Mr. Hottentote gives an account of his society, taking the English to task for what they do not know or do not understand about it. In presenting a defense of his society, Mr. Hottentote makes some direct comparisons between the two societies:

But we have no *Commerce with you,* so you know little of us. But you give us the Name of *Hottentotes,* from the word *Hottentote,* which we Repeat often in our *Dances* every *New Moon.* And you do but *Guess* at our *Religion* or *Government,* which because you know not, you *Fancy* we have None.

We have not such Stately *Edifices* as you in *England,* but we have *Hutts* and *Houses* which serve us for all the Conveniencies of Life that we want; but we Build them not so *Fine* as to be Afraid to make use of them, and live in the worst Part to save the *Best.* Our *Food* is *Plain* and *Natural,* and Adapted to our *Stomachs,* not our *Stomachs* to our *Meat.* Whence we have no *Surfeits,* and those *Diseases* are unknown to us which fill your *Bills* of *Mortality;* and we live Healthy and Strong to an *hundred Years* Generally, many to *one hundred* and *twenty,* or *one hundred* and *forty,* and are *Active* and *Robust* in our *Bodies.* (162)

Of course, Leslie is not here seriously attempting to defend a "Hottentot" way of life, but in making its spokesman more reasonable and sympathetic than the two English interlocutors, he diminishes them all the more. Not only does Leslie's "Hottentot" successfully hold his ground over his opponents (who sometimes take each other on), he proves to be the most dominant, skilled, and reasonable man in the verbal exchanges. The "Hottentot's" concluding piece of advice to both men is that they should "burn" their Bibles (232). This, of course, would make them even more like "Hottentots."

The debate carried on in travel narratives about whether or not the "Hottentots" had a religion brought the issue to the notice of John Locke, among others. As early as the 1690s, Locke invoked "Hottentots" in the debate concerning whether or not the idea of God is innate in humans. He argued that it is not, and his references to "Hottentots" help him to support his argument that there are no innate ideas, morals, or practical principles. Locke refers to "Navigation discovered . . . in these latter Ages, whole Nations, at the Bay of *Soldania,* in *Brasil,* in *Boranday,* and the *Caribee* Islands, *etc.* amongst whom there was to be found no Notion of a God, no Religion."[86] In 1695, Charles Gildon uses the "latest" travel narrative, probably Cowley's, to cast doubt on Locke's authority: "I know not whether the *Idea* of a God be *Innate* or no but I'm sure that it is very soon imprinted in the minds of Men; and I must beg Mr. *Locke's* pardon, if I very much question those Authorities he quotes from the Travels of some men, who affirm some Nations to have no notions of a Deity; since the same has been said of the Inhabitants of the *Cape of Good Hope,* which the last account of that place proves to be false."[87]

The unresolved discussion pertaining to the existence of a "Hottentot" religion lent itself to domestic debates as well. In 1730, John Jackson published *A Plea for Humane Reason: Shewing the Sufficiency of It in Matters of Religion* (1730), which earned the ire of Edmund Gibson, Bishop of London. Gibson retaliated in his *Second Pastoral Letter . . . Occasion'd by Some Late Writings, in Which It Is Asserted, "that reason is a sufficient guide in matters of religion, without the help of revelation"* (1730). Gibson's position was further defended by John Browne. Jackson responded with *Calumny No Conviction* (1731), and Gibson countered with *A Plea for Divine Revelation* (1731), where he argues for the necessity of both revelation and reason in religion. He uses a "Hottentot" reference to make his case:

> The question is, whether Human Reason can *of itself* discover all that is necessary to be known and done by men in order to a full discharge of all religious duties with the attainment of happiness? To which this Gentleman answers, yes sure, it is demonstrable that it can; *Because men may hearken to reason, if they please:* Or in other words, because men are free agents, therefore their reason can certainly discover all they want to know in matters of religion. Which I must confess, appears to my weak apprehension, to be much the same way of argumentation; as if I should conclude that a Hottentot has as good an understanding as our Author, because that Hottentot *may attend to what reason he has, if he pleases.* [88]

The discussion did not end here, however.

Jackson responds to Browne's and Gibson's works in *A Defense of the Plea for Human Reason: Being a Reply to a Book Entitled,* A Plea for Divine Revelation (London, 1731), where he recalls the "Hottentot" figure.

> My Lord, I must put this Author in mind of his *Hottentot,* who could not have argued worse; or else must call in question his *Honesty* for abusing me and Truth so grossly. Let him shew me, if he can, that human Reason of itself is not *sufficient* to bring Men to the Belief of the *Existence* of God as being a *Rewarder,* &c. and then he shall hear, whether in such a Case I allow it to be *sufficient* in Matters of Religion; let him produce his *Countrymen,* his *Hottentot,* his *Indian* or *Negroe,* whose Reason is not sufficient for this Knowledge.[89]

As this passage makes clear, Jackson was offended by Browne's insinuation that he is a "Hottentot."

English authors throughout the eighteenth century enjoyed a

tremendous amount of figurative play by maintaining that "Hottentots" are too savage to have a religion. *The Spectator no. 389* (27 May 1712) slyly refers readers to travel narratives in order to make a link between British atheists and "Hottentots":

> The Atheists are equally confounded, to which ever of these Causes we assign it; they have been so pressed by this last Argument from the general Consent of Mankind, that after great Search and Pains they pretend to have found out a Nation of Atheists, I mean that Polite People the *Hottentots*.
>
> I dare not shock my Readers with a Description of the Customs and Manners of these Barbarians, who are in every respect scarce one degree above Brutes, having no Language among them, but a confused *Gabble*, which is neither well understood by themselves or others.
>
> It is not however to be imagined how much the atheists have gloried in these their good friends and allies.[90]

Mr. Spectator goes on to propose that "we should always keep two or three Cannons ready pointed towards the Cape of *Good-Hope*, in order to shoot our Unbelievers into the Country of the Hottentots."[91] Similarly, in his "St. Paul's Church; Or, the Protestant Ambulators," Edward Ward attacks his enemies as being "Hottentot-like": But, Hottentot-like, in exceeding / All others in uncleanly feeding / How can such Mortals have a Notion / Of True Religion or Devotion?"[92]

Decades later, the anonymous author of *The Ranelean Religion Displayed* (1750) uses the subtitle of the work to establish a domestic connection: *In a letter from a Hottentot of Distinction, Now in LONDON, To his Friend at the Cape of good Hope. Containing the Reasons assign'd by the Raneleans for abolishing Christianity, together with a true Copy of their New Liturgy* (1750). The dedicatory epistle presents the voice of the "Hottentot of Distinction" reporting to his friend back home. As he explains it, their "Hottentot" emperor had sent him abroad to learn about European religions. His period of residence in London has convinced him that the English have replaced Christianity with a new religion that worships pleasure, as represented in his allusion to Ranelagh Gardens.

> the old Religion call'd Christianity, *which every Body, on account of its Antiquity, would be thought to esteem, tho' in reality, no Body Cares a Rush for it: For the Temples appropriated for this Worship are empty, even on high Festivals; and Dust and Cobwebs over-run their Walls; and its Followers are so divided about the Rites of this Worship, that, weary of Contending with one another,*

they seem with one Accord to forget it, and to embrace a Religion sprung up amongst them within this 100 *Years, call'd,* The Worship of Pleasure.[93]

Although somewhat jesting, these references that link those who have fallen away from the established church of the nation to "Hottentots" express the real anxiety felt by their authors. That they found such an effective satiric expression for one of the century's most contested issues testifies to how crucial the negative constructions of "Hottentot" were for them.

Charging that the nation was adopting "Hottentot" customs became a familiar complaint throughout the century. As we have seen, this message could be communicated in different tones of voice. Robert Graves's *The Spiritual Quixote* (1773) includes a not terribly serious reference to a narrative entitled "Literae Hottentoticae," written by a "beautiful young Hottentot" to her friends at the Cape, which gives "an account of the many barbarous customs and preposterous opinions which she had observed in our metropolis during her three years abode amongst us."[94] In July 1763, the *British Magazine* complained more seriously that "England . . . abounded greatly with such kinds of Hottentots." Likewise, Hannah More, in a letter to a Mrs. Rackett, dated 2 October 1779, refers to England as "this land of Hottentots and Savages."[95] In 1782, Horace Walpole complained that all the gossip in the press was making England "more savage than Hottentots where all private distresses are served up the next morning for the breakfast and entertainment of the public."[96]

Poets, pamphleteers, novelists, playwrights, and private citizens worked the idea that there was possible similitude between the British and the "Hottentots" to attack the spread of bad manners, ridiculous fashions, the affectations of the fashionable, or anything else they deemed inappropriate. Graves's *The Spiritual Quixote* (1773) plays with the idea that "Hottentots" and "fashionable" English can have a shared understanding. Mr. Wildgoose, who bemoans the fashions of the day, complains about the periwig: "But of late years, any man, that has a mind to look more considerable or more wise than his neighbours, goes to a Barber's, and purchases fifty shillings-worth of false hair (white, black, or grey) and hangs it upon his head, without the least regard to his complexion, his age, his person, or his station in life. And certainly, if an inhabitant of the Cape of Good Hope were to behold the stiff horse-hair buckles, or the tied wigs, of our Lawyers, Physicians, Tradesmen, or Divines, they would appear as barbarous and extraordinary to them, as the sheep's tripes and chitterlins about the neck of a Hottentot do to us."⁹⁷ The two women with whom he conversed, "forced a smile at Wildgoose's vehemence and far-fetched comparison" (187).

"Hottentot" references appear to have been especially useful for authors who wanted to warn against pride and excessive vanity. Bernard Mandeville invokes "Hottentots" in one of the remarks to his *The Fable of the Bees* (1714):

> Clothes were originally made for two Ends, to hide our Nakedness, and to fence our Bodies against the Weather, and other outward Injuries: To these our boundless Pride has added a third, which is Ornament; for what else but an excess of stupid Vanity, could have prevail'd upon our Reason to fancy that Ornamental, which must continually put us in mind of our Wants and Misery, beyond all other Animals that are ready clothed by Nature herself? It is indeed to be admired how so sensible a Creature as Man, that pretends to so many fine Qualities of his own, should condescend to value himself upon what is robb'd from so innocent and defenceless an Animal as a Sheep, or what he is beholden for to the most insignificant thing upon Earth, a dying Worm: yet while he is Proud of such trifling Depredations, he has the folly to laugh at the *Hottentots* on the furthest Promontory of *Africk*, who adorn themselves with the Guts of their dead Enemies, without considering that they are the Ensigns of their Valour those Barbarians are fine with, the true *Spolia opima*, and that if their Pride be more Savage than ours, it is certainly less ridiculous, because they wear the Spoils of the more noble Animal.⁹⁸

Vanity of a specifically female sort comes under scrutiny in Mary Barber's "A Letter Written for my Daughter, to a Lady Who Had Presented Her with a Cap" (1734). The poetic epistle presents a daughter's complaint that her mother will not let her wear the clothes she wants to wear, in this instance a cap. The first stanza has the daughter quoting her mother:

> Your late kind Gift let me restore;
> For I must never wear it more.
> My mother cries, "What's here to do?
> "A Crimson Velvet Cap for you!
> "You'll wear a *Coachman's* Cap in time:
> "Perhaps on Palfry pace along,
> "With ruffled Shirt, and *Tete-moutton;*
> "Banish the Woman from your Face,
> "And let the Rake supply the Place;
> "Delighted see the People stare,
> "And ask each other what you are?"

The poem's second stanza presents the daughter's own words.

> If she goes on to this dull Tune,
> Poor I must be a Quaker soon,
> She'll scarcely let me wear a Knot;
> But keeps me like a *Hottentot;*
> Says, Dressing plain, at small Expence,
> Shews better Taste, and better Sense.
> I'd take her Judgment, I confess,
> Sooner in any Thing, than Dress:
> A Science, which she little knows
> Who only huddles on her Cloaths.[99]

Besides the fact that "Hottentot" provides a convenient and silly rhyme with "Knot," it works well in illustrating the extent to which the daughter thinks her mother's demand is unfair. That the mother would keep her like a "Hottentot" is a (mock) horror to the girl, but not one she can countermand easily. Female vanity also came under Mary Wollstonecraft's scrutiny. She warned against the use of pomatum in her *Thoughts on the Education of Daughters* (1787). Calling the use (or overuse) of it "disgusting," she writes, "We laugh at the Hottenots, and in some things adapt their customs."[100] It is interesting to note that just a few years after writing this, Wollstonecraft wrote a positive review of Le Vaillant's travel narrative praising, in particular, its more sympathetic portrait of "Hottentots."

The idea that Britons could resemble "Hottentots" made possible the invention of what became an extremely common eighteenth-century personal insult—to call a fellow citizen a "Hottentot." In 1733, Paul Whitehead utilizes a "Hottentot" reference to complain about Alexander Pope: *"Thou* who didst let admiring Nations see, / A *Hottentot* of *English* Progeny."[101] In 1751, Lord Chesterfield proclaimed no less a man than Samuel Johnson a "Hottentot," writing that the "utmost I can do for him, is to consider him as a respectable hottentot."[102] Decades later, Horace Walpole also called Samuel Johnson a "Hottentot." Reflecting on Piozzi's anecdotes of Johnson, in a letter to Horace Mann (dated 28 March 1786), he writes:

> but his friends (of whom he made woeful choice) have taken care to let the world know that in behaviour he was an ill-natured bear, and in opinions as senseless a bigot as an old washer-woman—a brave composition for a philosopher!—let me turn from such a Hottentot to his re-

verse—to *you*— to you, the mild, benevolent, beneficent friend of mankind, and the true contented philosopher in every stage.¹⁰³

There are even sharper and more pointedly political uses of the "Hottentot" insult. Sheridan and Swift target a powerful country landlord, most probably Abel Ram, in *Intelligencer no. 2* (18 May 1728) for not showing proper civility to a distinguished man, most probably Swift himself.¹⁰⁴ Ram's coachman almost ran Swift down:

> Two *Clergy-men*, of some Distinction, Travelling to the Country for their Health, happened to set up together in a small Village, which was under the Dominion of a certain *Animal*, dignified with a *brace of Titles*, that of a *Militia-Collonel*, and a *Squire*. One of these Gentlemen standing in the Street, and observing a *Coach-man* driving his *Coach and four Horses* furiously against him, turned into the close Passage between his *Inn* and the *Sign-post*, but the *Coach-man*, instead of driving through the middle of the Street, which was the usual and most commodious way, turned short, and Drove full upon the Gentleman, without any Notice, so that he was on a sudden enclosed between the *fore-horses*.

The nobleman, however, refuses to criticize or punish his coachman to the extent that the "two clergymen" thought appropriate:

> His Friend who saw with Terror what had like to befallen him, full of Indignation, repaired immediately to the aforesaid *Squire* or *Collonel* (to whom he was told the *Equipage* belonged) with a Complaint against his *Coach-man*. But the *Squire* instead of expressing any Concern, or offering any Redress, sent the Doctor away with the following Answer. *Sir, I have a great Regard for your Cloath, and have sent my Coach-man to ask your Friend's Pardon; for one of your Servants this moment, told me what happened.* But, Sir, said the *Doctor*, do you think *that is sufficient?* I dare venture to affirm, if the like had befallen you, within the Liberties of my Friend, and you were brought to the same Danger by his Servant, he would not only have him Punished, but at the same time, he would discharge him his Service. Sir, (said the *Collonel*) *I tell you again, that I have sent my Coach-man to ask his Pardon, and I think that is enough,* which he spoke with some sturdiness; and well he might; for he had two *Cannons* at his Back. Good God, said the *Doctor* to himself, (when he got out of Gunshot) what a *Hottentot* have I been talking to, who so little values the Life of a Gentleman, and, as it happen'd, that very Gentleman, to whom the Nation hath in a particular manner been obliged!¹⁰⁵

The satire delivers a witty and polite attack on the powerful figure, but the complaint makes a larger point about the state of the nation. The clergyman's close call with death threatens the country as well. He is, after all, a man "to whom the Nation hath in a particular manner been obliged." In this way, Swift and Sheridan justify their attack on the squire and, in fact, hope that it will encourage their patriotic readers to join them in condemning this "Hottentot squire" who threatens their country.

Perhaps the century's most pointed domestic "Hottentot" representation appears in Christopher Smart's "Mother Midnight" (1751), where he employs it to cast shame on William Augustus, the duke of Cumberland. Playing on the nickname, "The Butcher," which Cumberland had earned for his ruthless treatment of Scottish rebels in the 1745 revolt, Smart's figure assaults the glory the nobleman received: "For my own Part was I not certified by the Writings of *Quintus Curtius* and others, I shou'd have concluded, that you was begot by an *Hottentot*, born of a Tygress, and educated by a Butcher. If a Man murders his Neighbour, he is try'd, condemn'd, executed, and hung in Chains with a very little Ceremony: But if he murders Ten Thousand Men, then it becomes *Glory*, and you have all the Poets, Painters, Printers, and Priests to celebrate him for the GOOD he has done."[106]

"Hottentot" references also provided a convenient way to attack the French. So virulently anti-French is Fielding's "Man of the Hill," in *Tom Jones* (1749), that he says he would rather "pass my life with the *Hottentots*, than set my Foot in *Paris* again."[107] His remark, which was clearly meant to shock, praises the "Hottentots" at the expense of the French: "They are a nasty People, but their Nastiness is mostly *without;* whereas in *France*, and some other Nations that I won't name, it is all *within*, and makes them stink much more to my Reason than that of *Hottentots* does to my Nose."[108] Oliver Goldsmith praises the English and ridicules the French in a "Hottentot" comparison in *The Citizen of the World*, letter 78:

> Another instance of this peoples breeding I must not forget. An Englishman would not speak his native language in a company of foreigners where he was sure that none understood him; a travelling Hottentot himself would be silent if acquainted only with the language of his country, but a Frenchman shall talk to you whether you understand his language or not; never troubling his head whether you have learned French, still he keeps up the conversation, fixes his eye full in your face, and asks a thousand questions, which he answers himself for want of a more satisfactory reply.[109]

In Moses Mendez's rendering of *The Double Disappointment* (1745), one character promises another that he will, "skiver you like a Rabbit you French Hottentot son of a whore."[110]

Many works of eighteenth-century fiction include characters who are likened to "Hottentots." Fielding's Lady Bellaston considers Squire Western something a little worse than a "Hottentot": "a Gentleman whom she honoured with the Appellation of *Hottentot.*"[111] In Richardson's *Clarissa* (1747–48), Lovelace refers to four of his acquaintances as "Hottentots." Sent by him to Clarissa, she is so shocked and disgusted by them that she writes to Anna Howe of her "escape" from their "very disagreeable company."[112] In letter 175, Lovelace admits to having "overplotted myself. To make my work secure, as I thought, I have frighted the dear creature with my four Hottentots, and I shall be a long time, I doubt, before I can recover my lost ground."[113] A "Hottentot" reference is used to describe Mr. Thornton, a character in Elizabeth Griffith's *The Delicate Distress* (1769), who appears to lack social graces: "There was such an aukward reserve, about poor Thornton, for the first three days he spent at Woodfort, that I looked upon him as a Hottentot: but that rough cast is now worn off, and he is really agreeable, and entertaining."[114] Smollett goes to the "Hottentot" well frequently; references to them figure in many of his novels, among them *The Expedition of Humphry Clinker* and *The Adventures of Ferdinand Count Fathom*. Robert Bage's *Mount Henneth* (1782) also includes "Hottentot" references.

The domestic examples of "Hottentots" testify to the special British fascination (or obsession) with them. No other people, real or imagined, were appropriated into the domestic discourse and national consciousness in the way "Hottentots" were. Images of "Hottentots" allowed the British to hold a mirror up to themselves, and in the glass they could see whatever it was they wanted to see about themselves, good and bad and/or consoling or discomforting. Moreover, the multiple valences to "Hottentot" helped to give British society the sense that it was on track and moving forward to claim its imperial destiny. With ideas and images of "Hottentots" in their minds, British men and women could be surer of themselves and more aware of some impulses they might have to steel themselves against. At the very least, "Hottentots" played a crucial role in showing the British what they they did not want to become.

5
Challenging the Constructions

AT LEAST SOME ENGLISH AUTHORS RESISTED AND CHALLENGED THE assumptions and conclusions made about "Hottentots." In *An Enquiry into the Morals of the Ancients* (1737), "George England" writes that wherever "Branches of Goodness" are practiced, "such a People are truly Polite, let them be *Hottentots*, or what we falsely think the lowest of Mankind."[1] William Macintosh goes so far as to employ the word "fiction" in his *Travels in Europe, Asia, and Africa* (1782) to address the disparity between the people he himself saw at the Cape and what had appeared in print about them: "They have been very much misrepresented in Europe: and it is surprising that the fictions which have been propagated concerning them, should so long have gained credit in the world."[2] Just as England was beginning its occupation of the Cape at the end of the eighteenth century, Samuel Fairfax recorded in his journal that "the poor Hottentots have been very much misrepresented in the general opinion entertained of them. They are a simple, innocent, harmless race, very tractable, and if pain is taken with them they might be turned to great use."[3] These more generous sentiments about "Hottentots" were not expressed in volumes that enjoyed widespread circulation, and so they never posed any serious challenges to the negative constructions.

An interesting way to measure the extent to which the English embraced the low ranking assigned to "Hottentots" is to examine the few popular texts that presented relatively positive descriptions of them. That there are not very many works which do so is telling in itself, nevermind the fact that they only began to appear decades after the spate of English-authored Restoration and early-eighteenth-century travel narratives. In fact, only two published works, both, not coincidentally, by foreign authors, ever really had the authority to destabilize how "Hottentots" were envisioned in Britain. The reception given to Kolb's *The Present State of the Cape of Good Hope* (1731) and Le Vaillant's *Travels into the Interior Parts of Africa*

(1790) reveals how crucial the "Hottentots" had become to the process of self and national definition taking place in England during the eighteenth century. As we will see, the strong responses to these two works successfully counteracted their more benevolent and generous intentions.

Peter Kolb's *The Present State of the Cape of Good Hope* presents the first eighteenth-century account of "Hottentots" that calls into question much of what had previously been written about them by seventeenth-century French, Dutch, and German travelers to the region. Kolb asserts his expertise on the basis of his own eight-year residence at the Cape, which lasted from June 1705 until April 1713. He attacks the European construction of "Hottentots" that made them out to be far worse than they seemed to him.

> It has been publish'd in several Languages, and is, I believe, at this day generally apprehended throughout *Europe*, that the *Hottentots* are so brutal a People as to be, in a Manner, incapable of Reflection: That they have no Sense of God or Religion; nor any Notion of Order or Oeconomy: That they are Nations of Savages, with hardly so much as a Tincture of Reason or Humanity. These are Excesses of the Imagination, which have made a very wretched People more wretched in *Europe* than they are at home: For the *Hottentots* are by no means so stupid and senseless as these Things amount to.[4]

Kolb's work was popular throughout Europe. First published in German in 1719 in a folio edition with engravings executed by Johann Jacob Schübler, it subsequently appeared in a two-volume Dutch edition in 1727. A two-volume English edition, which uses the original German edition as its source, was published in 1731, followed by another in 1738. A three-volume French edition, based on the Dutch translation, came into print in 1741.

Mary Louise Pratt correctly argues that Kolb "affirms the Hottentots above all as cultural beings."[5] His work presents more extensive descriptions of the Cape people than any previous volume. Kolb details their governmental, judicial, and religious systems, he provides a key to their vocabulary, and he describes in full their customs, ceremonies, and music, their practice of war, and their skill at the healing arts. Kolb stresses sameness (they are human) in the midst of difference (but they are not "civilized"). In no way does he view them as equal to Europeans. To him they are an ancient and inferior people; he compares them to the "*Jews* and the Old *Troglodytes*" (30).

Kolb's description of what he calls "Hottentot" "Invocations to

5: CHALLENGING THE CONSTRUCTIONS   153

the Moon" shows how he uses their religious worship to accept them into the human family, albeit with some ambivalence. He begins with a paragraph that details the basic scene. Notice, however, that his description emphasizes the relative strangeness of the "Hottentots" form of worship. Moreover, he awards himself a position of superiority; he sets the scene as if the "Hottentots" are putting on a display just for him.

> They throw their Bodies into a thousand different Distortions; and make Mouths and Faces strangely ridiculous and horrid. Now they throw themselves flat on the Ground, screaming out a strange unintelligible Jargon. Then jumping up on a Sudden, and stamping like Mad (insomuch that they make the Ground shake) they direct, with open Throats, the following Expressions, among others, to the Moon: *Mutschi Atzé. i.e. I salute you; you are welcome. Cherâqua kahá ehori Ounqûa. i.e. Grant us Fodder for our Cattle, and Milk in Abundance.* These and other Addresses to the Moon they repeat over and over, accompanying them with Dancing and Clapping of Hands. At the End of the Dance, they sing *Ho, Ho, Ho, Ho,* many Times over; with a Variation of Notes; which being accompanied with Clapping of Hands, makes a very odd and a very merry Entertainment to a Stranger. (97)

Kolb's representation of the language and voices of "Hottentots" in his description marks an important moment in the history of European depictions. Previously, English readers had only heard Terry's version of Cory's voice.

The concluding sentences place the ceremonies in a familiar context. Kolb clearly wants his European readers—who perform their own religious duties—to see "Hottentots" doing something they can relate to, even if they do not exert themselves in a similar manner.

> In Shouting, Screaming, Singing, Jumping, Stamping, Dancing, Prostration on the Ground, and an unintelligible Jargon, lie all their Formalities in the Worship of the Moon. In Rounds of these they continue the whole Night, and till pretty far of the next Day; never resting but by short Intervals when they are quite spent: At which Times they settle themselves into a squat Posture, holding their Heads between their Hands, and resting their Elbows upon their Knees. They lower their Voices too into a slow melancholy Hum; which they continue till they start up and go again to Singing and Dancing. These Intervals of Rest are so short and so few, that one would wonder where they find Strength and Spirit to furnish out such a Run of Noise and Action as they do in this Service. The Fervours of their Devotion are unequall'd. When they have done, they retire to their several Homes with as much

Chearfulness and Satisfaction as do any other People in the World from the Performance of their Religious Duties. (97–98)

Kolb's observation here that the "Hottentots" performed their religious duties in an "unequall'd" fashion establishes groundwork for a comparison between this society and European societies. Moreover, the concluding sentence's insistence that the "Hottentots" receive as much "Satisfaction" from their worship as do other people places them in the human family. Kolb is clearly viewing "Hottentots" from a relativist position, which marks the essential difference of his text from nearly all the other contemporaneous European-authored accounts.

Kolb had personal reasons for producing his more generous account of "Hottentots." He begins the narrative with an explanation that he went to the Cape to perform scientific observations in astronomy and meteorology for his former patron, Baron von Krosick, but he evidently returned home friendless and, more crucially, patronless: "My Friends in *Europe* were much wanting to their Promises to me of Support and Encouragement . . . and I was not a little shatter'd and reduc'd thro' their Neglect of me" (364). As might be expected from a man suffering from such disappointments, Kolb insinuates that some Europeans, presumably his former friends and patron, are less virtuous than "Hottentots." This subtext is evident in his description of "mutual Affection":

> The *Hottentots* are all Kindness and Good Will to one another. I have seen their mutual Liberalities many a Time, and with the highest Pleasure; and never saw any Thing like 'em in the Christian World . . . Is a *Hottentot's* Assistance requir'd by one of his Countrymen? He runs to give it. Is his Counsel ask'd? He gives it sincerely. Is his Countryman in Want? He relieves him, according to his Ability, with the utmost Readiness. One of the greatest Pleasures of the *Hottentots* certainly lies in their Gifts and Good Office to one another. (332–33)

It is hard to determine precisely how much Kolb's personal agenda influenced his more positive descriptions of "Hottentots," but clearly it played a role. His text can be questioned on other grounds as well.

Indeed, there are legitimate questions surrounding when and in what physical state Kolb composed his prose and executed the illustrations. W. Peter Carstens notes that Kolb went blind in April 1712, but regained his sight sometime after his return to Germany in 1713.[6] The text indicates that Kolb wrote his work only after his return to Europe, so it makes sense to ask what sort of notes he

5: CHALLENGING THE CONSTRUCTIONS

used during the composition process. The introductory passages assert that Kolb kept a journal, at least during his voyage to the Cape, and, certainly, he must have made notes of some kind while he was residing in Cape Town. In relation to the descriptions of the "Hottentots," Kolb says that much of the material is based on his own eyewitness experience with them, but some of it comes from the notes and observations of others: "I have finish'd my Detail of the *Hottentot* Nations . . . The Majority of these I visited my self, and had Accounts of the Rest from a great many Persons of Credit" (83). Kolb certainly had copies of the European sources he refutes at his desk as he wrote his book; his lack of reference to any English texts suggests he was either unfamiliar with them or that he did not know English.

At the time of its publication in London, English readers did not concern themselves at all with questions about the accuracy or reliability of Kolb's work—they were captivated by it. Kolb's work, actually, Guido Medley's translation of it, proved to be the right text at the right time. Although Kolb attacks the reliability of many of the previously printed accounts of "Hottentots," he does not provide much in the way of original and new material. What the volume offered readers was a seeming comprehensiveness, and they responded to it by remembering his descriptions and finding ways to use them in publications of their own. For example, the descriptions Kolb gives of "Hottentot" priests urinating on the participants of initiation, marriage, and funeral ceremonies almost instantly found their way into popular discourse. This information, however, had been reported previously in John Maxwell's (1707) and Edward Cooke's (1712) narratives, although the reading public was not so struck by it then to appropriate it. As we shall see, in 1731, they did so with gusto. Indeed, Kolb's work made quite a surprising and extraordinary impact on English readers.

The English translation of Kolb's work, published on 3 November 1730 (dated 1731 in the book), was noticed by the periodical press almost immediately upon its publication. It was a success despite the inexperience of the translator. Indeed, Kolb's work represents Guido Medley's only published work. Medley was clearly a man looking for funds and a patron. Medley's home address, in Spittlefields, an area known for its poverty, suggests his lack of financial security. Moreover, his decision to dedicate the work to John Montagu, a man who was not respected in high society circles, demonstrates that he was somewhat desperate in his search for a patron. Extant letters prove that he tried to win the notice and favor from Hans Sloane, then the President of the Royal Soci-

"The Hottentot Marriage," from Peter Kolb's *The Present State of the Cape of Good Hope* (London, 1731). Library Company of Philadelphia.

ety, writing to him three times between 3 August 1731 and 5 June 1735. In the last letter he thanks Sloane for recommending him to Montagu. If Medley had hoped that Sloane would arrange for his admittance into the society, he was disappointed. Whatever Medley went on to do in his life, he did so without any notice. His death is not recorded in any of the periodicals that usually acknowledge the demise of people of note.

Neither the accuracy of Kolb's observation or the reliability of Medley's translation was a point of contention when the work appeared in print, however. Of the two volumes, only the first (25 chapters, totaling 312 pages) describes and examines "Hottentot" societies. The twenty-seven engravings in volume one are far inferior to the ones that appeared in original German edition. Indeed, their poor quality is due to the fact that Medley (or someone) tried to trace them rather than hire an artist to copy them. Medley himself wields a heavy and, sometimes, curious editor's hand. At times he places himself in the work in such an obtrusive way that he undermines the text he is presenting. Moreover, the content of Medley's prefatory material is strange and inappropriate. For example, the preface is devoted to establishing Kolb's reliability, but Medley's thirteen page discussion concerning how the humors of authors influence their works hardly seems relevant in relation to the kind of narrative that follows. Medley asserts that Kolb's constitution was a phlegmatic one, which is, he writes, the one best suited to the writing of history: *"Phlegmatic* Writers certainly excel all others in Accounts of Fact. The *Phlegmatic* have no Eyes, indeed, for the *Inside* of Things; but they have excellent ones for the *Outside;* and give a Detail of a Thousand Particulars there which escape Men of other Complexions. They relate every Thing they see and hear, with the most religious Exactness, nor omitting the smallest or most indifferent Matter or Circumstance, they remember, tho' it be of neither Use nor Entertainment, nor any Thing at all to the Purpose" (xv). Medley undermines his own argument, however, by confessing that he does not "have the Honour to know him," although he swears that Kolb's writing proves "he is not subject to Transports of Imagination" (xvi). Medley's strongest argument in relation to Kolb's expertise is, curiously, one he does not make: Kolb resided longer at the Cape than any other author of representations of "Hottentots."

In fact, rather than make the simplest and most convincing argument available to him, Medley raises in the conclusion a new set of questions that cast suspicion on the accuracy and reliability of his own translation. He warns readers that his rendering of the text "is not so properly a Translation as an *Abridgment,"* explaining that Kolb is sometimes "very tedious" and in other places "runs out in Reflections that are neither very entertaining, nor very much to the Purpose" (xvii). Medley also expresses concerns about the apparent contradictions in the text, which he did not correct, and the organization, or what he calls "Method," that he feels compelled to rearrange in some places (xvii). Medley's preface attempts to end on an upbeat note, when he claims that "the *Original* is in great Esteem abroad, as the exactest History of the *Hottentots* the World has yet seen" (xviii). This is one of the few verifiable statements Medley makes in the preface, and it is not surprising that he uses Kolb's depiction of the "Hottentots" as the selling point for his translation.

Medley's skills as a translator can be attacked on at least two grounds. First, in regard to diction, he often selects extremely strong words, and he sometimes adds phrases of his own devising. For example, his translation of Kolb's attack on the previously published accounts of the "Hottentots" suggests his overly exuberant use of language: "FEW Histories have been handed into the World with so much Falshood and Imperfection as the Accounts we have hitherto had of the People about *Cape* of *Good Hope*. The Vanity of Travellers, the Prostitution of mercenary Pens, and the Credulity of Mankind were hardly ever more manifest than in Relations that have hitherto prevail'd concerning 'em" (25). A comparison of the same passage with the French translation suggests that the phrase "the Prostitution of mercenary Pens" is Medley's own invention. Even more striking than Medley's choice of diction and invention of phrases is the dramatic way he restructures and uses Kolb's histories of individual "Hottentots," especially the story concerning Claas. For example, Medley frames the first mention and history of him in such a way so that readers will regard him like a character in a tragedy: "And here I cannot help digressing upon the Story of this Man, in which there are Things so very affecting, that, far from doubting of the Reader's Pardon, I question whether, when he knows it, he will think he could have forgiven me the Suppression of a Matter that warms the Breast with such a Mixture of Indignation and Pity" (39). Medley's decision to tell Claas's story this early in translation shows that he wanted to shape the work to win sympathy for the "Hottentots" before he described what he regarded as "Hottentot" vices.

Briefly summarized, the first story about Claas that Medley relates explains how he became a victim of injustice. He had been a very happy man, but his happiness was destroyed when the "Tyrant Captain" of the "Hottentots" kidnapped his wife. His wife had earlier refused to acquiese to the chief's sexual desires. Frustrated, the chief uses his connection with the Dutch colonists to order Claas's removal from the village; Claas is charged with conspiring against the Dutch, and is arrested, tried, convicted, and sent to the prison on Robben Island. Upon hearing of Claas's downfall, a Dutch sea captain, who had earlier been rescued by Claas, testified to his benevolence before the directors of the Dutch East India Company. This testimony won Claas his freedom, but he returns to the kraal to find his cattle herd destroyed, and soon after his return he is murdered by the "Hottentot" chief. At the end of the volume, Medley returns to the figure of Claas, making him an exemplar of "Hottentot" hospitality to Europeans.[7]

Medley also emphasizes Kolb's positive views of "Hottentots" with a section of his own invention. He places "A Review of the Vices and Virtues of the Hottentots" at the end of the first volume, which presents material cobbled together from the sections of text he rearranged. Significantly, a comparable section does not appear in either the German original or in the French translation.

Rather than ameliorating the image of the "Hottentots" in British eyes or forcing a reappraisal of the negative constructions of them, Kolb's account seems to have confirmed for them the baseness of "Hottentot" society in a particularly appealing way. Indeed, contrary to the stated intention of its author, Medley's translation seems to have given eighteenth-century English readers proof that "Hottentot" society was the appropriate negative foil for them. In this way, it failed to accomplish one of Kolb's major goals, which was to get European readers to see how previous representations contain "so much Falshood and Imperfection" (25). A curious paradox thus exists in the reception of Kolb's work: readers accepted his descriptions as accurate, but they completely failed to see—or chose not to notice—the volume's message and purpose. The London periodical press, in particular, bears partial responsibility for the misreading.

Less than two months after *The Present State of the Cape of Good Hope* appeared in English, its descriptions of "Hottentot" ceremonies were being adapted for domestic application. As we saw in the previous chapter, there existed already a tradition of representing "Hottentots" in the domestic environment, but the depictions that derive their existence and authority from Kolb's text are particularly scatological and political. It is not surprising that the *Grub-Street Journal* drew first ink from Kolb's "Hottentot" well. As Bertrand A. Goldgar argues, this periodical shows the "inevitable connection between the literary and political worlds as the decade of the 1730s opened," and its "constant defenses" of Pope and Swift suggest its anti-Walpole stance.[8] The 24 December 1730 issue of the *Grub-Street Journal* presents an answer to an epigram that appeared in the *St. James's Evening Post*, the last line of which draws on Kolb's description of "Hottentot" priests urinating on the participants of ceremonial rituals:

> If none must be admir'd but Poets born,
> Admire a HOMER, and a VIRGIL scorn;
> Admire a HORACE, and contemn BOILEAU;
> Admire a DRYDEN, and despise a ROWE
> But if on such as these with scorn we look;
> What must be done to W____b, T____d, C____k?
> Scorn were too little from each honest Briton;
> These should be pump'd, duck'd, pillory'd, pist,
>   and sh____ on.[9]

The thrusts here, most probably aimed at Hugh Todd and Thomas Cooke, reference famous literary (and political) battles then taking place. Thomas Cooke, for example, attacked both Alexander Pope and Jonathan Swift in a number of works, and Pope returned the favor in The Dunciad, book 2, 130: "Cook shall be Prior, and Concanen, Swift."[10]

The editors of the *Grub-Street Journal* returned to *The Present State of the Cape of Good Hope* seven weeks later, dedicating almost the entire front page of the 18 February 1731 issue to it. The issue proved to be so popular that extra copies were printed. Mr. Bavius, the persona of the *Grub-Street Journal*, begins by referring to the controversy caused by the epigram published in the 24 December 1730 issue:

> HAVING observed that some Persons ignorant of the institution, and unacquainted with the customs of our Society, have been offended with an Epigram printed in our 51st. Journal; I think it incumpent upon me to inform them of their mistake. In that Epigram it was said of some of the most eminent of our Members, *These should be pump'd, duck'd, pillory'd, pist, and sh—t on;* which is so far from being any reflection on those worthy Gentlemen, that it is a very great compliment paid them.[11]

Mr. Bavius, the voice of the *Journal*, named after a poet Virgil mocks in Eclogue 3, then offers the following explanation; it will, he hopes, will satisfy those who accused him of disrespect.

> To *piss upon a man* is, in this country, commonly thought a term of reproach: but among the unprejudiced Hottentots, it is a mark of the highest honour. That honest people, unbias'd by the manners of other nations, follow the dictates of pure, untainted nature. *Kolben*, in his account of the *present state of the Cape of good Hope*, as I find it translated by the ingenious Mr MEDLEY, is very copious on this subject.[12]

The special attention given to Medley in this passage suggests that he is being mocked as well as the "Hottentots." The subsequent paragraphs quote extensively from his translation of Kolb's descriptions of initiation, marriage, knighthood, and funeral services. Bavius concludes this section of quotations with a reflection from Kolb's text that serves to heighten his own satire: "Strange! the different nations entertain of the same thing! the force, the witchcraft of custom! *To be piss'd upon* in Europe is a token of the highest Contempt; To be piss'd on in the Hottentot Countries is a token of the highest honour. *Pissing* is the glory of all the Hottentot Ceremonies."[13]

In the penultimate paragraph, Bavius launches a final attack at writers, like Thomas Cooke, who existed in Robert Walpole's favor:

> Thus far this ingenious Author; who has by this time, I hope, persuaded the reader, that there is no disgrace in being pist upon: since it is held in so much honour by whole nations; and I hope, for the future, that such learned and ingenious Authors, as shall have those honours conferred on them by our Society, will be universally treated with the more honour on that very account.[14]

The concluding paragraph testifies to the connection between literature and politics. Here Mr. Bavius cannot restrain himself from reminding readers that the political battles waged early on in the century continue still. The major reference is to Henry Sacheverell (1674–1724), the high church advocate whose sermons against toleration and occasional conformity caused such controversy in 1709–10. Notice is also taken of chaplain William Whiston (1667–1752) and mathematician Humphrey Ditton (1675–1715), who created what was seen as a ridiculous plan to determine longitude by firing a shell into the air.

> But moreover we are not without some instances of these honours even in our own Country. I well remember a certain Reverend Divine was in such esteem, that not only fans and other implements of the fair sex, but even vulgar utensils, nay, *Chamber-pots* were adorned with his picture. This surely would never have been done, if it had not been looked upon as a token of respect to *piss upon him*. And those ingenious Astronomers Messrs. Whiston and Ditton, had an Ode composed to their honour, the burden of which was
> Let Whiston and Ditton
> Be p——st on, be sh—t on.[15]

An indication of the popularity of this issue of the *Grub-Street Journal* is the notice taken of it in the February and March 1731 issues of the *Gentleman's Magazine*. In its own summary of what transpired, it pays a wry compliment to Bavius's efforts.

> Mr. *Bavius* clears up a passage which had offended some of his readers in an epigram inserted in one of his former journals. The line referr'd to is: *These should be pump'd, duck'd, pillory'd, piss'd, and sh—t on.*
> This, he says, is so far from a reflection, that it is a compliment paid to the gentlemen of their society, and marks of honour given their members. To prove this, he quotes *Kolben's* Account of the Cape of *Good Hope*.[16]

One month later, the March issue of the *Gentleman's Magazine* again refers readers to a "Hottentot" discussion in the *Grub-street Journal*.

The 4 March 1731 issue of the *Grub-Street Journal* features a letter from a figure named Belinda, who expresses her dismay about the 18 February issue. What we have here is a rather extraordinary example of the intersections of gender, literary, and party politics. Mr. Bavius presents "Belinda's" letter and its poetic attachment in full:

> I have hitherto read your weekly labours with pleasure: but give me leave to say, your Hottentot performance was such a nauseous piece of stupidity, that, if you don't speedily retrieve your honour, I shall wish some of you to be the happy Bridegrooms at the Cape of Good Hope; and can't now forbear expressing my female indignation, by presenting you with the following lines, as my present sentiments of your sinking Society, which, if you dare, you may print in your next.
>
> Long have I thought your Club to be
> A batchelor Society:
> A set of lively, brilliant Wits;
> But now 'tis plain you're marry'd Cits:
> Your sprightly joys seems past the full;
> *Just on the Point of growing dull*
> You have yourselves so much bepis'd,
> From off the stage you'll soon be his'd,
> Or may I ne'er by man be kis'd.[17]

The editor has the construct called "Belinda" unconsciously mark herself. Her strong comments not only poke fun at married men, but they also undermine her own expression of sentiments. This becomes apparent in Bavius's reply, which appears immediately after the poem.

On behalf of his society, Bavius attacks Belinda and all women who challenge or complain about marriage traditions by comparing them to author Eliza Haywood. Bringing Haywood into his argument also explains why the female correspondent is named "Belinda" (in her novel *The British Recluse* [1722] a character named Belinda is betrayed by a lover). Haywood herself was an easy target. Her 1721 desertion of her husband had attracted much public notice and comment.

> This Letter having been read, and some debate passed upon it, Mr. BAVIUS, by order of the Society, drew up their sentiments in the following manner. That they wondered so curious a Dissertation, supported by such full and faithful (tho' perhaps stupid) quotations, should give any offence to so ingenious a Lady; especially since the fair

5: CHALLENGING THE CONSTRUCTIONS 163

Hottentots were not represented there, as guilty of any indecent action towards men, but in a modest, passive manner, agreeable to the natural shamefacedness, and subjection of their sex, submitting in a decent posture to the ceremony of being *pissed upon,* as an emblematical introduction into the honourable state of matrimony. That this very Dissertation, at which this nice Lady was disgusted, had been so well relished by the Town, as to occasion the printing of an additional number of the *Journal* , in which it appeared. That however, from the last line of her verses, we have reason to hope, that she is not altogether irreconcileable, either to our Members, or to the ceremony itself, provided it were to be attended with the same consequents as among the Hottentots. That in this she has a great example to keep her in countenance, the beautiful, ingenious, and modest Mrs. ELIZA HAYWOOD, who was pleased, a few years since, to yield herself up a glorious prize to the vigorous Mr Curl, upon his out-pissing his Brother CHAPMAN: which whole Affair is admirably described in the beautiful Episode of the *Game of Pissing* in the second Book of the *Dunciad.*[18]

Pope's own attack on Haywood in *The Dunciad* stemmed from his anger at her for attacking Martha Blount in *Memoirs of a Certain Island* (1724), who is represented as "Marthalia" and is depicted as being a promiscuous and syphilitic woman.[19] The *Grub-Street Journal's* compliment to Pope and his work is in keeping with its consistent defense of Pope and Swift. Goldgar reminds us that the *Journal's* "literary and political prejudices reinforced each other, that in fact its literary judgments were at least in part colored by political considerations."[20] The March issue of the *Gentleman's Magazine* shies away from the political dimensions of these references; it does not reproduce Bavius's reply to Belinda, but merely summarizes her letter and reprints the poem.

Less than a year later, the *Gentleman's Magazine* (February 1732) continued to note other periodicals which used Kolb's text for domestic satire. This issue presents an account from the *Weekly Register* (dated 12 February 1732) that compares an English "Beau" to a "Hottentot."

The *Hottentots,* according to *Kolben,* wear a Crust, or Cap of Black Mortar; which seems to be the Parent of the Beau's Pomatum and Powder: and as their more Fat, Soot, and Butter denotes their Quality by the Quantity, our Beau takes Pains to display himself accordingly. The long Staves of our modern Heroes are a Mimickry of their *Hassagays.* If ours differ in the Obtuseness of their Heads, may it not better set forth the same Quality of their Understandings? It may therefore be proper to consult what Badge to put upon this new Order of Knights of the *Monkey-tail:* A Mixture of Colours, and a *proper Cap,* would do the Business, and save Thought. But since there is so much Likeness, our Heroes should carry some Token of their Etymology, and may hereafter be entitled *Totties*. This is pretty, and *pretty* is a Word they are fond of.[21]

The last sentence of this "Hottentot" reference might well be intending to cast an aspersion on the effeminacy on English beaux, likening them more to women than men.

A decade later, the *Gentleman's Magazine* (September 1741) presents an excerpt from *Common Sense* (dated 19 September 1741) that cites Kolb's description of an "Order of Knighthood among the Hottentots." In June 1754, the *Connoisseur*, a weekly humor magazine, mocks the idea of "noble Hottentots" by presenting the sad history of Tquassouw and Knonmquaiha, two "Hottentots" whose happy union was ruined by the trickery of the devil, who had disguised himself as a "Mynheer Van Snickersnee." The once-happy bride gave birth to a white child, and she was sentenced to death by clubbing. After her death, her "inconsolable husband" took to howling with the wolves, and one night he mysteriously disappears, never to be seen again.[22]

The periodical press was not alone, however, in finding Kolb's work useful for making serious or farcical judgments and comparisons. Tobias Smollett defers to Kolb and his work in several of his novels. In *The Adventures of Peregrine Pickle* (1751), Smollett likens Pipes's use of a cudgel to that of a "Hottentot" hunter at the Cape: "And let not the incredulous reader pretend to doubt the truth of this phenomenon, until he shall have first perused the ingenious Peter Kolben's Natural History of the Cape of Good Hope, where the inhabitants commonly use to strike fire with the shin-bones of lions which have been killed in that part of Africk."[23] James Carson argues persuasively that the reason Smollet presents relatively sympathetic accounts of "Hottentots" in his works is due to his debt to Kolb's volumes.[24] Carson and Louis Martz have both explored how Kolb's work clearly informs Smollet's description of Scottish Highlanders in *Humphry Clinker* (1771), and how it worked as a source text for his *The Present State of All Nations* (1768–69).[25]

The Present State of the Cape of Good Hope is the most cited text in entries about "Hottentots" in mid- and late-eighteenth-century travel collections, geography books, and encyclopedias of knowledge. It is named as a principal source in the English translation of Bernard Picart's *The Ceremonies and Religious Customs of the Idolatrous Nations* (1733); Thomas Astley's *A New General Collection of Voyages of Travels* (4 vols., 1745–47); Emanuel Bowen's *A Complete*

System of Geography (2 vols. ,1747); Thomas Salmon's *Universal Traveller* (1753) and *Modern History* (vol. 5, 1755), albeit not always in a complimentary fashion; Andrew Brice's *A New Universal Geographical Dictionary* (1759); *The Modern Part of an Universal History* (1760); John Newbery's *A World Display'd* (1759–61) and *A Curious Collection of Voyages* (vol. 10, 1761); Daniel Fenning's *A New System of Geography* (1764) and its later editions, which make a point of supporting Kolb against his detractors; John Knox's *A New Collection of Voyages, Discoveries and Travels* (1767); and, George Baldwyn's *Universal System of Geography* (1794).

Even if the periodical press refused to see the more generous purpose of Kolb's work, others did. Thomas Astley's *A New General Collection of Voyages and Travels* (1745–47) reminds readers of Kolb's attack on the excessively negative constructions of "Hottentots." The preface to volume three attacks the entrenched ideas about "Hottentots":

> *As touching the* Hottentots, *of whom so many different and romantic Stories have been propagated, we shall be able fully to satisfy the Curiosity of the Public by our Abstract of* Kolben's *Relation; which is so compleat, that he seems to have left nothing for future Travellers to add. We presume, the Reader will be both surprized and pleased with the agreeable Variety he finds in the Manners and Customs of these People; whom the Ignorance or Malice of most former Authors had represented as Creatures but one Degree removed from Beasts, and with scarce any thing human about them except the Shape: Whereas, in Fact, they appear to be some of the most humane and virtuous (abating for a few Prejudices of Education) to be found among all the Race of Mankind.*[26]

Throughout its Cape section, Astley's collection goes out of its way to support Kolb's authority. It even reprints one of his maps of the Cape. Significantly, the French translation of Astley's collection, executed by Prévost, also took to heart Kolb's and Astley's criticisms about how "Hottentots" had been misrepresented by others. Prévost's collection, in fact, helps to initiate the later eighteenth-century French construction of "Hottentots" as "noble savages."

Other geographies followed Astley's lead, but not always so enthusiastically. *Geography Made Familiar and Easy to Young Gentlemen and Ladies* (1748) presents an equivocal account at best: "The *Hottentots* about the *Cape of Good Hope* are not such Fools as they have been represented; they are honest and faithful to their Engagements, and very generous and hospitable. Indeed they are lazy, and delight in Nastiness, their Ornaments consisting of the unclean'd Guts of Animals, which they bear about them till they are quite dry, and then eat them."[27] The multiple editions of Daniel

Fenning's *A New System of Geography* (1764) also support and maintain Kolb's "defense" of "Hottentots." Fenning's first edition, published in 1764, uses Kolb's descriptions of "Hottentot" bodies and customs but, even more crucially, it takes both his stories about Claas and Van der Stel's "Hottentot" boy and presents them as absolute truth. Indeed, the one engraving in the first edition is entitled "Claas the Hottentot surrenders himself Prisoner to the Dutch Ensign."[28] The 1771 edition of Fenning's *Geography* asserts Kolb's authority even more strongly than the earlier ones, by resurrecting the old issue of how they are generally represented: "The Hottentots have been represented by some authors as being scarce above the level of the brutes, and as having neither understanding, nor any sense of order or decency, and as scarce possessing the least glimpse of reason and humanity: but this is far from being true. 'I have known many of them,' says the learned and judicious Mr. Kolben."[29] As late as 1777, Kolb's work is still being defended by no less an important authority than George Forster who, as a participant in Cook's second circumnavigation, had some personal knowledge of the Cape: "it is true that he has been misinformed in regard to some circumstances; and that others, chiefly relative to the colony, have at present another appearance than in his time: but he still remains the best author that can be consulted on the subject, and as such we will venture to refer our readers to him."[30]

That Kolb's work was granted such privileged status for so many decades is remarkable, especially when we consider his residence at the Cape ended in 1713. Indeed, it was not until the last decades of the eighteenth century that its authority began to be seriously challenged. Direct attacks began in 1770s. Significantly, criticism was voiced first by French authors, and thus it came into English in translations of their works. J. H. Bernardin de Saint Pierre's *A Voyage to the Isle of France, the Isle of Bourbon, and the Cape of Good Hope* (1775) says that Kolb's work is "full of . . . ridiculous fables."[31] In late 1776, a British reviewer of de la Caillé's *Journal Historique du Voyage fait au Cap de Bonne Esperance* (1776) wrote that Kolb "has too long deceived Europe by his false representations of the country he describes, after the suggestions of a set of men, whose views he was employed to serve."[32] A lengthy footnote accompanying the review makes a more personal criticism of the author, asserting that Kolb "passed the whole time of his mission with his bottle and his pipe."[33] A decade later, the *Monthly Review's* generally positive judgment of Anders (or Andrew) Sparrman's *A Voyage to the Cape of Good Hope* (1785) was based partly on its assessment that it was more accurate than Kolb's book.[34]

The sinking reputation of Kolb's work is confirmed in the first paragraph of a critical review of William Paterson's *A Narrative of Four Journeys into the Country of the Hottentots and Caffraria* (1789): "As the merit of Kolben's well-known description of the Cape of Good Hope has been impeached by respectable authority, we took up the present work with the pleasing expectation of being introduced into that obscure country, and to a familiar acquaintance with the natives . . . but in this hope, we were much disappointed."[35] Kolb's *The Present State of the Cape of Good Hope* also, quite naturally, fell out of favor because it was badly out of date by the second half of the century. Moreover, illustrated scientific travel narratives, some of which present extended accounts of travel at the Cape, began to appear, and British readers responded positively to the spirit of this emerging form.

In the last decade of the eighteenth century the negative constructions of "Hottentots" came under scrutiny in a variety of literary genres. In 1790, Tamary Hurrell published a collection of what she titled "tales of imagination on moral and interesting subjects," and one of them is called "The Hottentot."[36] Hurrell's work received good notices. The *Critical Review* records the author's intention in its positive review: "Mrs. Hurrell . . . tells us, that she received them [the stories] from a friend; that they are designed for the amusement of an idle hour, and that it has been the aim of the author to represent virtues of the most permanent good. The stories are interesting, the manners of the different nations well preserved, and the moral is in general unexceptional."[37]

Hurrell's decision to use a "Hottentot" in her tale makes sense; she takes what was thought to be the "worst" and transforms it into the "best." Indeed, she challenges many of the stereotypical notions one at a time, creating a "Hottentot" who is multilingual, wise, philosophical, well-traveled, Christian, compassionate, generous even to evil people, and, most crucially, not a sexual threat to the European woman. The tale relates, somewhat sketchily, two histories, one of a Dutch woman and the other of a "Hottentot." The briefiest of plot summaries does not do the tale justice: a male "Hottentot" rescues a Dutch woman from the clutches of a Dutch man who is about to rape her. In the character of Mrs. Van Frevil, Hurrell shows us the vulnerability of any European woman; threatened by a corrupt and immoral member of her own society, she finds she must rely on the goodness of a man others might consider a barbarian. Hurrell has created in Hacqua a character whom British readers would have considered an "acceptable" "Hottentot"; that is, he is an idealistic Christian who comes to view "Hottentots" from an European perspective. His defenses of "Hottentot" culture are rational ones, and the narrative makes it quite clear that, unlike "Cory," he has not returned to a "guts and garbage" existence but has chosen to live a truly natural lifestyle, and the one most in keeping with the traditions of his people.

The narrative begins with Hacqua, the "Hottentot," "throwing a random dart" (F5) in the direction of a hart, and killing, by accident, a man named Vanderstadt, who was about to make Mrs. Van Frevil "a victim to his brutal passion" (125). Mrs. Van Frevil found herself alone with Vanderstadt after a series of mishaps, which ultimately separated her from her husband after the three of them survived a Dutch East India Company shipwreck. When Mrs. Van Frevil and Hacqua encounter each other, she is "scared at his uncouth appearance" but reassured by the fact that he speaks Dutch and other languages. He takes her to his hut ("The Hottentot welcomed his fair companion to his lowly dwelling" [108]), and "afterwards he conducted her to the inward apartment, where he spread the softest skins for her to repose on, and then respectfully retired to the other, where he himself passed the night" (108–9). The next morning the two tell each other their personal histories: "The lady, on her side, was pleased to have an opportunity of relating her story, as she thought it would empower her to make the same request to her host, in whose life, she was persuaded, there must have happened some extraordinary turns of fortune; his appearance being that of a rude Hottentot, and his conversation of a civlized European" (109).

As Hacqua tells Mrs. Van Frevil his history, it is obvious that he understands the meaning behind the events of his life. At five years old, he was separated from his mother when they went into the woods to collect fuel. He was found by Father Angelo, "an elderly man in a black habit," who took him to Cape Town, where he had never been. Angelo renamed the boy Leontine and raised him: "Above all, he took pleasure in instructing me in the holy mysteries of the Christian Religion, which he inforced by a life of unexampled piety" (128). When Hacqua was 17, Angelo died, and Hacqua went to work as the Dutch governor's secretary. The governor had a son, named Fabrien, who "was not in reality what he seemed" (130). The town believed Fabrien to be a pious and exceptional young man, but after two years of acquaintanceship, Hacqua would learn otherwise. Fabrien had seduced the daughter of a captain stationed at the garrison, and the father wanted satisfaction. Using their friendship as a basis for emotional blackmail, Fabrien gets Leontine to agree to lie and say that it was he who seduced the girl, not Fabrien. The Captain, who turns out to be the father of Van Frevil's husband, challenges Leontine to a duel of sorts. Leontine wins their fight, believing, incorrectly it turns out, that he has killed the captain. Encountering Fabrien after the fight, Leontine finally figures out what a false friend he has, after which he runs away from the Cape.

The first evening of his escape finds him at a "Hottentot" village: "Spent with fatigue, I entered one of the huts, and was hospitably received by its owner, with whom I remained till my wounds were entirely healed and my strength recovered" (152). As he explains, while he was at the village he had the opportunity to see the "Hottentot" way of life, and his reaction to it is consistent with the French vision of "Hottentots."

> I was charmed with the simplicity of their manners, their unaffected benevolence, and the universal harmony that every where reigned throughout their societies. The ingratitude of Fabrien had disgusted me with the civilized part of mankind, among whom I had resided; I contrasted the virtues I perceived in the character of a people whom I had been taught to consider as barbarians, with the vices of more civilized individuals; my principles, I blush to speak it, were shaken, and I impiously dared to view the holy mysteries, in which I had been instructed by father Angelo, in no other light than as a cover for the worst of vices. "Here," said I, alluding to my nation, "nature flourishes in her pristine purity; here we may judge the hearts of men by their words, and read them in their countenances. In short, Madam, I was so far led away by my evil genius, that I resolved to renounce the Christian principles, and to embrace the religion and manners of my ancestors. I did not, indeed, adopt their idolatrous mode of worship; but, "I looked through Nature up to Nature's GOD." (152–53)

Hacqua goes on to explain that he assimilated into the society of "Hottentots": "I confess, with regard to their way of living, I adopted many customs which, at first, appeared aukward and disgusting to me; but use, which experience proves, can reconcile us to the greatest absurdities, in time surmounted my distaste" (153–54). Soon he married a beautiful woman, and he lived happily with her until she betrayed him (because of female vanity) by having an affair with another man. The chief of the village does not give Hacqua the justice he seeks, so he runs away and begins to travel the world. He tells Mrs. Van Frevil that his voyages took him to Egypt, Arabia, Persia, China, Japan, the Asiatic Isles, and "over a large part of Europe."

Hacqua returned to the Cape and eventually made his way to

the village where he was born. During one of his walks in the country, he heard a groan emanating from a small shed, and upon entering it he found an old man "seemingly at the point of death" (159). He revived the man, who, according to "Hottentot" custom, had been left there to die, and he soon discovers that the old man is his biological father. As a result of this reunion, Hacqua became acquainted with his entire family and began to live a somewhat reclusive existence amongst them. His life, he says, taught him the following lesson, which is in keeping with what most eighteenth-century British moralists believed:

> I had studied the character of many men, and the customs and laws of many nations, but had neglected the more useful study of *myself*. In this retirement from the world, I have had leisure to review my past life; I find that my misfortunes have, in general, originated from the irregularity and violence of my passions. I have been at war with mankind for their vices, but remembered not that I was myself imperfect. (164)

Conscious now of his own faults, Hacqua says that he feels "at peace with all mankind" (165). Hacqua insists on taking Mrs. Van Frevil to the Cape, from whence she can return to Holland to search for her husband. Lo and behold, she discovers her husband in Cape Town, and the reunited couple offer to take Hacqua to Holland "and share the wealth they possessed" (168). Hacqua declines their offer and lives the rest of his life in peace in his homeland, and Mrs. and Mr. Van Frevil return to Holland, "where they enjoyed many years of uninterrupted bliss" (169).

The mixed messages in this "moral and interesting" tale reflect many of the confusions and certainties of the late-eighteenth-century "contact zone."[38] The Van Frevil offer to take Hacqua to Europe and their willingness to share their wealth with him suggest that such a virtuous and tested couple as this one can find a way to live with "civilized" Africans, albeit on European soil. For his part, Hacqua understands that the proper place for him is not in European society but in his own, where he maintains a "civilized" existence because of his own sense of civility and self-knowledge. The work's numerous moral lessons were surely obvious to many readers: there are Europeans who do not live up to Christian ideals; that Christianity is a civilizing force; that an unprotected female is a vulnerable creature; that people are sometimes not what they appear to be; and, most crucially for our purposes, that even "Hottentots" are capable of being "civilized," and once saved, will not regress even in their homeland.

Also in 1790, English readers could find another romantic depiction of "Hottentots," this time in the form of a travel narrative. François Le Vaillant's *Travels into the Interior Parts of Africa, by the Way of the Cape of Good Hope, in the Years 1780, 81, 82, 83, 84, and 85* (1790) challenged British readers to view "Hottentots" in a radically different way. Le Vaillant's work followed a distinctly eighteenth-century French notion of "Hottentot," which constructed them as "noble savages" and exemplars of "Natural Men." A review of Le Vaillant's work in *Town and Country* addresses the particularly French characteristics of the work: "The Travels are highly entertaining and peculiarly interesting; but we must observe, that our author has carried the manners and prejudices of his countrymen into the wilds of Africa. We see, in every instance, the eager, the sanguine, the enthusiastic Frenchman."[39] In his narrative, Le Vaillant presents portraits of individual "Hottentots." He considers them as "pupils of nature," and he praises one of them, a young man he calls Klaas, for his "virtuous mind [that] was never corrupted by our elegant institutions."[40] In a section that recalls a dangerous moment when Klaas refused to leave his side, Le Vaillant proclaims "the worthy Klaas as my equal, my brother, and the confidant of all my pleasures, misfortunes, and secrets."[41]

Le Vaillant's work received an enthusiastic reception from Britain's more liberal literary and political circles. In fact, reviews of the work emanating from their pens often call into question the stereotypical conceptions of "Hottentots." For example, the review in the *Monthly Review* refers to the "Hottentots" as a "people, whom prejudice and calumny have represented as more hostile than their beasts of prey."[42] A few years later, when Mary Wollstonecraft reviewed Le Vaillant's second work, *New Travels into the Interior Parts of Africa* (1796), she writes that "the Hottentots have been considered as the most disgusting and brutal of 'the various tribes of the many peopled earth'; a real lover of mankind must then be highly gratified by the lively and artless pictures that occur in this narrative of the domestic virtues, and moral sensibility, of the untutored wanderers in those vast rocky deserts."[43]

The approval given to Le Vaillant's work by some prompted others to attack it and ridicule those who championed it. Elizabeth Hamilton's *Memoirs of Modern Philosophers* (1800) is principally interested in ridiculing William Godwin and Mary Hays, but Hamilton's references to Le Vaillant's work make it clear that she sees it as a threatening work. For Hamilton, it is dangerous not only because it is sympathetic to "Hottentots," but because any sort of identification with them runs contrary to emerging imperial ideals.

Hamilton makes her negative feelings about the Frenchman's work abundantly clear when she selects it as the life-changing text for the ridiculous Bridgetina Botherim and her circle of friends.

The day Bridgetina Botherim learns about the "Hottentots" is described as an "auspicious day"—one "of much importance; a day which opened upon her mind the grandest view, the most estatic prospect, that was ever presented to an enlightened imagination" (1:319). Her friend Glib is the one who shows her the light. His reaction to Le Vaillant's account of the Gonoquais "Hottentots" is far more coherent than Bridgetina's:

> his delight and admiration increased at every line, till at length, no longer able to contain his rapture, he ran hastily with the book in his hand to the back parlour, where Bridgetina, who had just then happened to call, was sitting with Mr. Myope and the Goddess of Reason. "See here!" said he, "See here, Citizen Myope, all our wishes fulfilled! All our theory realized! Here is a whole nation of philosophers, all as wise as ourselves! All on the high road to perfectibility! All enjoying the proper dignity of man! Things just as they ought! No man working for another! All alike! All equal! No laws! No government! No coercion! Every one exerting his energies as he pleases! Take a wife to-day: leave her again to-morrow! It is the very essence of virtue, and the quintessence of enjoyment!" (1: 320–21)

Bridgetina also is reduced to expostulations, but she can barely get a completed phrase out of her mouth. She first "cries": "The very ground-work of perfectibility!" (322). Next she "exclaims" before she is interrupted by Glib: "O Learned and amiable Hottentots!" (322). After he reads a passage about their marriages, she again "exclaims": "O enviable state of society, . . . O" (323). A few passages later, Glib reads aloud Le Vaillant's claim that they cannot count past ten to which Bridgetina again "cries": "Astonishing proof of the progress of mind" (326). Myope borrows the book from Glib to read the entire account, and when he is finished he makes a proposal:

> Here, said he, here, my friends, is the place—the only place to which, in this distempered state of civilization, a philosopher can resort with any hopes of comfort. Let us seek an asylum among these kindred souls. Let us form a horde in the neighbourhood of Haabas, and from the deserts of Africa send forth those rays of philosophy which shall enlighten all the habitable globe.

His plan appeared "charming to Bridgetina, who had, no doubt, that among the numerous philosophers of England a party would be formed every way agreeable to her wishes" (330).

5: CHALLENGING THE CONSTRUCTIONS 173

Indeed, so carried away with the idea of her impending emigration to Africa, Bridgetina drops loud hints about the "Hottentots" to Henry, the man she, in her fashion, "determined . . . should be her lover."

> She had not as yet thought proper to drop any hint of the proposed emigration; but by extravagant encomiums on the Hottentots, she sedulously prepared the way; and having prevailed on Henry to peruse the travels of Vaillant, she considered his praises of the work as a sufficient testimony of the impression it had made upon his mind. (2:35)

Bridgetina goes on to imagine her life in paradisical Africa among the "Hottentots" as an "extatic state of bliss! . . . a "dear delirium of delight!" (2:168). But Bridgetina never goes to Africa to live the life she imagined for herself. Indeed, by novel's end she fails even to get married, which is, of course, Hamilton's way of denying her any chance at happiness and a conventional life. Elizabeth Benger's *Memoirs of the Late Mrs. Elizabeth Hamilton* (1818) includes testimony to how the "Hottentotizing" of Bridgetina Botherim did indeed provide a necessary caution to at least one young British woman: "Of the positive good resulting from her work, the author received a most pleasing testimony in a letter from a young women, evidently of superior talents, who confessed she had detected herself in Bridgetina, and instantly abjured the follies and absurdities which created the resemblance.[44]

Maria Edgeworth also launched an attack on Le Vaillant for his generous view of "Hottentots." She makes him the "favourite traveller" of the socially maladjusted Mr. Forester in her *Moral Tales for Young People* (1801).

> Sitting down to dinner, eating, drinking, and behaving like other people, appeared to him difficult and disagreeable ceremonies. He did not perceive that custom had rendered all these things perfectly easy to every one else in company; and as soon as he had devoured his food his own way, he moralized in silence upon the good sense of Sancho Panza, who preferred eating an egg behind the door to feasting in public; and he recollected his favourite traveller, le Vaillant's enthusiastic account of his charming hottentot dinners, and of the disgust that he afterwards felt on the comparison of european etiquette and african simplicity.[45]

It is not a coincidence that Edgeworth's implicit warning about Le Vaillant's vision of the "Hottentots" was made as Pitt's ministry contemplated Britain's role and position in southern Africa. Conservative authors such as Edgeworth and Hamilton foresaw how a romantic notion of the "Hottentots" could be seductive to young men and women caught up in the revolutionary spirit of the times, as well as how it could be counterproductive to maintaining colonial rule.

Le Vaillant's text was also criticized for its focus on the author and its consequential tendency to relate his feelings rather than examine the landscape in a scientific way. John Barrow, whose own travel narratives became very popular, saw in Le Vaillant's work some "valuable matter, and ingenious observations," but he dismissed them as being "so jumbled together with fiction and romance, that none but those who have followed his steps can pretend to separate one from the other."[46] As we will see, Barrow could not embrace Le Vaillant's romantic vision of "Hottentots," nor could he rest easy with what he regarded as the Frenchman's tendency to make himself "an hero on every occasion." Indeed, Barrow's judgment of Le Vaillant on this score is stated quite definitively: "It is sometimes allowable for a traveller to be himself the hero of each little tale, but Monsieur Le Vaillant is an hero on every occasion."[47] Two decades into the nineteenth century, Le Vaillant's narrative was still being criticized for the egotism of the narrator-hero. Despite the fact that she thinks him an "author of veracity," Catherine Hutton complains in 1819 that "There is in Vaillant an air of romance that invalidates his testimony relating to facts; a desire to be thought the hero that lessens his real exploits."[48]

The very fact that Le Vaillant's romantic vision of "Hottentots" earned such a number of strong responses suggests the level to which it threatened a conservative agenda and program for the nation. This is why a periodical like the *Anti-Jacobin; or Weekly Examiner* felt it necessary, for example, to respond to Richard Payne Knight's poem, *The Progress of Civil Society* (1796), which argues that human beings are imperfect, and that the history of mankind is regressive rather than progressive. In a parody of Knight's work, the *Anti-Jacobin* mimics the style of the headings that *The Progress of Civil Society* uses at the start of each of its cantos. Clearly, what is being mocked here is the pretension to such a range of knowledge from an almost unbelievable combination of experiences and sources. The catalog progressively builds up momentum to the "Hottentot" references at the end.

> MARRIAGE being indissoluble, the cause of its being so often unhappy.—Nature's Laws not consulted in this point.—Civilized Nations mistaken.—OTAHEITE—Happiness of the Natives thereof—Visited

5: CHALLENGING THE CONSTRUCTIONS   175

by Captain COOK, in His Majesty's Ship the Endeavour—Character of Captain Cook.—Address to CIRCUMNAVIGATION.—Description of his Majesty's Ship the Endeavour—Mast, Rigging, Sea-sickness, Prow, Poop, Mess-room, Surgeon's Mate—History of Catching a Thunny-fish. Arrival at Otaheite.—Cast Anchor.—Land.—Natives astonished.—Love—Liberty—Moral Nature—Religious—Contrasted with EUROPEAN Manners—Strictness—License—DOCTOR'S COMMONS—Dissolubility of Marriage recommended—Illustrated by a Game at Cards—Whist—Cribbage—Partners changed—Why not the same in Marriage?—Illustrated by a River.—Love free. Priests, Kings.— German Drama.—KOTZEBUE's "Housekeeper Reformed."—To be translated.—Moral.—Employments of House-Keeping described.— HOTTENTOTS sit and stare at each other—Query WHY?—Address to the HOTTENTOTS.—History of the Cape of Good Hope.— Resume of the Arguments against Marriage.—Conclusion.[49]

With their invocation of "Hottentots," the editors of the *Anti-Jacobin* are relying on the prejudice against the "Hottentots" that already existed in their readers' minds.

As we have seen here, the British and continental European authors who challenged the negative constructions of "Hottentots" sometimes had personal and political reasons for doing so. Their voices, however, were so often met with an even louder response that it is possible to see how upsetting their works must have been to those who were more fully invested in demonizing "Hottentots." Indeed, the responses to the revisionist accounts insist on readjusting or resetting the constructions so that they become even more negative than before. The strength of such replies suggests that they are in some ways speaking for the nation as it seeks to define itself against "Hottentots," whether they lived at the Cape of Good Hope or in Britain itself.

6
An Information Age

The second half of the eighteenth century found more British men and women stopping at the Cape of Good Hope than ever before. The rise of natural history and other sciences, the colonial development of India and the founding of Australia as a colony, and, finally, in 1795, Britain's first occupation of the Cape brought them there. Although only a miniscule number of these travelers wrote narratives of their voyages or descriptions of the Cape and its people, those that did left us records that reveal as much, if not more, about themselves than whatever it was they were looking at. Indeed, it is ironic that so much information—or what passed for it—about "Hottentots" was actually disseminated during the second half of the eighteenth century, because by this point in time the actual Cape Khoikhoi were hardly a visible presence in and around Cape Town. Indeed, many travelers, such as George Forster, record their disappointment at not being able to see them: "The Hottentots or aboriginal inhabitants of this country, have retired into the interior parts, and their nearest *kraal* or village, is about a hundred miles from the Cape town . . . We had no opportunity to make new observations upon them, as we only saw a few individuals."[1]

Foster and other British travelers clearly arrived at the Cape with wild expectations about the people they called "Hottentots." John White's *Journal of a Voyage to New South Wales* (1790) suggests how the descriptions of previous travelers influenced his own observations:

> During my residence on shore, whenever I heard of any Hottentots being in town, I made a point of endeavouring to get a sight of them, in order to see whether their manners and appearance corresponded with the description of them given by travellers; such as being besmeared with grease, and decorated with the stinking entrails of animals; on which they likewise, when pressed by hunger, are said to feed.[2]

With images such as these in his mind, it is not surprising that when White actually saw "Hottentots," he found them "offensive" (96–97). Mary Anne Parker's *A Voyage round the World* (1795) makes a similarly dismissive comment, in this case about a "Hottentot" song: "to describe any part of it would be impossible; but, without a wish to offend, I must say that it appeared to me the very reverse of all that is musical and harmonious."[3] These and other later eighteenth-century travel narratives often present familiar representations of "Hottentots," definitively negative and unquestioning of the commonplace assumptions and judgments already made about them.

The very first representation of "Hottentots" written by an Englishwoman was penned by someone who had pretensions to being "a real Traveller." Indeed, the *Monthly Review* called Jemima Kindersley's *Letters from the Island of Teneriffe, Brazil, the Cape of Good Hope, and the East Indies* (1777) "the production of a real Traveller," and praised her for relating "a variety of amusing particulars with much ease and simplicity, and with every mark of fidelity."[4] En route to India to be with her husband, who was in the Royal Artillery, Jemima Kindersley stayed at the Cape for several months in late 1764 and early 1765, although she did not publish her collection of letters until a dozen years later.[5] Kindersley's description of "Hottentots" is included in the fifth letter she wrote at the Cape, dated March 1765. At the start of the letter, she lets slip that she expected to see strangeness: "I have purposely deferred giving you any account of the natives of this country, the Hottentots, till I could be assured that the strange accounts I heard of them were true; my eyes have convinced me that some of them are, and others I have from good authority."[6] The rest of the letter suggests, however, that Kindersley's exposure to "Hottentots" was limited at best, and she certainly does not report anything about them that has not been said before.

What she stresses most is what she sees as the "Hottentot" fondness for "spirituous" liquors. She pronounces it a "vice" the first of several times she mentions it: "Drunkenness and gluttony are the vices to which they are most addicted; having no moderation in either eating or drinking, but whenever it is in their power, indulge themselves in either to the greatest excess" (69). Gender might be a factor in Kindersley's failure to describe the physical stature and proportions of the "Hottenots," but her comments on their dress, cattle breeding, government, and language do not suggest that she had much curiosity about them. Her comments in regard to the debate about whether or not the "Hottentots" worship a god show only a begruding acknowledgment of their humanity: "It is a doubtful point whether they have any notion of a deity, as nothing like a religious ceremony is ever observed amongst them: but most of the Dutch are of opinion that they worship the sun; a very natural conjecture, for although they appear hardly a degree above the brute creation, still one must allow they have the faculty of thinking, consequently must attribute the earth, the sky, and all about them, to some superior power" (70). She calls "truly shocking" their much-reported custom of starving the elderly to death, although she has no way to confirm that such a tradition actually exists. In sum, Kindersley does not challenge any generally held notions about "Hottentots," nor does she seem to feel any special sympathy or generosity towards them.

As befits the wife of a colonial officer, Kindersley's representations are framed by a colonialist mentality rather than any historical or scientific interest. This predisposition is visible toward the end of the letter when she pronounces: "In all other respects they are the most quiet inoffensive people in the world" (71). What she has in mind here is revealed by the concluding paragraph, which confirms that the only "Hottentots" she saw are the ones who serve the Dutch. She gives a relatively positive report of them, yet she finds a way to diminish any compliment by remembering the oft-reported assertion that they will regress if they can.

> They sometimes become servants to the Dutch, and behave perfectly well; their honesty may be depended upon for any thing but liquor, but they have all, both men and women, such a strong natural propensity to intoxication that it is never to be conquered: those who are servants alter their appearance, and dress like slaves, but sometimes return among their own people, and to their own manners. (72)

It is, of course, impossible to know if Kindersley had either the "Cory" story or the history of Van der Stel's youth in mind when she wrote this passage, but these myths clearly hover over her conclusion. Other later eighteenth-century representations of "Hottentots" also suggest a growing colonialist sensibility, although the nation's designs had not yet been set on the Cape. William Macintosh's *Travels in Europe, Asia, and Africa* (1782) shows that he also can envision "Hottentots" as subjects. His word choice highlights the kinds of equations that colonialism sought to make: mild and tractable equals obedient, and quiet and inoffensive earns a ranking of useful: "The *Aborigines* of the country, who are called *Hottentots,* and who are of a mild and tractable disposition, have been easily reduced to the condition of obedient subjects. They are a quiet and inoffensive people, useful to the Dutch in many respects, particularly in the management of flocks and herds of cattle."[7] As we will see in the next chapter, Britain's seizure and occupation of the Cape demanded new constructions of "Hottentots," which are anticipated in this text.

The one truly surprising moment in Kindersley's account occurs in her description of "Hottentot" skin color: she writes that "they are by nature tolerably white, and not unhandsome" (68). Like many previous travelers, Kindersley goes on to explain that "Hottentots" "by degrees become almost jet black" because they grease themselves with oil. She does not explain what she means by the phrase, "tolerably white," but it does suggest her shock that any society would adopt a custom which, in effect, darkens their skin, especially if their complexion is fair enough to be considered white. Certainly, Kindersley's use of the phrases "tolerably white" and "not unhandsome" make visible a connection in her mind between whiteness and handsomeness. Her preference for white skin was shared by many in her society. Three years before the publication of Kindersley's narrative, Oliver Goldsmith's *An History of the Earth and Animated Nature* (1774) articulates the sentiment that white skin is the most "natural" to man: "Of all the colours by which mankind is diversified, it is easy to perceive that ours is not only the most beautiful to the eye, but seems the most advantageous."[8] Clearly, for Goldsmith, Kindersley, and others, white skin became the standard against which all other skin colors were found lacking. Their preference for white skin derived more from cultural and religious forces than any understanding of scientific fact or theory.

In addition to the emergence of British imperial vision, the second half of the eighteenth century marked the start of an information age that was energized by the observations of a select group of travelers. Call them naturalists or people who fancied themselves as such, these men were developing a new vocabulary that allowed them to catalog landscapes in strange and foreign places. This language of biological classification, systematized first by Carl Linnaeus, lent the naturalists a sense of mastery that shows up in their narratives, in relation to both content and style. No longer are fear, shock, or disgust the emotions that drive their descriptions. Their scientific orientation often helped to create and enforce a sense of distance between them and all they were looking at; their busy minds kept their emotions in check, most of the time. The spirit of this new information age is also evident in the frequent publication of encyclopedias and what we might define as textbooks of knowledge that seek to present authoritative and comprehensive visions of the world or of a particular subject. The representations of "Hottentots" in works such as *The Modern Part of an Universal History,* Goldsmith's *The History of the Earth and Animated Nature,* and the *Encyclopaedia Britannica* reflect the new scientfic sensibility, but this does not mean they present information that is accurate and free from bias. Indeed, very much a part of these works is an ethos of superiority and entitlement that is characteristic of those who assume their nation, their race, and their religion represent humanity's highest achievements to date.

John Hawkesworth's *An Account of the Voyages Undertaken by the Order of His Present Majesty for Making Discoveries in the Southern Hemisphere* (London, 1773), which presents the authorized narrative of Captain James Cook's first expedition, represents the first British-authored representation of "Hottentots" that reflects a scientific distance and vision. For example, unlike Kindersley's reaction to "Hottentot" skin greasing, the account in Hawkesworth's volume does not concern itself with making value judgments. Its description says that "their skins are of the same colour of soot, but that is in great measure caused by the dirt, which is so wrought into the grain that it cannot be distinguished from complexion"[9] What is striking about the representations in this text is not only the absence of emotional reactions to "Hottentots," but, at moments, their complimentary nature. For example, a description of "Hottentot" bodies relates that the sailors were impressed with their physique: "These are in general of a slim make, and rather lean than plump, but remarkably strong, nimble, and active. Their size is nearly the same with that of Europeans, as we saw some that were six feet high" (3:789). Characteristic of scientific accounts, other passages also show more of a tendency for neutrality. The representation of the "Hottentot" language underscores its difference and strangeness, but remains free of the gratuitous insults that, as we have seen, are common in British representations of it: "To a European, their language appears to be scarcely articulate; besides which it is distinguished by a very remarkable singularity. At very frequent intervals, while they are speaking, they cluck with the tongue against the roof of the mouth: these clucks do not appear to have any meaning, but rather to divide what they say into sentences" (3:789) This paragraph about language, in fact, concludes with a decided compliment: "Most of these Hottentots speak Dutch, without any peculiarity of pronunciation" (3:790).

More than anything else, Hawkesworth's edition makes clear

that Cook and his men arrived at the Cape with a tremendous curiosity about the "Hottentots." They were not able, however, to observe them as they hoped they could: "Of the natives of this country, we could learn but little except from report; for there were none of their habitations, where alone they retain their original customs, within less than four days journey from the town." The last paragraph, in fact, illustrates how Cook and his party arrived at the Cape with specific questions in mind, especially in relation to female genitalia:

> We were very desirous to determine the great question among the natural historians, whether the women of this country have or have not that fleshy flap or apron which has been called the *Sinus pudoris*, and what we have learnt I shall relate. Many of the Dutch and Malays, who said they had received favours from Hottentots women, positively denied its existence; but a physician of the place declared that he had cured many hundreds of venereal complaints, and never saw one without two fleshy, or rather skinny appendages, proceeding from the upper part of the *Labia*, in appearance somewhat resembling the teats of a cow, but flat; they hung down, he said, before the *Pudendum*, and were in different subjects of different lengths, in some not more than half an inch, in others three or four inches: these he imagined to be what some writers have exaggerated into a flap, or apron, hanging down from the bottom of the abdomen, of sufficient extent to render an artificial covering of the neighbouring parts unnecessary. (792)

Joseph Banks's journal, which remained unpublished for many years but served as one of Hawkesworth's principal source texts, does not include any information about this particular issue.[10] Banks's account does, however, testify to the power of past negative representations and the influence they had on the collective British idea of "Hottentots": "There remains nothing but to say a word or two concerning the Hottentots, so frequently spoken of by travellers, by whom they are generally represented as the outcast of the human species, a race whose intellectual faculties are so little superior to those of beasts, that some have been inclined to suppose them more nearly related to baboons than to men" (439). Banks's use of the word "some" suggests that he does not seem to embrace this notion of "Hottentots."

Banks and the Royal Society played a crucial role in creating the opportunity for the next British-authored account of the Cape. Indeed, on Banks's recommendation, King George III sent Francis Masson (1741–1805), born in Scotland but working as a gardener at Kew, on a two-year mission to the Cape in order to collect plants and seeds. Masson sailed from England on Cook's *Resolution*, arriving in Cape Town on 30 October 1772, and he soon began the first extensive inland tours of the country by a British subject. Masson returned to England in 1775, and wrote a fifty-page report of his "Botanical Travels" that was published in the *Philosophical Transactions of the Royal Society* (1776). The title of Masson's document well represents its main focus of interest, but he does include descriptions of "Hottentots." In fact, the kind of notice he takes of them seems determined by the level of their activity or subservience. At Lange Kloof, for example, Masson appears to think that servant "Hottentots" are better off than free ones. Servitude defines the existence of most of the "Hottentots" he sees: "The Hottentots are in general servants to the Dutch farmers; who give them wages, beads, and tobacco mixed with hemp; the latter, which intoxicates them, they are extremely fond of. A few free Hottentots still remain here, who live in their ancient manner; but who are miserable wretches, having hardly any stock of cattle."[11] Masson's comment on the "few free Hottentots" he sees is noteworthy because it suggests he connects their freedom with their misery. As we have seen, the general French construction and the one held by those in Britain with romantic sensibilities embraced the opposite point of view, idealizing the "Hottentot" lifestyle for the purity of its free and "natural" existence.

About three weeks after stopping in Lange Kloof, Masson arrived at a village of Gunaquas "Hottentots" whose activity and bravery prompted him to pay greater attention to them. Now he takes the time to describe them physically: "These Hottentots were remarkably well-shaped, and stouter made than any other Hottentots I have yet seen. They are also very bold in encountering wild beasts, particularly the lion, which often attacks their folds, and makes great havock" (294). His description of their bodies, especially of male genitalia, is free of condescending commentary and the use of subjective language:

> These Hottentots were all cloathed in *crosses,* or mantles, made of the hides of oxen, which they dress in a particular manner, making them as pliant as a piece of cloth: they wore the hairy side outwards. Their breast, belly, and thighs, were naked, except being crossed by a number of leathern straps round their middle. They had no other covering for their private parts, than a muzzle of leather exactly covering the extremity of the *penis,* and suspended by a leathern thong from their girdle, which was commonly ornamented with brass rings. (295)

Interestingly, Masson's observations of the females do not include any attempt to answer the "great question" about them: "The women were dressed almost in the same taste, except that a great number of small thongs of leather, suspended from their girdle, reached down to their knees, and in some measure concealed their nakedness" (295–96). What we find in Masson's *Botanical Travels* (1776) is that his interest in "Hottentots" is a dispassionate one.

William Paterson followed Masson into the interior. Paterson's patroness, the countess of Strathmore, sent him to the Cape to study botany. He spent three years there, making four separate tours into the interior from 1777 to 1779, traveling more than five thousand miles.[12] It took Paterson a decade to produce his *Narrative of Four Journeys into the Country of the Hottentots and Caffraria, 1777–1779* (1789), which is the first British-authored, book-length narrative devoted entirely to a description of Cape region. It was a popular work; a second edition was published soon after the first. Its importance in relation to representations of "Hottentots," however, is compromised by Paterson's extensive borrowing from Anders Sparrman's *A Voyage to the Cape of Good Hope*, which had appeared in an English edition in 1785. The only information in Paterson's narrative about "Hottentots" is a seven-page long footnote taken verbatim from Sparrman's work.[13]

Paterson's prefatory material suggests his own view of the "Hottentots," however. Significantly, it is far different from both Masson's and Sparrman's in that it seems to embrace quite a romantic view of "Hottentots" as "noble savages."

> The admirer of Nature has, in this country, a wide field for investigation: here he will discover objects amply sufficient to satisfy the most inquisitive taste: here he will find every object, simple and unadorned; and will behold, in the uncivilized Hottentot, those virtues, which he, perhaps, sought for in civilized society in vain. (3)

The narrative itself, however, contradicts the romantic spirit of the preface, a result, no doubt, of Paterson's dependence on Sparrman's work. Paterson was wise to make use of it.

Sparrman's credentials as a scientist—he had been one of Linnaeus's favorite students, and served as a medical doctor and professor of Physic at Stockholm—clearly helped his work to win such a positive reception. Also, he was a good friend to the British Royal Society. The English translation of his travel narrative, entitled *A Voyage to the Cape of Good Hope* (1785), proved to be extremely successful and influential from almost the moment it appeared. Indeed, Sparrman's work received so much praise that a review in the *Gentleman's Magazine* growled, "we cannot think it has all the merit that is ascribed to it.[14]

Sparrman's champions praised him partly by reflecting on the weaknesses of previously published accounts of "Hottentots."

> The extravagance, obscurity, and contradictions which are met with in authors concerning the people who inhabit the southern extremity of Africa, have induced us to extend the preceding extract to an unusual length. We have every reason which the case admits of for believing the Author to be an honest man; he appears to have been very industrious in his researches; and he certainly had greater opportunities, and has written more from his own immediate observation than any former writers.[15]

These compliments are, for the most part, justified. Barbara Stafford considers Anders Sparrman representative of the men who wrote the "illustrated factual travel accounts" that were becoming popular at this point in the eighteenth century. She draws a link between the scientific minds of the authors and the style of their narratives. Stafford sees in Sparrman an "asserted readiness to perceive the environment at first hand is clearly founded on an awareness of scientific method in which each concrete item is made to expose its material qualities and made to contribute to the knowledge of objective reality."[16]

Sparrman's descriptions of "Hottentots" were clearly of particular interest to later eighteenth-century British readers. With Kolb's work discredited by this point in time, they were looking for a reliable substitute and, to a great extent, they found it in Sparrman's work. In the preface to the volume, the editor and translator of the first English edition, probably George Forster, explains why this text is deserving of authority: "Physician, naturalist, and philosopher, neither human manners, nor civil institutions, rural oeconomy, nor police, nothing, in fine, escapes the keenness of his observation. Never relying on the relations of others, except when it is impossible for him to do otherwise, he sees every thing with his own eyes, and trusts only to the report of his own senses: and at the same time knows perfectly well (which is never the case with the ignorant traveller) both how to see and what to look for."[17] The point of this last phrase, that Sparrman "knows perfectly well . . . both how to see and what to look for," well captures the attention and privilege given to scientific authority in this information age.

Sparrman himself recognized that travelers had different skill levels at observation and representation. In his own introductory remarks, he, somewhat facetiously, tells readers what they will not find in his narrative, and in so doing he makes a serious comment about previous European constructions of "Hottentots": "Men with one foot, indeed, Cyclops, Syrens, Troglodytes, and such like imaginary beings, have almost entirely disappeared in this enlightened age. At the same time, however, many have been hitherto induced to give credit to tales almost as marvellous, with which authors, who have before me visited and described the Hottentots, have seasoned their relations, in order to make them go down the better with the public. So that the reader must not be surprised to find my accounts frequently differ much from those of various of my predecessors" (xv–xvi).

In comparison to previously published British accounts, Sparrman's representations of "Hottentots" seem emotionally distant. He tends to look at them in the same way he looks at the landscape all around him. For example, Sparrman's description of their use of a herbal ointment does not, as so many seventeenth- and early-eighteenth-century British representations do, emphasize so emphatically his own reaction to how "Hottentots" smell. Also, his use of a scientific vocabulary lends the prose an authority that serves to reinforce the distance between the observer and the observed.

> Besides the pleasure the Hottentots enjoy in besmearing their bodies from head to foot, they likewise perfume them with a powder of herbs, with which they powder both their heads and bodies, rubbing it in all over them when they besmear themselves. The odour of it is at the same time rank and aromatic *(Narcotico seu papaverino spirans)* and seems to come nearest to that of the poppy mixed with spices. The plants used for this purpose are various species of the *diosma,* called by the Hottentots *bucku,* and considered by them as possessing great virtues in curing disorders. Some of these species are very common round about the Cape; but one particular sort, which I am told grows about *Goud's-rivier,* is said to be so valuable, that no more than a thimble full of it is given in exchange for a lamb. (184)

This passage also provides a good illustration of how Sparrman's focus easily shifts from "Hottentot" to the landscape. This tendency is perhaps what prompts Mary Louise Pratt to see Sparrman's work as advancing "colonialist interests."[18] She believes that he "deterritorializes" the people of the Cape: "As the Khoikhoi are deterritorialized—extracted from the landscape in which they still live—they are thus taken out of economy, culture, and history too."[19] To be sure, Sparrman's main interest is not in the people who live in the region. His work is not, however, the first to "deterritorialize" the Cape people from their land. As we have seen, English sailors had been doing that since the early seventeenth century.

While Sparrman clearly does not feel any eagerness to champion "Hottentot" society, he also does not rush to condemn it. Indeed, at times he finds a way to compliment "Hottentot" products, without sounding like a "Hottentot" enthusiast or apologist the way Kolb does. For example, "Hottentot" shoes had a tremendous appeal to him. After providing details of them, he describes their advantages for anyone, "Hottentot" or European, who might wear them: "They sit as neat upon the foot as a stocking, and at the same time preserve their form. They are easily kept soft and pliable. . . . They are extremely light and cool. . . . They wear very well, as they are without any seam, or rather bottoms of the shoes, are both tough and yielding" (80). Sparrman's discussion of "Hottentot" shoes concludes with a justification for his tribute to them, which suggests his scientific sense and practicality: "I have brought home with me a pair of them, that I wore in my expedition into the country, that they may serve for a model, in case any body should be inclined to have a pair made by making a trial of them. Whatever is useful, whether it come from *Paris* or the country of the *Hottentots*, alike deserves our attention and imitation" (81).

Sparrman's observations of "Hottentot" genitalia also shows his awareness of previously printed descriptions. Before he presents his own representation, however, he, somewhat self-consciously, comments on those that were already available to readers.

> Notwithstanding the respect I bear to the more delicate part of my readers, the notoriety of the fact prevents me from passing over in this place those parts of the body, which our more scrupulous, but less natural manners forbid me to describe any ways than by the means of circumlocution, Latin terms, or other uncouth, and to most readers, unintelligible denominations and expedients. But those who affect this kind of reserve must pardon me, if I cannot wrap up matters with the nicety their modesty requires; as my duty obliges me to show how much the world has been misled, and the Hottentot nation been misrepresented; in as much as the Hottentot women have been described, and believed to be, in respect to their sexual parts, monsters by nature; and that the men were made such by a barbarous customs. It has been thought, for example, that these latter were, at the age of ten years, by a kind of castration, deprived of one of those organs which nature gives to every male, as being absolutely necessary for the propagation of his species; and that the former, or the women, have before their privy parts a natural veil or covering, a circumstance unheard of in females in any other part of the globe. (182)

These tortured sentences are of interest for two reasons: they consciously acknowledge female readers; and they, perhaps not with that same level of awareness, show how the genitalia of "Hottentots" came to serve in a synecdoche-like fashion to represent the whole of them. This is consistent with what Frantz Fanon believes happens when "the white man" considers the Negro: "one is no longer aware of the Negro but only of a penis; the Negro is eclipsed. He is turned into a penis. He *is* a penis."[20]

Sparrman's own description of "Hottentot" genitalia is as direct and definitive as possible.

> The men are at present by no means monorchides, though, perhaps the time has been when they were so . . . The women have no parts uncommon to the rest of their sex; but the *clitoris* and *nymphae*, particularly of those who are past their youth, are in general pretty much elongated; a peculiarity which undoubtedly has got footing in this nation, in consequence of the relaxation necessarily produced by the method they have of besmearing their bodies, their slothfulness, and the warmth of the climate. (182)

Sparrman's remarks did not end the public discussion of this subject, but the authority his text was granted resolved the question for many. One manifestation of his work's influence might well be that after its publication the British, to some extent, lessened their focus on what they called the female "organs of generation" and began to lampoon the buttocks of "Hottentot" women instead. Indeed, the case of the "Hottentot" Venus shows that the British found a way to continue to demonize the bodies of "Hottentot" females.

While it is certainly fair to see Sparrman's depiction of "Hottentots" as more scientific than not, this does not mean that it presents what some might be tempted to call a neutral or objective picture, if, indeed, such a thing is possible. It is clear throughout that Sparrman views and judges "Hottentots" as "unconstrained" and "rude" in comparison with Europeans; he often sets them up as the direct opposite of Europeans. This evaluation is evident, for example, in his description of their huts, where an unspoken point of comparison shows he uses European size as his standard.

> The highest of them are so low, that even in the center of the arch, it is scarcely possible for a middle-sized man to stand upright. But neither the lowness thereof, nor that of the door, which is but just three feet high, can perhaps be considered evidence as any inconvenience to a Hottentot, who finds no difficulty in stooping and crawling on all

fours, and who is at any time more inclined to lie down than stand. (195)

After a short explanation about the fireplaces, this part of the description concludes with a remark that shows that Sparrman could resort to using the same tendency for condescension and exaggeration as did less-educated Europeans. An animal simile he includes in his description of a "Hottentot" in his hut is especially striking.

> The door, low as it is, is the only place that lets in the day-light; and at the same time, the only outlet that is left for the smoke. The Hottentot, inured to it from his infancy, sees it hover round him, without feeling the least inconvenience arising from it to his eyes; while, rolled up like a hedge-hog, and wrapped up snug in his skin, he lies at the bottom of his hut, in the midst of this cloud, except that he is now and then obliged to peep out from beneath his sheep-skin, in order to stir the fire, or perhaps to light his pipe, or else sometimes turn the steak he is broiling over the coals. (196)

Despite the fact that Sparrman does not rank the "Hottentots" as the lowest of all human societies or use subjective words like "nasty" and "beastly" to describe them, his narrative reminds us that scientific minds are not necessarily free of the prejudices of their time.

Charles Peter Thunberg, a Swedish botanist, produced a narrative based on his residence at the Cape that English readers also enjoyed. Thunberg's account demonstrates much less scientific distance than Sparrman's work. Thunberg's *Travels in Europe, Africa, and Asia, Made between the Years 1770 and 1779* (London, 1793) appeared in three editions between 1793 and 1795. The *Annual Register* quoted extensively from it in 1793, and at the start of the nineteenth century, John Pinkerton included it in his collection of travel narratives. Thunberg made a number of trips into the interior, and these explorations convinced him that the "Hottentots" were a dying people: "As far as I had an opportunity of travelling last summer, both to the northward and eastward, in this extensive country, I met with but small remains of the once more or less numerous Hottentot nations, which, as late as the beginning of this century, still inhabited these vast plains."[21] Although Thunberg correctly understood what was happening to the "Hottenotots," he had little sympathy for them. His account is full of negative images and value-laden conclusions: "In a people so deeply plunged in sloth, and so overwhelmed with filth, as the Hottentots actually are, one would not expect to find the least trace of pride. It is however to be found even among these, the most wretched of the human race; for they not only adorn their bodies with all manner of finery as they conceive it to be; but when they are visited by strangers, paint their faces with various figures of brown and black paint."[22] Thunberg's depiction of "Hottentots" completely counters the "noble savages" championed by Le Vaillant in his *Travels into the Interior Parts of Africa* (1790) and *New Travels into the Interior Parts of Africa* (1796).

Throughout the second half of the eighteenth century, the British reading public also had access to other translations of foreign-authored travel narratives that included descriptions of the Cape, if not the "Hottentots." Several French narratives were very popular in Britain. Louis de Bougainville's *A Voyage round the World* appeared in English in 1772, and there were two editions of Jacques Henri Bernardin de Saint-Pierre's travel narrative over the course of twenty-five years.[23] Le Vaillant's two narratives were available in multiple editions throughout the 1790s. An English translation of a Dutch account written by John Splinter Stavorinus was published in 1798, and Bartholomaeo a Sancto Paulinus's 1796 travel narrative, translated first from the original Italian into German in 1798, appeared in English in 1800.[24]

Later eighteenth-century geography books demonstrate how the more scientific and colonialist travel narratives could help to ameliorate, at least somewhat, the negativity of representations of "Hottentots." Two of the most popular geography books of the time were Richard Brookes's *The General Gazetteer: Or, Compendious Geographical Dictionary* (1762) and William Guthrie's *A New Geographical, Historical, and Commercial Grammar* (1770). Brookes's *General Gazetteer* remained in active circulation from its first edition in 1762 through its eighteenth edition in 1827, and nineteenth-century editions based on it were published as late as 1842. Since the initial editions appeared decades before the scientific narratives were translated into English, they present descriptions of "Hottentots" that are in keeping with earlier depictions. The opening sentences of the first edition relate the traditional construction:

> The Hottentots are reckoned the nastiest people in the known world, and they have little or no religion. They are not so black as the negroes, and yet appear so, because they daub themselves with grease mixed with soot. All their dress consists in a skin which they throw on their shoulders, and a clout to hide their nakedness, but the women are provided with one by nature, of a considerable length, and in this they differ from all other women of the world.[25]

An "enumeration" of the "Hottentots" strange customs follows. Predictably, it tells familiar stories also. The second and third editions of Brookes's *Gazetteer,* published in 1766 and 1773 respectively, include slightly shorter, but equally negative, representations. Evidence suggests that the editors of the fourth through the seventh (London) editions of the *Gazetteer* (published in 1778, 1782, 1786, 1791) planned to include a separate entry for "Hottentots" in the "H" pages, as all mention of them is deleted from the Cape of Good Hope entry, but no representation does, in fact, appear in these editions.

A 1791 seventh edition published in Dublin includes a description of "Hottentots" on the "H" pages, as "Hottentots, the Country of the." It presents a much different picture from what was reported in earlier editions; in this one the focus seems to be on the "Hottentots' " relation to the Dutch colonial power.

> The natives live by grazing cattle, hunting, and fishing. They are allowed by the Dutch to have their own laws and customs, but are obliged to furnish their settlements with cattle, and assist them in their husbandry, &.c for which they receive provisions, brandy, tobacco & c.[26]

The Dublin edition also presents a description of "Hottentot" bodies that is different from the earlier editions, especially in reference to their skin color: "The men are of a moderate stature, the women small and of a black complexion."[27] Aside from this description of their appearance, the editors included well-known details about the customs and lifestyle of "Hottentots," especially in regard to their sexual habits ("all ages and sexes lie promiscuously"), their abandonment of their elderly parents and female infants, their religious customs, and their male initiation rituals.

A 1794 eighth edition published in London marks an important turning point for Brookes's *Gazetteer.* It reinstates a section on "Hottentots" in the "H" section. Significantly, this new description is based primarily on the information communicated in four late-eighteenth-century travel narratives, those by Sparrman, Paterson, Caille, and Le Vaillant. Following the travelers' lead, the 1794 edition of Brookes's *Gazetteer* does not attempt to make any sort of summary statement about "Hottentots" or proclaim them, as the first edition did, "the nastiest people in the known world." What we generally have here is a more neutral presentation of data, although at key moments a subjective and judgmental sentence or phrase communicates the common assumption that "Hottentots" are inferior people. This is evident at the end of the opening section, most of which is borrowed from Sparrman: "In fine, with respect to their shape, carriage, and every motion, their whole appearance indicates health and content. In their mien, moreover, a degree of carelessness is observable, that discovers marks of alacrity and resolution; qualities which, upon occasion, they certainly can exhibit."[28]

It is noteworthy that the editors of the *General Gazetteer* also consciously and deliberately shaped their own presentation of "Hottentots" by arranging and sometimes deleting sentences from their source materials in order to present either a more negative depiction or make a larger and more universal point. For example, they include a digression on female vanity from Abbé de la Caille's *Journal historique du voyage fait au Cap de Bonne-Espérance* (1763) that not only makes "Hottentot" women seem ridiculous, but is condescending to females generally.

> Such of the women, moreover, as are ambitious to please, adorn themselves with necklaces of shells: "for even in this country," says the abbé de la Caille, "the sex have their charms, which they endeavour to heighten by such arts as are peculiar to themselves, and would meet with little success elsewhere. To this end, they not only grease all the naked parts of their body, to make them shine, but they braid or plait their hair as an additional elegance. A Hottentot lady, thus bedizened, has exhausted all the arts of her toilette; and however unfavorable nature may have been to her, with regard to shape and stature, her pride is wonderfully flattered, while the splendour of her appearance gives her the highest degree of satisfaction.[29]

Immediately following this discussion of vanity, the editors present a statement that is, no doubt, intended as a warning to British women to remember their modesty: " 'Among the Hottentots', says Dr. Sparrman, 'as well as, in all probability, among the rest of mankind, dispersed over the whole globe, we must acknowledge the fair sex to be the most modest; for the females of this nation cover themselves much more scrupulously than the men.' "[30]

There is another substantive change in the 1794 edition, this in relation to "Hottentot" religiosity. Brookes's initial editions said they have "little or no religion," but here they are characterized as having no religion and, even more crucially, as not being interested in adopting one: "With respect to the Hottentots, in general, none of them seem to have any religion . . . nor do they appear willing to receive any instruction."[31] Signficantly, "Hottentots" began to be represented as capable of adopting Christianity after 1795, the year of the first British occupation of the Cape. In the 1794 edition, however, they are represented as having a belief in magic rather than religion: "All of them, however, have the firmest opinion in the power of magic; whence it might be inferred, that they believe in an evil being, analogous to what we call the devil; but they pay no religious worship to him."[32]

The 1794 edition makes a point of expanding its coverage of "Hottentots" to include those who live in interior sections of the country, courtesy of the later eighteenth-century travel narratives. Sparrman's negative description of the nomadic lifestyle of "Boshman [sic] Hottentot" is quoted almost verbatim. Interestingly, this description anticipates Britain's nineteenth-century election of the Bushmen to replace the "Hottentots" as humanity's most beast-like society: "As ignorant of agriculture as apes or monkies, they are obliged, like them, to wander over hills and dales, after certain wild roots, berries, and plants, which they eat raw."[33] In light of later revisions, it is also very significant that the 1794 edition awards a brief and positive mention to the Dutch colonists: "The whole of this country is naturally barren and mountainous; but the industrious Dutch have overcome all natural difficulties, and it produces, not only a sufficiency of all the necessaries of life for the inhabitants, but also for the refreshment of all the European ships that touch here."[34] As we will see, complimentary remarks about the Dutch colonists ceased once Britain gained control of the Cape.

A 1796 London abridgment of Brookes's *General Gazetteer* presents a considerably shorter account of the Cape "Hottentots" that is taken verbatim, but with substantial deletions, from the 1794 edition. The abridgment makes use of the sources without attributing the information to them, and it deletes comparisons to other native peoples as well as the section about female vanity. Significantly, the entry concludes with Sparrman's description of "Hottentot" huts, including the sentence with the animal simile: "The Hottentot, inured to it from his infancy, sees it hover round him, without feeling the least inconvenience arising from it to his eyes; while, rolled up like a hedge-hog, and wrapped up snug in his skin, he lies at the bottom of his hut, in the midst of this cloud, except that he is now and then obliged to peep out from beneath his sheep-skin, in order to stir the fire, or perhaps to light his pipe, or else sometimes turn the steak he is broiling over the coals."[35]

The 1797 tenth edition of Brookes's text acknowledges the British seizure of the Cape territory: "This fine Dutch colony surrendered by capitulation to the British arms, under general Alured Clarke and admiral Sir George Keith Elphinstone, September 16, 1795."[36] The description of "Hottentots, Country of the" is only slightly different from the one appearing in the 1794 eighth edition. Le Vaillant's representations of the Bushmen are deleted from the section, and the quotation from de la Caille's representation about the vanity of "Hottentot" women disappears as well, although it reappears, without attribution, in some later editions. The descriptions of the "Hottentot" huts and lifestyle remain unchanged, and the assertion that they have no religion, "nor do they appear willing to receive any instruction" appears as well. The eleventh through the seventeenth editions of *The General Gazetteer*, published 1800–1820, also adhere generally to the 1794 text. As we will see, editions published after the British colonial project began in the Cape colony are revised to reflect specific imperial and colonial concerns.

William Guthrie's *A New Geographical, Historical and Commercial Grammar* also shows the influence of the late-eighteenth-century narratives. First published in 1770, soon after the author's death, it appeared in nineteen editions by 1801, with five more released during the opening decades of the new century.[37] The earliest editions of Guthrie's work do not include any specific chapter devoted to the Cape of Good Hope and its people. They are, however, singled out for particularly negative notice in the last paragraph of a section, "OF AFRICA, from the Tropic of Cancer to the Cape of Good Hope."

> The history of this continent is little known, and probably affords no materials which deserve to render it more so. We know from the antients, who sailed a considerable way round the coasts, that the inhabitants were in the same rude situation 2000 years ago in which they are at present, that is, they had nothing of humanity about them but the form. This may either be accounted for by supposing that nature has placed some insuperable barrier between the natives of this division of Africa and the inhabitants of Europe, or that the former, being so long accustomed to a savage manner of life, and degenerating from one age to another, at length became altogether incapable of making any progress in civility or science. It is very certain that all the attempts of the Europeans, particularly of the Dutch at the Cape of Good Hope, have been hitherto ineffectual for making the least impression on these savage mortals, or giving them the least inclination or even idea of the European manner of life.[38]

This representation remained in place until the fourteenth edition appeared in 1794.

The 1794 edition presents a radically different picture of "Hottentots," principally because Le Vaillant's first narrative, which appeared in English in 1790, is extensively quoted in an entirely new chapter devoted to the "Country of the Hottentots." In fact, Le Vaillant's description of his thirty-six hour stay with the Gonaqua "Hottentots" is all that is presented in the chapter. At one point he makes a comparison between the Gonaqua and the Cape "Hottentots": "These people [the Gonaqua] did not resemble those degenerated and miserable Hottentots, who pine in the heart of the Dutch colonies, contemptible and despised inhabitants, who bear no marks of their ancient origin but an empty name; and who enjoy, at the expense of their liberty, only a little peace, purchased at a dear rate, by the excessive labour to which they are subjected on the plantations; and by the despotism of their chiefs, who are always sold to government."[39]

For this chapter's conclusion, the editors of *A New Geographical, Historical and Commercial Grammar* (1794) selected a paragraph from Le Vaillant's work that bluntly articulates his romantic French vision of "Hottentots."

> They are, however, (observes M. Vaillant) the best, the kindest, and the most hospitable of people. Whoever travels among them may be assured of finding food and lodging; and though they will receive presents, yet they never ask for any thing. If the traveller has a long journey to accomplish, and if they learn from the information he requires that there are no hopes of his soon meeting with other hordes, that which he is going to quit supply him with provisions as far as their circumstances will allow, and with every thing else necessary for his continuing his journey, and reaching the place of his destination. Such are these people, or at least such did they appear to me, in all the innocence of manners, and of a pastoral life. They excite the idea of mankind in a state of infancy.[40]

Such an extraordinary conclusion to the chapter suggests two things about the editors of *A New Geographical, Historical and Commercial Grammar*. Firstly, they were bold. Secondly, they were perceptive. They understood that British constructions of "Hottentots" were now open to some revision. It is important to remember that they made their editorial decisions before they and the rest of the nation could have known that British forces would soon be occupying Cape Town. Significantly, the editors of subsequent editions would not be so loyal to Le Vaillant; they replaced his text with a British-authored one soon after it became available to them.

Encyclopedias contributed to the new information age in ways that travel narratives and collections could not. The editors of these works gave themselves (and were generally granted) the authority to write what often became the accepted version of "truth." They did this partly by setting themselves up as the arbiters of travel narratives and other texts. For example, the "General Description of Africa" that begins the Africa volumes of *The Modern Part of an Universal History* (1760) calls into question the veracity of travel narratives: "And hence it is that we have hitherto been able to gain only so imperfect a knowledge of the inland parts of this vast continent, notwithstanding the vast number of authors who have attempted to give us more ample accounts of it; but who, by their pretended histories, descriptions, relations, memoirs, voyages, observations, and other as pompous as voluminous works, have rather helped to bewilder and benight their readers."[41] The editors of *The Modern Part of an Universal History* (1760) or the *Encyclopaedia Britannica* (1771) or any other late-eighteenth-century textbook of learning felt that they could "Survey mankind, from China to Peru," because their nation's boats predominated on the seas and because they took themselves and their literary projects seriously. In other words, their confidence is heightened by their sense of literary, racial, national, and geographic superiority. Their condescension in regard to Africans testifies to their Eurocentric and racialist, if not racist, perspective.

The chapter devoted to "Hottentots" in *The Modern Part of an Universal History* (1760) does not present any new information about them. The stated conclusion that "Hottentots" are the lowest of all African and human societies confirms what had been said previously by others: "no country or climate that we know of, hath as yet been able to make any change for the better in the subjects of that ungrateful republic; and that with respect to those *Hottentots* who live under the dominion of the *Dutch* company here, their condition is the most wretched and miserable not only of their whole nation, but, we may safely add, of all the *Africans*.[42] Although the editors quote Kolb's *The Present State of the Cape of Good Hope* (1731) throughout the entry, they clearly did not adopt his more open and generous view of "Hottentots." The representation of the "Hottentot" language serves as a good case in point. By deleting some phrases and conflating others, the editors undermine its validity as a language, which Kolb's work certainly does not do.

Present State (Kolb)
Their language is certainly a Composition of the strangest sounds that ever were utter'd by any People. Some will have it, that 'tis easily acquir'd by Strangers in all its Compass: Others, that it can never be acquir'd by a Stranger. Some look upon it as the Disgrace of Speech; others deny it the Name, as having Nothing of Sound or Articulation that is peculiar to Man in it, but resembling, say they, the Noise of irritated Turkey-cocks the Chattering of Magpies and the Hooting of Owls. And Dapper in particular says, 'tis disagreable to an European to hear it, much more to learn it. (31–32)

The Modern Part of an Universal History
Their language is a composition of the strangest and most disagreeable sounds, deemed by many the disgrace of speech, without human sound or articulation, resembling rather the noise of irritated turkies, the chattering of magpyes, and whooting of owls, justly considered the monster of languages, attainable only by youth, and children born in the country, and never to be acquired by strangers, the sound depending on extraordinary vibrations, inflexions, and clashing of the tongue against the palate.[43]

The editors of *The Modern Part of an Universal History* tend to overstate negative images of "Hottentots," which testifies to their use of "Hottentots" as the negative foil for British (or western European) society. "Hottentots" are depicted as being "sensible of the noble fruits reaped from industry by *Europeans*," but they are berated as being "the most lazy people in the universe: neither sex pares the nails of fingers or toes: they esteem thinking as labour, and, abhorring both as capital plagues, pass three parts in four of their lives with amazing stupidity in shameful idleness."[44]

The foil role assigned to "Hottentots" is even clearer at the chapter's end, when the editors ironically present a "Hottentot" view of the Dutch colonists.

> How much freer, happier, and nobler, is our race, who can range at will under the whole cope of heaven, wherever our wants or inclinations lead us, and find everywhere a rich supply ready prepared for us by the kind hand of nature, without our care of labour, who want neither storehouses nor magazines to secure our provisions and properties, nor castle and high walls to protect us and our families, but can live and sleep safe and fearless in our low huts or caves, or even under the open canopy of the skies, eat, drink, smoak, sing, and dance, race, hunt, and pursue every pleasure of life unrestrained and uncontrouled, whilst even our superfluities, and what would otherwise lie ne-

glected and despised by us, are more than sufficient to attract those mercenary and indigent slaves to come so far to purchase them from us, and bring us, in exchange for them, all that their country, art, or industry, produces, that may contribute to our use, our ornament, or delight.[45]

To ensure an unambiguous conclusion, however, the editors abandon irony and return to their most authoritative voice in a final section that serves to demonize other Africans in addition to "Hottentots":

Thus they think, and thus they balance the account between them and their masters; which, however strange and rhapsodical it may appear to us, we are assured, from a multitude of authentic witnesses, is the common language, not only of the Hottentots, but of the generality of the Africans, even of those, who, through the tyranny of the government they live under, are doomed to a still worse state of slavery and misery, and without those real advantages which this Hottentot nation enjoys to countenance their fond conceit, that they are the happiest and noblest, and the Europeans the most miserable and abject people that the sun shines upon.[46]

The echo of Edward Terry's early-seventeenth-century narrative in the last sentence is indicative of how the most common constructions of "Hottentots" remained current throughout the seventeenth and eighteenth centuries.

According to George S. Rousseau, the British reading public's hearty appetite for works of natural history developed in the second half of the eighteenth century. He argues that their particular fondness for Oliver Goldsmith's *An History of the Earth and Animated Nature* (1774) demonstrates how readers could embrace a work which might not pass critical muster.[47] Goldsmith had "Hottentots" in mind at several points in the work. His description of the breasts of Negro women recalls the illustration in Herbert's narrative: "The women's breasts, after bearing one child, hang down below the navel; and it is customary with them, to suckle the child at their backs, by throwing the beast over the shoulder. As their persons are thus naturally deformed, at least to our imaginations, their minds are equally incapable of strong exertions. The climate seems to relax their mental powers still the more than those of the body; they are, therefore, in general, found to be stupid, indolent, and mischievous" (228). Goldsmith's most lengthy discussion of "Hottentots" is located in a section devoted to "Quadrupedes of the Cow Kind," where he explains that they, more than any other society, "esteem" their bison. Indeed, Goldsmith's quite ridiculous description constructs "Hottentots" as being on the same level as their animals: "But it is among the Hottentots where these animals are chiefly esteemed, as being more than commonly serviceable. They are their fellow domestics, the companions of pleasures and fatigues; the cow is at once the Hottentot's protector and servant, assists him in attending his flocks, and guarding them against every invader . . . The backely lives in the same cottage with its master, and, by long habit, gains an affection for him; and in proportion as the man approaches the brute, so the brute seems to attain even to some share of human sagacity."[48] If passages like these are ones that helped Goldsmith's work to be such a popular success, we should not think the general public's interest in natural history reflected much scientific intelligence or sophistication.

Ironically, the encyclopedia that hoped to appeal to the more highly educated reader, the *Encyclopaedia Britannica* (1771), did not enjoy as much success as Goldsmith's work. It touted itself, however, as the most authoritative British encyclopedia of the century. Interestingly, the first edition does not even include a separate entry for "Hottentots." There is, however, a definition for "Caffraria," which names it as "the country of the Caffers, or Hottentots, in the most southerly port of Africa." The Dutch, however, are the only people acknowledged in it: "Most of the sea-coasts of this country are subject to the Dutch, who have built a fort near the most southern promontory, called the Cape of Good Hope."[49] The third edition of the *Encyclopaedia Britannica* (1797) was revised to include a separate entry for "Hottentots." While much of this eight-page-long section focuses on describing the native inhabitants, a description of the land is provided and compliments are paid to the colony the Dutch developed there: "It is naturally barren and mountainous; but the industry of the Dutch hath overcome all natural difficulties, and it now produces not only a sufficiency of all necessaries of life for the inhabitants, but also for the refreshment of all the Europeans who pass and repass that way."[50] Curiously, no mention is made of the September 1795 British seizure and occupation of the Cape, which suggests that the section was completed a few years before the publication of the third edition.

In its representation of "Hottentots," the editors of the *Encyclopaedia Britannica* make a decided effort to debunk many of the most negative seventeenth- and early-eighteenth-century descriptions of them. They succeed in doing so partly because they quote from the recent scientific narratives, specifically those by Forster,

Sparrman, Paterson, and Le Vaillant, and also because they repeatedly challenge earlier accounts. The discussion of the "Hottentot" language provides a good example of their method of attack. First they quote a source directly, in this case it is *The Modern Part of an Universal History,* and then they call it into question. Unbeknownst to the editors of the *Britannica,* this passage also shows them making their own mistake about the society's name.

> The natives of this country are called *Hottentots,* in their own language; a word of which it is vain to inquire the meaning, since the language of this country can scarce be learned by any other nation. The Hottentot language is indeed said to be a composition of the strangest and most disagreeable sounds, deemed by many the disgrace of speech, without human sound or articulation, resembling rather the noise of irritated turkies, the chattering of magpyes, and whooting of owls, justly considered the monster of languages, attainable only by youth, and children born in the country, and never to be acquired by strangers, the sound depending on extraordinary vibrations, inflexions, and clashing of the tongue against the palate.—If this account is true, however, it is obvious, that all the relations we have concerning the religion & c. of the Hottentots derived from themselves, must fail to the ground, as nobody can pretend to understand a language in itself unintelligible. The manners and customs of those people, however, are easily observable, whether they themselves give the relation or not; and if their language is conformable to them, it is no doubt of a nature sufficiently wonderful.[51]

What is most remarkable about the discussion of the "Hottentots" is its comfort with the assumption that they are full members of the human family. In this way, the *Encyclopaedia Britannica* presents a defense of "Hottentots."

The *Encyclopaedia Britannica* also shows an eagerness to make a more positive representation by not including some of Sparrman's most negative statements about "Hottentots." For example, the simile equating "Hottentots" and "hedge-hogs" does not appear, and what replaces it are phrases that argue the "Hottentots" live in houses that are natural and convenient for them: "The door, low as it is, alone lets in day-light or lets out the smoke: and so much are these people accustomed to live in such smoky mansions, that their eyes are never affected by it in the least, nor even by the mephitic vapour of the fuel, which to Europeans would be certain death."[52] The respect for difference here is noteworthy. Also indicative of the *Britannica's* more neutral stance is that at no point does it refer to the "Hottentots" as humanity's lowest society or its most beast-like people.

While post-1760 descriptions in travel narratives and encyclopedias certainly played a crucial role in enlarging some images and notions of "Hottentots," references to them in a wide range of philosophical and scientific works published during the 1770s and later also had a critical role in shifting the constructions. "Hottentots" proved to be convenient figures for later eighteenth-century advocates of progressive history. Joseph Priestley, for example, places a familiar construct into his more positive vision of human kind.

> I might enlarge much more than I have done in this preface on the *dignity*, and *utility*, of experimental philosophy; but shall only observe farther that it is nothing but a superior knowledge of the laws of nature that gives Europeans the advantages they have over the Hottentots, or the lowest of our species. Had these people never known Europeans, they could not have formed an idea of any mode of life superior to their own, though it differs little from that of the brutes. In like manner, science advancing, as it does, with an accelerated progress, it may be taken for granted that mankind some centuries hence will be as much superior to us in knowledge, and improvements in the arts of life, as we are now to the Hottentots, though we cannot have any conception what that knowledge, or what those improvements, will be.[53]

It is significant that after Priestley first sees "difference," he then sees some ground for analogy.

In a similar manner, "Hottentot" references came to figure in philosophical and political discourses that measured sameness as well as difference. John Millar's *The Origin of the Distinction of Ranks* (1771) argues that no matter the level of savagery or civility, "Man is every where the same." Millar uses travel narratives and collections for his source material as he "contemplate[s] the amazing diversity in the manners of different countries," to prove "that the untutored Indian and the civilized European have acted upon the same principles."[54] Millar sees the oppression of women as one of the distinguishing characteristics of "savage societies." It is in this context that he refers to Kolb's description of "Hottentot" courtship: "The form of courtship among the Hottentots, by which the lover is permitted to overcome the reluctance of his mistress, may be considered as a plain indication of similar manners, and exhibits a striking picture of primitive rudeness and simplicity."[55] Later in the chapter, Millar makes another "Hottentot" reference, stating that when a male "Hottentot" youth is initiated into the ranks of men, "it is usual for him to beat and abuse his mother, by way of triumph at being freed from her tuition. Such behaviour may happen in a rude country, where, after marriage is established, the superior strength of the husband has raised him to the head of his family, and where his authority has of course annihilated that of the wife, or at least greatly reduced her consideration and importance."[56]

Millar cites Kolb's text, specifically his rendition of the story of Van der Stel's youth, to illustrate "maladie du pays," which is felt in all countries "as they approach nearer to the ages of rudeness and simplicity." The "illness," steadfast loyalty to one's own culture and customs, is another mark of a "savage":

> The poorer the country in which he has lived, the more wretched the manner of life to which he has been accustomed, the loss of it appears to him the more insupportable. That very poverty and wretchedness, which contracted the sphere of his amusements, is the chief circumstance that confirms his attachment to those few gratifications which it afforded, and renders him the more a slave to those particular habits which he has acquired. Not all the allurements of European luxury could bribe a Hottentot to resign that coarse manner of life which was become habitual to him.[57]

In an explanatory footnote on the bottom of the page, Millar cites Kolb's text and provides a more detailed summary of the story of Van der Stel's youth. Significantly, at the end of the note, he misremembers the "Cory" story: "The English East-India Company made the like experiment upon two young Hottentots, but with no better success."[58] Millar's preference to see Cory or Van der Stel's youth as ill rather than as patriotic suggests how the British were still able to find ways to devalue the positive feelings of "Hottentots." To the British, patriotism is an emotion reserved for civilized people like themselves.

Lord Monboddo's *Of the Origin and Progress of Language* (1773) also demonstrates the resonance of Kolb's discussion of Van der Stel's youth. Monboddo uses it in a key passage to prove that it takes uncivilized societies a long time to develop: "And, I am persuaded, it is with wild men, as with wild fruits, which we know will not lose their savage nature at the first remove, but can only be tamed by continued culture for a succession of generation. And, accordingly, Kolben, in his account of the Hottentots, tells us, that it is not possible to tame a Hottentot, and reconcile him to Dutch manners, though taken quite young, and bred up in the European way; and he says, the experiment has been often tried, but never succeeded."[59] Monboddo makes this point to support his larger purpose, which is to explain and prove that language is not "natural" to society, that it takes time to develop. In this regard, Monboddo's work, by implication, links the much-favored eighteenth-century equation between the orangutan and wild men with previously published descriptions of "Hottentots" that likened them to apes and baboons (among them, Herbert and, more recently, Beeckman). Almost one hundred years later, *Blackwood's Edinburgh Magazine* remembered and mocked Monboddo's conclusion and, by extension, his source as well: "Lord Monboddo would have wandered among the Hottentots from kraal to kraal, blind and deaf to every sight and sound of nature, blind to everything save that glorious vision—alas! never destined to be realised—of a human child with the prehensile tail of a monkey."[60]

References to the "Hottentot" language figure centrally in the widescale debate about language taking place in the second half of the eighteenth century. James Dunbar, among others, discusses the "Hottentot" language in order to demonstrate that uncivilized societies have undeveloped or underdeveloped languages. Essay 3, "Of the Criterion of a Polished Tongue," in Dunbar's *Essays on the History of Mankind in Rude and Cultivated Ages* (1780) asserts that "The connexion of language and manners is an obvious connexion. They run parallel with each other, through different periods of their progress."[61] Articulation has an important place in Dunbar's conception of what makes for a "polished" language. He describes the "Hottentot" language as "not absolutely destitute of articulation," but "defective in this quality."[62] In his fifth essay, "Of the Rank of Nations, and the Revolutions of Fortune," Dunbar remembers the story of Van der Stel's youth: "Profound ignorance, and a contrariety, or repugnancy of customs and manners, account for that aversion, or contempt for strangers and foreigners, implied in the partial sentiments of savage and untutored minds. No information, no experience, no convinction can always conquer early prejudice: and the Hottentot, who returned from Europe, relapsed, we may believe, with all imaginable ease, perhaps with additional satisfaction, into the established habits of his country."[63]

Henry Home, lord Kames, also shows his familiarity with Kolb's text and with other travel narratives in his *Sketches of the History of Man* (1774). References to a variety of human societies help him to accomplish one of his central goals in the work, which is to attack Buffon's advocacy of monogenesis:

> M. Buffon, from the rule, That animals which can procreate together, and whose progeny can also procreate, are of one species, concludes,

that all men are of one race or species; and endeavours to support that favourite opinion by ascribing to the climate, to food, or to other accidental causes, all the varieties that are found among men. But is he seriously of opinion, that any operation of climate, or of other accidental cause, can account for the copper colour and smooth chin universal among Americans, the prominence of the *pudenda* universal among Hottentot women, or the black nipple no less universal among female Samoides?[64]

Kames continues to make "Hottentot" references as he presents his argument that the varieties of skin color testify to the existence of different human races. Part of his proof is dependent on information he learned from Kolb: "Let a European for years expose himself to the sun in a hot climate, till he be quite brown, his children will nevertheless have the same complexion with those in Europe. The Hottentots are continually at work, and have been for ages, to darken their complexion; but that operation has no effect on their children."[65]

Significantly, questions about the skin color of "Hottentots" did not receive any unusual amount of attention in the later eighteenth-century travel narratives. As we saw, Sparrman reports it as being "of a yellowish brown hue, somewhat resembling that of an European who has the jaundice in a high degree," and his description went largely unchallenged. What British travelers tended to stress in their descriptions is how "Hottentots" made themselves darker, how they, in effect, preferred to become the color of Negroes. Partly in response, perhaps, to these descriptions as well as to the larger discussion of skin color that was being conducted in philosophical and scientific discourses, there began to emerge in the mid eighteenth century a tendency to regard as minor and unimportant the differences in color between Negroes and "Hottentots." In short, as skin color became the major determining factor in racial classification, all sub-Saharan Africans became members of the same race.

We can find this position articulated in any number of works, from Blumenbach's *On the Natural Varieties of Mankind* (1776) to Goldsmith's *An History of the Earth and Animated Nature* (1774): "The Fourth striking variety in the human species is to be found among the Negroes of Africa. This gloomy race of mankind is found to blacken all the southern parts of Africa, from eighteen degrees north of the line, to its extreme termination, at the Cape of Good Hope."[66] Additionally, popular geographies, such as Guthrie's *A New Geographical, Historical and Commercial Grammar*, present this image and idea.

> In Africa, the human mind seems degraded below its natural state. To dwell long upon the manners of this country, a country so immersed in rudeness and barbarity, besides that it could afford little instruction, would be disgusting to every lover of mankind. Add to that, that the inhabitants of Africa, deprived of all arts and sciences, without which the human mind remains torpid and inactive, discover no great variety in manners of character. A gloomy sameness almost every where prevails; and the trifling distinctions which are discovered among them, seem rather to arise from an excess of brutality on the one hand, than from any perceptible approaches towards refinement on the other.[67]

Guthrie's preface remained in place without any substantive changes through all the eighteenth-century editions.

Those who wished to connect physical appearance, especially skin color, to national and moral character could also find many texts to support their position. David Hume makes this point in a footnote to the 1754 revision of his controversial essay, "Of National Characters" (1748): "I am apt to suspect the negroes and in general all other species of men (for there are four or five different kinds) to be naturally inferior to whites. There never was a civilized nation of any other complexion than white, nor even any individual eminent either in action or speculation."[68] Conversely, James Beattie, in *An Essay on the Nature and Immutability of Truth* (1770), strenuously objects to the racist and Eurocentric position Hume argues in "Of National Characters" (1748), but he also uses a "Hottentot" reference.

> That every practice and sentiment is barbarous which is not according to the usages of modern Europe, seems to be a fundamental maxim with many of our critics and philosophers. Their remarks often put us in mind of the fable of the man and the lion. If Negroes and Indians were disposed to recriminate; if a Lucian or a Voltaire from the coast of Guinea, or from the Five Nations, were to pay us a visit, what a picture of European manners he would present to his countrymen at his return! Nor would caricature, or exaggeration be necessary to render it hideous. A plain historical account of some of our most fashionable duellists, gamblers, and adulterers (to name no more) would exhibit specimens of brute barbarity, and sottish infatuation such as might vie with any that ever appeared in Kamschatka, California, or the land of the Hottentots.[69]

Beattie's insistence that Europeans can be as brute as "Hottentots" (and others) echoes Kolb's charge against those who disappointed him.

The theories of physiognomist Johann Casper Lavater advanced the argument that physical appearance is indeed related to moral character. Physiognomy was a popular subject in eighteenth-century Britain; in fact, it was so popular that it was satirized as well as championed.[70] The works of Lavater were especially influential. His *Essays on Physiognomy, Designed to Promote the Knowledge and Love of Mankind* (1789) declares quite definitively: "THAT there is national physiognomy, as well as national character, is undeniable. Whoever doubts of this can never have observed men of different nations, nor have compared the inhabitants of the extreme confines of any two. Compare a Negro and an Englishman, a native of Lapland and an Italian, a Frenchman and an inhabitant of Terra del Fuego. Examine their forms, countenances, characters, and minds."[71] Lavater's selection of Negro rather than "Hottentot" demonstrates how they were being used interchangeably by this point in time.

Neither science nor history, however, could yet prove conclusively why there was such variety in human features, be it skin color, facial structure, hair type, or physique, and what, if anything, all the differences signified. Perhaps one of the most unfortunate results of later eighteenth-century natural history is that it prompted some to merge Linnaeus's classifications with the longstanding notion of a "great chain of being."[72] Soame Jenyns does nothing unusual when he places "Hottentots" at the opposite end of the spectrum to certain British philosophers: "From this lowest degree in the brutal Hottentot, reason, with the assistance of learning and science, advances, through the various stages of human understanding, which rise above each other, till in a Bacon or a Newton it attains the summit."[73] William Smellie, one of the original editors of the *Encyclopaedia Britannica*, speaks even more directly to the link between the human and animal worlds.

> How many gradations may be traced between a stupid Huron, or a Hottentot, and a profound philosopher? Here the distance is immense—but Nature has occupied the whole by almost infinite shades of discrimination.
> In descending the scale of animation, the next step, it is humiliating to remark, is very short. Man, in his lowest condition, is evidently linked, both in the form of his body and the capacity of his mind, to the large and small orangoutang. These again, by another slight gradation, are connected to the apes, who, like the former, have no tails.[74]

Smellie's reference to a Huron shows the influence of Charles Bonnet's *The Contemplation of Nature* (1766), which compares Newton to a Scottish peasant. Smellie, a Scot, must certainly have wanted to find another target.

As humanity's most beastly society, the "Hottentots" played a crucial role in the misbegotten conflation of a classification system with the idea of a great chain of being. Peter Camper had hoped that his invention of the facial angle to measure the skulls of humans and beasts would benefit both natural history and art, but it was seriously misinterpreted and misused.[75] Stephen Jay Gould and others point out that he "did not define the facial angle as a device for ranking races or nations by innate worth or intellect."[76] Camper does, however, rank races by facial angle, with Africans on the bottom of the scale, representing those, he felt, who were the farthest from the ancient Greek ideal of beauty. Interestingly, at times Camper considers "Hottentots" as "not materially" different from negroes, but he also treats them as distinct. In his *The Connexion between the Science of Anatomy and the Arts of Drawing, Painting, Statuary* (1794), he explains why "Hottentots," among others, can never be called beautiful: "Laplanders, Tartars, Hottentots, and Brasilians, whose heads are very large in proportion to their bodies cannot please us or be deemed beautiful, no more than the Doric column could be called beautiful upon the revival of architecture."[77] Although Camper does not equate facial angle and range of intelligence in his work, many of his readers simply misinterpreted him or purposely misused his data.

The ubiquity of "Hottentot" representations in such a wide variety of later eighteenth-century texts testifies to the crucial role they continued to play in the collective consciousness. All the advances of the "Enlightenment" did little to shed significant new light on the negative constructions of "Hottentot." Authors could still be sure that their readers would know exactly what they meant when they used the word "Hottentot."

7
"The Most Wretched of the Human Race"

BRITAIN'S INTERESTS IN INDIA AND THE FAR EAST PROMPTED PITT'S ministry to turn their attention to the Cape of Good Hope.[1] Seizing it became a British objective in 1795, when France's dominance of the newly styled Batavian Republic raised the possibility that the French might come to control this gateway to the east. The Cape's crucial role in any British dream of empire was obvious to all. In 1784, Henry Rooke explained it this way: "Placed midway betwixt Europe and India, nature seems to have pointed it out to the ambitious powers that contend for wealth and empire in those distant regions . . . Great Britain, mistress of the East, where rich empires and flourishing settlements acknowledge her dominion . . . should not yet think her superiority firmly established or her possessions perfectly secure from her European rivals, while the Cape is in the hands of her enemies."[2] Pitt and Henry Dundas, the Secretary of War, ordered the seizure of the Cape, and by September 1795, the mission was accomplished.[3] For the next seven years the British controlled Cape Town and its environs, but they developed no plans to colonize the region. The Treaty of Amiens (1801) forced them to return possession of the Cape to the Dutch in February 1803. The outbreak of the Napoleonic Wars, however, reenergized British fear that the Cape might fall into unfriendly hands and, in 1805, Pitt's government ordered the military to invade the region once again. By January 1806, it was Britain's and would remain so until the 1910 formation of the Union of South Africa.[4]

British possession of the Cape forced traditional constructions of "Hottentot" to adapt to this new geopolitical reality.[5] The first four words of a memorandum written by General Robert Thomas Wilson reveal his awareness that the British occupation changed how "Hottentots" are represented: "Until the first possession of the Cape by the English the Hottentot had ever been repudiated as a Being that dishonored the Human Species—an Heathen incapable of civilization and the practice of moral Duties. The name was a term of reproach and the naturalist ashamed of his affinity to man endeavoured to class him amongst the vilest of Brutes."[6] Many post-1795 representations of "Hottentots" demonstrate that once the British counted the regions as theirs, they were ready to feel or, at least, to feign pity for those they had formerly regarded as beastly and unrecoverable. And by the second decade of the nineteenth century, there were pressing imperial reasons for what the 1812 edition of Guthrie's *A New Geographical, Historical, and Commercial Grammar* called a "favourable character of the Hottentots" at the Cape.[7]

Remarkably, late-eighteenth-century and early-nineteenth-century British visitors to the Cape often unambiguously articulate their awareness that the long-standing tradition of negative descriptions of "Hottentots" was misleading and inaccurate. Conscious of the constructions that had demonized "Hottentots" in the past, Lady Anne Barnard, at the Cape from 1797 to 1802, remembers the childhood images she held of them: "How unlike I found this place to the Cape of Good Hope as I painted it to myself in the nursery, where I supposed Christians living in Tents and Hottentots in Groupes skulking in the woods with their *Horns*."[8] John Harriott also mentions how the "Hottentots" have been "much misrepresented," and calls previous accounts "strangely exaggerated."[9] He keeps them in mind as he presents his own description of "Hottentots": "Their persons, instead of being homely and disgusting as represented, are on the contrary well shaped, and, for black people, more comely in countenance than the negro race."[10] Lady Barnard had the same reaction: "I was told the Hottentots were uncommonly ugly and disgusting, but I do not think them so bad. Their features are small and their cheek-bones immense, but they have a kind expression of countenance."[11]

Whether or not commentators criticized earlier representations as being misrepresentative, there was uniform recognition that the older publications about the Cape and its people were no longer valid now that the region belonged to Britain. Indeed, more positive rather than negative images of "Hottentots" served the personal agendas of individuals as well the imperial desire of the nation. The anonymous author of *Gleanings in Africa* (1806) strains a bit to adopt this viewpoint: "The figure of the Hottentot is, upon the whole, not unhandsome; many of them are tall, with limbs well proportioned, seemingly calculated for activity, and capable of enduring fatigue. When a Hottentot is in motion, he is altogether animation; his pace is so quick, that he seems rather to fly than to walk: . . . The eyes of the Hottentots are peculiarly lively and animated, and in many of the females whom I have seen, they bespeak a languishing softness, which, conjoined to a set of fine white teeth, render them sufficiently attractive."[12] Those who were still eager to delimit "Hottentots" as savages were often rebuked. Lady Anne Barnard, among others, was quick to point out that a certain level of European hypocrisy might be involved in maintaining the traditional constructions:

> The entrails of Animals says my European friends—how Savage! but mark you how every thing depends on the manner in which it is first presented to our imagination, you do not cry out Oh how savage! . . . on hearing Cramer bring forth melodious sounds from his violencello tho' it is done by fingering the entrails of the animals we are talking of.[13]

The somewhat self-serving British willingness to shift the general notion of "Hottentots," from that of the beastliest of human societies to an image of them as the world's most wretched people, did not completely erase the older, negative constructions, however. They were merely superseded.

Once Britain gained possession of the Cape it became easier to have sympathy for the sad condition of "Hottentots" at the Cape. Those who remained there began to be constructed as a people who suffered so terribly at the hands of Dutch colonists that they were approaching extinction. Many authors use strong language and dramatic images to render "Hottentot" wretchedness. *Gleanings in Africa* (1806) presents them as being "in a paroxysm of rage . . . their feelings trampled under, and their services ill requited," and imagines a far more glorious past for them:

> There can be little doubt that the Hottentots of the present day have lost much of their original independent character, from the connexion and intercourse with Europeans . . . In the vicinity of the Cape you no longer meet with hordes, who formerly united together under the command of a chief, and were wont to acknowledge his authority, and follow his standard. They may be said no longer to compose one distinct nation;—they are to be found scattered over the face of the colony, acting in the capacity of drudges or menial servants to the boors; —more dependent, and more in a state of slavery than if actually *slaves*.[14]

Signficantly, none of the early-nineteenth-century British representations identify colonialism per se as the force that caused the demise of "Hottentot" society. Instead, blame is directed at the

Dutch (or Boer) residents, who, according to Robert Percival's *An Account of the Cape of Good Hope* (1804), "have always behaved to them in such a manner, as if they were resolved to eradicate every feeling of humanity out of the breasts of these unfortunate people."[15] The previous English tendency to compliment generations of the colonial settlers, especially for their industry and development of the Cape, is replaced with condemnations for what is seen as their idleness and cruelty to "Hottentots." J. M. Coetzee convincingly argues that for the British, the Boer "betray the colonizing mission" on two counts: they remind the British that Europeans can regress, and their colonial rule has done nothing to prove that they have improved the land or the people of the region.[16]

Early-nineteenth-century British representations of the Boer recall some of the earliest European representations of "Hottentots. John Barrow accuses the Boer settlers of not using and developing the rich resources of the region: "Placed in a country where not only the necessaries, but almost every luxury of life might by industry be procured, he has the enjoyment of none of them. Though he has cattle in abundance he makes very little use of milk or of butter. In the midst of a soil and climate most favorable for the cultivation of the vine, he drinks no wine. He makes use of few or no vegetables nor roots."[17] Representations often picture the Boer as gross and "boorish." Barrow stresses what he sees as their disgusting eating habits, their abuse of power, and the idle routines of their daily existence.

> Three times a-day his table is loaded with masses of mutton, swimming in the grease of the sheep's tail. . . . The boor not withstanding has his enjoyments: he is absolute master of a domain of several miles in extent; and he lords it over a few miserable slaves or Hottentots without control. . . . Unwilling to work, and unable to think; with a mind disengaged from every sort of care and reflexion, indulging to excess in the gratification of every sensual appetite, the African peasant grows to an unwieldy size, and is carried off the stage by the first inflammatory disease that attacks him. (77)

Writing anti-Boer representations assumed extra urgency after it became clear that Britain must withdraw its forces from the Cape and return it to Batavian control in 1803.

The anti-Boer strategy in the British representations is partially, at least, driven by the knowledge that "Hottentots" could prove to be useful to Britain's imperial dreams. The journal of seaman Robert Warden, at the Cape from 1796 to 1797, makes this observation very early in the first British occupation: "If it were practicable to make these people steady, great advantages might accrue to the King and the Company."[18] After the first phase of British control ended in 1803, representations began to stress the improvement and progress seen in "Hottentots" during the eight-year occupation. Viscount George points to the "Hottentot" corps, native soldiers trained by British troops, as proof that "Hottentots" could be instructed for their own (and British) benefit. George's pro-British and anti-Dutch expression suggests that any sympathy he really had for "Hottentots" was limited at best.

> This inoffensive race, who formerly were only mentioned as sunk in sloth, drunkenness, and bestiality, have been brought forward, since the British possessed the colony, in a new and very different point of view. A large number of them have been embodied and taught European tactics; in consequence of which it has been discovered that they are intelligent, active, faithful, and brave; and that their former vices were owing to the Dutch, who, taking advantage of the inclination which all uncivilized nations have for spirits, had destroyed their strength by encouraging intoxication, and then degraded their minds by the most abject slavery.[19]

Significantly, British authors who represented the "Hottentot" corps before Britain was forced to return the Cape were oftentimes less complimentary. R. Renshaw, who was at the Cape as early as 1796, remembers: "During the time I remained in Africa, we raised a regiment of them, and clothed them in scarlet turned up with blue, of which they were wonderfully proud. We found them very tractable in the exercise, in which they became exceedingly expert; but when put to the test as soldiers, they proved cowards beyond description."[20] Although Renshaw slights the bravery of the troops, his account, at the very least, recognizes their ability to learn new skills.

Besides touting the accomplishments of "Hottentots" during this first period of occupation, British authors began to see them as willing to convert to Christianity. This marks a complete shift from previous representations. As we saw, eighteenth-century British accounts reported that the "Hottentots" had no religion and seemed completely averse to conversion. Supporters of British colonialism at the Cape were particularly eager, therefore, to present the opposite view. Descriptions of "converted Hottentots" became a standard trope in nineteenth-century representations. The subject was clearly a controversial one, however, and judging by how they framed their remarks, British writers took elaborate measures to ensure their audience would understand them in the proper context.

Lady Anne Barnard certainly appears to be conscious of audience when she recorded her impressions and feelings as she observed "Hottentots" at prayer. The opportunity came to her in 1798, the year after she and her husband established their residence as members of the British colonial administration at the Cape. As part of a tour of the region, they paid a visit to the Moravian missionary station at Genadendal on 10 May 1798. Her representation begins with an implied criticism of Europeans at worship: "I doubt much whether I should have entered St. Peters at Rome with the Triple Crown itself present in all its Ancient splendor with a more awed impression of the deity and his presence than I did this little Church of a few feet Square, where the simple disciples of Christianity dressed in the Skins of Animals knew no *purple* or *fine linen*, no pride . . . no hypocrisy. I felt as if I was creeping back *1700 years*, to hear from the rude but inspired lips of Evangelists the simple sacred words of wisdom and purity."[21]

Barnard places her description of "Hottentots" at prayer in a historical context, as if this provides her audience with an acceptable explanation for the group's acceptance of Christianity.

> The Service began after the Presbyterian form with a psalm. Then indeed the note that raised itself to Heaven was an affecting one, about 150 Hottentots joined in the 23rd psalm in a tone so sweet, so loud, but so just and true that it was impossible to hear it without being surprised. . . . Mild and tender by nature, oppressed by the Dutch and often sinking under it, the poor creatures blessed God as they listened, while the artless tears of gratitude and Hope fell down on their Sheep Skins. . . . Not a Hottentot did I see in this congregation that had a bad passion in the Countenance, I watched them closely, all was sweetness and attention. I was even surprised to observe so few *vacant* eyes, and so little curiosity directed to *ourselves*.[22]

The notice Barnard takes here of her own reaction to this occasion is particularly interesting; clearly, she is still trying to reconcile the traditional negative constructions of "Hottentots" she was raised to have with what she sees before her.

Londoners could see living proof of Christianized "Hottentots" in late 1803, when Reverend Kicherer, who had been sent to the Cape by the London Missionary Society, brought three "converted Hottentots" to Britain. As far as I can determine, these were the first Cape people in London since Cory's kidnapping brought him there in 1613. The timing of Kicherer's appearance in England, in relation to Britain's surrender of the Cape, suggests how complicit missionary societies could be in promoting the idea of the British empire. The party's very presence in London argued that the government should recapture the Cape. On at least two occasions in November (and perhaps early December), the missionary and his protégés were presented at prayer meetings to answer questions and to show the public the "first fruits of the South African mission."[23] The December 1803 issue of the *Evangelical Magazine* published an extensive account of the first meeting on 7 November along with background material and written testimonials from others, including, significantly, the "Hottentots." The material presented in this issue demonstrates that "Hottentots" have certain abilities, such as language and literacy, which Europeans had never granted to them previously.

According to the *Evangelical Magazine*, Kicherer, who spoke "imperfect English," began the presentation by providing a description "of the state in which he first found the Hottentots of that country, their wildness, their ignorance of all religion, and their extreme laziness and filthiness."[24] The account then becomes a transcript of the questions asked and the answers given by John, Mary, and Martha, who are referred to throughout as the "three converted Hottentots." Undoubtedly, fiction plays a role here in much the same way it did in travel narratives. The opening questions and answers suggest the presence of the traditional constructions of "Hottentots," such as they had no religion and were more like beasts than human beings.

> Q. What did you know of God before the Missionaries came? A. We knew nothing at all of Him; we did not know there was any God.—Q. What did you then think of yourself? A. I thought I was like a beast; and that when I died, there would be an end.—Q. What have you since learned about yourself? A. I have learned that I am a poor wicked creature.[25]

It is significant that this account lends the "Hottentots" such command of English, suggesting that not only can they pray like the English, but they can also sound like them. Their suspicious facility with the language might very well be driven by the catechistical style of instruction.

A representation of the evening's effect on the audience suggests how warmly Kicherer and his party were received by London crowds. The description also makes a reference to skin color that indicates how the issue had been resolved.

> It is easier to conceive than to describe the sacred pleasure which filled the minds of a large assembly of Christians, when they thus beheld "Ethiopia stretching forth her hands to God," and heard some of Afric's tawny race singing the praises of our common Lord. Indeed, the voice of joy and praise was uncommonly loud and fervent when the congregation sung that doxology, "Praise God, from whom all blessings flow!" and, we trust, a sincere tribute of praise was offered up to God,who had thus granted to the Heathen "Repentance unto life."[26]

This account, as well as many nineteenth-century travel narratives, suggests that once "Hottentots" became British subjects and willing converts to Christianity, their skin color became a less significant marker of absolute difference.

The *Evangelical Magazine* also presents background information about Kircherer's Zak River mission station, which shows how the new construction of "Hottentots" sits atop the older negative images of them.

> We understand that when he commenced his work at Zak River, he found only thirty-six inhabitants: the people in general roamed about the country like wild beasts, in quest of prey. But, by his judicious management, about 600 persons were brought, and, in a great measure, kept together. He has been indefatigable in instructing them, both by preaching and catechizing. About 300 are now worshippers of God; and he has no doubt of the real conversion of about forty; even the little children can give a good reason of the Christian hope! It is worthy of observation, that when these poor Africans are enlightened, a great change takes place in their outward conduct and appearance. Those who before were almost naked, clothe themselves with decency;—from being extremely filthy, they learn to be clean;—and from that laziness which prevails among them while Heathens, they learn to be diligent, and to cultivate the earth for their subsistence. Thus, while the gospel brings to them a spiritual salvation, it becomes also the mean of civilizing, we might also say of humanizing them; and this affords an additional argument for Missionary zeal.[27]

It is not coincidental that this section and the introductory material combined exceed the amount of space allotted to the transcription of the answers given by the "converted Hottentots" to the assembly. The *Evangelical Magazine* is being mindful of how it frames its positive account of the "converted Hottentots."

By the time a *Supplement to the Evangelical Magazine for the Year*

7: "THE MOST WRETCHED OF THE HUMAN RACE" 215

1803 was ready for press, and with additional public meetings to report on, the magazine's cautious strategy was dropped. Indeed, a "sketch" of the meeting at the Scots Church (London), on 21 November 1803, is presented almost entirely as a transcript of questions put to Kicherer and the three converts. The two women appear to have been far more loquacious than John. In answer to a question about "how they expect to be supported in the trying hour of death," Kicherer first translates a response from John, which is followed by a much longer one from Martha. It is impossible to know if the flaws in the language derive from Kicherer or Martha, but the answer, no doubt, is fully correct.

> I wish I could say all she tell to me, but it impossible. She say, she trust there shall be many here who have pity for themselves, and for others,—compassion for own soul and soul of others; but wish it was all, but perhaps it was not all; perhaps some here now not have compassion on own soul. O, that they would take counsel of poor Hottentot, she say! but Lord Jesus shew them compassion. See from such people as poor Hottentot,—see if such people, when they go to Jesus Christ, be saved, he will save them too, when they come like poor sinner: if they know not how to come like poor sinner, Christ will learn them; if they ask him, and not wait till to-morrow. We all now here; but perhaps last time some hear dear gospel. Tell to them that no people go to Christ, but Christ save them, when they like to be saved: that Christ never say "I won't save them." This is part of what she say, but not so good.[28]

The evening's program ended with the "converted Hottentots" singing the One Hundred Thirtieth Psalm. Also, a hymn sung by them appears in the poetry section of the supplement.

Although Kicherer and his companions left London on 12 December 1803, the *Evangelical Magazine* continued to keep the story of their visit alive throughout the initial issues of 1804. The opening pages of the January 1804 issue use the visit to remind readers of the society's mission. Significantly, it employs the "voice" of a "Hottentot" woman to issue the reminder.

> IT was a severe, but just reproach on the general disregard of the perishing Heathen, which was lately uttered by a poor Hottentot woman in one of our assemblies:—"It is a great pity," said she, "and a great sin, that they who so long enjoyed great plenty of the bread of life, did not give one crumb to the poor heathen; but that God was very good who had forgiven this great sin, and had blessed the little bit they had lately given so much"; and now, she hoped that Christians would sin

no longer against God, in witholding the bread of life, but would abound in giving it more and more.²⁹

Following this is a four-page history of Kicherer's efforts at the Zak River mission. The issue's "Religious Intelligence" column provides a description of the party's departure from London as well as more personal information about the Hottentots themselves. The poetry section features a poem celebrating the visit, entitled "The Hottentots in London," and the issue concludes with "A Hymn to Jesus. Sung by the Hottentots."

"The Hottentots in London" is of particular interest. In describing how Christianity has "civilized" "Hottentots," the poem's middle stanzas demonstrate the great shift underlying British constructions of them. The third, fourth, and fifth stanza present the traditional view. Here the very humanity of the "Hottentots" is questioned. They are likened to animals, and they are denied a language and any notion of religion:

> Who are those of Olive hue,
>   Varied forms of human race,
> Uttering language harsh and new,
>   Strangers from some distant place?
> Children these of Nature rude
>   In a land of darkness born;
> By oppression's rod subdued,—
>   Europe's ridicule and scorn.
>
> Wand'ring wild o'er Afric's plain,
>   Their untutor'd hordes abound,
> And degraded life maintain,
>   Like the brutes that graze around.
> Naked, but as filth arrays;
>   Artless, but as want constrains;
> Lawless, but as passion sways,
>   Or as hopeless slav'ry chains.
>
> Knowing not their Maker's name;
>   Having not the means to know;
> Void of decency and shame,
>   And unconscious of their woe;—
> Life with them was but a state,
>   To be wretched and to die;
> And their everlasting fate,
>   Waken'd not an anxious sigh!³⁰

The imagery changes completely in the subsequent stanzas which depict the great change in the "Hottentots" as a result of their acceptance of Christianity.

> What a change in these is wrought!
>   Trophies rich of grace divine:
> From Death's gloomy shadows brought,
>   Humble lights for God to shine!
> What could break old habit's force,
>   Stem the holds of sin, secure,
> Turn corrupted Nature's course,
>   Into channels clean and pure.
>
> Mark them,—savage once, and wild;
>   Now adorn'd with smiles serene,
> Gentle, teachable, and mild
>   Decent look and pious mean.
> Hark! Religion joy doth bring,
>   Tuning grateful, cheerful praise;
> Sweetly Jesus' love they sing
>   In their native simple lays.[31]

As we see here, the ideal "Hottentot" is "Gentle, teachable, and mild." Representations like this one, in poetic form or not, were often republished. A copy of this poem, for example, appeared subsequently in *An Extract from the Reverend Mr. Kicherer's Narrative of His Mission in South Africa* (1804). Publications like these broadcast the message that Britain's colonizing mission could, if given the chance, transform and save the "Hottentots."

The *Evangelical Magazine* could not leave the story of the "three converted Hottentots" alone. In February 1804, it provides yet another transcript of the answers given by the "three converted Hottentots" at a prayer meeting. The April 1804 issue presents an "affecting Anecdote of a Hottentot Youth" sent to them by a "Mariner" about a homesick eleven year old boy who commited suicide in order to be reunited with his mother. "Mariner" sent the anecdote because he had been so moved by reading in previous issues of "the great good which hath been done by the means of Missionary labours amongst the Hottentots."[32] The May issue features an "Interesting Incident" arising from the 21 November 1803 prayer meeting at Scots Church (London). It explains that a "negro boy," curious about the two Hottentot women, made his way to the church vestry door. When the two saw him, they "flew to him . . . with much maternal affection," and put questions to him in Dutch.

He did not understand them, but someone translated their questions for him. What they wanted to know was if he "loved the Lord Jesus Christ," and when he did not respond affirmatively to it, "their mortification was extreme; their countenances fell; they were grieved to find a native of Africa, who had enjoyed the privileges of this country, unacquainted with the Redeemer."[33] Stories about converted "Hottentots" continued to appear in the *Evangelical Magazine* for years to come. The February 1805 issue relates the history of "Cupido," who, "was before his conversion, as notorious a sinner as was ever known." The story and the name given to this figure testifies as to how "Hottentots" continued to serve symbolic levels of meaning in the British consciousness. The March 1805 issue notes the successful conversions of more "Hottentots" to Christianity.[34]

Missionary societies were not alone in presenting the case for the expanding British empire. John Barrow was the first of many to use his publications to argue for permanent British occupation and colonization of the Cape. Barrow went to Cape Town in 1797 to serve as private secretary to Lord Macartney, then British governor there. Ordered to undertake three inland expeditions from 1797 through 1799, Barrow had ample opportunity to see more of the Cape than any previous British visitor. His preparation for these journeys included reading eighteenth-century accounts of the region, which he did not find useful. Barrow distrusted them because he knew that most of the authors did not venture very far from the Cape, and that they often merely repeated stories about "Hottentots" without knowing if they were true or not. He even attacks Sparrman on these grounds: "*Sparrmann*, the Swede . . . by his indefatigable labours, supplied a very extensive and satisfactory account of the natural productions, especially in the animal kingdom, of those parts of the settlement over which he travelled; but he was credulous enough to repeat many of the absurd stories told of the Hottentots by his predecessor *Kolbe*, with the addition of others collected from the ignorant boors."[35] Barrow charges that previous authors have "abused" the world with "ridiculous and false accounts" that have "generally much traduced and misrepresented" the "Hottentot" character.[36] Barrow could find no satisfaction in these earlier texts because they do not reflect the kind of vision he has of the region. He was among the first group of British men and women who saw colonial possibilities for themselves and their nation at the Cape, and thus for him the really serious flaw in the older texts is that they did not provide the information that could help to advance their nation's colonial project.

Not surprisingly, the authorial stance Barrow adopts in his *An Account of Travels into the Interior of Southern Africa in the Years 1797 and 1798* (1801) reflects his imperial sensibility. Barrow's colonialist description of "Hottentots" presents them as a "mild, quiet, and timid people; perfectly harmless, honest, faithful; and, though extremely phlegmatic, they are nevertheless kind and affectionate to each other, and by no means incapable of strong attachments."[37] Barrow does not show any special curiosity for the "Hottentots." He is not any more interested in them than he needs to be; he makes quick and easy conclusions when he writes about their bodies and customs. Judging them by British standards, he finds them inferior on almost every count: "Except in the preparation of poisons, making bows and arrows, musical instruments, coarse earthen ware, and sewing together the skins of sheep for their winter garments with sinews of the intestines of animals the Hottentots may be said to be entirely ignorant of arts and manufactures."[38]

Barrow was sent into the interior to gather information about the territory, to make sure the Boer farmers accepted British rule, and to get a better sense of the native societies (those he calls "Hottentots," "Bushmen" [the !Kung] and "Kaffers" [the Xhosa]). Traveling in that capacity, he is master of what he sees, and he rarely, if ever, expresses any personal feelings. His prose is specific, descriptive, scientific, and technical where it needs to be, and, above all, it seems sure of its own authority. Mary Louise Pratt says that Barrow's language "suggests the fantasy of dominance and appropriation."[39] Barrow was so angry about the British surrender of the Cape that, in 1804, he published a second volume to his *Travels*. It hardly presents any record of his travels, however. In fact, just one of the book's six chapters discusses, and that in very sketchy detail, an account of an expedition into the interior of the country. Every chapter's real purpose is dedicated to arguing that British repossession of the Cape of Good Hope is essential to the well-being of Britain. Barrow's pro-empire stance demands that he envision "Hottentots" at the particular expense of the Boer colonists. He condemns the Boer for not encouraging the "Hottentots," whom he calls a "race of men, of willing and intelligent minds."[40]

The more sympathetic constructions of "Hottentots" at the Cape does not mean that the British completely erased the traditional constructions of "Hottentots" from their minds. As we have seen, they considered the Boer as white "Hottentots" or worse. Representations of the Dutch colonists written during this first phase of the British occupation often depict them as even lower than the

"Hottentots." James Forbes remembers the "Hottentots" as "a mild, amiable, gentle race compared with the Dutch boers and yeomanry of the Cape," and citing the narratives written by Barrow and Percival, he says the Boer farmers who lived in the interior are "no better than the savages, and in clemency, urbanity, and other social virtues, far inferior to the Hottentots among whom they dwell."[41] Situating the Boers and the "Hottentots" together allowed British writers to argue that the "other" European inhabitants of the Cape region were not only below the British on any national chain of being, but they were in the process of descending even lower. Moreover, British representations of the Boer often went on to claim they were dangerous as well as degenerate: in a downward spiral themselves, they were blocking the "Hottentots" from ascending the human chain. It is only a slight overstatement to say that the road to the Anglo-Boer war began in these early years of the nineteenth century with publications like Barrow's.

We can never know, of course, if Barrow would have presented such a revisionary representation or expressed an equal amount of pity and compassion for "Hottentots" if Britain had not come to possess the Cape. Clearly, central to Barrow's vision of "Hottentots" is his confidence that they would help British emigrants and, thus, further Britain's interests: "The emigrants would have the great and immediate advantage of the assistance of the Hottentots—a quiet, intelligent, and industrious race, too happy at the idea of serving English families, from whom they know they will receive kind treatment."[42] At the same time, Barrow's sympathy might well have been sincere. In a posthumously published autobiographical memoir, he makes remarks consistent with his earlier expressions. There he describes "Hottentots" as "docile creature[s] who can be "moulded into any shape that his superiors think fit," and he uses the words "cruel" and "inhuman" to discuss the treatment they received from the Boers.[43]

To a great extent, Barrow's view of the "Hottentots" became the official British position on them. British writers and editors of geographies and encyclopedias displayed their preference for Barrow over Le Vaillant, Sparrman, or Kolb by awarding the highest authoritative status to their own countryman.[44] Indeed, Barrow's representation of "Hottentots" as a dying race—worse off than slaves—make up the last words in the entry on them in the 1812 and subsequent editions of Guthrie's *A New Geographical, Historical, and Commercial Grammar*:

> These weak people, the most helpless, and in their present condition perhaps the most wretched of the human race, duped out of their possessions, their country, and their liberty, have entailed upon their miserable offspring a state of existence to which that of slavery might bear the comparison of happiness. It is a condition, however, not likely to continue to a very remote posterity. The name of Hottentot will be forgotten or remembered only as that of a deceased person of little note."[45]

The comparison Barrow makes between "Hottentots" and slaves is not unusual for its time.

Once Britain held the Cape, the abolitionist movement began to show an interest in "Hottentots." In his *Walks and Sketches at the Cape of Good Hope* (1803), Robert Semple writes that "domestic slavery has at all times and in all nations been productive of much evil," and he acknowledges that even though the Hottentot "has not the name of slave . . . his condition is not on that account in the least more desirable."[46] Semple expresses his view that the law binding "Hottentots" to serve their masters for twenty-five years is tantamount to slavery: "his master enjoys twenty five years of his serveices for the prime of his life, and may then cast him off to seek his break elsewhere" (45). *An Account of the Colony of the Cape of Good Hope, with a View to the Information of Emigrants* (1819) depicts "Hottentots" as being "wholly subdued, by the Dutch, to a sort of service worse than slavery" and reckons that "the Hottentot, in the remoter parts, is exposed to as cruel usage as any of the West India slavedrivers can exercise."[47] Considering the "Hottentot" and the slave as just about one and the same, abolitionist authors framed their view of Cape "Hottentots" as less than free and, like the slaves, in need of protection and liberation.

British policy at the Cape in regards to "Hottentots" attempted to address, if not ameliorate, their unique status. The measures put in place by DuPre Alexander, second earl of Caledon, the first British governor at the Cape after the 1806 recapture, suggest that he endorsed what came to be seen as the "liberal" positions.[48] What became known as Caledon's "Hottentot" Code, enacted by proclamation on 1 November 1809, limited the movements of "Hottentots" but awarded them certain legal rights. As well, in May 1811, Caledon created the Judges of Assize, who were comissioned to travel through the country to hear, among other things, complaints made against Dutch farmers by their indigenous laborers.

Twentieth-century historians have viewed Caledon's code from a variety of perspectives. Vincent T. Harlow puts a positive spin on the code, recognizing that while the code "continued the economic dependence of the Hottentot labourer upon his farmer employer by tying him to a fixed place of abode . . . it was also designed to provide him with protection and saved the remnant of this unfortunate people from destruction."[49] Susan Newton-King, in addressing the implications of the "Hottentot" code, focuses instead on how it served to control the population:

> First, it was now legal to compel any Khoisan not in government service to serve the colonists, for without a pass he could not legally be anywhere at all. . . . The second implication . . . was that it gave to the local officials extensive opportunities for patronage in the sphere of labour distribution.[50]

Timothy Keegan also argues that the ordered registration of the Khoikhoi population and the required service contracts between them and their employers actually gave Europeans more power over them. He points out that once the code was in place, the Khoi needed approval to move their place of residence, and they could be detained if they did not have the passes they were required to carry. All this, Keegan believes, "enabled officials, even the lowliest, to control the lives of Khoi, and forcibly to contract out those Khoi without formal employment or without passes to colonists with influence, thereby greatly extending official powers of patronage."[51]

The enacting of Ordinance 50 in July 1828 effectively (confirmed on 15 January 1829) made defunct the pass laws that were instituted with Caledon's code. It also afforded apprentices and children far more protection and legal rights, and it confirmed that "Hottentots" could buy or possess land. Predictably, British authors put a positive spin on the new law. In relation to the plight of "Hottentots," George Thompson cited Ordinance 50 as proof of "the beneficent Government of England": "But happier times are now dawning upon them; and in the new arrangements about to be introduced, and the better code of laws soon to be conferred upon the Colony, the Hottentot race will find, I trust, that their case has not been overlooked by the beneficent Government of England."[52] British abolitionists, authors, and editors represented their nation as being better for and kinder toward "Hottentots" and slaves than were the Dutch colonists. A revised twenty-fourth edition of Guthrie's *A Geographical, Historical, and Commercial Grammar* (1827) asserts that "the British colonists are more liberal, friendly, and hospitable, than the Dutch, and less tyrannical in the treatment of their Hottentot and Malay slaves."[53]

7: "THE MOST WRETCHED OF THE HUMAN RACE"

Secular and religious periodical literature continued to print accounts testifying to the positive changes in the "Hottentots" since the start of the British colonial era. In 1808, the *Annual Register* describes and celebrates "Hottentot Devotion in South Africa":

> DECEMBER 24th, being Christmas-eve, many Christians, Hottentots, and slaves, came hither, and joined our congregation in celebrating Christmas with us. . . . Our church was crowded with attentive hearers, who, with us, adored our incarnate God and Saviour, praising him with heart and voice, that he came into the world to save sinners. . . . The congregation of believing Hottentots at Baviansklöof consists of 496 persons.[54]

Belief that "Hottentots" had accepted Christianity served to change their status completely. Faithful "Hottentots" can be figured as recovered, and equal in this way with others, be they English or African. Reverend C. I. Latrobe describes the success of the settlements of the United Brethren in his *Journal of a Visit to South Africa in 1815 and 1816* (1818): "Whoever charges the Hottentots with being inferior to other people of the same class, as to education and the means of improvement, knows nothing of them. They are possessed of good sense and even of considerable gifts, in speaking on various subjects, within the reach of their apprehension."[55]

The shared interests of the missionaries and the British government is evident in a London Missionary Society pamphlet, entitled *Mantis, the Soothsayer; Or, The Hottenots' God. A Conversation between a Missionary and a Hottentot; With an Account of the Insect* (1818, 2nd ed. in 1820). It pictures a "Hottentot" wagon driver remembering the insect he used to worship. The pamphlet reports the conversation as having taken place between missionary Evan Evans and his driver:

> July 15 [1817].—Experienced much pleasure this morning in conversing with the driver of our waggon, concerning the state of ignorance in which his nation was involved, before the Missionaries came among them. He showed me a small insect, which the farmer call *the Hottentots' God,* and which, in fact, they used to worship. This man said to me, "Oh, Sir! it is impossible for me to say how thankful I am to the good men over the great waters, because they have sent you, their servant, to teach poor Hottentots. But it is God, the Almighty God, who put this in the hearts of the good men in England; he said to them, "The poor Hottentots in Africa know nothing of me, the true God; they worship

a poor insect, that even they themselves can tread to death with their naked feet."[56]

The effectiveness of representations like this one should not be underestimated. Early-nineteenth-century readers believed in the "truth" of these kinds of accounts in the same way that eighteenth-century readers embraced what they read in travel narratives.

Early-nineteenth-century travel narratives emphasize the positive rather than focus on the negative, a strategy which stands in start contrast to the tendencies of seventeenth- and eighteenth-century representations. Maria Graham, at the Cape in April 1811, reports she was "delighted" with the "Hottentot" camp she saw at Wyneberg, because "eight hundred of that savage people have been civilized and taught the arts of society."[57] To her, they seem to be "as well as any peasants I remember to have seen. Their houses, furniture, and clothes, are all of their own manufacture, for they are ingenious and expert at any handicraft for which they have a pattern."[58] Graham's likening of "Hottentots" to the peasants she saw regularly in Britain is indicative of how the British were now much more willing to see "sameness" rather than insist on "difference." Poor but pristine is also a motif in John Campbell's description. Campbell, traveling at the Cape for the London Missionary Society in 1812, describes the situation of the forty or so "Hottentot" families who reside in the Moravian settlement at Groene Kloof, about thirty-five miles from Cape Town: "Their houses, though mean huts, were clean, and their dress, upon the whole was decent, though there were some exceptions."[59] Campbell's description of his departure from this station is purposefully evocative and visual:

> On clearing the thicket, and passing the end of the village, we found about forty Hottentots in a group, who sang a farewell hymn, which we answered by singing, "Praise God from whom all blessings flow, & c." The whole looked as if we had returned to the Paradisiacal age. Dreadful must be the wickedness of that part of the world where such institutions as these can be opposed. Great good they may effect, but harm they cannot do. The government of the colony, highly to their honour, has been kind to them. The poor Hottentots, in their own way, all bid us Farewell, which was returned, and not by any one without emotion. They stood looking after us as long as we were in sight.[60]

Campbell's reference to Eden presents an echo to the sixteenth-century accounts that declared the place a paradise. What he is suggesting is that with the Cape under British rule, and with the success the missionaries have had in converting "Hottentots," a true garden has at last been created there.

Another mark of the emerging colonialist rhetoric in descriptions of "Hottentots" is the tendency to incorporate them into the imperial economic plan. In September 1818, the British government offered free passage, land, and cash to those who organized parties of emigrants to the Cape. In 1820, more than four thousand Britains made the journey to begin development of the British Cape Colony. These new residents understood that it would have been counterproductive for them to view "Hottentots" as their adversaries or incidental to their mission at the Cape. David Spurr believes the "ultimate aim of colonial discourse . . . seeks to dominate by inclusion and domestication rather than by a confrontation which recognizes the independent identity of the Other"; its "impulse" is "to see the colonized people as ultimately sympathetic to the colonizing mission and to see that mission itself as bringing together the peoples of the world in the name of a common humanity."[61] Many settlers and visitors, such as William Wilberforce Bird, quickly realized how essential the "Hottentots" were to the success of the British colonial project, all of which increased the importance of the efforts to bring them into Christianity's fold.

> The Hottentots, both men and women, are shepherds, ox-herds, leaders of waggons; and the men drivers of them: and these duties are so absolutely required in the colony, that the greatest distress to the community would follow, were this class entirely domesticated. There is no part of the population so necessary to be encouraged and kept up, as the Hottentot, and none whom the government should guard with more constant protection.[62]

Bird had some doubts about how much "Hottentots" could be improved, however. He clearly feared that it was in the "Hottentot" nature to be somewhat nomadic: "All that any one interested in Cape comforts can bring himself to wish, with respect to what is called improvement in the Hottentot, is that, instead of continuing to be a wandering heathen, he might become a wandering Christian."[63] His doubts aside, Bird's representation of a wandering Christian "Hottentot" is still noticeably positive ("quick in capacity, and the progress of his intellect rapid").[64]

The image of a wandering or roaming "Hottentot" is also central to a sentimental and romantic construction that begins to emerge in this early stage of British colonization. There is a tendency in these representations to construct a former "Hottentot" nation that lived in harmony with itself and its surroundings, which serves to heighten any comparison with their present situation. In *Travels in the Interior of Southern Africa* (1822), William Burchell recounts what he imagined about "Hottentots" before he came ashore in 1810: "As I looked upon the mountains and the shore, my imagination carried me back to that period when its peaceable inhabitants, the simple Hottentots, roamed freely over the country, enjoying the liberty of nature, nor dreaming that a day could ever arrive when they must resign all to some unknown race of men, coming upon them from the ocean."[65] This image of "Hottentots" does not figure them as noble savages per se. Rather, it constructs them as victims of the Dutch, and now in need of rescue by the British.

Thomas Pringle's sonnet "The Hottentot," first published in 1827, shows all the tendencies of this emerging Cape colonialist construction: a yielding "Hottentot" figure, an idealization of the "Hottentot" past, and a condemnation of Boer cruelty and oppression:

> Mild, melancholy, and sedate he stands,
> Tending another's flocks upon the fields—
> His father's once—where now the white-man builds
> His home, and issues forth his proud commands:
> His dark eye flashes not; his listless hands
> Support the boor's huge firelock; but the shields
> And quivers of his race are gone: he yields,
> Submissively, his freedom and his lands.
> Has he no courage?—Once he had—but lo!
> The felon's chain hath worn him to the bone.
> No enterprise?—Alas! the brand, the blow
> Have humbled him to dust—his HOPE is gone.
> "He's a base-hearted hound—not worth his food"—
> His master cries;—"he has no *gratitude!*"[66]

Significantly, Pringle's negative reference to the Boer in lines six and seven is made less specific in a 1834 version, which describe the "Hottentot's listless hand" as: "Lean on the shepherd's staff; no more he wields / The Libyan bow—but to th'oppressor yields."[67] Pringle's revision is a polemical one that might well reflect his own activities in the abolitionist movement after his return to Britain in 1827, when he served as secretary to the Anti-Slavery Society. Pringle raises the issue of skin color in a note he wrote about the last phrase, "he has no gratitude," where he explains that "such was the common allegation of the colonists respecting the Hottentots, and frequently have I heard it repeated. My own experience enables me totally to deny its truth. But as a body, how could *gratitude* be *then* expected from them by the white men?"⁶⁸

Whatever sympathy early-nineteenth-century British colonialists might have had for the "Hottentots" at the Cape, it was not often articulated in their belletristic envisionings of them. Indeed, negative images of "Hottentots" continued to find expression in the poetry and novels of the time. George Marshall's *Epistles in Verse, between Cynthio and Leonora* (1812) invokes eighteenth-century stereotypes of "Hottentots," poetically rendering them as stupid, naked, and filthy.

> But now th'untutor'd natives of these plains
> Demand my song, uncouth and barb'rous swains!
> Scarce human form the squalid figures boast,
> Within, the mental spark in darkness lost!
> Naked, they stare around with wild grimace,
> Filth is their ornament, their cov'ring grease!
> When round their limbs the recent hide they throw,
> 'Tis garbage makes the Hottentot a beau!⁶⁹

Those Britons who opposed the missionary enterprise also employ the familiar negative images of "Hottentots." The *Edinburgh Review* (July 1806) attacks the "mistaken zeal" and the "misplaced expense" of those who want to preach "the most abstruse mysteries of our holy religion, to tribes of [Hottentot] savages who can scarcely count ten."⁷⁰ Charles Isaac Mungo Dibdin locates "Hottentots" in "The Age, a Satire" (1807): "To herd with some strange, unenlighten'd race, / With whom such actions ne'er entail disgrace; / Who, poor in spirit, and of manners rude, / Love the mean 'luxury of doing good.'/ There let him crawl his round, like some old wife, / And call the Hottentot-existence—Life."⁷¹

Significantly, marginalized British populations, such as Scots and women, continued to be depicted as British "Hottentots." They were envisioned as impolite, dirty, and savage, and, indeed, the representations reinforce these stereotypes. Susan Ferrier employs a "Hottentot" reference to make a class-oriented insult. In her novel *Marriage* (1818), two of her characters, an English bride and her maid, complain of being taken to Scotland. The maid demands that the driver who brought them there take them home: "A pretty way of travelling, to be sure, it will be," continued she, "to go bumping behind a dirty chaise-driver; but better to be shook to a jelly altogether, than stay amongst such a set of *Oaten-*

toads."[72] The maid's mispronunciation and her snobbery in relation to the driver is meant to suggest that she is a bit of an "oaten-toad" herself.

Unlike the eighteenth-century representations of British "Hottentots," which often suggest how they threatened the nation, nineteenth-century references do not show any serious worry or concern that society will degenerate or is at peril because of them. British "Hottentots" are represented as lacking politeness, taste, and social grace, but they are dismissed in a comic fashion rather than satirically roasted. In her novel *The Wanderer; Or, Female Difficulties* (1814), Frances Burney is being somewhat ironical when she has Mrs. Ireton, a rude character based on her stepmother,[73] distance herself from a Hottentot: " 'Pray, Ma'am,' Mrs. Ireton cried, 'permit me to enquire—' her eye angrily, yet cautiously, glancing at Mr. Giles, 'to what extraordinary circumstance I am indebted, for having the honour of receiving your visitors? Not that I am insensible to such a distinction; you won't imagine me such a Hottentot, I hope, as to be insensible to so honourable a distinction.' "[74] Burney, of course, is using the reference as a signal to the reader. Readers are left little doubt that Mrs. Ireton is, in fact, deserving of the "Hottentot" association.

Representations of "Hottentot" females continue to adhere to the traditional constructions. Lucy Aikin's *Epistles on Women* (1810) imagines "Hottentot" females as stupid and idle: "And vacant Hottentots, short labour done, / Toy, pipe, and carol in the evening sun."[75] More seriously, "Hottentot" females continue to represent a sexual woman as opposed to a maternal one. A section of Thomas Hood's "Little O'Patrick—An African Fact" (pre-1845) pictures a "Hottentot" woman trying to seduce Little Patrick: "She came to accept him for life in her arms, / And stretch'd her thick lips to a broad grin of love, / A Raven preparing to bill like a Dove, / With a soul full of dread he declined the grim bliss."[76] Moreover, "Hottentot" females continue to raise the possibility of perversion in the British consciousness. Herbert's charge of bestiality is remembered in Charles Maturin's gothic novel, *Melmoth the Wanderer* (1820), when the superior of a convent is described as having "no more idea of the intercourse between the sexes, than between two beings of a different species. The scene that he beheld could not have revolted him more, than if he had seen the horrible loves of the baboons and the Hottentot women, at the Cape of Good Hope."[77]

The British attention to female "Hottentot" genitalia continued well into the nineteenth century, despite the best efforts of William Somerville, a young Scottish doctor, who submitted a twenty-six-page report on the subject to the Royal Society in 1805.[78] Somerville's report addresses "the great questions" about "Hottentot" women. A description and pencil sketch demonstrate the falseness of previous descriptions of female genitalia. At the very start of his report, Somerville comments on "the ignorance and credulity that has caused other travellers to falsely record their impressions of Hottentot women."[79] "Hottentot" women go "on through life performing every healthy function, fulfilling the duties of her sex just as perfectly as any other women."[80] Somerville says he found that "from within the Vulva descends a loose flabby substance, wrinkled in appearance, which being superficially examined has given rise to the erroneous terms of flap or apron."[81] Also, he quite deliberately addresses the representations that accuse "Hottentot" women of being immodest.

> It is but justice to the modesty of the Hottentots to say, that I have constantly found as many difficulties on the part of the women to submit to the exposure of those parts which a closer inspection required, as in all probability would have occurred in persuading an equal number of females of any other description to undergo examination. Some it is true, of abandoned character from greater intercourse with white people than their untutored countrywomen in remoter parts of the settlement, scrupuled not to exhibit themselves for a stipulated price. But I have seen high bribes scorned and every offer that temptation could hold out rejected with contempt by Hottentot maidens almost naked, the indecency of whose attire would have provoked the censure of a wanton on London streets.[82]

Fascination with the figure of the "Hottentot" female, as well as the demonization of her, continued to hold currency in the nineteenth century because it proved to be such a useful vent for any number of British domestic and imperial anxieties.

Issues of race, gender, and British politics converge in belles-lettres and visual representations of Saartjie Baartman, the "Hottentot" Venus, who was displayed in London in 1810.[83] Her nickname alone suggests the link between "Hottentot" females and sexuality. Despite the name assigned to her, Baartman was not, in fact, a Cape Khoikhoi woman. She was from the Bushmen society, and she had their characteristic steatopygia (deposits of fat on her buttocks), which struck Europeans as misshapen and gross. Alexander Dunlop, the man who brought her to England, exhibited her so that her buttocks could be examined. The *Times* (26 November 1810) provides a description of the scene:

a stage raised about three feet from the floor, with a cage, or enclosed place at the end of it; that the Hottentot was within the cage; that on being ordered by her keeper, she came out, and that her appearance was highly offensive to delicacy . . . The Hottentot was produced like a wild beast, and ordered to move backwards and forwards, and come out and go into her cage, more like a bear in a chain than a human being . . . She frequently heaved deep sighs; seemed anxious and uneasy; grew sullen, when she was ordered to play on some rude instrument of music . . . And one time, when she refused for a moment to come out of her cage, the keeper let down the curtain, went behind, and was seen to hold up his hand to her in a menacing posture; she then came forward at his call, and was perfectly obedient. . . . She is dressed in a colour as nearly resembling her skin as possible. The dress is contrived to exhibit the entire frame of her body, and spectators are even invited to examine the peculiarities of her form.[84]

According to Lindfors and others, members of the African Association pressed a suit against Dunlop and his partner.[85] The case was heard on 24 November 1810; the suit was dismissed because it was found that Baartman consented to her own display. The exhibition did not last much longer, however, and Baartman disappeared from public view. In 1814, she went to Paris, and was exhibited there, causing the same kind sensation as she did in England. She died in Paris on 29 December 1815; her body was autopsied and dissected by G. Cuvier and, possibly, J. J. Virey, who published a report on her remains in the *Journal Universel des Sciences Médicales* (1816).[86]

Baartman's display in London prompted much occasional verse. All of it dismisses her in a light-hearted way. The following four lines present a representative verse: "A rump she has (though strange it be), / Large as a cauldron pot, / And this is why men go to see / This lovely Hottentot."[87] The visual representations of the "Hottentot" Venus are even more interesting than the poetry, because they make visible the intersections of politics and gender. These depictions of the "Hottentot" Venus place her with prominent male political figures; she is thus given the power to ruin the reputations of British men who associate with her. The political rumor in the autumn months of 1810 was that Spencer Perceval's very weak ministry, which had been in power since October 1809, was about to fall, and that William Wyndham Grenville would organize a new ministry.

Heath's "Love at First Sight, or A Pair of Hottentots with an Addition to the Broad Bottom Family," depicts a nude Grenville greeting a nude Venus holding a staff of government. Both have

William Heath, "Love at First Sight, or A Pair of Hottentots with an Addition to the Broad Bottom Family." Permission of the Pierpont Morgan Library.

C. Williams, "Prospects of Prosperity, or Good Bottoms Going into Business." Permission of the Pierpont Morgan Library.

large bottoms. He says to her: "at Last I have met with a True Broad Bottom real Flesh no Deception!!! I wonder if Broad Bottoms would breed in this Country." She responds in pidgin English: "Me hear of your Bottom, me Long to See it, me write to you about it!!!" A figure representing Lord Temple says, "Charming Indeed, oh I am so pappy [sic] the Family is not Extinct."[88] His mistaken diction works on two levels. It suggests the next generation might lose their ability to speak English, which answers Grenville's question about whether or not they could breed in Britain, and it refers to Temple's father, the marquis of Buckingham, who is pictured standing behind Grenville. Buckingham, Grenville's brother, does not look at all pleased by the imminent exchange about to occur between his brother and the "Venus Hottentot," and he says, "ah' sure a Pair were never seen so justly formed to meet by Nature."

Williams's "Prospects of Prosperity, or Good Bottoms Going into Business," has a figure representing Grenville rush forward to embrace an almost naked "Hottentot" Venus.[89] His rump is almost as large as hers. The words out of his mouth address the similarity of their situations: "My dear Sartjee I come to congratulate you, you are going to trade on your own bottom I find. I expect soon to be in the same situation myself." Her answer, spoken in pidgin English, suggests that the dawning of his government will help her out: "Ah! glad of dat broder broady, good ting! me got only half my bottom belong to me no do much good wid dat." The following year, Williams produced another print depicting the "Hottentot" Venus. This one, however, has the duke of Clarence in its satiric sights.[90]

In 1816, years after she had left Britain, her influence (or the idea of it) is addressed satirically in *The Talents Run Mad; or, Eighteen Hundred and Sixteen* (1816). In a dialogue between the author and his friend, the friend laments that men shun "our fair ones' European charms, / And woos the brown embrace of Afric arms."[91] A footnote on the bottom of the page explains:

> Woos the brown embrace of Afric arms.—It is well known, that divers gentlemen, stricken in years, paid the most delicate attentions to the Hottentot Venus. As for that idle story of the good Mr. B.—, no one now believes a syllable of it. The facts of the interview were these. Mr. B—having called on Venus, naturally began the conversation by remarking that it was a fine day. Venus agreed with him; and no sooner did she observe that the day before had also been fine, then he agreed with her. He then took the opportunity of hoping that the next day

might be as fine; and she did not omit so favorable an occasion of likewise hoping that it might. In short, there was not a drop of rain difference in their opinions; and Mr. B.—concluded a conversation, replete with weather, by converting Venus to Christianity.[92]

Satire like this is meant to be amusing and offensive, and this one succeeds on both counts. The "Hottentot" Venus appears to enjoy the power given to her to infect those who carry the nation into the future. And for their part, the diseased and giddy men have degenerated enough to respond to her. The poem's reference to the Venus's conversion to Christianity indicts the church as well. Appearing in print before emigration to the Cape began in earnest, *The Talents Run Mad* poses a serious warning to those who might be tempted by the "charms" of "Hottentot" females.

As the British Cape Colony developed, fascination with "Hottentots" waned. According to Timothy Keegan, after abolition in 1834, notice taken of them certainly declined."[93] Representations of "Hottentots" can be found in the British periodical press only when there were outbreaks of hostilities in the colony, changes in colonial policy, or upon the publication of a controversial travel narrative. The British were more interested in the new and extensive representations of Xhosa and Zulu societies, who were getting in the way of their expanding colony. The nineteenth-century construction of "Hottentots" that fixed them as a victimized and dying people worked as a sort of self-fulfilling prophecy.

The British visitors to the Cape Colony who wrote letters and travel narratives just about universally recognize that the "Hottentots" will disappear. Those who supported missionary societies and the abolition of slavery usually adopted a "liberal" attitude in relation to "Hottentots." In the letters Lady Margaret Herschel, wife of the astronomer John Herschel, wrote while she lived in Cape Town (1834–38), she constantly refers to the "Hottentots" as the "poor Hottentots." They are objects of her pity because she felt that they were being crushed by heartless "tyranny."

> This same Cape of Good Hope is soiled & blackened by human nature in some of its worst shapes—one of which is *tyranny* over the black population. . . . Only three weeks ago the families of three hundred Hottentots who have been fighting *for* the Colony, have been turned out, at a day's warning of their Cottages near Uitenhage, & from their fields of ripening corn & pumpkins while their Husbands & Brothers were at a distance under arms, just because the farmers at Uitenhage asked the Governor to give *them* the land for grazing. It is said that Government had only given the land to the Hottentots *on sufferance*, but they

were not allowed the common kindliness of being *suffered* to wait to eat what they had planted & sowed—the curses of the Hottentot soldiers when they heard of it "were loud & deep," & a mutiny is to be feared, which will be represented in Colonial Reports as an act of savage treachery & ingratitude. When such wickedness is acted in high places, one can only bite one's lips & hold one's breath & turn away as from an incurable disease, & in a place like this we at last learn the lesson to shut our eyes & ears lest we should listen to a string of utter falsehoods or truths worse than any fiction—& this is one reason why I prize my home employments so much & cling to them as to an anchor of safety & defence.[94]

While Margaret Herschel rails against colonial tyranny, she also finds positive things to say about "Hottentots." She does not regard them as "nasty" or "stupid," and she does not berate them for idleness. Significantly, she does not cast doubt on the sincerity of the "Hottentots" at the mission settlements who converted to Christianity, as do so many other British travelers. After returning to Cape Town from a visit to the Moravian mission at Genadendal, Herschel describes a moment from that trip: "Coming out of one cottage half an hour *before* morning service on the Sunday we found the *whole* congregation assembled in groups on the green *waiting* for the Bell. I thought how different from the lagging droppers in of an English church."[95] Herschel's willingness to see British people as not measuring up to a "Hottentot" standard is unusual.

British visitors to the Cape who represent "Hottentots" as being responsible for their own demise generally blame them for not being able to adapt or live up to British standards. Alfred W. Cole articulates this view in his travel narrative of the Cape Colony: "wherever the foot of civilization treads, the native tribes melt away."[96] Not surprisingly, Cole does not support the efforts of missionary societies to "improve" the "Hottentots." He thinks the missionaries "begin at the wrong end. They strive to make Christians before they have made men out of barbarians"; he does not recognize the converted as such—"they attend the chapels of the missionary station; but notwithstanding their religion, they are filthy drunkards, almost to a man, and to a woman too."[97] Additionally, he charges that the "Hottentots" at the missionary stations have other reasons for converting:

> the Hottentot Christian feels himself a more important person, from the notice taken of him by the missionaries and their friends . . . it is of very great pecuniary advantage to him. Each missionary station has a

tract of land belonging to it, on which are built the chapel, the schoolhouse, the minister's residence & c. A Hottentot has only to go and attend the school and chapel regularly, and to play the devout well, when he will be allowed to erect a hut on the land, and a small piece of ground will be given him as a garden. He will be supplied with implements and seeds, and by doing a little work about once a week he can thus live all the rest of the time in idleness.[98]

Similarly, Harriet Ward expresses disdain not only for "Hottentots" but also for those who champion them: "from the smoky hut of the indolent Hottentot—and from the tent and bivouac of the soldier—let the voice of Truth be heard! Ye philanthropists—fallacious reasoners on subjects of which ye know nothing certain, who romanticize about savages and slavery till ye get entangled in a web of metaphysics of your own weaving."[99]

Almost all these representations use or imply the past tense when speaking about "Hottentots." In June 1837, the *Saturday Magazine* does so in its description of them as a weak and nonthreatening people: "The Hottentots, before they submitted to the yoke of the Dutch, were divided into numerous independent tribes, and possessed a character resembling that of the best-disposed Bushmen, with whom they were no doubt identical, but the state of slavery in which they now exist has, in most cases, destroyed the buoyancy of their disposition, and they are now generally a mild, kind, and timid people."[100] In 1850, Napier's *Excursions in Southern Africa* declares them extinct, reporting that the "Quaiquae" "as a nation, may be said now no longer to exist."[101] Napier does not extend much sympathy to those who managed to survive: "the Hottentots of the present day—in number probably not a tithe of their forefathers, are, with few exceptions, scattered over the face of the country in the shape of domestic servants, of vagrants, or of worse than useless idlers at different missionary establishments within the colony."[102] It is only partially true to say that "Hottentots" stopped being constructed as the most savage of all human peoples because they ceased to exist as a viable society. By the time the British stretched themselves through the Cape colony, their agents of empire had little reason to fear any moment of contact between themselves and "Hottentots." Throughout much of the nineteenth century, the title of humanity's lowest people was placed on the Bushmen people, who were sometimes called "wild Hottentots," and later on the Zulu and other societies who were demonized as savage and backward Africans.

Negative ideas and images of "Hottentots" lingered in the British and western consciousness, however. Later nineteenth-century belles-lettres representations of "Hottentots" never adopted more sympathetic constructions. In the pages of British novels, poems, or newspapers, "Hottentots" continued to represent beast-like humans or pagans. Robert Leighton depicts Hottentots with a Scottish accent in his *Scotch Words, and the Bapteesement o' the Bairn* (1869). Employing such a traditional construction lets him separate the religious from the heathens: Ye're richt, guidman, rather than hands like his / Bapteese the bairn, we'll keep it as is— / For aye an outlin' wi' its kith an' kin / A hottentot, a heathen steep'd in sin!"[103] The heathen here is not pictured as a serious threat—he is just a "Hottentot." In *The Mill on the Floss*, George Eliot employs "Hottentot" representations to criticize Maggie Tulliver's wealthy Aunt Pullet. As Susan Meyer points out in her *Imperialism and Home: Race and Victorian Women's Fiction*, Mrs. Pullet, as "the embodiment of the civilized," is reduced through her comparison to a Hottentot figure.[104] William Makepeace Thackeray invokes the "Hottentot" Venus for a comparison in *Vanity Fair*.[105] Charles Dickens's "Tom Tiddler's Ground" features a hermit named Mr. Mopes, who steeps "himself in soot and grease and other nastiness," and gives his career more renown than if he had been an "ordinary Christian or decent Hottentot."[106] These negative belles-lettristic representations suggest that no matter Britain's imperial dominance around the world, the collective British imagination still had a need for demonizing "Hottentots."

Conclusion:
Remembering "Hottentots"

IMAGES OF "HOTTENTOTS" AS SIMPLE, UNCIVILIZED, AND WEIRD OR barely human people, survived into the twentieth century. Indeed, members of the general public were probably not even aware that their views of "Hottentots" had derived from European invention. Early-twentieth-century representations come in variety of presentational forms, and they make for some odd entries in cultural history. America's most curious "Hottentot" representation is found in the ranks of a Negro League baseball team, named the Terra Haute Hottentots. Beyond its obvious play with alliteration, the name suggests the color-driven climate of American society, if not also an owner's attempt to demean the players on his team. "Hottentot" representations can also be found in other forms of popular culture.

Musical representations of "Hottentots" were especially popular at the turn of the century. As we have seen, images of dancing "Hottentots" were often used in eighteenth-century travel narratives and other sources to mock and degrade the Cape Khoikhoi, and the early-twentieth-century representations continue this tradition. The titles alone of two pieces of instrumental music, Alan Macey's "The Hottentots: Cocoa Nut Dance" (1896) and Theodore F. Morse's "Happy Hottentots: Dance Unique" (1904), fetishize them for their dancing style. The musical representations continue the practise of sexualizing "Hottentot" females. In 1901, Harry Von Tilzer composed a song called, "My Lady Hottentot," and, five years later, Marie Cahill enjoyed a hit with "The Hottentot Love Song."

In February 1916, Al Jolson starred in *Robinson Crusoe, Jr.*, a self-styled "musical Extravaganza," which featured a song called "Happy Hottentots." The lyrics present "Hottentots" as cannibals:

> 'Way down in the jungle, those Hottentot are playing
> 'Way down in the savaged, down in the ravaged land
> . . . .

> If a victim comes along, they'll take him right away
> When he hears their raggy song, he'd better start to pray,
> For they will take him and bake him a while,
> Oh, those dancing Hottentots upon that ragtime isle.[1]

Other early-twentieth-century musical "Hottentot" representations include Ethel Waters's song, "The Hottentot Potentate," and Laura Elizabeth Richards's *The Hottentot and Other Ditties: Words and Melodies* (1939).

Perhaps the century's most extensive dramatic representation of "Hottentot" can be found in Victor Mapes and William Collier's farce, *The Hottentot*, which played at the George M. Cohan Theater on New York's Broadway in 1920. The "Hottentot" in question is a race horse, first described as a "nasty brute, with a cranky and dangerous disposition," although he redeems himself by winning a race at a Long Island steeplechase track. At play's end, voices in the fashionable crowd are rooting him on:

> *Ollie:* Look at the Hottentot take that water jump! (*Waving his cap.*) A race, a race. By Jove, it's a race. (*All commence to yell 'Hottentot, Hottentot.' Crowd off stage takes it up.*) The Hottentot wins!
> Sam enters. [He was riding the horse, and he presents the winner's trophy to Peggy]
> *Sam:* (*Tries to speak, can't, nods. After a pause*) We got off to a pretty bad start, but when the Hottentot gets going, he's some horse—I'll tell the world.[2]

Two film versions of the play appeared: a silent picture in 1922 and a talkie in 1929, and both received excellent reviews. *Movie Picture World* called the 1922 film "one of the very best and most highly amusing comedies yet brought to the screen."[3] The later version also won acclaim for its "natural laughs"; the reviewer for *Variety* punned that the production "is exceptionally well mounted."[4]

More famously, the specter of "Hottentots" can be seen in the form of "Tottenhots" in the Oz series, first appearing in *The Patchwork Girl of Oz* (1913). They present a weird parable of European colonization of the Cape. The "Tottenhots" are described as being "a tribe of fun-loving night people who live in . . . a collection of houses that look like large overturned kettles with hatches on top. They are small, dusky people with scarlet colored hair that stands straight up like wires. They wear skins around the waist for clothing and have bracelets on their ankles and wrists, necklaces, and large pendant earrings."⁵ In *The Patchwork Girl of Oz,* Dorothy, Ojo, and friends have trouble with the "Tottenhots" at first contact.

> The black dots grew larger as they advanced and although the light was dim Dorothy thought they looked like big kettles turned upside down . . . By this time Dorothy had discovered they were people, tiny and curiously formed, but still people . . . the little girl turned to the queer creatures and said: "who are you?"
> They answered this question all together, in a sort of chanting chorus, the words being as follows:
> We're the jolly Tottenhots;
> We do not like the day,
> But in the night 'tis our delight
> To gambol, skip and play.
>
> We hate the sun and from it run,
> The moon is cool and clear,
> So on this spot each Tottenhot
> Waits for it to appear.
>
> We're ev'ry one chock full of fun,
> And full of mischief, too;
> But if you're gay and with us play
> We'll do no harm to you.⁶

The "Tottenhots" and Dorothy and her band have a misunderstanding that results in both parties being hurt or scared. The "Tottenhots" disappear, but then reappear. A "Tottenhot" challenges Dorothy and company:

> It was just a little rough-house, that's all, said the Tottenhot. "But the question is not if WE will behave, but if YOU will behave? We can't be shut up here all night, because this is our time to play; nor do we care to come out and be chewed up by a savage beast or slapped by an angry girl. That slapping hurts like sixty; some of my folks are crying about it. So here's the proposition: you let us alone and we'll let you alone."⁷

Needless to say, this proposition the "Tottenhots" present to Dorothy and her company has a strange and eerie resonance. If only the "Tottenhots" had been left alone!

The representations in the above-mentioned texts reveal that no matter their dominance, Britain and America have a need for contructions of "Hottentots.' But twentieth-century history proves to us that the desire and need to demonize other cultures is not only a European trait. In mid-twentieth-century South Africa, the accession to power of Daniel Malan's Reunified National Party (called the National Party after 1951), the advent of the apartheid system, and, most specifically, the Population Registration Act of 1950, meant that the descendents of the Cape Khoikhoi were classified as "colored." Perhaps no government order demonstrates the brutality of the National Party's apartheid system more fully than the destruction of District Six in Cape Town. In 1966, the South African government issued an order to raze District Six, the residential area of Cape Town where most of the "colored" population lived. Fifty thousand to sixty thousand people were made homeless and were forced to relocate to townships on the Cape Flats, miles outside of Cape Town. Allister Sparks, who has written that "the road from slavery to apartheid was across the broken backs of the Khoikhoi," characterized the new townships as "soulless places, frightened and frightening."[8] Fuad Petersen, one of the thousands uprooted, described their loss of community: "When we were evicted from District Six, we lost more than our home. We lost neighbours and friends whom we could rely on in times of sickness or other misfortune. The government gave us another home, but it couldn't give us a sense of belonging."[9] Once again, whatever was left of the Cape Khoikhoi population was dispossessed.

At the close of the twentieth century, South Africa has set its country on a path that seeks to honor and remember the great diversity of its people. Indeed, the recent initiation of majority rule has reenergized the rights movement by and for indigenous peoples. A new generation of "Hottentot" representations and references have helped spread the message of this new movement. Organizations such as the Griqua National Congress are helping to raise the public's level of awareness of what happened to the Cape Khoikhoi and other Khoisan peoples. New cultural spaces are being created, and older ones are being transformed. December 1994 marked the opening of the District Six Museum in Cape Town, which intends to serve "as a reminder that forced removals must never happen again."[10] In 1996, the South African National Gallery mounted a show detailing how the Bushmen people have been abused and misrepresented by museums, science, and popular culture.[11] And, finally, Robben Island and its infamous prison are now in the public trust as a museum.

Significantly, the figure of the "Hottentot" Venus is playing an especially unique role in the revisioning of South Africa. In 1979, Stephen Gray, one of South Africa's most well-known writers and editors, published a collection of poetry entitled, *Hottentot Venus and Other Poems*. The speaker in the volume's title poem is presented as Saartjie Baartman ("they called me the Hottentot

Venus").[12] Throughout she speaks for herself, reflecting on her history and fame. She does so in a voice that is unafraid and challenging.

> I know my rights I put down my foot
> and the Tuileries Gardens shake I put down
> my foot and the Seine changes course I put
> down my foot and the globe turns upside down
> I rattle my handful of bones and the dead arise.[13]

Of course, Gray's use of her figure also works symbolically. The Saartjie Baartman in his book speaks for all the Khoikhoi and San peoples, generations of whom suffered under colonialism's agents and rules.

Representations of the "Hottentot" Venus have become central to the conscience and consciousness of the indigenous peoples' rights movement. The Griqua National Congress has mounted a campaign to have her remains returned to South Africa from the Musee de l'Homme, where they have been held since her death. Her story has recently been told by Zola Maseko, a South African film director. His film about her, "The Life and Times of Sara Baartman: The Hottentot Venus," was shown at the 1999 London film festival.[14]

Late-twentieth-century American writers have also found her a compelling figure for feminist construction. In Elizabeth Alexander's title poem, "The Venus Hottentot," she describes what she would do if she could rise up from Cuvier's autopsy table.

> If he were to let me rise up
> from this table, I'd spirit
> his knives and cut out his black heart,
> seal it with science fluid inside
> a bell jar, place it on a low
> shelf in a white man's museum
> so the whole world could see
> it was shriveled and hard,
> geometric, deformed, unnatural.[15]

Significantly, Alexander's Venus is not in full control of her situation; she needs Cuvier's figure to "let" her rise up. The poem presents her highly personal dream of revenge.

Suzan-Lori Parks's 1996 play about the "Hottentot Venus," entitled *Venus*, projects multiple cultures (French, British, American, South African) and histories into the landscape of this figure's life.¹⁶ Parks explains her approach as follows: " 'Tell all the Truth but tell it slant,' as Emily Dickinson says. With *Venus* my angle is this: *History, Memory, Dis-Memory, Remembering, Dismembering, Love, Distance, Time, a Show.*"¹⁷ In the play, Parks purposefully employs unconventional form and language to stress the business of nineteenth-century exhibitions and the circus atmosphere of Venus's life. Parks uses role doubling, dialect, sounds, historical footnotes, and a chorus in order to reveal some truth about the roles/characters. For example, in a scene that has the character called "Mother-Showman" explaining who Venus is to the spectators, Parks neatly summarizes—in four lines—the traditional constructions of "Hottentots," from the story of Cory to the Venus.

> Ladies and Gents: The Venus Hottentot
> Shes been in civilization a whole year and still hasnt learnd nothing!
> The very lowest rung on Our Lords Great Evolutionary Ladder!
> Observe: I kick her like I kick my dog!¹⁸

Parks's use of a dog comparison provides an eerie echo of the numerous early-seventeenth-century English accounts that referred to Cory and the Cape people as dogs.

By devoting more than one role to Venus, Parks pays special attention to the different stages of her life. "The Girl" is shy, but tempted by money. "The Venus" is sometimes compliant, sometimes assertive, and often questioning about what is being done to her. Despite her situation, as the Bride-to-Be she still believes in love (or longs to believe in love). Venus's penultimate speech in the play, spoken after other characters announce her death, presents her own summation of her life.

> Tail end of the tale for there must be uh end is that Venus, Black Goddess, was shameless, she sinned or else completely unknowing thuh Godfearin ways, she stood showing her ass off in her iron cage. When Death met Love Death deathd Love and left Love tuh rot *au naturel* end for thuh Miss Hottentot. Loves soul, which was tidy, hides in heaven, yes, that it Loves corpse stands on show in museum. Please visit.¹⁹

Venus closes the play by asking for kisses, and thus to some extent she remains a sexual being. In Parks's rendering of her, she has voice (in her own language) and power at the close of the play.

Late-twentieth century representations of powerful and knowing "Hottentots" mark a radical and welcome departure from the traditional constructions.

Significantly, these new "Hottentot" representations, for the most part, do not pretend to speak for the Khoikhoi peoples. That would be impossible. Instead they present a chorus of voices that actively insist in the repudiation of the traditional constructions, which began to be assembled when the English envisioned a society on to which they could vent their frustrations and inscribe their own nightmares. Negative constructions of "Hottentots" sustained the English for so long that we must not attempt to excuse them simply as an inevitable and reflex consequence of individual and collective confusions and fears. As I have explored through my analysis of precolonial literary representations, the kind of prejudice that developed against "Hottentots" was the result of a process that requires time, texts, and ideology. Indeed, the English demonization, diminishment, and dismissal of them was a chosen and learned activity. Eager students, the early-modern English enthusiastically accepted the lessons that taught them they were superior to "Hottentots." They conveniently ignored or forgot that the Khoikhoi peoples lay underneath their constructions of "Hottentots," but we must not.

Notes

INTRODUCTION

1. Dan Jacobson, "The Road to Griquatown,"*Times Literary Supplement,* 1 April 1994, 3.
2. See, for example, Danby P. Fry, *The Word "Hottentot": Articles extracted from the Transactions of the Philological Society* (London, 1866; rpt. Pretoria: The State Library, 1971), 1, and Alan Barnard, *Hunters and Herders of Southern Africa: A Comparative Ethnography of the Khoisan Peoples* (Cambridge: Cambridge University Press, 1992), 9.
3. Barnard, 156.
4. Ibid., 160.
5. John Parker, *Books to Build An Empire: A Bibliographical History of English Overseas Interests to 1620* (Amsterdam: N. Israel, 1965), 158.
6. Wallace T. MacCaffrey points this out in his *Elizabeth I: War and Politics, 1588–1603* (Princeton: Princeton University Press, 1992), 541.
7. Lawrence Stone, *The Crisis of the Aristocracy, 1558–1641* (Oxford: Oxford University Press, 1967), 15.
8. Parker, 229.
9. Janssen's memorandum is discussed and quoted in Richard Elphick's *Khoikhoi and the Founding of White South Africa* (Johannesburg: Ravan Press, 1985), 87–88.
10. See Allister Sparks, *The Mind of South Africa* (New York. Alfred A. Knopf, 1990), 29–30.
11. Historian Shula Marks has written the most authoritative accounts of Khoisan resistance. See her "Khoisan Resistance to the Dutch in the Seventeenth and Eighteenth Centuries," *Journal of African History,* xiii, 1 (1972): 55–80.
12. Herman Giliomee and Richard Elphick present the following popoulation statistics to mark the European growth rate in the entire Cape Colony: 125 in 1670; 788 in 1690; 1,693 in 1711; 2,540 in 1730; 4,511 in 1750; 7,736 in 1770; c. 20,000 in 1798; 42,975 in 1820. See their "The Structure of European Domination at the Cape, 1652–1820," *The Shaping of South African Society, 1652–1800* (London, 1979), 360.
13. *The Oxford History of South Africa,* 206.
14. Monica Wilson, "The Hunters and Herders," *A History of South Africa to 1870,* eds. Monica Wilson and Leonard Thompson (Cape Town & Johannesburg: David Philip, 1982), 68. Monica Wilson estimates the total Khoikhoi population south of the Orange River in 1652 to be about 200,000 (68).
15. Percy Ward Laidler and Michael Gelfand take this census from Theal's work. See Gelfand and Laidler, *South Africa: Its Medical History* (Cape Town: C. Struik, 1971), 145.
16. Chinua Achebe, "An Image of Africa," *Research in African Literatures,* vol. 9 (1978), 2.

17. See, for example, *Africa and Africans As Seen by Classical Writers*, ed. Joseph E. Harris (Washington, D.C.: Howard University Press, 1977) and Eldred D. Jones, *The Elizabethan Image of Africa* (Charlottesville: University of Virginia Press, 1971).

18. Margaret T. Hodgen, *Early Anthropology in the Sixteenth and Seventeenth Centuries* (Philadelphia: University of Pennsylvania Press, 1964), 54.

19. Edward Aston, *The Manner and Customs of All Nations* (London, 1611), 48–49.

20. Thomas Stephens in Richard Hakluyt, *The Principal Navigations* (London, 1599), 2:100.

21. John Jourdain, quoted in R. Raven-Hart, *Before Van Riebeeck: Callers at South Africa from 1488 to 1652* (Cape Town: C. Struik, 1967), 42.

22. J.M. Coetzee, *White Writing: On the Culture of Letters in South Africa* (New Haven: Yale University Press, 1988), 3.

23. Benedict Anderson, *Imagined Communities* (London: Verso, 1991), 5–7.

24. Bernard W. Sheehan, *Savagism and Civility: Indians and Englishmen in Colonial Virginia* (Cambridge: Cambridge University Press, 1980), 6.

25. Andrew Hadfield and Willy Maley, eds., *Representing Ireland: Literature and the Origins of Conflict, 1534–1660* (Cambridge: Cambridge University Press, 1993), 7.

26. Ibid., 7.

27. Hayden White, *Tropics of Discourse: Essays in Cultural Criticism* (Baltimore: Johns Hopkins University Press, 1978), 151.

28. Rose A. Zimbardo, "Satiric Representation of Venereal Disease: The Restoration versus the Eighteenth-Century Model," *The Secret Malady*, ed. Linda E. Merians (Lexington: University Press of Kentucky, 1996), 183.

29. Philip D. Curtin, *The Image of Africa: British Ideas and Action, 1780–1850* (Madison: University of Wisconsin Press, 1964), 30.

30. Winthrop D. Jordan, *White Over Black: American Attitudes Toward the Negro, 1550–1812* (Chapel Hill: Institute of Early American History and Culture, 1968), 11.

31. James Walvin, *England, Slaves and Freedom, 1776–1838* (Mississippi: Univ. Press of Mississippi, 1986), 77.

32. John Maxwell, "An Account of the Cape of Good Hope," *Philosophical Transactions of the Royal Society*, vol. 25 (1706–7), 2424.

33. Willem Ten Rhyne's account, *A Short Account of the Cape of Good Hope*, was first published in 1686. It did not appear in English until it was excerpted in the Churchill Collection (1704). This translation comes from *The Early Cape Hottentots*, ed. I. Schapera and B. Farrington (Cape Town: Van Riebeeck Society, 1933), 113.

34. Michael Streak, *The Afrikaner As Viewed by the English*, 30

35. Georges Louis Leclerc, Count de Buffon, *Histoire Naturelle*. This is the English translation that appeared in *Barr's Buffon*, 1792, 296.

36. Abbé Raynal, *A Philosophical and Political History of the Settlements and Trade of the Europeans in the East and West Indians* (London, 1783), 309.

37. Edward Said, *Orientalism* (New York: Vintage Books, 1979), 43.

38. See Mary Louise Pratt, *Imperial Eyes: Travel Writing and Transculturation* (London and New York: Routledge, 1992); David Spurr, *The Rhetoric of Empire: Colonial Discourse in Journalism, Travel Writing, and Imperial Administration* (Durham: Duke University Press, 1993); Sara Suleri, *The Rhetoric of English India* (Chicago: University of Chicago Press, 1992); Jyotsna G. Singh, *Colonial Narratives/Cultural Dialogues: Discoveries of India in the language of colonialism* (London and New York:

Routledge, 1996); Simon Gikandi, *Maps of Englishness: Writing Identity in the Culture of Colonialism* (New York: Columbia University Press, 1996); Ann McClintock, *Imperial Leather: Race, Gender, and Sexuality in the Colonial Contest* (London and New York: Routledge, 1995).

Chapter 1: First Contact

1. George Abbot, *A Briefe Description of the Whole World* (London, 1599), cix.
2. Richard Zouch, *The Dove: Or Passages of Cosmography* (London, 1613), c.
3. Francis Drake in Richard Hakluyt, *Principal Navigations* (London, 1598), 3:1580.
4. The expedition had left Plymouth on 10 April 1591.
5. Barker, quoted in *Principal Navigations* (London, 1598–99), 2:103.
6. Ibid.
7. Ibid.
8. Foster Rhea Dulles, *Eastward Ho!* (London: Bodley Head Ltd., 1931), 82.
9. *The Description of a Voyage Made by Certaine Ships of Holland into the East Indies*, trans. W. P. (London, 1597), 4.
10. Ibid., 5.
11. Ibid.
12. Ibid.
13. The unlikeliness of the picture suggests to M. Van Wyk Smith the influence of the earliest European image of the inhabitants of "Allago," which was done by Hans Burgkmair in the early sixteenth century for Balthasar Sprenger's *Die Merfart und Erfarung nüwer Schiffung und Wege* (Munich, 1508). See his article, " 'The Most Wretched of the Human Race': The Iconography of the Khoikhoin (Hottentots), 1500–1800," *History and Anthropology*, 5, no. 3–4 (1992): 291.
14. John Huighen Van Linschoten, *His Discourse of Voyages into ye Easte and West Indies* (London, 1598), 75.
15. Ibid., 76.
16. Van Wyk Smith, op. cit., 292.
17. *The History and Description of Africa. Done into English in the Year 1600*, 3 vols. (London: Hakluyt Society, 1896), 1:19–20.
18. Ibid., 68.
19. Ibid., 69.
20. Ibid., 68–69.
21. Kim F. Hall, *Things of Darkness: Economies of Race and Gender in Early-Modern England* (Ithaca: Cornell University Press, 1995), 30.
22. See Anthony Gerard Barthelemy, *Black Face, Maligned Race* (Baton Rouge: Louisiana State University Press, 1987), 12–13. Kim F. Hall, op. cit., 31.
23. John Speed, *A Prospect of the Most Famous Parts of the World* (London, 1646), 5–6.
24. Excerpts from Davies appeared in *Principal Navigations* (1599) and *Purchas His Pilgrimes* (1625). My source here is Davies, as quoted in *Before Van Riebeeck*, ed. Major R. Raven-Hart (Cape Town: C. Struik, 1967), 20. Raven-Hart's work will subsequently be cited as *BVR*.
25. *Voyages of Sir James Lancaster to Brazil and the East Indies*, edited with an introduction by Sir William Foster (London: Hakluyt Society, 1940), 81.
26. *A Letter Written to the Right Worshipfull the Governours and Assistants of the East Indian Marchants in London* (London, 1603), 2.

27. "The Last East-Indian Voyage," included in *The Voyage of Sir Henry Middleton to the Moluccas,* ed. Sir William Foster (London: Hakluyt Society, 1943), 9. All further quotations from this narrative will be cited parenthetically.

28. Hayden White, *Metahistory: The Historical Imagination in Nineteenth-Century Europe* (Baltimore: Johns Hopkins University Press, 1973), 6–7.

29. Edward Terry, *A Voyage to the East Indies* (London, 1655), 14.

30. Patrick Copland, quoted in R. Raven-Hart, *Before Van Riebeeck: Callers at South Africa from 1488 to 1652* (Capetown: C. Struik, 1967), 59.

31. Thomas Herbert, *A Relation of Some Yeares Travaile* (London, 1634), 14. Herbert also stopped at the Cape on his homeward journey in 1629 (7–21 September), but he does not mention this stay, which was much longer than his first one, in his narrative.

32. Edward Michelbourne, quoted in *BVR* , 32.

33. Mary Louise Pratt, *Imperial Eyes* (London: Routledge, 1992), 27.

34. Edward Michelbourne, quoted in *BVR*, 32.

35. Samuel Purchas, *Purchas His Pilgrimes* (London, 1625), 514.

36. Ralph Standish, quoted in *BVR,* 57–58.

37. Abdul R. JanMohamed, "The Economy of Manichean Allegory: The Function of Racial Difference in Colonialist Literature," *"Race," Writing, and Difference,* ed. Henry Louis Gates, Jr. (Chicago: University of Chicago Press), 79.

38. John Jourdain, quoted in *BVR,* 44.

39. Edward Terry, *A Voyage to the East Indies* (London, 1655), 14.

40. Ralph Standish, quoted in *BVR,* 57.

41. Edward Michelbourne, quoted in *BVR,* 33.

42. Captaine Robert Coverte, *A True and Almost Incredible Report of an Englishman, That (Being Cast Away in the Good Ship Called the* Assention *in Cumbaya at the Farthest Part of the East Indies) Travelled by Land through Many Unknowne Kingdomes and Great Cities* (1612; reprint, New York: De Capo Press, 1971), 6.

43. *Voyages of Sir James Lancaster,* op. cit., 80.

44. Ibid., 123.

45. Ibid.

46. Jourdain, quoted in *BVR,* 41.

47. Milward, quoted in *BVR,* 70.

48. Thomas Herbert, 1634, 16.

49. Thomas Herbert, 1638, 18.

50. *Shakespeare's Europe: A Survey of the Condition of Europe at the End of the Sixteenth Century,* ed. Charles Hughes (New York: Benjamin Blom, 1967), 483.

51. *Voyages of Sir James Lancaster,* op. cit., 123.

52. William Keeling, quoted in *BVR,* 37.

53. John Jourdain, quoted in *BVR,* 41–42.

54. Edward Michelbourne, quoted in *BVR,* 42.

55. *The Embassy of Sir Thomas Roe to the Court of the Great Mogul, 1615–1699,* 2 vols., ed. William Foster (London: Hakluyt Society, 1899), 1:11.

56. Coverte, op. cit., 5.

57. John Jourdain, quoted in *BVR,* 42.

58. Terry, 1655, 18.

59. Nicholas Withington, quoted in *BVR,* 60.

60. Ibid., 42.

61. Herbert, op. cit., 1634, 16.

62. Nicholas Downton, in *BVR,* 48.

63. Mary Douglas, *Purity and Danger: An Analysis of the Concepts of Pollution and Taboo* (1966; reprint, London: Routledge, 1991), 2.

64. I am indebted to Mary Douglas here. In the same passage I quoted above, she writes, "dirt offends against order."

65. Thomas Herbert, op. cit., 1634 edition, 15.

66. Mario Perniola, "Between Clothing and Nudity," in *Fragments for a History of the Human Body*, part two, ed. Michel Feher with Ramona Naddaff and Nadia Tazi (New York: Zone, 1989), 237.

67. Edward Michelbourne, quoted in *BVR*, 33.

68. Patrick Copland, quoted in *BVR*, 59.

69. Milward, quoted in *BVR*, 70.

70. Herbert, 1634, 15; 1638, 17.

71. Copland, quoted in *BVR*, 59.

72. Standish, quoted in *BVR*, 58.

73. Copland, quoted in *BVR*, 60.

74. Herbert, op. cit., 1634, 15.

75. Samuel Purchas, *Purchas His Pilgrimmage*, 3rd ed. (London, 1617), 866.

76. Terry, 1665, 332.

77. Herbert, op. cit., 1634, 17.

78. Ibid., 16.

79. Herbert, 1638, 17.

80. Van Wyk Smith, op. cit., 293 and 296.

81. P. J. Marshall and Glyndwr Williams, *The Great Map of Mankind: Perceptions of New Worlds in the Age of the Enlightenment* (Cambridge: Harvard University Press, 1982), 36.

82. Kim F. Hall, "Sexual Politics and Cultural Identity in *The Masque of Blackness*," in *The Performance of Power: Theatrical Discourse and Politics*, ed. Sue Ellen Case and Janelle Reinelt (Iowa City: University of Iowa Press, 1991), 13.

83. Lancaster, op. cit., 103.

84. *Purchas His Pilgrimage*, op. cit., 865.

85. *The Last East-Indian Voyage*, quoted in *The Voyage of Henry Middleton*, op. cit., 9.

86. Log, quoted in *BVR*, 37.

87. Nicholas Dowton, quoted in *BVR*, 48.

88. Withington, quoted in *BVR*, 60.

89. Edward Terry, *A Voyage to East-India* (London, 1665), 332.

90. Ivan Hannaford, *Race: The History of an Idea in the West* (Baltimore: Johns Hopkins University Press, 1996), 171.

91. In this regard, William Cunningham's *The Cosmographical Glasse* (1559) presents a conversation between Philo. and Spoud:

> *Philo:* What wil you coiecture then of those people that are blacke, face, body & all externe partes of them, doeth it not come of the heate of the Sone?
> *Spoud:* It must needes so be, and I have sene men of that colour, & we call them Aethiopians.
> *Philo:* Very well, & do not you beleue that the countrey where they dwell, must of force be under the beames of the Sone?
> *Spoud:* Els it could not folow that ther colour should so much differ fro ours. (66–67)

92. Richard Eden, *The Decades of the Newe World or West India* (London, 1555), 310.

93. Winthrop Jordan, *White over Black: American Attitudes toward the Negro, 1550–1812* (Chapel Hill: University of North Carolina Press, 1968), 9.
94. *The Three Voyages of Martin Frobisher,* ed. Richard Collinson (New York: Burt Franklin, 1867), 55–56.
95. Ibid., 56.
96. Benjamin Braude, "The Sons of Noah and the Construction of Ethnic and Geographical Identities in the Medieval and Early Modern Periods," *William and Mary Quarterly* 54, no. 1 (January 1997): 103–42.
97. Ibid., 138.
98. Herbert, op. cit., 1634, 14.
99. Herbert, op. cit., 1638, 16.
100. Ibid.
101. Herbert, op. cit., 1665, 17.
102. Herbert, op. cit, 1638, 19.
103. Herbert, op. cit., 1665, 20–21.

Chapter 2: Spreading the Word

1. Philip L. Barbour, "Samuel Purchas: The Indefatigable Encyclopedist Who Lacked Good Judgment," in *Essays in Early Virginia Literature,* ed. J. A. Leo Lemay (New York: Burt Franklin and Company, 1977), 36.
2. *Purchas His Pilgrimage* (London, 1613), 2.
3. James P. Helfers believes that Purchas met Hakluyt "around 1610," but he offers no definitve proof of their acquaintanceship. See his "The Explorer or the Pilgrim? Modern Critical Opinion and the Editorial Methods of Richard Hakluyt and Samuel Purchas," *Studies in Philology* 94, no. 2 (spring 1997): 164. Loren E. Pennington writes that Hakluyt "was so impressed with the *Pilgrimage* and its author that he threw open his archives for Purchas to draw upon in expanding subsequent editions of the work," but he does not provide a source for this statement. See his "*Hakluytus Posthumus:* Samuel Purchas and the Promotion of English Overseas Expansion," *The Emporia State Research Studies* 14, no. 3 (1966): 6.
4. Derek Hirst, *Authority and Conflict: England, 1603–1658* (Cambridge: Harvard University Press, 1986), 114.
5. Ibid.
6. Braude, op. cit., 137.
7. Robert Coverte, op. cit., 6.
8. "Modesty had almost forbidden me to recite that, which may with some easily obtaine a *Plaudite*, in the last Act and finishing of this Chapter, concerning the Caffares. *Linschoten* shall recite it for me. They live, saith he, like beasts (he speaketh of those which live neere Mosambique, and those especially more within the Land) they are blacke as pitch, with flat noses, thicke lippes, some have holes both above and under in their lippes, and, as it were, other mouthes in their cheekes, wherein they thrust small bones to beautifie themselves: for which cause they rase and seare their bodies with irons. If they will make a divellish forme and picture, they represent a white man in his apparell, as thinking nothing more ugly. Some also file their teeth as sharpe as needles. They have Villages wherein they dwell together, and in every Village a Lord or King, to whom they are subject. Religion and Faith are unknowne to them. They use mutuall warres, and some eat mans flesh. When they take prisoners in war, or kill their enemies, they observe a more beastly testimony of their great valour, which is after this manner.

They cut off their privy members (to deprive them of all hope of generation) and then drie them well for preservation: after which, they come before the King with great reverence, in the presence of the principall men of the Villages, and there take these members, so dried, one by one in their mouthes, and spit them on the ground at the Kings feet, which the King with great thankes accepteth; and the more to honor them, causeth them all to be taken up, and given to them againe, which is from thenceforth an ensigne of their Knight-hood. For they take all those members, and tie them on a string like a bracelet or chaine; and at all solemne meetings, as when they marry, or goe to a Wedding or Feast, the Bride, or wives of these Knights, doe weare that chaine about their neckes, being, saith our Author, among them as great an honor as the Golden Fleece, or the renowned Garter with us, and their wives as proud, as if some Crowne or Scepter had befallen them" (*Purchas His Pilgrimage*, 1613, 581).

9. In the second edition, this paragraph can be found in chapter 7 rather than chapter 8 (the Cape section).

10. Samuel Purchas, *Purchas His Pilgrimage*, 2nd edition (London, 1614), 867.

11. Walter Raleigh, *The English Voyages of the Sixteenth Century* (Glasgow: James MacLehose and Sons, 1906), 133.

12. Barber, op. cit., 38.

13. Parker, op. cit., 49.

14. *Purchas His Pilgrimes*, 514.

15. Loren E. Pennington also argues that Purchas's embrace of empire was gradual. See his article, op. cit., 5–39.

16. *Purchas His Pilgrimage*, 1613, 632.

17. Barbour writes that Smith and Purchas became friends in 1611. See Barbour's *The Complete Works of Captain John Smith*, 3 vols., ed. Philip L. Barbour (Chapel Hill: Univesity of North Carolina Press, published for the Institute of Early American History and Culture, 1986), 1: xlvi.

18. *Purchas His Pilgrimages*, 1613, 635. This sentence was not revised in the 1614 and 1617 editions.

19. Sheehan, *Savagism and Civility*, op. cit., 48.

20. *Purchas His Pilgrimages*, 1617, 943.

21. The fourth edition of *Theasaurus Geographicus* (1728) is a good example of a text that casts doubt on conversion stories.

22. Peter Burke, "America and the Rewriting of World History," in *America in European Consciousness, 1493–1750,* ed. Karen Ordahl Kupperman (Chapel Hill: University of North Carolina Press, 1995), 33–51.

23. J. N. L. Baker makes this point in an article, "Academic Geography in the Seventeenth and Eighteenth Centuries," included in his *The History of Geography* (New York: Barnes and Noble, 1963), 16.

24. Robert Stafforde, *A Geographical and Anthologicall Description of All the Empires and Kingdomes Both of the Continent and Ilands in This Terrestriall Globe* (London, 1607), 37.

25. Ibid., 41.

26. See J. N. L. Baker's "Nathanael Carpenter and English Geography," in Baker, op. cit., 2–13. Baker speaks of Carpenter's lack of influence on subsequent English geography on page 11. In his *The Beginnings of the Teaching of Modern Subjects in England* (1909; reprint, London, 1971), Foster Watson cites John Webster's *Examination of Academies* (1654) as identifying Carpenter's work as the textbook of choice (100).

27. Ibid., 8.

28. Nathanael Carpenter, *Geography Delineated Forth in Two Bookes* (Oxford, 1625), chapter 14.
29. Peter Heylyn, *Microcosmus: A Little Description of the Great World* (London, 1639), 9.
30. Peter Heylyn, *Microcosmus: A Little Description of the Great World* (London, 1627), 734.
31. Peter Heylyn, *Cosmographie*, vol. 4, part 1 (London, 1652), 77.
32. *Dictionary of National Biography*, s.v. "Peter Heylyn."
33. *Cosmography*, op.cit., 78.
34. Peter Heylyn, *Cosmographie* (London, 1657), 993. The later editions use the more conventional spelling of the word cosmography.
35. *Cosmography*, 1703, 924.
36. Samuel Clarke, A Geographical Description of All the Countries in the Known World (London, 1671), 70. First edition of this work was published in 1657.
37. S. Clark, *A New Description of the World* (London, 1689).
38. Ibid., 177.
39. Ibid., 177–78.
40. William Byrd, for example, owned copies of Heylyn, Bohun, and Varenius. See the forthcoming *The Commonplace Book of William Byrd II*, ed. Kevin J. Berland, Jan K. Gilliam, and Kenneth A. Lockridge (Williamsburg: Omohundro Institute for Early American Culture and History). I am grateful to Kevin Berland for the information he has shared with me about William Byrd.
41. The title page of Laurence Echard's *A Most Compleat Compendium of Geography* (London, 1691) makes this common claim.
42. Edmond Bohun, *A Geographical Dictionary* (London, 1688), n.p.
43. The title pages of the subsequent editions credit a Mr. Bernard with the additions and corrections. In his autobiography, Bohun asserts that Bernard's additions were responsible for the accusation made against him that he was a Jacobite. See *The Diary and Autobiography of Edmund Bohun, Esq.*, ed. S. Wilton Rix (privately printed by Reed Crisp, Ipswich, 1853), 92–93. Bernard's 1693 preface justifies the edition.
44. *A Geographical Dictionary*, begun by Edmund Bohun and continued by Mr. Bernard (London, 1693), 67.
45. The *Dictionary of National Biography* entry on Blome records a remark from Wood: "This person Bloome is esteemed by the chiefest heralds a most impudent person, and the late industrious Garter (Sir W. D[ugdale]) hath told me that he gets a livelihood by bold practices" (*DNB*, s.v. "Richard Blome").
46. Richard Blome, *A Geographical Description of the Four Parts of the World Taken from the Notes and Workes of the Famous Monsieur Sanson, Geographer to the French King, and Other Eminent Travellers and Authors* (London, 1670), 65.
47. See I. Schapera's introduction to his translation in *The Early Cape Hottentots*, ed. I. Schapera and B. Farrington (Cape Town: Van Riebeeck Society, 1933), 2–3.
48. John Ogilby, *Africa* (London, 1670), 24. Subsequent quotations from this source will be cited in the text.
49. Schapera, op. cit., 4.
50. Ibid., 7.
51. Ibid., 45.
52. Laurence Echard, *A Most Compleat Compendium of Geography* (London, 1691), 140.
53. Laurence Echard, *A Most Compleat Compendium of Geography*, 2nd ed. (London, 1691), 170–71.

54. Patrick Gordon, *Geography Anatomiz'd: Or, The Compleat Geographical Grammar* (London, 1693), 174–75.

55. Patrick Gordon, *Geography Anatomiz'd: Or, The Compleat Geographical Grammar* (London, 1699), 322.

56. Ibid., 322–23.

57. Ibid., 323.

58. See the *DNB* entry on Moll.

59. Herman Moll, preface to *A System of Geography* (London, 1701).

60. Jonathan Swift, *Gulliver's Travels and Other Writings*, ed. Louis A. Landa (Boston: Houghton Mifflin Co., 1960), 229.

61. Moll, op. cit., 118.

62. *Thesaurus Geographicus or The Compleat Geographer* (London, 1722), 184.

63. See Schapera and Farrington, op. cit., 83.

64. *Atlas Geographus: Or, a Compleat System of Geography (Ancient and Modern) for Africa* (London, 1714), 4:578–79.

Chapter 3: The Story of Cory

1. There is some debate about "Cory's" name. Some modern commentators suggest that it could refer to the Cape Khoikhoi society he belonged to, probably the Gorachouqua, but the English did not have this information at the time of his capture and abduction. It seems more likely that Cory was the name chosen for him by the English, and it well might derive from the word "corybant." As Purchas explains in another section of *Purchas His Pilgrimage* (1614), "Of Ionia and the Neighbor Countries," the corybantes "were a shaven order of Priests, who, ravished with a sacred fury, played upon Cimbals, and danced, shaking their heads to and fro, drawing others into the same rage of superstition" (379). For another presentation of facts about Cory, see Hans Werner Debrunner, *Presence and Prestige: Africans in Europe* (Basel: Basler Afrika Bibliographien, 1979), 57–58.

2. Nicholas Downton, quoted in *BVR*, 66.

3. Edward Blitheman, quoted in *BVR*, 71; both letters are dated 20 February 1615.

4. Edward Dodsworth, quoted in *BVR*, 64.

5. Ibid.

6. John Jourdain, quoted in *BVR*, 88.

7. Ibid.

8. Ibid.

9. Thomas Elkington, quoted in *BVR*, 67.

10. Richard Baker, quoted in *BVR*, 78.

11. Walter Peyton, quoted in *BVR*, 72.

12. Ibid. Edward Dodsworth, also at the Cape in June 1615, likewise records Cory as remembering Thomas Smith very kindly (*BVR*, 67–69).

13. Nathaniel Salmon, quoted in *BVR*, 90.

14. William Minors, quoted in *BVR*, 114.

15. Historical Manuscripts Commission, *Report on Manuscripts in the Welsh Language*, vol. 1, part 3 (London: Her Majesty's Stationary Office, 1898), 1012. Debrunner also cites a source that says the same, op. cit., 58.

16. Samuel Purchas, *Purchas His Pilgrimage* (London, 1617), 867.

17. Samuel Purchas, *Purchas His Pilgrims* (London, 1625), 215.

18. The sermon was published on 11 September 1646.

19. Edward Terry, ΥΕΥΔΕΛΕΥΘΕΡΙΑ: Or, Lawlesse Liberty (London, 1646), A4.
20. Edward Terry, *The Merchants and Mariners Preservation and Thanksgiving. Or, Thankfulnesse Returned for Mercies Received* (London, 1649), 15.
21. Terry, 1665, 331.
22. Terry, 1777, 432.
23. Terry, 1655, 19–20.
24. Terry, 1665, 332.
25. Ibid., 332–33.
26. Ibid., 333.
27. Terry, 1655, 21–22.
28. Ibid., 22–23.
29. Terry, 1665, 333.
30. Ibid.
31. Terry, 1655, 24.
32. Ibid., 25.
33. Peter Heylyn, *Cosmographie in Four Books* (London, 1657), 994.
34. This stamp of approval appears in the dedicatory epistle.
35. Herbert, 1665, 20.
36. S. Clark, *A New Description of the World* (London, 1689), 178.
37. John Harris, *Navigantium atque Itinerantium* (London, 1705), 1:143.
38. William Funnell, *A Voyage round the World* (London, 1707), 291.
39. Alexander Hamilton, *A New Account of the East Indies* (Edinburgh, 1727; London, 1737), 3.
40. *A New General Collection of Voyages and Travels*, 4 vols. (London, 1745–47), 3: 347.
41. Thomas Salmon, *Modern History*, 5 vols. (London, 1755), 5: 35.
42. Edward Pettit, *The Visions of Government etc. Wherein the Antimonarchical Principles and Practices of all Phanatical Commonwealths-men, and Jesuitical Politicians are discovered, confuted, and exposed* (London, 1686), 209. Ray William Frantz was the first to notice this reference. See his *The English Traveler and the Movement of Ideas, 1660–1732* (1934; reprint, Lincoln: University of Nebraska Press, 1967), 157.
43. Kenneth Parker mentions these exchanges in his article, "Telling Tales: Early Modern English Voyagers and the Cape of Good Hope, *The Seventeenth Century*, 10, no. 1 (spring 1995): 141. Parker misattributes Roe's representation with Terry's.
44. Horace Walpole, *Journal of the Reign of King George the Third, from the Year 1771 to 1783*, ed. with notes by Doran (London, 1859), 2:319.
45. Maria Edgeworth, *Leonora*, cited in *Oxford English Dictionary*, s.v. "hottentot."
46. Equiano, *The Interesting Narrative of the Life of Olaudah Equiano, Written by Himself*, ed. Robert J. Allison (New York: Bedford Books of St. Martin's Press, 1995), 99–100.
47. Thomas Bluett, *Some Memoirs of the Life of Job, the Son of Solomon the High Priest of Boonda in Africa* (1734), 31–33. London.
48. Henry Louis Gates Jr., "James Gronniosaw and the Trope of the Talking Book," in *Studies in Autobiography*, ed. James Olney (New York and Oxford: Oxford University Press, 1988), 52.
49. Quobna Ottobah Cugoano, *Thoughts and Sentiments on the Evil and Wicked Traffic of the Slavery and Commerce of the Human Species* (1787), collected in *Unchained Voices*, ed. Vincent Carretta (Lexington: University Press of Kentucky, 1996), 150–51.

50. *Unchained Voices* (1996) includes the note Cugoano appended to his work's table of contents, see 179–80.

51. Simon de la Loubère, *A New Historical Relation of the Kingdom of Siam* (London, 1693), 185.

52. John Nieuhoff,*Voyages and Travels to the East-Indies* in *A Collection of Voyages and Travels*, 4 vols., ed. Awnsham and John Churchill (London, 1704), 2: 188.

53. Ibid.

54. The last political prisoners left Robben Island in 1991; those convicted of criminal infractions were held on the island until Sept. 1996. The island now functions as a cultural site and museum.

55. John Maxwell, "An Account of the Cape of Good Hope," *Philosophical Transactions of the Royal Society of London* 25 (1706–7): 2427.

56. Peter Kolb, *The Present State of the Cape of Good Hope*, 2 vols., tr. Guido Medley (New York: Johnson Reprint Corporation, 1968), 1: 106–107. All subsequent quotations from this source will be noted in the text.

57. *A New General Collection*, op. cit., 3: 366.

58. What is interesting is that the French edition presents the story (Prévost, *Histoire Générale Des Voyages, ou Nouvelle Collection De Toutes Les Relations de Voyages*. Paris, 1749), and Rousseau quotes it verbatim in *Discours sur l'origine et les fondemens de l'inegalite parmi les Hommes* (Amsterdam, 1755):

> "Il revit au Cap après la mort du Commissaire. Peu de jours après son retour, dans une visite qu'il rendit à quelques Hottentots de ses parens, il prit le parti de se dépouiller de sa parure Européenne pour se révêtir d'une peau de Brebis. Il retourna au Fort, dans ce novel ajustement, chargé d'un pacquet qui contenoit ses anciens habits, & les présentant au Gouvernour il lui tint ce discours. *"Ayes la bonté, Monsieur, de faire attention que je renonce pour toujours à cet appareil. Je renonce aussi pour toute ma vie à la Religion Chretienne, ma resolution est de vivre & mourrir dans la Religion, la manniére & les usages de mes Ancêtres. L'unique grace que je vous demande est de me laisser le Collier & le Coutelas que je porte. Je les garderai pour l'amour de vous."* Aussi-tôt sans attendre la réponse de Van der Stel, il se déroba par la suite & jamais on ne le revit au Cap. (Rousseau, 258–59)

59. Andreas Mielke, "Hottentots in the Aesthetic Discussion of Eighteenth-Century Germany," *Monatshefte*, 80, no. 2 (1988): 142.

60. Ibid., n.44, 147.

61. James P. Carson has written a fine examination of Smollett's "Hottentot" references in his article, "Britons, 'Hottentots,' Plantation Slavery, and Tobias Smollet," *Philological Quarterly* 75, no. 4 (fall 1996): 471–99.

62. Tobias Smollett, *A Compendium of Authentic and Entertaining Voyages*, 7 vols. (London, 1756), 4:192.

63. Thomas Salmon, *Modern History* (Dublin, 1755), 1: 35.

64. George Augustus Baldwyn's *A New, Royal, Authentic, Complete, and Universal System of Geography; Or, A Modern History and Description of the Whole World* (1794) also includes this same engraving of him.

65. The engraving is dated 16 July 1785, but the name of the artist is not given. It appears on page 376 in the 1785 edition.

66. Charles Theodore Middleton, *A New and Complete System of Geography* (1778), 1:384.

67. The letter is dated 12 December 1761. *New Letters of David Hume*, ed. Ray-

mond Klibansky and Ernest C. Mossner (Oxford: Clarendon Press, 1954; rpt. 1969), 220.

68. Henry St. John, *Letters on the Study and the Use of History*, 2 vols. (London, 1752), 1: 29–30.

69. Ibid.

70. James Dunbar, *Essays on the History of Mankind in Rude and Cultivated Ages* (London, 1780), 160.

71. *The New Royal Geographical Magazine* (London, 1794), 302.

72. James Prior, *Narrative of a Voyage in the Indian Seas* (London, 1820), 9–10.

Chapter 4: "Hottentots" at Home and Abroad

1. William Petty, quoted in Winthrop D. Jordan, *White over Black: American Attitudes toward the Negro, 1550–1812* (Chapel Hill: University of North Carolina Press, 1988), 225.

2. Philip Edwards, *The Story of the Voyage: Sea-Narratives in Eighteenth-Century England* (Cambridge: Cambridge University Press, 1994), 2.

3. Robert Boyle, "General Heads for a Natural History of a Countrey," *Philosophical Transactions of the Royal Society* (London, 1666), 188.

4. Ray William Frantz, *The English Traveller and the Movement of Ideas, 1660–1732* (1934; reprint, Lincoln: University of Nebraska Press, 1967), 17, 30, 38, 55.

5. Percy Adams, *Travel Literature and the Evolution of the Novel* (Lexington: University Press of Kentucky, 1983), 97. See chapter 3, "The Truth-Lie Dichotomy."

6. Richard Blackmore, *The Nature of Man* (London, 1711), 7.

7. John Dyer, "The Fleece," xxx.

8. Edward Barlow, *Journal of His Life at Sea in King's Ships, East and West India-Men, and Other Merchantmen, from 1659–1703*, transcribed by Basil Lubbock, 2 vols. (London: 1934), 1: 239.

9. John Ovington, *Voyage to Suratt* (1696), 489.

10. William Funnell, *A Voyage round the World* (1707), 289.

11. John Maxwell, "An Account of the Cape of Good Hope," *Philosophical Transactions of the Royal Society* (1707), 2425.

12. Edward Cooke, *A Voyage to the South Sea and round the World* (London, 1712), 70.

13. Woodes Rogers, *A Cruising Voyage round the World* (London, 1712), 420.

14. Ambrose Cowley, *Voyage round the Globe* (London, 1687), 34–35.

15. Ovington, op. cit., 492.

16. Beeckman, op. cit., 180.

17. Alexander Hamilton, *A New Account of the East Indies* (1727; reprint, London, 1737), 3.

18. Thomas Southerne, *Oroonoko*, ed. Maximillian E. Novak and David Stuart Brown (Lincoln: University of Nebraska Press, 1976), 59. In a footnote the editors suggest that Hottman's name might be a reference to Hotspur. I am grateful to Susan Iwanisziw for alerting me to Hottman's existence in Southerne's play.

19. Ovington, op. cit., 497.

20. Lockyer, op. cit., 288.

21. Ogilby, op. cit., 24.

22. Daniel Defoe, *Atlas Maritimus* (London, 1728), 237.

23. Stephen Addington, *The Youth's Geographical Grammar* (London, 1770), 180.

24. Ambrose Cowley, *Voyage round the Globe* (London, 1687), 35.

25. Simon de la Loubère, *A New Historical Relation of the Kingdom of Siam* (1693), 184.

26. William Dampier, *A New Voyage round the World* (London, 1697), 536–37. There were five editions of this work printed before 1703. All of my quotes are from the first edition.

27. *The Six Voyages of John Baptiste Tavernier* (1678), 205.

28. See Emile Boonzaier, Penny Berens, Candy Malherbe, and Andy Smith, *The Cape Herders: A History of the Khoikhoi of Southern Africa* (Cape Town: David Philip, 1996), 43–47. There were also ritualistic occasions when men and women would rub themselves with a ceremonial fat or grease.

29. Ambrose Cowley, *Voyage round the Globe* (London, 1687), 35.

30. William Funnell, *A Voyage round the World* (London, 1707), 289–90.

31. A translation of this account appears as an appendix in Gabriel Dellon's *Voyage to the East Indies* (London, 1698), 14. Rennefort was at the Cape from December 1666 to January 1667.

32. Ten Rhyne's account is in *A Collection of Voyages and Travels* (London, 1704), 4:835.

33. Ovington, op. cit., 486.

34. Maxwell, op. cit., 2424–26.

35. *A New General Collection of Voyages and Travels*, 4 vols. (London, 1745–47), 3:348.

36. Robert Morden, *Geography Rectified* (London, 1693), 525.

37. Alexander Hamilton, *A New Account of the East Indies* (1727; reprint, London, 1737), 4.

38. Emily Brittle, *The India Guide; Or, Journal of a Voyage to the East Indies in the Year 1780, in a Poetical Epistle to Her Mother* (Calcutta, 1785), 84.

39. Ovington, op. cit., 489.

40. Funnell, op. cit., 290–91.

41. Cowley, op. cit., 36.

42. Charles Lockyer, *An Account of the Trade in India* (London, 1711), 300.

43. Dampier, op. cit., 541.

44. John Maxwell, "An Account of the Cape of Good Hope," op. cit., 2425.

45. Pascoe Thomas, *A True and Impartial Journal of a Voyage to the South-Seas and round the Globe* (London, 1745), 340. Thomas was the mathematics teacher on the *Centurion*, the flagship of Commodore George Anson's fleet. Other members of Anson's expedition also published narratives, but they did not include any descriptions of "Hottentots" in them.

46. Samuel Pepys, *The Diary of Samuel Pepys*, ed. Robert Latham and William Matthews (Los Angeles: University of California Press, 1970), 3:298.

47. Mary Louise Pratt, "Scratches on the Face of the Country; or, What Mr. Barrow Saw in the Land of the Bushmen," *"Race," Writing, and Difference*, ed. Henry Louis Gates Jr. (Chicago: University of Chicago Press, 1985), 139.

48. *The Six Voyages of John Baptiste Tavernier* (1678), 204.

49. *A Relation of the Voyage to Siam* (1688), 72.

50. *A New Historical Relation of the Kingdom of Siam* (1693), 185.

51. Ovington, op. cit., 495.

52. Maxwell, op. cit., 2426–27.

53. Daniel Beeckman, *A Voyage to and from the Island of Borneo in the East Indies* (1718), 184.

54. Anonymous, "Account of the Loss of the Ship *Johanna*" mss., The Royal Society, London.

55. Ovington, op. cit., 497.

56. Christopher Schweitzer, *A Relation of Two Several Voyages Made to the East Indies* (London, 1700), 238.

57. Willem Ten Rhyne, "An Account of the Cape of Good Hope and the Hottentotes," *A Collection of Voyages and Travels,* op. cit., 4:836.

58. Edward Cooke, *A Voyage to the South Sea and round the World* (1712), 70.

59. Jennifer L. Morgan, " 'Some Could Suckle over Their Shoulder': Male Travelers, Female Bodies, and the Gendering of Racial Ideology, 1500–1770," *William and Mary Quarterly* 54, no. 1 (January 1997): 192.

60. Tavernier, op. cit., 206.

61. Leguat's narrative appears in R. Raven-Hart's *The Cape of Good Hope, 1652–1702: The First Fifty Years of Dutch Colonisation as Seen by Callers at Cape Town* (Cape Town: A. A. Balkema, 1971), 111.

62. Percy Adams, *Travel Literature and the Evolution of the Novel* (Lexington: University Press of Kentucky, 1983), 103.

63. Edward Long, *The History of Jamaica* (London, 1774), 2:353.

64. Ibid., 2:364.

65. *The Spectator,* ed. and with an introduction by Donald F. Bond, 5 vols. (Oxford: Clarendon Press, 1965), 5:157.

66. Felicity A. Nussbaum, *Torrid Zones: Maternity, Sexuality, and Empire in Eighteenth-Century English Narratives* (Baltimore: Johns Hopkins University Press, 1995), 1.

67. Ruth Perry, "Colonizing the Breast: Sexuality and Maternity in Eighteenth-Century England," *Eighteenth-Century Life* 16, n.s. 1 (February 1992): 188.

68. George Alexander Stevens, "A Pastoral," in *Songs, Comic and Satyrical* (Philadelphia, 1778), lines 13–18.

69. *The Literary Works of Matthew Prior,* ed. H. Bunker Wright and Monroe K. Spears (Oxford: Clarendon Press, 1971), 1:496.

70. John Locke, *An Essay Concerning Human Understanding,* ed. and with an introduction by Peter H. Nidditch (Oxford: Clarendon Press, 1975), 92. Interestingly, Locke's "Hottentot" reference was remembered decades after it appeared in print. In his *Dialogue of the Dead between Lock (sic) and Montaigne,* Matthew Prior depicts the deceased philosopher saying the following: "Hear me a little; from these plain Propositions I go on to greater Discoveries, that an Infant in the Cradle cannot make a Syllogism half so well as a Sophister in the Schools, and that a Hottentote is not so learned in the Bay of Sardaignia as he would have been if his Friends had Educated him at Oxford, or Cambridge" (*The Literary Works of Matthew Prior,* ed. H. Bunker Wright and Monroe K. Spears [Oxford: Clarendon Press, 1971], 1:496).

71. Ovington, op. cit., 498.

72. Cowley, op. cit., 35.

73. Samuel Johnson, *Journey to the Western Islands of Scotland,* ed. Pat Rogers in *Johnson and Boswell in Scotland* (New Haven: Yale University Press, 1993), 67–69.

74. *Journals of Dorothy Wordsworth, Recollections of a Tour Made in Scotland (1803),* ed. E. de Selincourt, 2 vols. (London: Macmillan and Company, 1959), 1:259. Elizabeth A Bohls points out another time Dorothy quotes William in her journal, as when he described a ferryman's house near the Trossachs as "Hottentotish" (Elizabeth A. Bohls, *Women Travel Writers and the Language of Aesthetics, 1716–1818* [Cambridge and New York: Cambridge University Press, 1995], 195.)

NOTES

75. Quoted in James P. Carson, "Britons, 'Hottentots,' Plantation Slavery, and Tobias Smollet," *Philological Quarterly* 75, no. 4 (fall 1996): 497, n. 45.
76. Evan Lloyd, "Conversation" (London, 1767), lines 11–15.
77. Joseph Thurston, "The Fall" (London, 1732).
78. Jonathan Swift, "A Letter on the Fishery," *Directions to Servants and Miscellaneous Pieces, 1733–1742*, ed. Herbert Davis (Oxford: Basil Blackwell, 1964), 112.
79. John Wesley, "The Imperfection of Human Knowledge," *The Works of John Wesley*, vol. 2, ed. Albert C. Outler (Nashville, Tennessee: Abingdon Press, 1985), 2:579–80.
80. Equiano's *The Interesting Narrative of the Life of Olaudah Equiano, or Gustavus Vassa, the African*, ed. and with an introduction by Robert J. Allison (Boston: Bedford Books of St. Martin's Press, 1995), 97.
81. Gilbert Burnet, *An Introduction to the Third Volume of the History of the Reformation of the Church of England* (London, 1714), 27–28.
82. Gilbert Burnet, op. cit., 56.
83. See the entry for Leslie in the *DNB*.
84. William Higden, a divine, who was named prebendary of Canterbury in 1713, published pamphlets supporting the taking of oaths from 1709 to 1710. Daniel Eilon thinks that Leslie's work influenced Swift's characterization of Yahoos ("Swift's Yahoo and Leslie's Hottentot," *Notes and Queries* (December 1983): 510–12.
85. Charles Leslie, *The Finishing Stroke: Being a Vindication of the Patriarchal Scheme of Government* (1711), 128.
86. Locke, Essay Concerning Human Understanding, op. cit., 87–88.
87. Charles Gildon, quoted in Ray William Frantz, op. cit., 148.
88. Edmund Gibson, *A Plea for Divine Revelation: In Answer to a Letter to the Right Reverend the Lord Bishop of London Called a Plea for Human Reason* (London, 1731), 18–19.
89. John Jackson, *A Defense of the Plea for Human Reason: Being a Reply to a Book Entitled,* A Plea for Divine Revelation (London, 1731), 57.
90. *The Spectator,* op. cit., 4:461.
91. Ibid., 4: 462.
92. Edward Ward, "St. Paul's Church; Or, the Protestant Ambulators (London 1716), lines 150–53.
93. *The Renelean Religion Displayed: In a Letter from a Hottentot of Distinction, Now in LONDON, To His Friend at the Cape of Good Hope. Containing the Reasons Assign'd by the Raneleans for Abolishing Christianity, Together with a True Copy of Their New Liturgy* (London, 1750), iv–v.
94. Robert Graves, *The Spritual Quixote* (London, 1773), 242.
95. Hannah More to Mrs. Rackett, 2 October 1779. Dorchester Record Office, D/RAC:88.
96. Walpole's letter is addressed to Lady Ossory, and is dated 7 January 1782. *Horace Walpole's Corresondence*, ed. W. S. Lewis, Warren Hunting Smith and George L. Lam [New Haven: Yale University Press, 1971], 25:636.)
97. Robert Graves, *The Spiritual Quixote* (1773), 186–87.
98. Bernard Mandeville, *The Fable of the Bees*, ed. F. B. Kaye, 2 vols. (1924; reprint, Oxford: Clarendon Press, 1957), 1:127.
99. *Poetry of Mary Barber* (New York: Edwin Mellen Press, 1992). I am grateful to Betty Rizzo for this reference.
100. Mary Wollstonecraft, *Thoughts on the Education of Daughters*, in *The Works of Mary Wollstonecraft*, ed. Janet Todd and Marilyn Butler (New York: New York University Press, 1989), 4:17.

101. Paul Whitehead, "The State Dunces" (London, 1733), lines 299–300.

102. Philip Dormer Stanhope, earl of Chesterfield, *Letters to His Son on the Art of Becoming a Man of the World and a Gentleman*, 2 vols. (New York: Chesterfield, 1917), 1:384.

103. *Horace Walpole's Correspondence*, op. cit., 25:636.

104. See the headnote to the piece in James Wolley's edition of *The Intelligencer* (Oxford: Clarendon Press, 1992), 50. I am grateful to James Woolley for this reference.

105. Ibid., 52.

106. Christopher Smart, *The Midwife* 2, no. 1 (24 April 1751), 30. I am indebted to Betty Rizzo for this reference.

107. Henry Fielding, *Tom Jones*, ed. Sheridan Baker (New York: W. W. Norton and Company, 1973), 367. This section was revised by Fielding in later editions.

108. Ibid.

109. *Collected Works of Oliver Goldsmith*, ed. Arthur Friedman (Oxford: Clarendon Press, 1966), 2:321.

110. Moses Mendez, *The Double Disappointment* (London, 1745). The work was first performed in 1745. In 1760, the insult was slightly revised to read, "I'll rub your Pate for you, you *French* Hottentot." (34).

111. Henry Fielding, *Tom Jones*, ed. Sheridan Baker (New York: W. W. Norton and Company, 1973), 666.

112. Samuel Richardson, *Clarissa*, ed. and with an introduction and notes by Angus Ross (Middlesex: Penguin Books, 1985), 542.

113. Ibid., 574.

114. Elizabeth Griffith, *The Delicate Distress*, ed. Ricciardi and Staves (Lexington: University Press of Kentucky, 1997), 24. I am indebted to Betty Rizzo for this reference.

Chapter 5: Challenging the Constructions

1. George England, *An Enquiry into the Morals of the Ancients* (1737), 169.

2. William Macintosh, *Travels in Europe, Asia, and Africa*, 2 vols. (London, 1782), 1:218.

3. Samuel Fairfax, "Journal of My Own Proceedings at the Cape: September 1797," *The State* 2 (1909):589.

4. Peter Kolb, *The Present State of the Cape of Good Hope* (New York and London: Johnson Reprint Corporation, 1968), 37.

5. Mary Louise Pratt, *Imperial Eyes: Travel Writing and Transculturation* (London and New York: Routledge, 1992), 43.

6. Peter Kolb, op. cit., xi.

7. See pages 1: 334–36 for this Claas story.

8. Bertrand A. Goldgar, *Walpole and the Wits: The Relation of Politics to Literature, 1722–1742* (Lincoln: University of Nebraska Press, 1976), 94.

9. *Grub-Street Journal 51*, 24 December 1730.

10. See the *DLB* entries for Thomas Cooke and Hugh Todd. *The Poems of Alexander Pope*, ed. John Butt (New Haven: Yale University Press, 1963), 380.

11. *Grub-Street Journal 59*, 18 February 1731.

12. Ibid., n.p.

13. Ibid., n.p.

14. Ibid., n.p.

15. Ibid., n.p.
16. *Gentleman's Magazine,* February 1731, 62.
17. *Grub-Street Journal 61,* 4 March 1731.
18. Ibid., n.p.
19. Maynard Mack, *Alexander Pope: A Life* (New York: W. W. Norton and Company, 1985), 411.
20. Goldgar, op. cit., 97.
21. *Gentleman's Magazine,* February 1732, 602.
22. *Connoisseur* 21, 20 June 1754, 121–26.
23. Tobias Smollett, *The Adventures of Peregrine Pickle,* ed. and with an introduction by James L. Clifford (London: Oxford University Press, 1964), 86. See James P. Carson, op. cit., for an excellent analysis of Smollet's references to and treatment of "Hottentots."
24. Carson, op. cit., 491.
25. See Carson, op. cit. Carson cites and accepts as correct Louis L. Martz's argument that Smollett was the author-editor of the eighth volume of *The Present State of All Nations.* See Martz's *The Later Career of Tobias Smollett* (New Haven: Yale University Press, 1942).
26. *A New General Collection of Voyages and Travels,* 4 vols. (London, 1745–47), 3:A2.
27. *Geography Made Familiar and Easy to Young Gentlemen and Ladies* (London, 1748), 258–59.
28. Interestingly, later editions, published in the 1785 and 1787, changed the title of this illustration to "The History of a Generous Hottentot," which makes a far more positive statement.
29. Daniel Fenning, *A New System of Geography* (London, 1771), 365.
30. George Forster, *A Voyage round the World in His Britannic Majesty's Sloop, Resolution* (London, 1777), 1:79.
31. J. H. Bernardin de Saint Pierre, *A Voyage to the Isle of France, the Isle of Bourbon, and the Cape of Good Hope* (London, 1775), 256. In his preface, the English translator of this work invokes Oliver Goldsmith's name: "The Reader is here presented with a Translation of a Work, which the late Doctor Goldsmith admired for the accuracy and ingenuity of its Observations, and for the Spirit of Benevolence and Philanthropy which breathes through the whole. He wished it to be done into English, and had he lived, his correcting Hand would have rendered the Translation more worthy of the Author and of the Public favour, than in the state in which it is now submitted" (n.p.). That Goldsmith admired this text for its "Benevolence" is particularly interesting, especially when we consider how negatively Goldsmith represented "Hottentots" in his own *History of the Earth and Animated Nature* (1774).
32. *Monthly Review,* December 1776, 544–45.
33. Ibid., 545.
34. *Monthly Review,* June 1786, 518.
35. *Monthly Review,* August 1790, 398.
36. Tamary Elizabeth Hurrell appears to be a previously undiscovered author. She was born in 1738, daughter to the celebrated actors William Pritchard and Hannah Vaughan Pritchard. She was single at the time of her mother's death in 1768, but she later married Allen Hurrell (1741–1809), a farmer in Cambridgeshire. She gave birth to a son in September 1779. *Tales of Imagination, on Moral and Interesting Subjects* (Dublin, 1790) appears to be the only work she published in her life. The dedicatory epistle to Lady Caroline Paget relates that Hurrell "is

a daughter of the late Mrs. Pritchard, attended Lady Caroline Paget as English preceptress" (vi). See the entry for the mother in the *Biographical Dictionary of Actors, Actresses, Musicians Dancers, Managers & Other Stage Personnel in London, 1660–1800.*

37. *Critical Review*, August 1790, 220.
38. I am using Mary Louise Pratt's term here. See *Imperial Eyes*, op. cit., 6–7.
39. *Town and Country*, August 1790, 356.
40. Le Vaillant, *Travels into the Interior Parts of Africa, by the Way of the Cape of Good Hope, in the Years 1780, 81, 82, 83, 84, and 85* (1790), xx.
41. Ibid.
42. *Monthly Review, Appendix to the First Volume*, January–April 1790, 481.
43. Mary Wollstonecraft, review of *New Travels into the Interior Parts of Africa*, vol. 25 *Analytical Review* (1797), in *The Works of Mary Wollstonecraft*, vol. 7, ed. Janet Todd and Marilyn Butler (New York: New York University Press, 1989), 480.
44. Elizabeth Ogilvy Benger, *Memoirs of the Late Mrs. Elizabeth Hamilton: With a Selection from Her Correspondence, and Other Unpublished Writings*, 2 vols. (London, 1818), 1:132–33.
45. Maria Edgeworth, *Moral Tales for Young People*, vol. 1 (New York and London: Garland Publishing, 1974), 4–5.
46. John Barrow, *An Account of Travels into the Interior of Southern Africa*, 2 vols. (London, 1804), 2:21.
47. Ibid.
48. Catherine Hutton, *The Tour of Africa* (London, 1819), 2: vi.
49. *Anti-Jacobin; Or, Weekly Examiner*, 2 April 1798, vol. 2 (London, 1799), 97. I am indebted to April London and Jim Butler for this reference.

Chapter 6: An Information Age

1. George Forster, *A Voyage round the World in His Britannic Majesty's Sloop Resolution* (London, 1777), 79.
2. John White, *Journal of a Voyage to New South Wales* (London, 1790), 96.
3. Mary Anne Parker, *A Voyage round the World* (London, 1795), 55.
4. *Monthly Review* (September 1777), 243–45. The review also makes one negative comment about the work, complaining that it has "little of that philosophical penetration so desirable in travellers" (243).
5. Born in 1741, she married Nathaniel Kindersley on 19 April 1762. After he was sent to India with his regiment, she and an infant son left England in the spring of 1764 to join him there, and as a family they lived in or around Calcutta until his death in 1769. Finding herself a widow at 28 years of age, and entitled to a pension of £130 a year, she returned to England at some point thereafter.
6. Jemima Kindersley, *Letters from the Island of Teneriffe, Brazil, the Cape of Good Hope, and the East Indies* (London, 1777), 68.
7. William Macintosh, *Travels in Europe, Asia, and Africa*, 2 vols. (London, 1782), 1:217–18.
8. Oliver Goldsmith, *An History of the Earth and Animated Nature*, 8 vols. (London, 1774), 2:232.
9. John Hawkesworth, *An Account of the Vaoyages Undertaken by the Order of His Present Majesty for Making Discoveries in the Southern Hemisphere*, 3 vols. (London, 1773), 3:789.
10. *Journal of the Right Honourable Sir Joseph Banks during Captain Cook's First Voy-*

age in the H.M.S. Endeavour in 1768–1771, ed. Joseph D. Hooker (London: Macmillan and Company, 1896). The description of the "Hottentots" appears on pages 439–42.

11. Francis Masson, "Mr. Masson's Botanical Travels," *Philosophical Transactions of the Royal Society,* vol. 66 (1776), 290.

12. Forbes, *Pioneer Travellers in South Africa* , 91–92.

13. The review of Paterson's work in *Monthly Review* (August 1790) particularly complains about this borrowing from Sparrman (400). The review in the *Gentleman's Magazine* (September 1789) guesses that "Mr. P thought he could not give a better" description of "Hottentots" than the one Sparrman provides (830).

14. *Gentleman's Magazine,* vol. 55 (November 1785), 903.

15. *Monthly Review* (June 1786), 514.

16. Barbara Maria Stafford, *Voyage into Substance: Art, Science, Nature, and the Illustrated Travel Account, 1760–1840* (Cambridge: Massachusetts Institute of Technology Press, 1984), 34.

17. Anders Sparrman, *A Voyage to the Cape of Good Hope* (London, 1785), vi. Sparrman's work was first published in Swedish in 1783, but it was quickly translated into other European languages, appearing in a German edition in 1784, the first of four English editions was released in 1785, and Dutch and French editions were printed in 1787.

18. Pratt, op. cit., 52.

19. Ibid., 53.

20. Frantz Fanon, *Black Skin, White Masks* (New York: Grove Weidenfeld, 1967), 170.

21. Charles Peter Thunberg, *Travels in Europe, Africa and Asia, Made between the Years 1770 and 1779,* 3rd ed., 4 vols. (London, 1795), 1: 304.

22. Thunberg, "Character of the Hottentots," *Annual Review* (1793), 290.

23. Saint-Pierre's work appeared as *A Voyage to the Island of Mauritius. By a French Officer, and Translated by John Parish* (London, 1775) and *A Voyage to the Isle of France, the Isle of Bourbon and the Cape of Good Hope, with Observations and Reflections upon Nature and Mankind* (London, 1800).

24. John Splinter Stavorinus, *Voyages to the East Indies,* translated by Samuel Hull Wilcocke (London, 1798) and Bartholomaeo a Sancto Paulinus, *A Voyage to the East Indies* (London, 1800).

25. *The General Gazetteer: Or, Compendious Geographical Dictionary.* Originally compiled by R. Brookes, (London, 1762), S1.

26. *The General Gazetteer: Or, Compendious Geographical Dictionary.* Originally compiled by R. Brookes, Revised by W. Guthrie and E. Jones, 7th ed. (Dublin, 1791), n.p.

27. Ibid., n.p.

28. *General Gazetteer; Or, Compendious Geographical Dictionary,* by R. Brookes, 8th ed., (London, 1794), n.p.

29. Ibid., n.p.

30. Ibid., n.p.

31. Ibid., n.p.

32. Ibid., n.p.

33. Ibid., n.p.

34. Ibid., n.p.

35. *Brookes' General Gazetteer Abridged* (London, 1796), n.p.

36. See the entry for "Good Hope, Cape of" in *The General Gazetteer,* 10th ed. (London, 1797), n.p.

37. A final edition of the work, edited by H. A. Davenport, appeared in 1843. Like Brookes's work, there were also probable pirate editions of the work published in Dublin and Scotland, and perhaps more legitimate early-nineteenth-century editions published in the United States. There was also a French edition, published in 1801. Because Guthrie died the year this work was first published, all the subsequent editions were brought out by unnamed editors.

38. William Guthrie, *A New Geographical, Historical, and Commercial Grammar*, 3rd ed. (London, 1771), 596.

39. William Guthrie, *A New Geographical, Historical, and Commercial Grammar* (London, 1794), 762.

40. William Guthrie, *A New Geographical, Historical, and Commercial Grammar* (London, 1794), 767.

41. *The Modern Part of an Universal History*, vol. 14 (London, 1760), 2.

42. *The Modern Part of an Universal History*, vol. 15 (London, 1760), 540.

43. Ibid., 487.

44. Ibid., 494.

45. Ibid., 541.

46. Ibid., 541–42.

47. Rousseau, "Science Books and Their Readers in the Eighteenth Century," in *Books and Their Readers in Eighteenth-Century England,"* ed. Isabel Rivers (Leicester: Leicester University Press, 1982), 223.

48. Oliver Goldsmith, *An History of the Earth and Animated Nature*, 8 vols. (London, 1774), 3:21–22.

49. *Encyclopaedia Britannica; Or, A Dictionary of Arts and Sciences*, 3 vols. (Edinburgh, 1771), vol. 1. I am grateful to Liz Denlinger for checking this source for me.

50. *Encyclopedia Britannica; Or, A Dictionary of Arts and Sciences*, 10 vols. (Edinburgh, 1797), 8:684–85.

51. *Encyclopedia Britannica; Or, A Dictionary of Arts and Sciences*, 10 vols. (Edinburgh, 1797), 8:683

52. Ibid., 687.

53. Joseph Priestley, *Experiments and Observations on Different Kinds of Air*, 3 vols. (London, 1790), 1:xxxi. Priestley's work was first published in 1774.

54. John Millar, *The Origin of the Distinction of Ranks* (London, 1771), ii.

55. *The Origin of the Distinction of Ranks* (1806; reprint, London 1990), 29.

56. Ibid., 49–50.

57. Ibid., 143.

58. Ibid., 144.

59. Monboddo, *Of the Origin and Progress of Language* (London, 1773), 300–301.

60. *Blackwood's Edinburgh Magazine*, vol. 68 (August 1850), 231.

61. James Dunbar, *Essays on the History of Mankind in Rude and Cultivated Ages* (London, 1780), 109.

62. Ibid., 128.

63. Ibid., 160.

64. Henry Home, *Sketches of the History of Man*, 2 vols. (Edinburgh, 1774), 1:12.

65. Ibid., 15.

66. Goldsmith, op. cit., 2:226.

67. Starting with the first editions in 1770, numerous subsequent editions of Guthrie's text have the same preface, which is where this passage appears. I am quoting here from the 1798, 17th edition, xi.

68. David Hume, "Of National Characters," quoted in Emmanuel Chukwudi Eze's *Race and the Enlightenment* (London: Blackwell Publishers, 1997), 33.

69. James Beattie, quoted in Eze, op. cit., 37.

70. In 1763, John Clubb published a satire *Physiognomy; Being a Sketch Only of a Larger Work upon the Same Plan* (London, 1763).

71. J. C. Lavater, *Essays on Physiognomy*, trans. Thomas Holcroft, 3 vols. (London, 1789), 3:85.

72. Winthrop D. Jordan explains that Linnaeus himself did not rank the various classes of "man" in an hierarchical fashion, but ideas about ranks of man, based on physical characteristics, can be found in a number of seventeenth-century English texts. See Jordan's discussion in chapter 6 of his *White over Black*, op. cit., 221.

73. Soame Jenyns, "Disquistions on Several Subjects," *The Works of Soame Jenyns*, 4 vols. (London, 1790), 3:184–85. Quoted in Carson, op. cit, 495, n. 18, and in Jordan, *White over Black*, op. cit., 224.

74. William Smellie, *Philosophy of Natural History*, 2 vols. (Edinburgh, 1790), 1:521.

75. Stephen Jay Gould, "Petrus Camper's Angle," *Bully for Brontosaurus: Reflections in Natural History* (New York: W. W. Norton and Compnay, 1991), 233. Also, see Miriam Meijer's *Race and Aesthetics in the Anthropology of Petrus Camper* (Amsterdam and Atlanta: Rodophi, 1999) for a comprehensive study of Camper and race.

76. Ibid.

77. *The Works of the Late Professor Camper, on the Connexion between the Science of Anatomy and the Arts of Drawing, Painting Statuary*, trans. T. Cogan (London, 1794), 87.

Chapter 7: "The Most Wretched of the Human Race"

1. The first time the British thought about seizing the Cape was in 1781. The alliance between the United Provinces and France in the American War for Independence led the British to fear that France could gain a presence at the Cape. Britain declared war on Holland on 20 December 1780 and, in early 1781, orders were issued to Commodore Johnstone to sail to the Cape and occupy it. A French fleet led by Suffren beat the British force there, however, so Johnstone and his ships were forced to abandon their mission.

2. Henry Rooke,*Travels to the Coast of Arabia Felix and from Thence to the Red Sea and Egypt to Europe* (London, 1784), 33–35.

3. See *Cambridge History of the British Empire*, vol.8, 2nd ed., ed. Eric A. Walker (Cambridge: Cambridge University Press, 1963). Chapter 7, "The British Occupations, 1795–1806," written by Vincent T. Harlow, is particularly relevant to the point I am making here.

4. See L. C. F. Turner, "The Cape of Good Hope and the Anglo-French Conflict, 1797–1806," *Historical Studies, Australia and New Zealand* 9 (May 1961): 368–77. The British still had no immediate or formal plans to develop the Cape as a colony in 1806, but when the Netherlands gave up any claim to the area in 1815, they announced their intention to create the Cape colony

5. For a different and more theoretical account of a newly emergent discourse of the Cape, see Kenneth Parker, "Fertile Land, Romantic Spaces, Uncivilized Peoples: English Travel-Writing about the Cape of Good Hope, 1800–1850,

in *The Expansion of England: Race, Ethnicity and Cultural History*, ed. Bill Schwarz (London: Routledge, 1996), 198–231.

6. British Library, ADD. MS. 30,097, f. 54.

7. This is a phrase used in the 1812 edition of Guthrie's *A New Geographical, Historical, and Commercial Grammar* (London, 1812), 822. Significantly, it begins the concluding paragraph of the description of them.

8. *The Cape Journals of Lady Anne Barnard, 1797–1798*, ed. A. M. Lewin Robinson with Margaret Lenta and Dorothy Driver (Cape Town: Van Riebeeck Society, 1994), 193.

9. John Harriott, *Struggles through Life* , 2nd ed. (London, 1808), 237.

10. Ibid.

11. Lady Anne Barnard, *South Africa a Century Ago* (Oxford: Basil Blackwell, 1925),15. Barnard's letter is dated 10 August 1797.

12. *Gleanings in Africa* (London, 1806), 229–30.

13. *The Cape Journals of Lady Anne Barnard, 1797–1798*, ed. A. M. Lewin Robinson with Margaret Lenta and Dorothy Driver (Cape Town: Van Riebeeck Society, 1994), 336.

14. *Gleanings in Africa*, op. cit., 228.

15. Robert Percival, *An Account of the Cape of Good Hope* (1804), 82.

16. J. M. Coetzee, *White Writing: On the Culture of Letters in South Africa* (New Haven: Yale University Press, 1988), 31–32.

17. John Barrow, *An Account of Travels into the Interior of Southern Africa* (London, 1804), 76. Subsequent citations from this source will be acknowledged in the text.

18. "The Journal of Robert Warden, Seamen, at the Cape, 1796–7," introduced by A. M. Lewin Robinson, *Quarterly Bulletin of the South African Library* 7, nos. 3 and 4 (1953): 75.

19. George, Viscount Valentia, *Voyages and Travels to India, Ceylon, the Red Sea, Abyssinia, and Egypt*, 3 vols. (London, 1809), 1:44.

20. R. Renshaw, *Voyage to the Cape of Good Hope and up the Red Sea* (Manchester, 1804), 17.

21. Anne Barnard, *The Cape Journals of Lady Anne Barnard, 1797–1798* (Cape Town: Van Riebeeck Society, 1994), 330–31.

22. Ibid., 331.

23. *Evangelical Magazine* (December 1803), 32. There were meetings on 7 and 21 November, and there was a third meeting, at Surrey Chapel, whose date is not given in the *Evangelical Magazine*. Kicherer and his companions left London on 12 December 1803, and they returned to the Cape via Holland in 1805. In her book, *Mission Stations and the Coloured Communities of the Eastern Cape, 1800–1852*, Jane Sales reports that two of three "converted Hottentots" became drunkards at Graaff-Reinet, "though the missionary periodical continued to print pious letters from them as late as 1812." See *Mission Stations and the Coloured Communities of the Eastern Cape, 1800–1852* (Cape Town: A. A. Balkema, 1975), 13.

24. *Evangelical Magazine* (December 1803), 545.

25. Ibid.

26. Ibid., 595–96.

27. Ibid., 547.

28. *Supplement to the Evangelical Magazine for the Year 1803* (London, 1803), 595–96.

29. *Evangelical Magazine* (January 1804), 5.

30. Ibid., 46.

31. Ibid.

32. *Evangelical Magazine* (April 1804), 172.

33. *Evangelical Magazine* (May 1804), 200.

34. On pages 86 and 135 of the respective issues.

35. John Barrow, *An Account of Travels into the Interior of Southern Africa* (London, 1804), 15–16. Subsequent citations from this source will be acknowledged in the text.

36. John Barrow, *An Account of Travels into the Interior of Southern Africa in the Years 1797 and 1798,* 2nd ed. (London, 1806), 101.

37. Ibid.

38. John Barrow, *An Account of Travels into the Interior of Southern Africa in the Years 1797 and 1798* (1801), 160. All subsequent quotations from this source will be made in the text.

39. Mary Louise Pratt, *Imperial Eyes: Travel Writing and Transculturation* (London: Routledge, 1992), 60. Pratt's reading of Barrow and other travel narratives that describe southern Africa is far more polemical than mine.

40. John Barrow, *An Account of Travels into the Interior of Southern Africa,* vol. 2 (London, 1804), 48–49.

41. James Forbes, *Oriental Memoirs* (London, 1813), 186.

42. John Barrow, *An Autobiographical Memoir of Sir John Barrow,* (London, 1847), 248.

43. Ibid., 242–43.

44. For example, Abraham Rees's *The Cyclopaedia* (3rd ed., 1819) corroborates and cites Barrow's works, and adopts his anti-Boer position. The entry on "Hottentots" explains their demise as coming from "the neglect or oppression with which they have been treated by the colonists has contributed to corrupt and degrade them" (n.p.).

45. John Barrow, *An Account of Travels into the Interior of Southern Africa in the Years 1797 and 1798,* 2nd ed. (London, 1806), 93–94.

46. Robert Semple, *Walks and Sketches at the Cape of Good Hope* (London, 1803), 27 and 41.

47. *An Account of the Colony of the Cape of Good Hope, with a View to the Information of Emigrants* (London, 1819), 85–86.

48. See Susan Newton-King, "The Labour Market of the Cape Colony, 1807–1828," and Stanley Trapido, " 'The friends of the Natives'," in *Economy and Society in Pre-Industrial South Africa,* ed. Shula Marks and Anthony Atmore (London: Longman, 1980), 171–207 and 247–74.

49. *Cambridge History of the British Empire,* 206.

50. Susan Newton King, op. cit., 177.

51. Timothy Keegan, *Colonial South Africa and the Origins of the Racial Order* (Charlottesville: University Press of Virginia, 1996), 54.

52. George Thompson, *Travels and Adventures in Southern Africa* (London, 1827), 30. Twentieth-century historians, such as Robert Ross, Susan Newton-King, and Stanely Trapido have argued convincingly, however, that the laws created to protect and "emancipate" the Khoikhoi were actually counterproductive to real freedom and liberation.

53. William Guthrie, *A Geographical, Historical, and Commericial Grammar* (1827), 731.

54. *The Annual Register* (1808), 34.

55. C. I. Latrobe, *Journal of a Visit to South Africa in 1815 and 1816* (1818; reprint, New York: Negro Universities Press, 1969), 45. There was a second edition of his work published in 1821.

56. *Mantis, the Soothsayer; Or, The Hottenots' God. A Conversation between a Missionary and a Hottentot; With an Account of the Insect* (London, 1818, 2nd ed. in 1820), n.p.

57. Maria Graham, *Journal of a Residence in India* (Edinburgh, 1812), 173.

58. Ibid.

59. John Campbell, *Travels in South Africa, Undertaken at the Request of the Missionary Society*, 2nd ed., corrected (London, 1815), 7.

60. Ibid., 8.

61. David Spurr, *The Rhetoric of Empire: Colonial Discourse in Journalism, Travel Writing, and Imperial Administration* (Durham: Duke University Press, 1993), 32.

62. William Wilberforce Bird, *State of the Cape of Good Hope in 1822* (London, 1823), 67–68.

63. Ibid.

64. Ibid.

65. William Burchell, *Travels in the Interior of Southern Africa*, 2 vols. (London, 1822), 1:5.

66. Thomas Pringle, "The Hottentot," as it was first published in George Thompson's *Travels and Adventures in Southern Africa* (London, 1827), 25.

67. Pringle revised the poem and included it in his *African Sketches* (London, 1834), 101. See the notes to *The African Poems of Thomas Pringle*, op. cit., 111.

68. Ibid.

69. George Marshall, *Epistles in Verse, between Cynthio and Leonora, in Three Cantos, Descriptive of the Voyage to and From the East Indies* (Newcastle, 1812), 124.

70. *Edinburgh Review* 8, no. 16 (July 1806): 434. Quoted in C. Duncan Rice, "The Missionary Context of the British Anti-Slavery Movement," in *Slavery and British Society, 1776–1846*, ed. James Walvin (Baton Rouge: Louisiana State University Press, 1982), 152.

71. Charles Isaac Mungo Dibdin, "The Age, a Satire," in *Mirth and Metre Consisting of Poems, Serious, Humorous, and Satirical* (London, 1807).

72. Susan Ferrier, *Marriage* (Finland: Penguin, 1986), 16. I am grateful to Betty Rizzo for this reference.

73. Katherine Rogers makes this connection in the entry she wrote on Burney for *A Dictionary of British and American Women Writers, 1660–1800*, ed. Janet Todd (London: Methuen and Company, 1987), 65.

74. Frances Burney, *The Wanderer; Or, Female Difficulties*, ed. Margaret Anne Doody, Richard L. Mack, and Peter Sabor (Oxford: Oxford University Press, 1991), 608. I am grateful to Betty Rizzo for this reference.

75. Lucy Aikin, *Epistles on Women* (London, 1810), 43.

76. Thomas Hood, "Little O'Patrick—An African Fact," *The Complete Poetical Works of Thomas Hood* (London: H. Frowde, 1906), 241.

77. Charles Robert Maturin, *Melmoth the Wanderer* (Lincoln: University of Nebraska Press, 1961), 160–61.

78. Somerville's report, entitled "On the Structure of Hottentot Women," can be found at the Royal Society. *Letters and Papers*, Decade 12 (1805).

79. Ibid., 1.

80. Ibid., 12.

81. Ibid., 18.

82. Ibid., 16.

83. See Paul Edwards and James Walvin, *Black Personalities in the Era of the Slave Trade* (Baton Rouge: Louisiana State University Press, 1983), 171–82. Their work presents the contemporary accounts of her, such as the advertising bill, a

poem, letters of protest written on her behalf, and the report from the court about her case. Also, see Richard D. Altick, *The Shows of London: A Panoramic History of Exhibitions, 1660–1862* (Cambridge: Harvard University Press, 1978), 268–73. Also, see Richard D. Altick, *The Shows of London: A Panoramic History of Exhibitions, 1660–1862* (Cambridge: Harvard University Press, 1978), 268–73; Percival R. Kirby, "The Hottentot Venus," *Africana Notes and News* 6 (1949): 55–62, and, also by Kirby, "More about the Hottentot Venus," *Africana News and Notes* 10 (1953): 124–34; Stephen Jay Gould, "The Hottentot Venus," *Natural History* 91, no. 10 (July–December 1982): 20–27; Bernth Lindfors, " 'The Hottentot Venus and Other African Attractions in Nineteenth-Century England," *Australasian Drama Studies* 1 (1983): 83–104.

84. *Times*, 26 November 1810, 3, as quoted in Bernth Lindfors, op. cit., 87.
85. Lindfors, op. cit., 87.
86. J. J. Virey, *Journal Universel des Sciences Médicales*, vol. 3 (1816): 225–34.
87. Edwards and Walvin, op. cit. , 178–81.
88. Dorothy George, *Catalogue of Political and Personal Satires*, 11577, 8:947.
89. Dorothy George, *Catalogue of Political and Personal Satires*, 11580, 8: 949.
90. See George, *Catalogue*, 11748, vol. 9.
91. *The Talents Run Mad; or, Eighteen Hundred and Sixteen* (London, 1816), 19.
92. Ibid., 19–20.
93. Keegan, op. cit., 127.
94. *Lady Herschel: Letters from the Cape, 1834–1838,* ed. Brian Warner (Cape Town: Friends of the Cape Town Library, 1991), 88–89. Her letter is dated 15 December 1835. The "Kaffir" War she refers to was taking place on the eastern frontier of the colony; the British forces were using some of the "Hottentot" soldiers to fight the war.
95. Ibid., 124.
96. Alfred W. Cole, *The Cape and the Kaffirs* (London, 1852), 78.
97. Ibid., 42–43.
98. Ibid., 147.
99. Harriet Ward, *Five Years in Kaffirland,* 2 vols., 2nd ed. (London, 1848), 1:27–28.
100. *Saturday Magazine*, 10 June 1837, 218.
101. Edward Hungeford Delaval Elers Napier, *Excursions in Southern Africa*, 2 vols. (London, 1850), 1:104.
102. Ibid.
103. Robert Leighton, *Scotch Words, and the Bapteesement o'the Bairn* (London, 1869), lines 53–56.
104. Susan Meyer, *Imperialism at Home: Race and Victorian Women's Fiction* (Ithaca: Cornell University Press, 1996), 138.
105. See Deborah A. Thomas, "Miss Swartz and the Hottentot Venus Revisted," *The Thackeray Newsletter* 36 (November 1992): 1–5.
106. Charles Dickens, "Tom Tiddler's Ground," in *Christmas Stories* (London: J. M. Dent and Sons, 1971), 271.

Conclusion

1. "Happy Hottentots," music by Sigmund Romberg and lyrics by Harold Atteridge. Included in the score for *Robinson Crusoe, Jr.* (New York: G. Schirmer, 1916), 3–6.

2. Victor Mapes and William Collier, *The Hottentot* (New York: S. French, 1922), 38 and 109–10.

3. Review of "The Hottentot," *Moving Picture World*, 22 December 1922, 774. A positive review of the film also appeared in *Variety*, 22 February 1923, and it was considered one of the "best moving pictures of 1922–23," by Robert E. Sherwood, who published a volume listing the year's best films *(The Best Moving Pictures of 1922–23* [Boston: Small, Maynard and Company, 1923), 102. I am indebted to Kevin J. Harty for these references.

4. Review of "The Hottentot," *Variety*, 11 September 1929, 18. I am indebted to Kevin J. Harty for this reference.

5. This is the summary description of them presented on an L. Frank Baum website: www.halcyon.com/piglet/. I am indebted to Jessy Randall for this reference.

6. See chapter 19, "The Trouble with Tottenhots." The text comes from the website, op. cit.

7. Ibid.

8. Quoted in *The Illustrated History of South Africa* (Pleasantville, New York: Reader's Digest Association, 1988), 433.

9. Allister Sparks, *The Mind of South Africa* (New York: Alfred A. Knopf, 1990), 84 and 87.

10. This is the declaration on the museum's web site, http://www.districtsix.co.za.

11. The title of the show was "Miscast—Negotiating the Presence of the Bushmen."

12. Stephen Gray, "Hottentot Venus," *Hottentot Venus and Other Poems* (London: Rex Collings, 1979), 1.

13. Ibid., 2.

14. Maseko's film was included in the Forty-Third London Film Festival (1999). I am indebted to Kevin J. Harty for this information.

15. Elizabeth Alexander, *The Venus Hottentot* (Charlottesville: University Press of Virginia, 1990), 7.

16. The play's original run of New York performances earned mixed reviews. *Theater Week* called the production "daring" and "unsettling," praising the abilities of both the playwright and the director to bring to the stage a work whose central image is "scary, ugly, beautiful" (20 May 1996, 16–18). The production was directed by Richard Foreman, and it was a joint production of the New York Shakespeare Festival and the Yale Repetory Theater. Less complimentary reviews of the first production appeared in *Theatre Journal* (May 1997, 223–25), *Variety* (6–12 May, 1996, 211–12) and *New York* (27 May, 1996, 83). I am indebted to Kevin J. Harty for these references.

17. Suzan-Lori Parks, *Venus* (New York: Theatre Communications Group, 1997), 166.

18. Ibid., 45.

19. Ibid., 161.

Bibliography

Abbot, George. *A Briefe Description of the Whole World.* London, 1599.
An Account of the Colony of the Cape of Good Hope, with a View to the Information of Emigrants. London, 1819.
"Account of the Loss of the Ship Johanna." MSS., 1682, The Royal Society, London.
Achebe, Chinua. "An Image of Africa." *Research in African Literatures* 9 (1978): 1–15.
Adams, Percy. *Travel Literature and the Evolution of the Novel.* Lexington: University Press of Kentucky, 1983.
Addington, Stephen. *The Youth's Geographical Grammar.* London, 1770.
Aikin, Lucy. *Epistles on Women.* London, 1810.
Alexander, Elizabeth. *The Venus Hottentot.* Charlottesville: University Press of Virginia, 1990.
Altick, Richard D. *The Shows of London: A Panoramic History of Exhibitions, 1660–1862.* Cambridge: Harvard University Press, 1978.
Anderson, Benedict. *Imagined Communities.* London: Verso, 1991.
Annual Register. "Hottentot Devotion in South Africa." London, 1808. 34.
Anti-Jacobin; Or, Weekly Examiner, 2 April 1798.
Aston, Edward. *The Manner and Customs of All Nations.* London, 1611.
Atlas Geographus: Or, A Compleat System of Geography. London, 1711–17.
Baker, J. N. L. "Academic Geography in the Seventeenth and Eighteenth Centuries." In *The History of Geography: Papers by J. N. L. Baker,* 14–32. New York: Barnes and Noble, 1963.
———. "Nathanael Carpenter and English Geography in the Seventeenth Century." In *The History of Geography: Papers by J. N. L. Baker,* 1–13. New York: Barnes and Noble, 1963. 1–13.
Baldwyn, George Augustus. *A New, Royal, Authentic, Complete, Universal System of Geography; Or, A Modern History and Description of the Whole World.* London, 1794.
Banks, Joseph. *Journal of the Right Honourable Sir Joseph Banks during Captain Cook's First Voyage in the HMS Endeavour in 1768–1771.* Edited by Joseph D. Hooker. London: Macmillan and Company, 1896.
Barber, Mary. *Poetry of Mary Barber.* New York: Edwin Mellen Press, 1992.
Barbour, Philip L., ed. *The Complete Works of Captain John Smith.* 3 vols. Chapel Hill: Published for the Institute of Early American History and Culture, University of North Carolina Press, 1986.
———. "Samuel Purchas: The Indefatigable Encyclopedist Who Lacked Good Judgement." In *Essays in Early Virginia Literature Honoring Richard Beale Davie,*

edited by J. A. Leo Lemay, 35–52. New York: Burt Franklin and Company, 1977.

Barlow, Edward. *Journal of His Life at Sea in King's Ships, East and West India-Men, and Other Merchantmen from 1659–1703.* Transcribed by Basil Lubbock. 2 vols. London: Hurst and Blackett, 1934.

Barnard, Alan. *Hunters and Herders of Southern Africa: A Comparative Ethnography of the Khoisan Peoples.* Cambridge: Cambridge University Press, 1992.

Barnard, Lady Anne. *The Cape Journals of Lady Anne Barnard, 1797–1798.* Ed. by A. M. Lewin Robinson, with Margaret Lento and Dorothy Driver. Cape Town: Van Riebeeck Society, 1994.

———. *South Africa a Century Ago: Letters Written from the Cape of Good Hope, 1797–1801.* Oxford: Basil Blackwell, 1925.

Barrow, John. *An Account of Travels into the Interior of Southern Africa in the Years 1797 and 1798.* London, 1801.

———. *An Account of Travels into the Interior of Southern Africa.* London, 1804.

———. *An Account of Travels into the Interior of Southern Africa in the Years 1797 and 1798.* 2nd ed. London, 1806.

———. *An Autobiographical Memoir of Sir John Barrow,* London, 1847.

Barthelemy, Anthony Gerard. *Black Face, Maligned Race.* Baton Rouge: Louisiana State University Press, 1987.

Beeckman, Daniel. *A Voyage to and from the Island of Borneo in the East Indies.* London, 1718.

Benger, Elizabeth Ogilvy. *Memoirs of the Late Mrs. Elixabeth Hamilton.* 2 vols. London, 1818.

Bird, William Wilberforce. *State of the Cape of Good Hope in 1822.* London, 1823.

Blackmore, Richard. *The Nature of Man.* London, 1711.

Blackwood's Edinburgh Magazine, "African Sporting." 68 (August 1850) 245.

Blome, Richard. *A Geographical Description of the Four Parts of the World Taken from the Notes and Works of the Famous Monsieur Sanson, Geographer to the French King, and Other Eminent Travellers and Authors.* London, 1670.

Bluett, Thomas. *Some Memoirs of the Life of Job, the Son of Solomon the High Priest of Boonda in Africa.* London, 1734.

Bohls, Elizabeth A. *Women Travel Writers and the Language of Aesthetics, 1716–1818.* Cambridge: Cambridge University Press, 1995.

Bohun, Edmond. *A Geographical Dictionary.* London, 1688.

Bond, Donald F., ed. *The Spectator.* 5 vols. Oxford: Clarendon Press, 1965.

Boonzaier, Emile, Penny Berens, Candy Malherbe, and Andy Smith. *The Cape Herders: A History of the Khoikhoi of Southern Africa.* Cape Town: David Philip, 1996.

Boyle, Robert. "General Heads for a Natural History of a Countrey." In *Philosophical Transactions of the Royal Society,* 188. London, 1666.

Braude, Benjamin. "The Sons of Noah and the Construction of Ethnic and Early Modern Identities in the Medieval and Early Modern Periods." *William and Mary Quarterly* 54, no. 1 (January 1997): 103–42.

Brittle, Emily. *The India Guide: Or, Journal of a Voyage to the East Indies in the Year 1780, in a Poetical Epistle to Her Mother.* Calcutta, 1785.

Brookes, Richard. *The General Gazetteer.* London, 1761.

———. *The General Gazetteer*. London, 1791.
———. *The General Gazetteer*. London, 1794.
———. *The General Gazetteer*. London, 1796.
———. *The General Gazetteer*. London, 1797.
Burchell, William. *Travels in the Interior of Southern Africa*. 2 vols. London, 1822.
Burke, Peter. "America and the Rewriting of World History." In *America in European Consciousness, 1493–1750*, 33–51, edited by Karen Ordahl Kupperman. Chapel Hill: University of North Carolina Press, 1995.
Burnet, Gilbert. *An Introduction to the Third Volume of the History of the Reformation of the Church of England*. London, 1714.
Burney, Frances. *The Wanderer; Or, Female Difficulties*. Edited by Margaret Anne Doody, Richard L. Mack, and Peter Sabor. Oxford: Oxford University Press, 1991.
Campbell, John. *Travels in South Africa, Undertaken at the Request of the Missionary Society*. 2nd ed. London, 1815.
Camper, Petrus. *The Works of the Late Professor Camper*. Translated by T. Cogan. London, 1794.
Carpenter, Nathanael. *Geography Delineated Forth in Two Bookes*. Oxford, 1625.
Carretta, Vincent, ed. *Unchained Voices*. Lexington: University Press of Kentucky, 1996.
Carson, James P. "Britons, 'Hottentots,' Plantation Slavery, and Tobias Smollet." *Philological Quarterly* 75, no. 4 (fall 1996): 471–99.
Clark, S. *A New Description of the World*. London, 1689.
Coetzee, J. M. *White Writing: On the Culture of Letters in South Africa*. New Haven: Yale University Press, 1988.
Cole, Alfred W. *The Cape and the Kaffirs*. London, 1852.
Collinson, Richard, ed. *The Three Voyages of Martin Frobisher*. 1867. Reprint, New York: Burt Franklin, 1963.
Comaroff, John, and Jean Comaroff. *Ethnography and the Historical Imagination*. Boulder: Westview Press, 1992.
Connoisseur 21 (20 June 1754), 121–26.
Cooke, Edward. *A Voyage to the South Sea and round the World*. London, 1712.
Coverte, Robert. *A True and Almost Incredible Report of an Englishman That . . . Travelled by Land through Many Unknowne Kingdomes and Great Cities*. 1612. Reprint, rpt. New York: De Capo Press, 1971.
Cowley, Ambrose. *Voyage round the Globe*. London, 1687.
Critical Review, August 1790.
Cugoano, Quobna Ottobah. *Thoughts and Sentiments on the Evil and Wicked Traffic of the Slavery and Commerce of the Human Species*. In *Unchained Voices*, edited by Vincent Carretta. Lexington: University Press of Kentucky, 1996.
Cunningham, William. *The Cosmographical Glasse*. London, 1559.
Curtin, Philip D. *The Image of Africa: British Ideas and Action, 1780–1850*. Madison: University of Wisconsin Press, 1964.
Dampier, William. *A New Voyage round the World*. London, 1697.
Davis, David Brion. "Constructing Race: A Reflection." *William and Mary Quarterly* 54, no. 1 (January 1997): 7–18.

Debrunner, Hans Werner. *Presence and Prestige: Africans in Europe.* Basel: Basler Afrika Bibliographien, 1979.

Defense of the Plea for Human Reason. London, 1731.

Defoe, Daniel. *Atlas Maritimus.* London, 1728.

Dellon, Gabriel. *Voyage to the East Indies.* London, 1698.

Description of a Voyage Made by Certaine Ships of Holland into the East Indies. Translated by W. P. London, 1597.

Dibdin, Charles Isaac Mungo. *Mirth and Metre, Consisting of Poems, Serious, Humorous, and Satirical.* London, 1807.

Dickins, Charles. "Tom Tiddler's Ground." In *Christmas Stories.* London: J. M. Dent and Sons, 1971.

Douglas, Mary. *Purity and Danger: An Analysis of the Concepts of Pollution and Taboo.* 1966. Reprint, London: Routledge, 1991.

Dulles, Foster Rhea. *Eastward Ho!* London: Bodley Head, 1931.

Dunbar, James. *Essays on the History of Mankind in Rude and Cultivated Ages.* London, 1780.

Dyer, John. *The Fleece: A Poem, in Four Books.* London, 1757.

Echard, Laurence. *A Most Compleat Compendium of Geography.* 1st ed. London, 1691.

———. *A Most Compleat Compendium of Geography.* 2nd ed. London, 1691.

Eden, Richard. *The Decades of the Newe World or West India.* London, 1555.

Edgeworth, Maria. *Moral Tales for Young People.* 3 vols. New York: Garland Publishing Co., 1974.

Edwards, Paul, and James Walvin. *Black Personalities in the Era of the Slave Trade.* Baton Rouge: Louisiana State University Press, 1983.

Edwards, Philip. *The Story of the Voyage: Sea-Narratives in Eighteenth-Century England.* Cambridge: Cambridge University Press, 1994.

Eilon, Daniel. "Swift's Yahoo and Leslie's Hottentot." *Notes and Queries* (December 1983): 510–12.

Elphick, Richard. *The Khoikhoi and the Founding of White South Africa.* Johannesburg: Ravan Press, 1985.

Encyclopaedia Britannica; Or, A Dictionary of Arts and Sciences. 3 vols. London, 1771.

Encyclopaedia Britannica; Or, A Dictionary of Arts and Sciences. 10 vols. London, 1797.

England, George. *An Enquiry into the Morals of the Ancients.* London, 1737.

Equiano, Olaudah. *The Interesting Narrative of the Life of Olaudah Equiano, Written by Himself.* Edited by Robert J. Allison. New York: Bedford Books of St. Martin's Press, 1995.

Evangelical Magazine, "Hottentots." December 1803. 545–50.

Evangelical Magazine, "Minutes of the Questions put to the Reverend Mr. Kicherer." *Supplement for the Year 1803.* 591–97.

Evangelical Magazine, "Mr. Kicherer's Mission to the Hottentots." January 1804. 5–8.

Evangelical Magazine, "Anecdote of a Hottentot Youth." April 1804. 172.

Evangelical Magazine, "Interesting Incident." May 1804. 200.

Eze, Emmanuel Chukwudi. *Race and the Enlightenment*. London, Blackwell Publishers, 1997.

Fairfax, Samuel. "Journal of My Own Proceedings at the Cape, September 1797." *State* 2 (1909): 580–89.

Fanon, Frantz. *Black Skin, White Masks*. New York: Grove Weidenfeld, 1967.

Fenning, Daniel. *A New System of Geography*. London, 1771.

Ferrier, Susan. *Marriage*. London: Penguin Books, 1986.

Fielding, Henry. *Tom Jones*. Edited by Sheridan Baker. New York: W. W. Norton and Company, 1973.

Forbes, James. *Oriental Memoirs*. London, 1813.

Forbes, Vernon S. *Pioneer Travellers of South Africa*. Cape Town: A. A. Balkema, 1965.

Forster, George. *A Voyage round the World*. London, 1777.

Foster, William, ed. *The Embassy of Sir Thomas Roe to the Court of the Great Mogul*. 2 vols. London: Hakluyt Society, 1899.

———. *The Voyage of Sir Henry Middleton to the Moluccas*. London: Hakluyt Society, 1943.

———. *Voyages of Sir James Lancaster to Brazil and the East Indies*. London: Hakluyt Society, 1940.

Frantz, Ray William. *The English Traveler and the Movement of Ideas, 1660–1732*. 1934. Reprint, Lincoln: University of Nebraska Press, 1967.

Fry, Danby P. *The Word "Hottentot": Articles Extracted from the Transactions of the Philological Society*. 1866. Reprint, Pretoria: State Library, 1971.

Funnell, William. *A Voyage round the World*. London, 1707.

Gates, Henry Louis Jr. "James Gronniosaw and the Trope of the Talking Book." In *Studies in Autobiography*, edited by James Olney. New York and Oxford: Oxford University Press, 1988.

Gates, Henry Louis Jr., ed. *"Race," Writing and Difference*. Chicago: University of Chicago Press, 1985.

Gentleman's Magazine, February 1731. 62.

Gentleman's Magazine, February 1732. 602.

Geography Made Familiar and Easy to Young Gentlemen and Ladies. London, 1748.

George, Dorothy M. *Catalogue of Prints and Drawings in the British Museum: Political and Personal Satires*. 11 vols. London: British Museum, 1870–1954.

George, Valentia. *Voyages and Travels to India, Ceylon, the Red Sea, Abyssinia, and Egypt*. 3 vols. London, 1809.

Giliomee, Herman, and Richard Elphick, "The Structure of European Domination at the Cape, 1652–1820." In *The Shaping of South African Society, 1652–1820*, edited by Giliomee and Elphick, 359–90. Cape Town and London: Longman, 1979.

Gleanings in Africa. London, 1806.

Goldgar, Bertrand A. *Walpole and the Wits: The Relation of Politics to Literature, 1722–1742*. Lincoln: University of Nebraska Press, 1976.

Goldsmith, Oliver. *The Collected Works of Oliver Goldsmith*. 5 vols. Edited by Arthur Friedman. Oxford: Clarendon Press, 1966.

———. *An History of the Earth and Animated Nature*. 8 vols. London, 1774.

Gordon, Patrick. *Geography Anatomiz'd: Or, The Compleat Geographical Grammar.* London, 1699.

Gould, Stephen Jay. *Bully for Brontosaurus: Reflections in Natural History.* New York: W. W. Norton and Company, 1991.

———. "The Hottentot Venus." *Natural History* 91, no. 10 (July-December 1982): 20–27.

Graham, Maria. *Journal of a Residence in India.* Edinburgh, 1812.

Graves, Robert. *The Spiritual Quixote.* London, 1773.

Gray, Stephen. *Hottentot Venus and Other Poems.* Cape Town: David Philip, 1979.

Griffith, Elizabeth. *The Delicate Distress.* Edited by Cynthia Booth Ricciardi and Susan Staves. Lexington: University Press of Kentucky, 1997.

Grub-Street Journal 51, 24 December 1730.

Grub-Street Journal 59, 18 February 1731.

Grub-Street Journal 61, 4 March 1731.

Guthrie, William. *A New Geographical, Historical, and Commercial Grammar.* London, 1771.

———. *A New Geographical, Historical and Commercial Grammar.* London, 1794.

———. *A New Geographical, Historical and Commercial Grammar.* London, 1812.

———. *A New Geographical, Historical and Commercial Grammar.* London, 1827.

Hakluyt, Richard. *The Principal Navigations.* London, 1598–99.

Hall, Kim F. "Sexual Politics and Cultural Identity in *The Masque of Blackness.*" In *The Performance of Power: Theatrical Discourse and Politics,* edited by Sue Ellen Case and Janelle Reinelt. Iowa City: University of Iowa Press, 1991.

———. *Things of Darkness: Economics of Race and Gender in Early-Modern England.* Ithaca: Cornell University Press, 1995.

Hamilton, Alexander. *A New Account of the East Indies.* 1729. Reprint, London, 1737.

Hannaford, Ivan. *Race: The History of an Idea in the West.* Baltimore: Johns Hopkins University Press, 1996.

Harris, John, comp. *Navigantium atque Itinerantium.* 2 vols. London, 1705.

Hawkesworth, John. *An Account of the Voyages Undertaken by the Order of His Present Majesty for Making Discoveries in the Southern Hemisphere.* London, 1773.

Helfers, James P. "The Explorer or the Pilgrim? Modern Critical Opinion and the Editorial Methods of Richard Hakluyt and Samuel Purchas." *Studies in Philology* 94, no. 2 (spring 1997): 160–86.

Herbert, Thomas. *A Relation of Some Yeares Travaile.* London, 1634.

———. *A Relation of Some Yeares Travaile.* London, 1638.

———. *A Relation of Some Yeares Travaile.* London, 1665.

Heylyn, Peter. *Cosmographie.* London, 1652.

———. *Cosmographie.* London, 1657.

———. *Cosmographie.* London, 1703.

———. *Microcosmus: A Little Description of the Great World.* London, 1627.

———. *Microcosmus: A Little Description of the Great World.* London, 1639.

Hirst, Derek. *Authority and Conflict: England, 1603–1658.* Cambridge: Harvard University Press, 1986.

Historical Manuscripts Commission. *Report on Manuscripts in the Welsh Language.* Vol. 1, part 3. London: Her Majesty's Stationary Office, 1898.

Hodgen, Margaret T. *Early Anthropology in the Sixteenth and Seventeenth Centuries.* Philadelphia: University of Pennsylvania Press, 1964.

Home, Henry. *Sketches of the History of Man.* 2 vols. Edinburgh, 1774.

Hood, Thomas. *The Complete Poetical Works of Thomas Hood.* Edited by Walter Jerrold. London: H. Frowde, 1911.

Hughes, Charles, ed. *Shakespeare's Europe: A Survey of the Condition of Europe at the End of the Sixteenth Century.* New York: Benjamin Blom, 1967.

Hume, David. *New Letters of David Hume.* Edited by Raymond Klibansky and Ernest C. Mossner. 1954. Reprint, Oxford: Clarendon Press, 1969.

Hurrell, Tamary Elizabeth. *Tales of Imagination.* Dublin, 1790.

Hutton, Catherine. *The Tour of Africa.* London, 1819.

Illustrated History of South Africa. Pleasantville, New York: Reader's Digest Association, 1988.

JanMohamed, Abdul R. "The Economy of Manichean Allegory: The Function of Racial Difference in Colonial Literature." In *"Race," Writing and Difference,* edited Henry Louis Gates Jr., 78–106. Chicago: University of Chicago Press, 1985.

Jacobson, Dan. "The Road to Griquatown." *Times Literary Supplement* (1 April 1994): 3.

Jenyns, Soame. *The Works of Soame Jenyns.* 4 vols. London, 1790.

Jordan, Winthrop D. *White over Black: American Attitudes toward the Negro, 1550–1812.* Chapel Hill: Institute of Early American History and Culture, 1968.

Keegan, Timothy. *Colonial South Africa and the Origins of the Racial Order.* Charlottesville: University Press of Virginia, 1996.

Kindersley, Jemima. *Letters from the Island of Teneriffe, Brazil, the Cape of Good Hope, and the East Indies.* London, 1777

Kirby, Percival R. "The Hottentot Venus." *Africana Notes and News* 6 (1949): 55–62.

———. "More about the Hottentot Venus." *Africana Notes and News* 10 (1953): 124–34.

Kolb, Peter. *The Present State of the Cape of Good Hope.* Translated by Guido Medley. 2 vols. 1731. Reprint, New York: Johnson Reprint Corporation, 1968.

Laidler, Percy Ward, and Michael Gelfand. *South Africa: Its Medical History.* Cape Town: C. Struik, 1971.

Latrobe, C. I. *Journal of a Visit to South Africa in 1815 and 1816.* 1818. Reprint, New York: Negro Universities Press, 1969.

Lavater, J. C. *Essays on Physiognomy.* Translated by Thomas Holcroft. 3 vols. London, 1789.

Leclerc, Georges Louis. *Barr's Buffon. Buffon's Natural History.* 10 vols. London, 1797–1807.

Leighton, Robert. *Scotch Words and the Bapteesement o'the Bairn.* London, 1869.

Leo, Africanus. *The History and Description of Africa.* 3 vols. London: Hakluyt Society, 1896.

Leslie, Charles. *The Finishing Stroke.* London, 1711.

A Letter Written to the Right Worshipfull the Governours and Assistants of the East India Merchants in London. London, 1603.

Le Vaillant, François. *Travels into the Interior Parts of Africa.* London, 1790.

Lindfors, Bernth. "The Hottentot Venus and Other African Attractions in Nineteenth-Century England." *Australasian Drama Studies* 1 (1983): 83–104.

Lloyd, Evan. *Conversation.* London, 1767.

Locke, John. *An Essay Concerning Human Understanding.* Edited by Peter H. Nidditch. Oxford: Clarendon Press, 1975.

Lockyer, Charles. *An Account of the Trade in India.* London, 1711.

Long, Edward. *The History of Jamaica.* 3 vols. London, 1774.

Loubère, Simon de la. *A New Historical Relation of the Kingdom of Siam.* London, 1693.

MacCaffrey, Wallace T. *Elizabeth 1: War and Politics, 1588–1603.* Princeton: Princeton University Press, 1992.

Macintosh, William. *Travels in Europe, Asia, and Africa.* 2 vols. London, 1782.

Mack, Maynard. *Alexander Pope: A Life.* New York: W. W. Norton and Company, 1985.

Mandeville, Bernard. *The Fable of the Bees.* Edited by F. B. Kaye. 2 vols. 1924. Reprint, Oxford: Clarendon Press, 1957.

Mantis, the Soothsayer: Or, The Hottentots' God. London, 1818.

Mapes, Victor, and William Collier. *The Hottentot.* New York: Samuel French, 1922.

Marshall, P. J., and Glyndwr Williams. *Great Map of Mankind: Perceptions of New Worlds in the Age of Enlightenment.* Cambridge: Harvard University Press, 1982.

Maturin, Charles Robert. *Melmoth the Wanderer.* Lincoln: University of Nebraska Press, 1961.

Marks, Shula. "Khoisan Resistance to the Dutch in the Seventeenth and Eighteenth Centuries." *Journal of African History* 13, no. 1 (1972): 55–80.

Marshall, George. *Epistles in Verse.* Newcastle, 1812.

Masson, Francis. "Mr. Masson's Botanical Travels." *Philosophical Transactions of the Royal Society* 66 (1776): 268–317.

Maxwell, John. "An Account of the Cape of Good Hope." *Philosophical Transactions of the Royal Society* 25 (1706–7): 2423–33.

Meijer, Miriam. *Race and Aesthetics in the Anthropology of Petrus Camper.* Amsterdam and Atlanta: Rodophi, 1999.

Merians, Linda E., ed. *The Secret Malady.* Lexington: University Press of Kentucky, 1996.

Meyer, Susan. *Imperialism at Home: Race and Victorian Women's Fiction.* Ithaca: Cornell University Press, 1996.

Middleton, Charles Theodore. *A New Complete System of Geography.* 2 vols. London, 1778.

Mielke, Andreas. "Hottentots in the Aesthetic Discussion of Eighteenth-Century Germany." *Monatshefte* 80, no. 2 (summer 1988): 135–48.

Millar, John. *Observations Concerning the Distinction of Rank in Society.* London, 1771.

———. *The Origin of the Distinction of Ranks.* 4th ed. 1806. Reprint, London: Thoemmes Antiquarian Books Ltd., 1990.

Modern Part of an Universal History. 44 vols. London, 1759–66.

Moll, Herman. *A System of Geography.* London, 1701.

Monboddo, James Burnet. *Of the Origin and Progress of Language.* 6 vols. Edinburgh, 1773.

Monthly Review, December 1776. 544–45.

Monthly Review, September 1777. 243–45.

Monthly Review, June 1786. 518.

Monthly Review, August 1790. 398.

Monthly Review, Appendix to the First Volume, January–April 1790. 481.

Morden, Robert. *Geography Rectified.* London, 1693.

More, Hannah. Letter to Mrs. Rackett, 2 October 1779. D/RAC:88. Dorchester Record Office.

Morgan, Jennifer L. " 'Some Could Suckle over Their Shoulder': Male Travelers, Female Bodies, and the Gendering of Racial Ideology, 1500–1700." *William and Mary Quarterly* 54, no. 1 (January 1997): 167–92.

Moving Picture World, 22 December 1922.

Napier, Edward Delaval Hungerford Elers. *Excursions in Southern Africa.* 2 vols. London, 1850.

New General Collection of Voyages and Travels. 4 vols. London, 1745–47.

New Historical Relation of the Kingdom of Siam, A. London, 1693.

Newman, Gerald. *The Rise of English Nationalism: A Cultural History.* New York: St. Martin's Press, 1987.

Newton-King, Susan. "The Labour Market of the Cape Colony, 1807–1828." In *Economy and Society in Pre-Industrial South Africa,* edited by Shula Marks and Anthony Atmore, 171–207. London: Longman, 1980.

———. " "The Friends of the Natives." In *Economy and Society in Pre-Industrial South Africa,* edited by Shula Marks and Anthony Atmore, 247–74. London: Longman, 1980.

Nieuhoff, John. *Mr. John Nieuhoff's Voyages and Travels to the East-Indies.* In *A Collection of Voyages and Travels,* edited by John and Awnsham Churchill, 2:186–89. 4 vols. London, 1704.

Nussbaum, Felicity A. *Torrid Zones: Maternity, Sexuality, and Empire in Eighteenth-Century English Narratives.* Baltimore: Johns Hopkins University Press, 1995.

Ogilby, John. *Africa.* London, 1670.

Ovington, John. *Voyage to Suratt.* London, 1696.

Oxford History of South Africa. Edited by Monica Wilson and Leonard Thompson. 2 vols. New York: Oxford University Press, 1969.

Parker, John. *Books to Build an Empire: A Bibliographical History of English Overseas Interests to 1620.* Amsterdam: N. Israel, 1965.

Parker, Kenneth. "Fertile Land, Romantic Space, Uncivilized Peoples: English Travel-Writing about the Cape of Good Hope, 1800–1850." In *The Expansion of Empire: Race, Ethnicity and Cultural History,* edited by Bill Schwarz, 198–231. London: Routledge, 1996.

———. "Telling Tales: Early Modern English Voyagers and the Cape of Good Hope." *Seventeenth Century* 10, no. 1 (spring 1995): 121–49.

Parker, Mary Anne. *A Voyage round the World*. London, 1795.

Parks, Suzan Lori. *Venus*. New York: Theatre Communications Group, 1997.

Pennington, Loren E. "Hakluytus Posthumus: Samuel Purchas and the Promotion of English Overseas Expansion." *Emporia State Research Studies* 14, no. 3 (1996): 5–39.

Pepys, Samuel. *The Diary of Samuel Pepys*. Edited by Robert Latham and William Matthews. 11 vols. Los Angeles: University of California Press, 1970–83.

Percival, Robert. *An Account of the Cape of Good Hope*. London, 1804.

Perniola, Mario. "Between Clothing and Nudity." In *Zone: Fragments for a History of the Human Body, Part Two*, edited by Michel Feher with Ramona Naddaff and Nadia Tazi. New York: Zone, 1989.

Perry, Ruth. "Colonizing the Breast: Sexuality and Maternity in Eighteenth-Century England." *Eighteenth-Century Life* n.s. 1, 16 (February 1992): 185–213.

Petit, Edward. *The Visions of Government*. London, 1686.

Plea for Divine Revelation. London, 1731.

Pope, Alexander. *The Poems of Alexander Pope*. Edited by John Butt. New Haven: Yale University Press, 1963.

Pratt, Mary Louise. *Imperial Eyes*. London: Routledge, 1992.

Prévost, Abbé. *Histoire Générale Des Voyages, ou Nouvelle Collection de Toutes Les Relations de Voyages*. Paris, 1749.

Priestley, Joseph. *Experiments and Observations on Different Kinds of Air*. 3 vols. London, 1790.

Pringle, Thomas. *The African Poems of Thomas Pringle*. Edited by Ernest Pereira and Michael Chapman. Durban: Killie Campbell Africana Library, 1989.

Prior, James. *Narrative of a Voyage in the Indian Seas*. London, 1820.

Prior, Matthew. *The Literary Works of Matthew Prior*. Edited by H. Bunker Wright and Monroe K. Spears. 2 vols. Oxford: Clarendon Press, 1971.

Purchas, Samuel. *Purchas His Pilgrimage*. London, 1613.

———. *Purchas His Pilgrimage*. London, 1614.

———. *Purchas His Pilgrimage*. London, 1617.

———. *Purchas His Pilgrimes*. London, 1625.

Raleigh, Walter. *The English Voyages of the Sixteenth Century*. Glasgow: James MacLehose and Sons, 1906.

Ranelean Religion Displayed. London, 1750.

Raven-Hart, R. *Before Van Riebeeck: Callers at South Africa from 1488 to 1652*. Cape Town: C. Struik, 1967.

Raynal, Guillaume-Thomas-François. *A Philosophical and Political History of the Settlements and Trade of the Europeans in the East and West Indies*. Translated by J. O. Justamond. 8 vols. London, 1783.

Rees, Abraham. *The Cyclopaedia*. 3rd ed. London, 1819.

Relation of the Voyage to Siam. London, 1688.

Renshaw, R. *Voyage to the Cape of Good Hope and up the Red Sea*. Manchester, 1804.

Rhyne, Willem Ten. *An Account of the Cape of Good Hope and the Hottentots*. In *A*

Collection of Voyages and Travels, edited by John and Awnsham Churchill, 4:829–45. 4 vols. London, 1704.

Rice, C. Duncan. "The Missionary Context of the British Anti-Slavery Movement." In *Slavery and British Society,* edited by James Walvin, 150–63. Baton Rouge: Louisiana State University Press, 1982.

Richardson, Samuel. *Clarissa.* Edited by Angus Ross. Middlesex: Penguin Books, 1985.

Rix, Wilton S., ed. *The Diary and Autobiography of Edmund Bohun, Esquire* Ipswich: Reed Crisp, 1853.

Robinson, A. M. Lewin, "The Journal of Robert Warden, Seamen, at the Cape, 1796–97. *Quarterly Bulletin of the South African Library* 7, nos. 3–4 (1953): 68–79.

Rogers, Pat, ed. *Johnson and Boswell in Scotland.* New Haven: Yale University Press, 1993.

Rogers, Woodes. *A Cruising Voyage round the World.* London, 1712.

Romberg, Sigmund, and Harold Atteridge. *Robinsoe Crusoe, Jr.* New York: G. Schirmer, 1916.

Rooke, Henry. *Travels to the Coast of Arabia Felix and from Thence to the Red Sea and Egypt to Europe.* London, 1784.

Rousseau, George S. "Science Books and Their Readers in the Eighteenth Century." In *Books and Their Readers in Eighteenth-Century England,* edited by Isabel Rivers. Leicester: Leicester University Press, 1982.

Rousseau, Jean-Jacques. *Discours sur l'origine et les fondemens de l'inegalite parmi les hommes.* Amsterdam, 1755.

Said, Edward. *Culture and Imperialism.* New York: Alfred A. Knopf, 1993.

———. *Orientalism.* New York: Vintage Books, 1979.

Saint Pierre, J. H. Bernardin de. *A Voyage to the Isle of France, the Isle of Bourbon, and the Cape of Good Hope.* London, 1775.

Salmon, Thomas. *Modern History.* 5 vols. London, 1755.

Saturday Magazine. 10 June 1837.

Schapera, Isaac, and B. Farrington, eds. *The Early Cape Hottentots.* Cape Town: Van Riebeeck Society, 1933.

Schweitzer, Christopher. *A Relation of Two Several Voyages Made to the East Indies.* London, 1700.

Selincourt, E. de, ed. *Journals of Dorothy Wordsworth, Recollections of a Tour Made in Scotland (1803).* 2 vols. London: MacMillan and Company, 1959.

Semple, Robert. *Walks and Sketches at the Cape of Good Hope.* London, 1803.

Sheehan, Bernard W. *Savagism and Civility: Indians and Englishmen in Colonial Virginia.* Cambridge: Cambridge University Press, 1980.

Sherwood, Robert E. *The Best Moving Pictures of 1922–23.* Boston: Small, Maynard and Company, 1923.

Singh, Jyotsna G. *Colonial Narratives/Cultural Dialogues: "Discoveries" of India in the Language of Colonialism.* London: Routledge, 1996.

Smart, Christopher. *The Midwife 2.* 24 April 1751.

Smellie, William. *Philosophy of Natural History.* 2 vols. Edinburgh, 1790.

Smith, Van Wyck. " 'The Most Wretched of the Human Race': The Iconography of the Khoikhoin (Hottentots), 1500–1800." *History and Anthropology* 5, nos. 3–4 (1992): 285–330.

Smollett, Tobias. *The Adventures of Peregrine Pickle*. Edited by James L. Clifford. Oxford: Oxford University Press, 1964.

———. *A Compendium of Authentic and Entertaining Voyages*. 7 vols. London, 1756.

Southerne, Thomas. *Oroonoko*. Edited by Maximillan E. Novak and David Stuart Rodes. Lincoln: University of Nebraska Press, 1976.

Sparks, Allister. *The Mind of South Africa*. New York: Alfred A. Knopf, 1990.

Sparrman, Anders. *A Voyage to the Cape of Good Hope*. London, 1785.

Speed, John. *A Prospect of the Most Famous Parts of the World*. London, 1646.

Spurr, David. *The Rhetoric of Empire: Colonial Discourse in Journalism, Travel Writing, and Imperial Administration*. Durham: Duke University Press, 1993.

St. John, Henry. *Letters on the Study and the Use of History*. 2 vols. London, 1752.

Stafford, Barbara Marie. *Voyage into Substance: Art, Science, Nature, and the Illustrated Travel Account*. Cambridge: Massachusetts Institute of Technology Press, 1984.

Stafforde, Robert. *A Geographical and Anthologicall Description of All the Empires and Kingdomes Both of the Continent and Ilands in This Terrestrial Globe*. London, 1607.

Stanhope, Philip Dormer. *Letters to His Son on the Art of Becoming a Man of the World and a Gentleman*. 2 vols. New York: Chesterfield, 1917.

Stevens, George Alexander. *Songs, Comic and Satyrical*. Philadelphia, 1778.

Stone, Lawrence. *The Crisis of the Aristocracy, 1558–1641*. Oxford: Oxford University Press, 1967.

Streak, Michael. *The Afrikaner as Viewed by the English, 1795–1854*. Cape Town: C. Struik, 1974.

Swift, Jonathan. *Gulliver's Travels and Other Writings*. Edited by Louis A. Landa. Boston: Houghton Mifflin Company, 1960.

———. "A Letter on the Fishery." In *Directions to Servants and Miscellaneous Pieces, 1733–1742*, edited by Herbert Davis. Oxford: Basil Blackwell, 1964.

Talents Run Mad; or, Eighteenth hundred and sixteen. London, 1816.

Tavernier, Jean Baptiste. *The Six Voyages of Jean Baptiste Tavernier*. London, 1678.

Terry, Edward. ΥΕΥΔΣΛΣΥΘΕΡΙΑ *Or, Lawless Liberty*. London, 1646.

———. *The Merchants and Mariners Preservation and Thanksgiving. Or, Thankfulnesse Returned for Mercies Received*. London, 1649.

———. *A Voyage to the East Indies*. London, 1655.

———. *A Voyage to the East Indies*. London, 1665.

———. *A Voyage to the East Indies*. London, 1777.

Theasaurus Geographicus. 4th ed. London, 1728.

Thomas, Pascoe. *A True and Impartial Journal of a Voyage to the South Seas and round the Globe*. London, 1745.

Thomas, Deborah A. "Miss Swartz and the Hottentot Venus Revisited." *Thackeray Newsletter* 36 (November 1992): 1–5.

Thompson, George. *Travels and Adventures in Southern Africa*. London, 1827.

———. "Character of the Hottentots." *Annual Review* (1793): 285–91.

Thunberg, Charles Peter. *Travels in Europe, Africa and Asia, Made between the Years 1770 and 1779*. 3rd ed. 4 vols. London, 1795.

Thurston, Joseph. *The Fall*. London, 1732.

Todd, Janet, ed. *A Dictionary of British and American Women Writers, 1660–1800*. London: Metheun and Company, 1987.

Town and Country (August 1790): 356.

Turner, L. C. F. "The Cape of Good Hope and the Anglo-French Conflict, 1797–1806." *Historical Studies: Australia and New Zealand* 9 (May 1961): 368–77.

Van Linschoten, John Huighen. *His Discourse of Voyages into ye Easte and West Indies.* London, 1598.

Variety, 11 September 1929.

Virey, J. J. *Journal Universel des Sciences Médicales* 3 (1816): 225–34.

Walpole, Horace. *Horace Walpole's Correspondence.* Edited by W. S. Lewis, Warren Hunting Smith, and George L. Lam. 48 vols. New Haven: Yale University Press, 1937–83.

———. *Journal of the Reign of King George the Third, from the Year 1771 to 1783.* London, 1859.

Walvin, James. *England, Slaves and Freedom, 1776–1838.* Mississippi: University Press of Mississippi, 1986.

Ward, Edward. *St. Paul's Church; Or, the Protestant Ambulators.* London, 1716.

Ward, Harriet. *Five Years in Kaffirland.* 2nd ed. 2 vols. London, 1848.

Warner, Brian, ed. *Lady Herschel: Letters from the Cape, 1834–1838.* Cape Town: Friends of the Cape Town Library, 1991.

Watson, Foster. *The Beginnings of the Teaching of Modern Subjects in England.* 1909. Reprint, Yorkshire: Scolar Press, 1971.

Wesley, John. "The Imperfection of Human Knowledge." *The Works of John Wesley*, edited by Albert C. Outler. 2 vols. Nashville: Abingdon Press, 1985.

White, Hayden. *Metahistory: The Historical Imagination in Nineteenth-Century Europe.* Baltimore: Johns Hopkins University Press, 1973.

———. *Tropics of Discourse: Essays in Cultural Criticism.* Baltimore: Johns Hopkins University Press, 1978.

White, John. *Journal of a Voyage to New South Wales.* London, 1790.

Whitehead, Paul. *The State Dunces.* London, 1733.

Wilson, Monica, and Leonard Thompson. *A History of South Africa to 1870.* Cape Town: David Philip, 1982.

Wollstonecraft, Mary. *The Works of Mary Wollstonecraft.* Edited by Janet Todd and Marilyn Butler. 7 vols. New York: New York University Press, 1989.

Woolley, James, ed. *The Intelligencer.* Oxford: Clarendon Press, 1992.

Zouch, Richard. *The Dove: Or, Passages of Cosmography.* London, 1613.

Index

Abbot, George, 32, 61, 62
abolitionist movement, 139–40; interest in "Hottentots," 221, 226
Account of the Colony of the Cape of Good Hope, An, 221
Achebe, Chinua, 19
Adams, Percy, 119, 134
Addington, Stephen, 124
Africans: European construction of, 19–20; influence of classical representations in early modern English depictions of, 19–20, 32–33, 58
Africanus, Leo, 36
Aikin, Lucy, 228
Alexander, Du Pre, 221. *See also* Caledon's code
Alexander, Elizabeth, 242
America: English colonization of, 23
Americans: early English depictions of, 23–24, 68–70, 102
Anderson, Benedict, 22
Annual Register, the, 188, 223
Anti-Jacobin; or Weekly Examiner, the, 174
Astley, Thomas, 101, 109, 127, 164, 165
Aston, Edward, 20
Atlas Geographus, 85–86
Ayton, Richard, 138

Baartman, Saartjie ("Venus Hottentot"), 136, 229–34, 237, 241–43
Bage, Robert, 150
Baker, J. N. L., 70
Baker, Richard, 89
Baldwyn, George Augustus, 102, 165
Banks, Joseph, 181
Barber, Mary, 146
Barbour, Philip L., 67
Barker, Edmund, 33
Barlow, Edward, 120

Barnard, Alan, 14, 15
Barnard, Lady Anne, 208, 209, 212
Barrow, John, 174, 210, 218–19, 220
Barthelemy, Anthony, 37
Beattie, James, 204
Beeckman, Daniel, 123, 132
Behn, Aphra, 104, 105
Best, George, 57
Bird, William Wilberforce, 225
Blackmore, Richard, 119
Blackwood's Edinburgh Magazine, 202
Blitheman, Edward, 88
Blome, Richard, 78, 81
Blount, Martha, 163
Bluett, Thomas, 104
Blumenbach, Johann Friedrich, 203
Blumenberg, Hans, 25
body: depictions of "Hottentots," 34
Boemus, 32
Boer. *See* Dutch
Bohun, Edmund, 77, 81
Bonnet, Charles, 205–6
Bougainville, Louis de, 189
Bowen, Emanuel, 164
Boyle, Robert, 118
Braude, Benjamin, 57, 64
Brice, Andrew, 165
British: construction of themselves as superior colonial masters, 222; early attitudes to trade, 16–17; emigration to the Cape Colony, 225; seizure and occupation of the Cape, 176, 193, 207, 219
British Magazine, the, 145
Brittle, Emily, 128
Brome, Charles, 77
Brookes, Richard: the *General Gazetteer,* 189–93
Buffon, Georges-Louis, Comte de, 28, 202
Burchell, William, 226

284

INDEX 285

Burnet, Gilbert, 140–41
Burney, Frances, 228
Bushmen, 192

Cahill, Marie, 238
Caillé, Abbé de la: *Journal Historique Du Voyage fait au Cap de Bonne Esperance*, 166, 190, 191
Caledon's code, 221–22
Campbell, John, 224
Camper, Peter, 206
cannibalism: allegations of, 34, 39, 50, 65, 76, 77, 78, 82–83, 139, 238–39; allegation refuted, 17
Cape of Good Hope: classical descriptions of, 32; earliest English descriptions of, 33; European fear of seas and voyage sickness, 20–21, 39, 40, 44; figuring it as a garden, 22, 44, 45–46; naming of, 20
Cape Town: colonization of, 17–18, 68; European use of harbor, 16; growth of city, 18
Carpenter, Nathanael, 70
Carson, James, 164
Churchill, Awnsham and John, 83, 84
civility, 46, 47, 59, 94, 108, 148, 170, 193, 200
Claas: story of, 158
Clark, S., 75, 99
Clarke, Samuel, 75
Coetzee, J. M., 22, 210
Cole, Alfred W., 235
Collier, John, 112
Collier, William, 239
Common Sense, 164
Connoisseur, the, 164
Cooke, Edward, 120, 133, 155
Cooke, Thomas, 159, 161
Copland, Patrick, 22, 44, 52, 56
Cory: story of, 23, 30, 74, 87–117, 168, 178, 201
Coverte, Robert, 47, 49, 64–65
Cowley, Ambrose, 122, 125, 129, 137
Critical Review, the, 167
Cugoano, Quobna Ottobah, 105–6
Cunningham, William, 32
Curtin, Philip D., 25

Dampier, William, 125, 129
Dapper, Olfert, 78–80

Davies, John, 37–39
Defoe, Daniel, 124
Description of a Voyage Made by Certaine Ships of Holland, 33–34
Dias, Bartholomeu, 15, 20
Dibdin, Charles Isaac Mungo, 227
Dickens, Charles, 237
Diderot, Denis, 28
District Six Museum, 241
Ditton, Humphrey, 161
Dodsworth, Edward, 88
Douglas, Mary, 51
Downton, Nicholas, 50, 55, 87–88, 91
Drake, Sir Francis, 33
Dunbar, James, 115, 202
Dunlop, Alexander, 229
Dutch: attitudes about skin color, 27; blamed for demise of "Hottentots," 209–10, 219, 226; as Boer "Hottentots," 210, 219–20, 221; British praise of colonists at Cape, 192, 198; constructions of "Hottentots," 27
Dyer, John, 119

East India Company (Dutch), the, 16, 17, 33, 106
East India Company (English), the, 21, 39; reports about Cory, 87–91
Echard, Laurence, 81–82
Eden, Richard, 56
Edgeworth, Maria, 103, 173
Edinburgh Review, the, 227
Edwards, Philip, 118
Eliot, George, 237
Elizabeth I, 16
Elkington, Captain Thomas, 45, 68, 88–89
Encyclopaedia Britannica, 180, 195, 198–99, 205
England: early claim of Cape, 16, 73; slave trade, 25; social conditions, 16. *See also* Great Britain
Enquiry into the Morals of the Ancients, 151
Equiano, Olaudah, 103
Evangelical Magazine, the, 213–18

Fairfax, Samuel, 151
Fanon, Frantz, 187
female: descriptions of breasts, 52–53, 134, 197; genitalia, 52, 132–34, 181,

187, 203, 228–29; modesty or immodesty, 52–53, 75, 133, 182–83; sexuality and the sexualized female, 134, 135, 136, 228–34; stereotypical descriptions of Africans, 133–34, 135–36; vanity, 146, 169, 191, 194
Fenning, Daniel, 112, 165, 166
Ferrier, Susan, 227
Fielding, Henry, 149, 150
Forbes, James, 220
Forster, George, 166, 176, 184
Frantz, Ray William, 118
French: attacks on Kolb, 166; English comparisons of them to "Hottentots," 13, 149; English critique of French construction, 171–74; romantic construction of "Hottentots," 27–28, 165, 171, 182
Funnell, William, 101, 120, 125–26, 128–29

Gama, Vasco da, 15
Gates, Henry Louis, 105
Gentlemen's Magazine, the, 161–62, 163, 164, 183
geography, 70–71, 76–77; influence of classical texts, 32; new style texts of, 77–78
Geography Made Familiar and Easy to Young Gentlemen and Ladies, 165
George, Viscount Valentia, 211
Gibson, Edmund, 143
Gildon, Charles, 142
Gleanings in Africa, 208, 209
Goldgar, Bertrand A., 159, 163
Goldsmith, Oliver, 149, 179, 180, 197–98, 203
Gordon, Patrick, 82–83
Gould, Stephen Jay, 206
Graham, Maria, 224
Graves, Robert, 145–46
Gray, Stephen, 241
Green, John, 101–2, 109
Griffith, Elizabeth, 150
Griqua National Congress, 241, 242
Grub-Street Journal, the, 159–60, 163
Guthrie, William: and *A New Geographical, Historical, and Commercial Grammar*, 189, 193–95, 203–4, 208, 220, 222

Hacke, William, 83
Hacque: story of, 168–70
Hadfield, Andrew, 24
Hakluyt, Richard: and *Principal Navigations*, 18, 21, 33, 60, 61
Hall, Kim, 37, 55
Ham: use of biblical figure to cast aspersion on dark skin color, 56–57
Hamilton, Alexander, 101, 123, 127
Hamilton, Elizabeth: and *Memoirs of Modern Philosophers*, 171–73
Harlow, Vincent T., 221–22
Harriott, John, 208
Harris, John, 83, 100
Hawkesworth, John, 180
Haywood, Eliza, 162–63
Heath, William, 230–31
Herbert, Sir Thomas, 20, 44, 48, 50, 51, 52, 53, 57–58, 98–99, 137
Herschel, Lady Margaret, 234–35
Heylyn, Peter, 65, 71–72; and *Cosmography*, 72–74, 84, 97–98
Hirst, Derek, 62
Hoadly, Benjamin, 141
Hodgen, Margaret T., 19
Homes, Henry, lord Kames, 202–3
Hood, Thomas, 228
"Hottentots" (representations of): bodies, 34, 50, 51, 52–53, 54–55, 78, 83, 122, 180, 181, 182, 185, 186, 191, 208–9; customs, 84, 119, 154, 177–78, 200, 209, 219; demise, 220–21, 234–36; diet, 49–50, 65; dress, 34, 51–52, 74, 78, 122–23, 163, 182, 186, 189; general description, 45, 46, 72, 74, 75–76, 85–86, 189; government, 35, 80, 81; houses, 35, 122, 137, 138, 187–88, 224; language, 34–35, 47, 48, 74, 81, 83, 84, 119, 180, 196, 199, 202; name, 14, 81–82; religion, 35, 80, 81, 128–30, 152, 153–54, 177–78, 189, 191–92, 199, 211–12, 223; sexuality, 79, 131, 134–35, 186; skin color, 26–27, 28, 33, 36, 55–58, 63–64, 70, 84, 124–27, 179, 203–4; stealing, 48–49; trading, 33, 34, 39, 40–43, 47–48, 65, 88, 89
Houtman, Cornelius, 34, 37
Hume, David, 114–15, 204
Hurrell, Tamary, 167–70
Hutton, Catherine, 174

idleness, 120, 122, 123, 210
Intelligencer, the, 148–49
Ireland: English oppression of, 139
Irish, native: English representations of, 18–19, 24, 51; similarities with "Hottentots," 24, 48, 53, 137

Jackson, John, 143
Jacobson, Dan, 14
JanMohamed, Abdul R., 45–46
Janssen, Leendert, 17
Jenyns, Soame, 205
Johnson, Samuel, 137–38; called a "Hottentot," 147–48
Jolson, Al, 238
Jourdain, John, 21–22, 46, 47, 48, 50, 88

Keegan, Timothy, 222, 234
Keeling, William, 48, 55
Khoikhoi: contact with Europeans, 15–16, 18; ethnography of, 14–15; names of societies, 15; population of, 18; resistance to Dutch, 17; social organization of, 15
Kicherer, Reverend, 212–15; narrative of, 217; Zak River Mission Station, 214, 216
Kindersley, Jemima, 177–79
Knight, Richard Payne, 174
Knox, John, 165
Kolb, Peter, 30, 151, 184, 195; attacks on *Present State*, 166–67; *Present State of the Cape of Good Hope*, 152–59; influence and use of *Present State*, 160, 164–66, 201

Lancaster, James, 33, 39, 47
Last East-Indian Voyage, The, 39–43, 55
Latrobe, Reverend C. I., 223
Lavater, Johann Casper, 204–5
Leguat, François, 134
Leighton, Robert, 237
Leslie, Charles, 141–42
Letter Written to the Right Worshipfull East Indian Marchants in London, 39
Linnaeus, Carl, 179
Linschoten, John Huighen van, 35
Lloyd, Evan, 138–39
Locke, John, 103, 136–37, 142
Lockyer, Charles, 123, 129

London Missionary Society, the, 223, 224
Long, Edward, 134–35
Loubère, Simon de la, 106, 125, 131

Macey, Alan, 238
Macintosh, William, 151, 178
male: genitalia, 130–32, 182, 186, 187
Maley, Willy, 24
Mandeville, Bernard, 146
Mantis, the Soothsayer, 223
Mapes, Victor, 239
Marshall, George, 227
Marshall, P. J., 55
Martz, Louis, 164
Maseko, Zola, 242
Masson, Francis, 181–83
Maturin, Charles, 228
Maxwell, John, 26, 107, 120, 127, 129–30, 132, 155
Medley, Guido, 155–58, 160
Mendez, Moses, 13, 149
Meyer, Susan, 237
Michelbourne, Sir Edward, 44, 47, 49, 51
Middleton, Charles Theodore, 114
Middleton, David, 52
Middleton, Henry, 40
Mielke, Andreas, 111
Millar, John, 200–201
Milward, John, 52
missionary societies at the Cape of Good Hope, 129
Modern Part of an Universal History, The, 180, 195–97
Moll, Herman, 83–84
Monboddo, James Burnett, Lord, 201–2
Monthly Review, the, 166, 171, 177
Moravian Mission (Genadendal), 212, 235
Morden, Robert, 81, 127
More, Hannah, 145
Moreri's Dictionary, 81
Morgan, Jennifer L., 133
Morse, Theodore F., 238
Moryson, Fynes, 48

Napier, Edward Delaval Hungerford Elers, 236
native: depiction of native societies,

18–19, 23, 24, 68–70; fear of going "native," 22, 94–95, 100
Newbery, John, 165
Newman, Gerald, 22
Newton, Isaac, 78
Newton-King, Susan, 222
Nieuhoff, John, 106
Nussbaum, Felicity A., 135

Ogilby, John, 15; *Africa*, 15, 78–81
Ordinance, 50, 222
Ovington, John, 120, 122, 123, 126, 128, 131–32, 133, 137

Parker, John, 68
Parker, Mary Anne, 177
Parks, Suzan-Lori, 242–43
Patchwork Girl of Oz, The, 239–40
Paterson, William, 167, 183, 190
Paulinus, Bartholomaeo a Sancto, 189
Pepys, Samuel, 130
Percival, Robert, 210
Perniola, Mario, 51
Perry, Ruth, 135–36
Petersen, Fuad, 241
Pettit, Edward, 102
Petty, William, 118
Peyton, Walter, 89–90
Picart, Bernard, 164
Pinkerton, John, 188
Pliny: *Natural History*, 20, 32
Pocahontas, 23, 69
Pope, Alexander, 160, 163
Pory, John, 36
Prat, William, 32
Pratt, Mary Louise, 44, 131, 152, 185, 219
Prévost, Antoine-François, Abbé, 109, 165
Prideaux, John, 70
Priestly, Joseph, 200
Pringle, Thomas, 226
Prior, James, 116
Prior, Matthew, 136
Purchas, Samuel, 18, 60; *Purchas His Pilgrimage*, 52–53, 55, 61–65, 90; *Purchas His Pilgrimes*, 67–68, 90–91

Ranelean Religion Displayed, The, 144
Raymond, Captain George, 33

Raynal, Guillaume Thomas François, Abbé, 28
Relation of Two Several Voyages Made to the East Indies, A, 133
Rennefort, Urbain Souchu de, 126
Renshaw, R., 211
Richards, Laura Elizabeth, 239
Richardson, Samuel, 150
Robben Island, 107, 241
Roe, Sir Thomas, 49
Rogers, Captain Woodes, 122
Rooke, Henry, 207
Rousseau, George S., 197
Rousseau, Jean-Jacques, 28, 109–11
Royal Society, the, 118, 181, 229; *Philosophical Transactions of*, 182

Sacheverell, Henry, 161
Said, Edward, 31
St. James's Evening Post, the, 159
St. John, Henry, viscount of Bolingbroke, 115
Saint Pierre, J. H. Bernardin de, 166, 189
Salmon, Nathaniel, 90
Salmon, Thomas, 102, 111, 165
Saturday Magazine, the, 236
Schapera, Isaac, 14, 79, 80
Scots: likened to "Hottentots," 114–15, 137–38, 227–28; 237
Semple, Robert, 221
Sheehan, Bernard, 23, 69
Shelburne, Lord, Sir William Petty, 114
Sheridan, Thomas, 13
skin color: debate over "Hottentot" skin color, 124–27; theories about variety of human skin colors, 63–64, 71–72
slavery: at the Cape of Good Hope, 17; business of, 25; and skin color, 25, 26, 57–58
Sloane, Hans, 155
Smart, Christopher, 149
Smellie, William, 205–6
Smith, John, 69
Smollett, Tobias, 112–12, 150, 164
Somerville, William, 228–29
Southerne, Thomas, 123
Sparks, Allister, 241

Sparrman, Anders, 166, 183–88, 190, 191, 192, 203, 218
Spectator, the, 135, 144
Speed, John, 37
Spurr, David, 225
Stafford, Barbara Marie, 184
Stafforde, Robert, 70
Standish, Ralph, 45, 47, 52
Stanhope, Philip Dormer, Lord Chesterfield, 147
Stavorinus, John Splinter, 189
Stephens, Thomas, 20–21, 33
Stevens, George Alexander, 136
Streak, Michael, 27
Swift, Jonathan, 13, 84, 134, 139, 148, 160

Talents Run Mad, The, 233
Tavernier, Jean Baptiste, 81, 125, 131, 133
Ten Rhyne, Willem, 27, 85, 126, 133
Terry, Reverend Edward, 13, 44, 46, 53, 56, 90, 91–97, 98
Thackeray, William Makepeace, 237
Thomas, Pascoe, 130
Thompson, George, 222
Thunberg, Charles Peter, 188–89
Thurston, Joseph, 139
Todd, Hugh, 159
Town and Country, 171
travel literature, 20–21, 31, 118–19, 195; doubts about the veracity of, 119; scientific travel narratives, 167, 184
True and Large Discourse of Voyage of 20 April 1601, A, 47

United Brethren, 129

Vaillant, François Le, 151, 171, 174, 189, 190, 194
Van Riebeeck, 17, 18
Van Wyk Smith, 35, 55
Varenius, 78
Von Tilzer, Harry, 238

Walpole, Horace, 103, 145, 147
Walvin, James, 25–26
Ward, Edward, 144
Ward, Harriet, 236
Warden, Robert, 210–11
Waters, Ethel, 239
Weekly Register, the, 163–64
Wells, Edward, 78
Welsh: likened to "Hottentots," 138
Wesley, John, 139
Whiston, William, 161
White, Hayden, 24, 40
White, John, 176
Whitehead, Paul, 147
Willebrand, Christian Ludwig, 111
Williams, C., 232–33
Williams, Glyndwr, 55
Wilson, General Robert Thomas, 207
Withington, Nicholas, 50, 56
Wollstonecraft, Mary, 147, 171
Wordsworth, Dorothy, 138
Wreede, Georg Frederick, 78

Zimbardo, Rose, 25
Zouch, Richard, 32